To John,

a good friend

and Capful

Jim Healy

10/98

Golfing before the Arch

A History of St. Louis Golf

by

Jim Healey

DEDICATION

To Deb, Shari and Tim

FORWARD

Golfing before the Arch has two distinct meanings; first and foremost it is what occurred prior to the physical construction of our area's symbol; the time prior to 1966. Secondly though, it refers to the present activity; the golfing that takes place throughout the area that surrounds the arch. In the symbolic sense we go before someone, or some presence, to honor them and ourselves. In this same manner, as we golf, we honor those who have gone before us and given us the history we have today.

ACKNOWLEDGMENTS

This book, like all such efforts, would not have been possible without the help and support of several key individuals; Larry Etzkorn in particular is deserved of singular mention for his ongoing support and patience at my seemingly never-ending phone calls and questions, as I picked his brain about district and local events.

Ultimately, this project would not have been possible without the support of four individuals - friends - for whose support I am forever indebted; Bob O'Connell, Steve Neusel, Greg Klapp and Larry Cardinale.

Many others helped by contributing information on their careers and the career of others, while still others pointed me in the proper direction to obtain new data that I hope will make this book enjoyable for the reader. Among these are; Bart Collida, Delores Williams, Ellen Port, Jim Tom Blair, Bob Cochran, Jim Holtgrieve, Don Bliss, Scott Thomas, David Lucks, Marianne LeButt, Mahlon Wallace, Dick Shaiper, Bob Goalby, Jay Haas, Jerry Haas, Judy Rankin, Bob Green, Steve Spray, Garth Bayer, Jerry Tucker, Mike Tucker, Herb Matter, Malinda Miller-Huey, Ronald Foulis, Jeff Smith, Patti Sturgis, Barb Berkmeyer, Marcella Rose, Jim Manion, Bob Mason, Tom Wargo, Keith Foster, Gary Kern, Nancy Scranton, Heather Drew, Paula Eger, Kevin Conroy, John Hayes, Brian Hayes, Dave Furlong, Jim Offer, Bob Compton, Tom Hulverson, Msgr. Thomas Durkin and Mike Byrne. Many of these shared with me their scrapbooks and their memories, not only of themselves and their loved ones, but of golfers throughout the area, so that we might all enjoy their accomplishments.

Introduction

"In golf when we hit a foul ball, we got to go out and play it"
...Sam Snead speaking to baseball great Ted Williams

Golf in St. Louis has a long, varied and significant history. Some of the games best players, contributors and architects have spread their love of golf throughout the world from the banks of the Mississippi. We have had our share of national champions and championships. We have world class courses for the public and private player. We have players, both amateur and professionals, whose names are recognized where ever knowledgeable golfers assemble. Local designers have given us some of their best work and have taken it to other states (and countries) to share their sport. Nationally known architects vie for contracts in the area...where previously few ventured. True, there are cities who have more courses, and maybe better players, but we can hold our own against the best for our affection for the game and our place in its history.

This is not to say that class struggles, depressions, two World Wars and countless small-minded individuals, municipal and county boards and your normal run-of-the-mill political in-fighting at almost all levels, did not do their best, at times, to stop golf course expansion. But, on occasion, they did the right thing for golf and for golfers, as courses did flourish, taxes were paid and golfers enjoyed their surroundings (or as the saying goes, "...*a bad day on the course beats a good day anywhere else*".)

Despite having only three courses in the City of St. Louis proper, and two of those are nine holers, golfers throughout the area have shown their love and appreciation for the game by journeying outward. This may explain in part, why it took golf longer in St. Louis to grow when compared to cities like Chicago. Having to travel many miles over dusty roads to stand in line for a tee time is not conducive to the growth of any activity, let alone one that required an investment in equipment such as golf requires. Couple that with the sheer diffi-

culty of mastering the game and it is little wonder that golf grew slowly outside of the private clubs.

The rise of the early courses also dictated where future courses would be laid out and northwest St. Louis County with the Country Club and Field Club prior to 1900 captured the early sites. Shortly after the 1900's began, the Normandy area captured two clubs when Glen Echo CC and Normandie CC were started. Other clubs, lost forever, sprang-up in Kinloch, Florissant, Forest Park, Jefferson Barracks, Tower Grove Park, and Bel Nor. These were shortly followed by Algonquin and Westwood (known today as Westborough) in Southwest county, along with Sunset Hill (though today it has dropped the "Hill").

Despite the obstacles that presented themselves to the average golfer—golf clubs were hard to get, membership in clubs was selective and teachers were few—golf did flourish, if only at the Country Club level. Through the 20's and into the 50's golf grew much in line with the population. The year 1953 marked a watershed for golf throughout the country; it was the first time in years there was actually a significant growth in course development, following several very flat periods. During the 60's, 70's and early 80's golf grew, but more likely at resort locations than in your neighborhood. The late 80's and 90's have seen a resurgence of golf at all levels with public and private courses being built in most major metropolitan areas.

In the Bi-State area we have seen 40 new courses since the mid-80's; almost one-third of all the courses located throughout the area; with 34 being open to the public. The total number of courses throughout the Greater St. Louis Area stands at over 130 of which approximately 100 are open to the public. With the larger number of facilities, golf is booming. Latest statistics point to almost 350,000 golfers throughout the metropolitan area, with women comprising almost 30% and almost 46% of all new golfers.

But this book is not just about the growth or number of courses in the Area, for that is a matter of economics and demographics. Nor is it about the number of "firsts", of which we could boast, though these will be noted for their historical significance. Rather this is more about those individuals who contributed to that growth, who had the vision to see that spending 4 hours in the company of friends was not what Churchill observed *"a good walk in the park spoiled"*, but more about testing your ability and frailties in front of others, while at the same time enjoying their camaraderie. It is the ever-present desire to excel in sport while observing a civility in the execution. And it's about the social aspect of belonging.

Golf in its early days was a fairly closed activity. The Clubs were fostered by the wealthy to provide a place for the family to enjoy the company of others in their social class. At many Clubs it remains the same today, as minorities, women and those with less than the years-salary for initiation fees, are resigned to look-in. This is not to chastise those who belong to clubs; for it is they who kept the sport alive through depressions and wars. It was their love of golf that kept the spirit alive and has enabled golf at all levels to thrive. It is perhaps this symbol of golf that, unlike almost any other major sport - except possibly tennis - draws the ire of those who would ban all such gathering places. But it was the private facilities that employed the likes of Hagen, Hogan, Nelson and Snead during those early days when winning paychecks had only three zeros —sometimes only two— which paid them monthly stipends, and allowed them to pay their bills while they were creating their legends on the course.

Public golf grew out of the desire of those without the wealth to enjoy golf, and on occasion, the Country Club life-style, albeit if only for hours at a time. The first public course, Van Courtland Park in the Bronx, opened with 9 holes in 1895, and expanded to 18 holes in 1899 under the direction of architect Tom Bendelow. The first public courses in the Gateway area were Rock Springs in Alton which opened in 1912, followed shortly by Forest Park in 1913. As mentioned earlier, there were obstacles to overcome, but as more Scots and Englishmen (and the occasional Irishman) brought their love of the game with them, it did spread throughout the area.

The sport is very democratic: it makes no concession for ability, the elements or luck. Your ability to execute the shot is all that matters. Golf can be challenging for the bold, deflating for the foolhardy and miserable for the hacker. On the Tour you make the cut, you make money (at least official money); if you're home on too many weekends, you can kiss your endorsements (and your exemption) good-bye. If you're a Steve Jones, you can take 3 years off to recover from an accident and still win the US Open. If you're Davis Love III, you'll think all year about those three putts! And if you're Tom Lehman you wondered for years when you're day will come...then it finally did at Royal Lytham! And if you're Tiger Woods, well...what more needs to be said!

But too much money for finishing an also-ran has left the sport in a very awkward position. A player actually made a million dollars one year, and didn't win a tournament! As Trevino lamented, *"...if you're putting for the win and make it, you win $250,000; if you miss it you only win $150,000. It does soften the blow"!* The PGA or USGA or LPGA or somebody (maybe IMG's Mark McCormack) gave us the idea that the money list was what mattered. And unfortunately we have come to believe this, much to our amazement. Do we actually believe that because Peter Jacobsen wins more in one tournament than Sam Snead did in an entire season that he is somehow better than Snead? Or Hogan or Nelson or Sarazen? And does being 30th on the all time money list really count when winning 18 tournaments in one year as Nelson did in 1945 netted him only $50,000! Today, if he won just 11 as Hogan did in 1948 or Snead with 10 wins

Introduction

in 1950, he would net well in excess of $2,000,000, maybe even $3,000,000!

Winning is what should matter. And to the true competitor (not just the guy trying to "hang-on"), it is what drives them. Money is the fortunate by-product. Whether your name is Norman, Irwin, Kite, Nicklaus, Palmer, Lehman, Holtgrieve, Blair, Bliss, Lucks or Cochran it is the desire to win that keeps them competitive. As Shoeless Joe said in Field of Dreams, *"I would have played for meal money"*. Even for a man about to face death as Lou Gehrig was in 1939, he considered himself *"...the luckiest man on the face of the earth"* just to have had the opportunity to play that wonderful sport. This is the attitude that drives all great athletes...to compete against the best and be victorious...to test yourself in the most challenging of situations. For some it's the weekly nassau, for others it's the club championship and for the very fortunate, it's a national title.

Golf offers opportunities and challenges for all. From the Senior Tour, which gives those who couldn't make the cut on the Tour a chance to say they beat Nicklaus, Trevino and Palmer (and today Irwin and Floyd), to those who believe that "Tiger" Woods will become the next Nicklaus. To the Nike Tour which provides many with the opportunity to see if they "really" can compete at the next level; to the PGA & LPGA Tours which provides the ultimate challenges for the very talented to test themselves against the best each week; to the Oldsmobile Scramble and the countless of other tournaments that provide us with the challenges we crave while allowing us to exorcise the demons inside who tell us, deep at night, that we really could win the "US-something", if only given the chance.

So we travel to the latest upscale course that promises 4 hour rounds, "Country Club atmosphere for a day" (and frequently, a price to match) search-ing for smooth greens, manicured fairways, and tees we could almost putt off of! The quality of courses has improved to the point where we no longer accept a poorly conditioned one. This appalls many who

say we are spending too much on chemicals and conditioning at the expense of what the sport of golf was originally intended. St. Andrews in Scotland, in particular, is famous for being mistaken by Sam Snead when, upon viewing it for the first time, thought it must be an old abandoned course. We expect Augusta-type fairways and greens, fair rough, water you can see and sand we can putt out of. This is not traditionally what mother-nature provides.

The golf architect must attempt to mold from a piece of land a layout that can command a $40 green fee, perhaps a few homes, move golfers around in 4 hours at 7-10 minute intervals over 7,000 yards with a slope of 130, while satisfying environmental concerns, keep course maintenance at a minimum all while making it look natural. Anyone applying for this job?

Finally it is about what golf means to the individual. To the non-player we can never really explain this sufficiently. From the character-building it brought to Bobby Jones to the anguish it bestows on a Greg Norman, golf is one of the true sports where you are expected to call your own fouls and follow the rules, however severe or penal they may appear. No "head-butting" allowed here! To those who have stood over a putt of three feet, whether for the club championship or a fifty-cent skin, we all feel the same kindred sense of fear as we look at the 4 1/2" cup and wonder whether the 1.68" ball can really fit! (Actually 2 1/2 balls could fit at once!!) We will try a variety of clubs and putters, training aids and videos all in the quest for par. They promise us to cut our handicap in half, or knock 5 strokes off our round, and if they all worked, we would all be shooting in the 60's! Yet sadly, 95% of us will never achieve our dream. But quitting is not in our mind-set. For we remember the well-struck tee shot, or the high, graceful approach or the curling 15 footer. These are the memories that bring us back. These are the feelings we want to experience once again. This is why we play the game.

Golfing Before the Arch

Jimmy Manion
nicknamed "Little Dynamite" for his
mighty drives
and firery temper

From 1915-1935 there were a few
St. Louisans who were recognized
throughout the country as they
travelled from event to event...and
who were considered among the
favorites whenever they teed it up.
Jimmy Manion and Eddie Held were
perhpas the best of this early group!

Eddie Held
Winner of the 1st USGA Amateur
Publinks in 1922.

"If my recollections can do no more perhaps they may help to refresh those of the reader, so much more vivid and better worth recalling, so that he loses himself for a little while in a pleasant reverie of the links."
...Bernard Darwin (1944)

Golf arrived in St. Louis a little late. The east coast was alive with courses, but the movement west was a little slower. Whether Foxboro GC or the Dorset Club or St. Andrews (NY) was the first club that is still in existence, all three having begun between 1886-88, is not the issue here. Golf was being played in Chicago in 1892 and in the early 1890's in New York, Pennsylvania, Massachusetts, Vermont, Virginia, Illinois, Ohio, California, Georgia, New Hampshire and South Carolina. Quincy (IL) had a Club in 1898 and there were courses in Kansas City, St. Joseph and Omaha prior to 1895, though many of these would later be abandoned for various reasons. Courses were built in Peoria and Springfield (IL) in this period that still exist. When the Chicago GC moved to Wheaton from Downers Grove and established their 18 hole layout in 1895, the first 18 hole course in America, it marked the beginning of the growth of golf in America. But golf would not be played in the Bi-state area with any regularity until 1896. But once it came, courses would begin to develop throughout the area — at least for a time!

A *"Golf Guide"* published in 1899 listed every known course in America. This Guide lists a total of 10 courses in Missouri; two in Kansas City and eight

in the St. Louis Area. They were the St. Louis Field Club, St. Louis CC, St. Louis Jockey Club, St. Louis Athletic Club, Kinloch Club, Normandy Heights GC, Carondelet Park Links and Jefferson Barracks Links. As noted by the Guide *"...the above six clubs maintain golf links of one kind or another, in addition to the better known courses of the St. Louis Field Club and the Country Club"*. Another source comes

St. Louis CC after the fire of 1896. Located on Hanley Road on the grounds which is Polo Drive and Davis Place today.

from *"The Golfers Green Book"* published in 1906 by Joseph E. G. Ryan for the Western Golf Association. This publication states there were four courses in St. Louis that belonged to the Association; St. Louis Country Club, Glen Echo, Normandie and St. Louis Field Club. By 1900 the Country Club and the Field Club had also joined the US Golf Association.

One distinction that must be made is that of a Club versus a course. Courses did spring up at various times, but those associated with "Clubs" received the recognition. So while a links may have been built in a park, unless it was part of a "Club" it was not deemed worthy of much recognition.

St. Louis CC

St. Louis Country Club was originally located in Bridgeton in 1892, where enough room existed for the construction of a Polo field, which was the primary interest at the time. Early club founders John Shepley, Marshal Hodgman, Irwin Smith and James Scudder owned a farm in Bridgeton and offered to lease it for a polo club. Many sons of prominent St. Louisans, in particular Clay Pierce, Walter McKittrick and Ted Steedmann, had learned of polo while attending eastern colleges and they were anxious to create a similar environment here. With initially only 15 members there was some interest in the new game of golf, but here polo was king. In fact, the logo for St. Louis CC has two horseshoes intertwined in the design. The site chosen was known as the Collier Farm. It had a two-story building that could serve as a clubhouse in addition to stables and a barn, all located on 253 acres. It had another important ingredient to serve as a Country Club; a narrow-gauge rail line connected the Bridgeton site with Florissant and with Ferguson. It then connected with the Olive Street horsecar line just west of Grand and on to downtown. The ride out would take about an hour. The land was bounded by Fee Fee Church Road, just south of Utz Lane, and would be near Dunn Road. This site today is part of the present Brown Campus area.

When the expected northwest

St. Louis CC layout Clayton - 1896		
Hole		**Yardage**
1	Mid Field	335
2	North Road	320
3	Fair View	265
4	Look Out	290
5	Hill Top	485
6	Road Side	300
7	Tribulation	300
8	Lone Oak	395
9	Home	245
		2,935

migration of the city ceased to develop, and instead the move westward toward Forest Park took over (down Lindell and the Central West End), the club decided in 1894 to look for another site. In November of that year the club purchased an option on the McCausland homestead at Clayton and Hanley Road plus an additional 200 acres from the Davis brothers, Sam, Dwight and John, that was adjacent to the McCausland property. At $1,000 per acre the deal was concluded early in 1895 with the new clubhouse completed in 1896. Clayton was still rather rural, and would not become a city until 1913 so the club felt that they had the room they would need. With the new location, and plans for golf as well, membership would quickly grow to 250.

The Club site was on a high piece of ground on Hanley Road and was bounded by Clayton Road on the south, North and South Road on the west and the Chicago-Rock Island and Pacific Railroad tracks on the north. Today the area is Davis Place and Polo Drive. The clubhouse was an ornate, three-story colonial frame building 144 feet long facing Hanley

Glen Echo CC 1904

Rd. A covered 15 foot veranda extended around two sides of the building that commanded a view of the tennis, golf and polo facilities. Transportation to the club was a concern and there was an on-going dispute regarding the use of Forsyth due to a right-of-way issue. To solve this, and assist the members getting access to the club from the city, the members privately constructed Wydown Boulevard, running from Hanley to Forest Park.

The original nine holes were laid out in 1896 as the now 300-member Country Club contracted with James Foulis, the head professional at Chicago Golf Club and brother of Robert Foulis, to construct 9 holes. In keeping with tradition from Scotland each of the holes were named and in most cases they reflected the shape or look of the hole. This was the first course constructed in the area.

Golf appears to have begun on October 8, 1896, according to an article in the *St. Louis Republic* "*...the good old Scots-English game of golf received its formal christening in St. Louis Yesterday afternoon when the first Golf Tournament given by the St. Louis Country Club was played under the most favorable conditions*".

In 1897 a fire consumed the handsome clubhouse and all that remained in the smoking ruins was the chimney. "*Burned like a straw stack*" was the headline in the *Republic* so members went back to the architect of the original building, J.L. Mauran and agreed to rebuild. The clubhouse was rebuilt in 1898 and about $80,000 was spent to completely refurbish the facility and grounds.

As Clayton grew, the rural environs began to disappear. Streetcar tracks now ran through the property (golfers had to avoid the wires on their tee shots, or re-tee the ball) so the club, in 1910, contem-

St. Louis Field Club - 1900

plated a move to another site with more room still further west. In 1911, the board negotiated a purchase of land owned by the Archbishop of St. Louis [referred to in documents simply as "the Archbishops land"] at Ladue and Price Roads. The purchase price was to be $227,000 or $1,000 per acre. To help negotiate the deal, since most of the members of the Country Club were not Catholics, they hired a prominent church member to be the intermediary with Lindell. The Archbishop agreed to the sale and then used the proceeds to buy a tract of land on Laclede Station Road where Kenrick Seminary would later be built.

The Country Club president was William F. Boyle. Other officers and directors were B.B. Graham, D.S.H. Smith, Daniel Taylor, A.L. Shapleigh, J.F. Shapley, F.W. Oliver and Walter McKittrick. The Greenkeeper-Pro was Ed McNamara, who would serve for several seasons. Judge Boyle would serve as president of the club for 15 years.

The Field Club

The **St. Louis Field Club** was located in "Bissell, MO" and "*..on the Burlington Railroad, near St. Louis; a Field Club station is on the links.*" The site was thirteen miles north of the city and was "*..accessible by railroad, or a carriage road, and is about an hour's ride from the downtown district by bicycle.*" The land is described as "*...a pretty piece of high ground, consisting of forty-five acres.*" There are records that point to the St. Louis Field Club being loosely organized around 1892 with a membership of 127, and constructing a course in late 1897.

The club was officially organized on October 8, 1897 with 102 members, and the first golf medal was awarded to Rayburn Bissell for his victory in the match-play championship that year. Records indicate that its members were competing in the Western Golf Association Amateur, along with members from St. Louis CC in 1902; but no other area clubs are mentioned.

Located in what is today part of Riverview Gardens on Bellefontaine Road near the historic General Daniel Bissell House, Club President D.O. Ives along with A.L. Kenneth are given credit for the course design, though John McGee will be given credit in a later article as the architect of the Field Club course. There is no mention of collaboration between the two groups, so perhaps McGee did the design while Ives and Kenneth did the on-site construction. In the first formal matches recorded, on May 6, 1898, a foursome went out on the links, which though barely two months old and quite wet, displayed the beauty that was ex-pected. McGee, playing left-handed, had been playing golf for almost ten years, and he recorded a 79 over the 9 holes. Other scores ranged into the 100's. Records referred to Harry S. Cullin as vice-president, F. Rayburn Bissell as club secretary and Ed McNamara as Greenkeeper. McNamara was a rather colorful player & green-keeper while at the Field Club, and was the Club's first golf professional. He later left the golf business and became a St. Louis policeman. Early biographies of him show him with a golf club while another pictures him in his officers uniform.

The site was most likely chosen as the Bissell family had approximately 1,200 acres in the area [down from the 2,500 they had prior to 1844] and the land appeared well-suited for a course. When the club was organized in 1893, golf was not being played in the area, and at that time the Country Club had no plans for a course. But there may have been a

few "gutties" hit around the property until the course was completed. The Bissell house was built in 1818 and it is the original home that stands on the site today. The Bissel's trace their roots back to the mid-1600's when the first crossed from England to the new country. Legend

Florissant Valley CC - c.1898 - located in Bel-Nor. Members attempted, without success, to duplicate St. Louis CC. Facility had polo ponies and golf in 1898.

has it that when Paul Revere made his historic ride to Concord and Lexington, it was a Bissell ancestor who took the news south from Boston, and with less historical significance since he did not run into the redcoats. General Daniel Bissell was awarded his stars by none other than General George Washington. A signed declaration of this fact adorns the walls of the home.

James R. Bissell noted the location of the house and golf course as he recalled from 1915, and placed them in a 1983 drawing. The course was located across the road [Bellefontaine] toward the Railroad tracks. A frame structure was constructed to serve as the clubhouse, but like so many of the day, it caught fire and burned to the ground. Rayburn Bissell then built a new home to be used as a clubhouse, this one made of brick, on

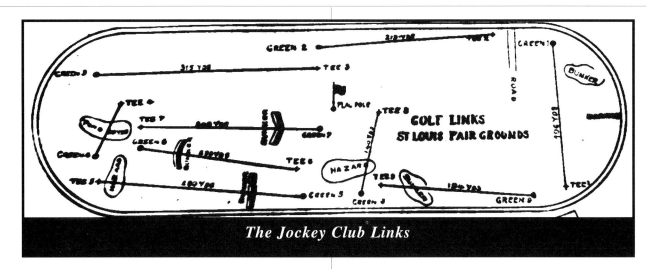

The Jockey Club Links

the east side of Bellefontaine just north of the Bissell Home. It would serve until the club moved.

Plans for a new, larger clubhouse in 1898 never materialized and the club continued to operate from the new site for a few more years. Finally on July 6, 1900, a new clubhouse opened for the members. The Club was also plagued with transportation problems as the rail line to their site was in jeopardy. Like the Country Club, the Field Club realized that the migration in St. Louis was moving west, not northwest and the club also voted for a move southward.

When the Club moved to the Normandy area, on a parcel of land owned by the Lucas Family in 1910, the club changed its name to Bellerive and built 18 holes on what is now the University of Missouri-St. Louis campus. The Bellerive name was in recognition of the French history in the area as Captain Louis Ange de Bellerive was the last French commander in North America and the first governor of St. Louis. The club stayed at the site for 50 years before relocating once again, this

Players at the Fair Grounds who failed to replace a piece of "cut sod" following a stroke would be fined $5, and this would be strickly enforced.

Jockey Club Links		
No	Bogey	Yardage
1	4	196
2	4	219
3	5	315
4	3	90
5	5	280
6	5	233
7	5	249
8	4	140
9	4	194
	39	**1916**

time on Ladue Rd. at Mason at it's present site.

Many of the early clubs did not remain open long, and many moved to more favorable locations. In some cases fire destroyed the clubs and the records, and the members simply did not rebuild but moved to other clubs. As noted earlier, six early clubs began with good intentions, but circumstances brought many to their eventual demise.

The Jockey Club

The *St. Louis Jockey Club*, the Delmar Jockey Club and the Kinloch Jockey Club were early race tracks throughout the area, as racing occupied significant parts of the sports pages. But the St. Louis Jockey Club is the only one that laid out a golf course within the infield of their 60-acre race track [the course in the infield of the Indy 500 had nothing new on St. Louis!]. Technically named *The St. Louis Golf Club*, [also referred to as the *Fair Grounds Links,* as well as just *The Jockey Club*] the course had several advantages. It was the closest club to the downtown area which made it perfect for early morning or late afternoon play. It was also fairly short, so a round could be played in well under two hours. It was also very flat, making it very easy for all to play, especially the ladies in their long dresses. In fact, as the club grew in popularity, the ladies began to outnumber the men on the links. Finally they had an outstanding professional in Occley Johnson, formerly of the Chicago Golf Club, and the course was considered the best maintained of the early clubs and members were very protective about the grounds. The Club here was a second or third club for many and except for the Country Club members, all believed it was the best conditioned in the area. On one occasion, a rodeo was being contemplated for the infield. The thought of hooves and roundups taking place was too much for members to bear. Johnson considered fencing off the greens to protect them, such was the care which the links received.

The Jockey Club itself was an old St. Louis institution, dating back to the Civil War. It had, for years, managed the annual Harvest Fair which included the Veiled Prophet Parade, the major social event for the city, which lasted for a month at a time. We know that they also held a 13-day race schedule during this event at Fairgrounds Park. The Harvest Fair was no small event limited to local activities, as such dignitaries as Abraham Lincoln, Stephen Douglas, William Tecumseh Sherman and Horace Greeley attended on various occasions.

The clubhouse was a

Kinloch Club - 1899

large three-story mansion that was on North Grand next to the track. In the early 1900's horse racing was one of the main forms of entertainment and local papers carried results from all over the country, and news on jockeys, horses, trainers and turf conditions dominated the sports columns.

When the golfers club at the Jockey Club was organized in 1898, it's members were allocated to a room on the third floor of the clubhouse. The prominent members of the Jockey Club were members of the Field Club, the Kinloch Club, Florissant Valley Club and the Country Club.

C. Norman Jones, with the St. Louis Brewing Association, had introduced golf to the members. But he is best remembered not for his play, but for the stylish clothes he wore on the course, reminiscent of the stylish Englishmen and Scots who came to America to seek their fortune.

The course officially opened on April 22, 1898 with an exhibition between two Foulis brothers, David and Jim, both Chicago area professionals who

Triple A Clubhouse 1901

would play important parts in the design of several area courses. Jim Foulis was noted as *"the greatest driver [of golf] in America. He holds the record for the long distance drive, having sent the ball on one occasion the enormous distance of 308 yards."* Though the grounds were wet, the newspaper article noted that Foulis frequently drove within 50 yards of a 315 yard hole. Oddly, Foulis used only three clubs for the entire match; the driver, mashie and putter. However, the putting surface was in such poor shape, the course was barely two months old and very wet on that day, that it often took them three to four strokes to hole out after getting to the green. For the 27 holes they played, Jim had a 123 and Dave a 125, with scores of 41-43-39 and 44-38-43. Par for the course was listed at 39. Jim Foulis had designed the course and remarked how the greenkeeper, [Occley Johnson] had done a fine job keeping it in shape. Some golfers had been playing early in the month, but the April 1898 opening marks the Jockey Club as the second links officially opened in the area. Like the Country Club, it would be a private club, but it was open year round and thus received much more play.

The members received quite a bit of attention as they played golf the morning before big races, or prior to attending baseball at the nearby Robinson Field (later Sportsman's Park) home of the St. Louis Browns. The course continued to host Ladies tournaments, but as time went by, the layout within the track was not conducive to good course conditioning as the fairways became hard as asphalt. Following the Worlds Fair in 1904, horse-racing fell out of grace with the powers-that-be in Jefferson City, particularly due the money being wagered on the ponies. So when para-mutual betting was abolished in 1905, the club's days were numbered. The racetrack was dismantled shortly thereafter, and the clubhouse was razed as the land was sold to the city for a Fairgounds Park.

Early view of the Normandie Course looking toward #4

Florissant Valley CC

The exclusive *Florissant Valley CC* was formed in the late 1890's and was located in Normandy Heights [thus the golf course was often mistakenly referred to as the Normandy Heights Club]. The club, like several others in the area, leased property from the land-wealthy J.B.C. Lucas family.

The Lucas family follows it's roots back to France where, in 1784, the patriarch of the US clan, Jean Baptiste Charles Lucas, took an interest in the revolution taking place in America. Siding with the patriots, he received a letter of introduction from the US Ambassador to France, Benjamin Franklin, recommending his services to Thomas Jefferson. He had also met John Adams on his travels to Europe, so Lucas was well known in US circles. Years later, when Jefferson became president, he appointed Lucas, who by then was an attorney, as the commissioner of Land Claims and Judge of the Territorial Court in the newly created Louisiana Purchase area.

As so many early settlers of the area were French, it became natural for Lucas to settle here and become an aristocrat-of-sorts among his former countrymen. He purchased a considerable amount of land, especially after the New Madrid earthquake of 1812, and by the late 1800's owned some 1,500 acres on their farm in the Normandy-Berkeley-Kinloch-Pasadena Hills-Bel Nor area. When Wilson P. Hunt, son of Ann Lucas and Theodore Hunt, gained control of the property through his mother-in-law Anne B. Lucas, he built his mansion on the land and planted hundreds of trees, many imported from France. Lucas & Hunt Road in north county reflects their significance in the area. But by 1927, the remaining land was sold to another group of investors, and 10 years later the remaining property was sold at auction on the courthouse steps in Clayton to Rice Emerson, whose family still owns the property.

In the spring of 1899, the 40 member *Florissant Valley Club* laid out nine holes in what is today Bel-Nor, just north of Normandie GC and situated south of Natural Bridge Road. Like the Country

Triple A Club - 1903 after moving to present site

Club, they also had polo ponies and a large barn. But with only 40 members, they could not maintain all the facilities, so the golf course was turned back into pasture by 1905. When the old Lucas mansion, which was being used as the clubhouse, burned in 1912 the members never rebuilt, though the Florissant Valley Club remained as a dining club till 1946, but at another site.

Kinloch CC

The *Kinloch Club* was also located on a portion of the Lucas property; at Lucas-Turner Place. It's grounds were part of the Harry Smith Turner property, another member of the Lucas family who had established his home in the area prior to the Civil War. The Kinloch Club was regarded as the most exclusive of the early clubs. Its members were among the most wealthy and influential St. Louisans, paying a $1,700 entry fee to join. Several of them formed one of the earliest phone companies, the Kinloch Telephone Company, whose Chairman was a member of the Anheuser family. Golf was played here, according to a Globe-Democrat article, during 1898. The exact reason for it's demise is unclear. One story noted the increased

Sunset CC (then called Sunset Hill CC) c. 1910 when it was primarily a dinner club. Golf would arrive here in 1917.

assessments as a possible reason. But one incident apparently played a big part in the drama. When a young, wealthy St. Louisan attempted to join, a member with whom he had had a serious disagreement, openly voiced his opposition to other members. The applicant withdrew his name, rather than face a blackball. At the next meeting a very heated discussion ensued. Shortly after this incident, several members met at the St. Louis Club and on August 10, 1899, they formed the *Log Cabin Club* . This departure all but marked the end of the Kinloch Club, though it would continue for a few more years, it would never again have the same significance.

Triple A Club

The *Triple A Club,* or St. Louis Amateur Athletic Association, [the two names are often used interchangeably] came into being on August 11, 1897, as the club leased land in the northwestern section of Forest Park [near the site of the present 18 hole golf course]. The original plan called for about 2,000 invitations to be sent to interested participants, and the club organizers planned to purchase the clubhouse of the Pastime Athletic Club for their clubhouse, though this never materialized, as a new building was constructed and opened on June 5, 1898. The group was to be the St. Louis member of the Amateur Athletic Union [AAU].

Early on, it's members were mainly interested in baseball and track, with the first golf matches held in October 1898. Initially the club opened with only 6 holes. Aware that golf was an 18-hole event, six holes meant you would go around it three times and still have a match. But as more golfers appeared, and the course became more crowded, money was freed-up, and the additional 3 holes were completed in December 1898.

At this time, no area club had an "official" 18-hole layout and the local Newspapers began to decry this as a blemish on the area as major national events overlooked St. Louis as a consequence.

By the summer of 1900, four clubs openly spoke about lengthening their links to 18 holes; Triple A, the Country Club, the Field Club and the new, much-publicized Mound City Golf Club [soon renamed Glen Echo]. But it was at Triple A where the initial 18 flags were in holes, not at Normandie or Glen Echo, St. Louis or the Field Club.

In April 1901, as the courses were beginning to open for the season, the following article appeared in the Post-Dispatch; "*Walter L. Gilliam, chairman of the golf committee of the St. L. A.A.A. says that the Forest Park links will be in very fair condition after a few weeks' sunshine and spring showers. He says the entire 18 holes have been sodded and need only a little cutting and trimming. The fair greens are now being rolled and mowed. There is a large and growing contingent of golfers in this club.*" And in June 1901 the Globe-Democrat had an article that stated "*...the eighteen holes at the Forest Park Athletic Association is said to be among the finest in this part of the country*".

But the joy of their new-found links would be short-lived. Unfortunately for the club, the July 30 1901 Globe-Democrat noted that with the World's Fair approaching, the clubhouse needed to be torn down and the club moved to a new location in the park. The site chosen is the present site in the southeast corner of the park. Money given to the Club by the city to pay for their move and new building did not go far enough, so it was decided to build only 9 holes.

On April 2, 1902 the Triple A players were competing against the Country Club, Field Club, Glen Echo and Normandie in a series of matches to be held during the spring, with the championship being held at the Field Club on June 21. The Women's championship was being held in conjunction with the men's, and their championship was held at the Fair Grounds [Jockey Club] on October 4.

The Triple A club operated as a private club until 1981, when it went public, though memberships are available. Today, it is one of the few courses that take no reservations and walk-on's are always welcome.

Normandie Clubhouse - opened in April, 1902

Tower Grove Park Links

All of the previously mentioned clubs were essentially private, or at least memberships were required. As interest grew, politicians began to call for public venues. A proposal was made to establish free-links at *Forest Park*, *Carondelet Park* and *Tower Grove Park*. Mayor Ziggenheim barely knew what golf was, but like any good politician he was quoted as saying *"...golf, oh yes, isn't that the game for skinnies? Well, if that's what the people want, then we'll give it to them."* As best as can be determined, the only links built during this period were at **Tower Grove Park**. Newspapers indicate that links were scheduled to be laid out at Carondelet and Forest Park, but no record exists to verify this.

The **Carondelet Park Links** referred to in the *"Golf Guide"* most likely referred to the six-hole course at **Tower Grove Park** in 1898, which was expanded to nine holes in 1901. What makes this club unique is that it was formed by early St. Louis women golfers, most disenchanted with the rules applying to playing opportunities at the Country Club. From the May 19, 1901 *Globe-Democrat*

article; *"Out at the Tower Grove Park, the ladies will play golf and no lone man may enter into the sacred precincts of the grove unless some woman waits for him. He may play with his wife, or if unmarried, and with a sweetheart among the players, he may also play golf. So if any unattached man is seen wandering within the limits of the links you will know that his possibilities are about to become probabilities"*.

They formed their club in 1898 at the Wednesday Club Women's Meeting, as a place they could take their children to learn the game. The club also had a professional instructor, Mr. George Norman, a pro from St. Louis CC, whose task it was to teach the ladies and children the game. However, when the ladies selected someone to lay-out their course, they selected a Mr. John McGee from the Field Club! Located in the northwest corner of the park, the ladies constructed *"a small, but elegant clubhouse"* where they gathered, usually each Thursday to play.

An article in the Globe-Democrat on April 13, 1902, announced the annual meeting of the Tower Grove park golf club, where new officers

*Harry Allen
Early State Champion
and one of the founders
of Bellerive CC*

*Don Anderson
Another State
Champ
who found compet-
ing against Manion,
Held and Wolff a
difficult task.*

*Tommy Armour
The Silver Scot, so
named as his hair
turned grey over the
years. Came over as
an Amateur and
became one of the
great Pro's of the
day.*

*Jesse Carleton
One of the founders
of Glen Echo, he
later would also help
in the founding of
Sunset CC.*

The 9th Tee at Glen Echo - 1903

were elected for the coming year. Mrs. Charles W. Scudder was re-elected as president and Mrs. Thomas Neidringhaus as vice president. The membership fee was reduced from $15 to $10 because of the good financial condition of the club. A junior tournament was planned for June 1, and for regular members on June 4. Most of the families maintained memberships at other private clubs during this time, and must have changed some of those club's rules, as the course ceased operations in 1903.

Jefferson Barracks Links

The *Jefferson Barracks* course was most likely the first of at least two that were constructed at the military site; each probably abandoned as space was needed for troops during the War periods. We must remember, laying-out a course often consisted of a large field with some type of marker to note the hole location. It did not mean a closely-mowed surface or even a defined fairway, at least not until a few years later. They literally were, at times, pastures or fields that were for the time, serving no other use.

Despite the construction of St. Louis CC in 1896 by Jim Foulis as well as his design of the Jockey Club, it appears that few clubs utilized "professional" architects to layout their courses.

Instead they relied on local professionals to accomplish this task. Glen Echo and Normandie followed this approach when they gave birth to tees and greens in 1901 and contracted with the Foulis' once more.

Log Cabin Club

As noted earlier, the *Log Cabin Club* was not born from a need for another club, as much as dissatisfaction with the Kinloch Club. Following the incident mentioned earlier, the members began preparing to depart from the Club. They had scouted sites all summer and found a site just west of the Country Club on the Clymer farm. A lease on the land was secured by Thomas Niedringhaus, Charles Hodgman, Alexander Euston, Richard Everett, David Evans, Emile Glogau, Henry Lewis and C. Norman Jones. They hired Professional James Mackrell from the Country Club to lay-out their new course. [Robert Foulis would also be given credit] An old log cabin nearby served as the inspiration for the club's name. The site of the original clubhouse is today the Ladue City Hall on Clayton Road. Getting to the site required traveling a streetcar line to that site and then a carriage ride to the club. The clubs original nine holes would "merge" with the neighboring Bogey Club in 1912 to allow the members access to a full eighteen.

The Log Cabin Club also has the distinction of being the oldest club in St. Louis to remain at one location through the years, having begun in 1899 at the same site. A very select membership of usually no more than 60 members, the club has hosted some of the countries most distinguished leaders, including Dwight Eisenhower in 1947 and President Teddy Roosevelt and former President Grover Cleveland during the 1904 Worlds Fair. The original Clymer house served the club until 1981 when it was consumed in a fire and the club built a new facility. Today the new clubhouse sits on the east side of Clayton Road just west of the Bogey Club site.

Algonquin CC

The *Algonquin Club* was organized in 1899 as its members were playing golf over a 9 hole course in Webster Park. Originally located near the present site of Gore Ave. and the RR tracks in Webster Groves, the Algonquins were a bold group, challenging all comers, and for a few matches in 1900, going undefeated. The land in Webster Park was sprinkled with homes, one of which was the McKinnie homestead which sat in the middle of the course. But as 1901 turned, more homes were built on the land, and the space for golf was reduced. As one home was built, you could no longer tee from the 8th tee to hit toward the green, so the course had to be re-routed around the lot. Other land was considered, and they even considered merging with the Triple A club, which was also undergoing a space problem, though theirs was due to the coming 1904 Worlds Fair. Finally on June 25, 1903, Arthur Deacon, Bart Adams, Allen McKinnie, W.S. Avis and Kent Jarvis met to form the new club. A name not mentioned was Mrs. Kent Jarvis. She was a very active golfer and perhaps the driving forces behind the new Club. Later that year they purchased the 54 acre Jackson Farm [at Jackson and

Charles McGrew was the father-in-law of another famous St. Louisan, Albert B. Lambert, an early backer of Charles Lindbergh's flight to Paris, and name-sake of our international airport. Lambert also won the 1907 Missouri Amateur and is credited with winning the Paris Olympic championship in 1900. His trophy for this win resides at the USGA Museum in Far Hills, New Jersey.

Berry Roads] and created first the new nine hole course. The construction of their clubhouse was completed in 1904. Nine years later in 1913 they would add more land, enlarge the clubhouse and complete nine new holes.

Financing the improvements at Algonquin was accomplished by rather novel means. Instead of the traditional assessments or increase in the dues, the members issued bonds subscribed by the members to cover the costs.

Conditions in 1904 at the club were sparse, no phones, no caddies, no golf professional and no automobiles. The club did arrange with the Missouri Pacific RR for a stop near the present site of the 4th green, and the Lockwood Avenue streetcar also provided another means of getting to the club.

Creating a club in the southwest section of the city was somewhat risky. All the other clubs, with the exception of the Tower Grove Club and Jefferson Barracks, had been organized in the northwest or west sections of the area. [The Tower Grove and Jefferson Barracks clubs being the other exceptions but they were unique in their membership make-up and perhaps as a result, no mention is made of these two clubs being included in the early inter-club matches of which the other clubs participated]

Another factor facing each club was keeping them in good condition. Maintenance at clubs was difficult at best, as mowing was accomplished with horse-drawn mowers. It was a continual task as you would finish the nine holes and it would be time to begin again.

The location of each club has one outstanding feature; each was built on or near a Railroad line! In

> *Robert Foulis*
> *Architect, Greenkeeper and early agronomist. Designed with his brother James, Normandie, Glen Echo, Sunset CC Bogey Club, Log Cabin and the original Bellerive CC. Pro at Normandie, Glen Echo and Bellerive. Was also a pro at Onwentsia in Chicago prior to arriving in St. Louis. Was head greenkeeper at Normandie, Glen Echo, Bellerive at the same time. Consulted on almost every course in the area prior to 1930 including Triple A, Ruth Park, Algonquin, Kirkwood, Westwood and Forest Park.*

the late 1890's, carriages were the normal mode of transport and public transportation was generally streetcars; so to venture "6-8 miles to the club" was not made without some thought and a degree of adventure. So in many ways the site of the early clubs was dictated by the location of the Rail lines. One newspaper account noted that the possible closing of a rail line could seriously threaten the future of the Field Club since members could not make the journey easily, a situation which the club said they were working to rectify by providing alternate means of transportation. This may point us in the direction as to why they abandoned the Bellefontaine area for a more attractive site in the

No	Hole	Yards	Par	No	Hole	Yards	Par
1	Lilac	276	4	10	Hard Scrabble	414	5
2	The Valley	481	5	11	Hillside	271	4
3	The Glen	178	3	12	Westward Ho	246	5
4	Spooks	280	4	13	Echo	321	4
5	Long Drive	548	6	14	Dew Drop	149	3
6	Road Way	242	4	15	The Lake	360	4
7	Boomerang	415	5	16	Punch Bowl	423	5
8	The Alps	435	5	17	Old Hickory	400	5
9	The Fountain	148	3	18	Sweet Home	411	5
		2,973	39			3,175	40

Glen Echo CC (circa 1906)

Normandy area in 1910; there were already other clubs nearby and transportation was much easier.

Of the courses created prior to 1900, none remain today. Of the Clubs there are four; St. Louis, Bellerive (The Field Club), Triple A and Log Cabin. But at the turn of the century two organizations would be founded that would, to this day, do battle over their history.

Glen Echo & Normandie

The Glen Echo club was organized in 1900 by some very prominent St. Louisans including Murray Carleton, Herman Luyties, Festus Wade, Julius Koehler, Selwyn Edgar and George A. Meyer. They negotiated a lease with Mr. William Hunt for 167 acres of the Lucas property. But the driving force behind *Glen Echo* was

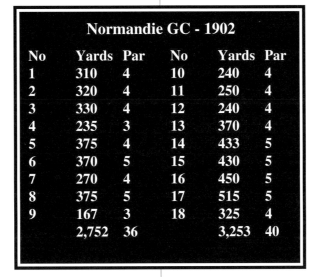

No	Yards	Par	No	Yards	Par
\multicolumn{6}{c}{**Normandie GC - 1902**}					
1	310	4	10	240	4
2	320	4	11	250	4
3	330	4	12	240	4
4	235	3	13	370	4
5	375	4	14	433	5
6	370	5	15	430	5
7	270	4	16	450	5
8	375	5	17	515	5
9	167	3	18	325	4
	2,752	36		3,253	40

Colonel George S. McGrew. McGrew helped foster enthusiasm for the new club as he gave speeches and presentations to area golfers. One such presentation was about his recent trip to England and Scotland, where he played a match with Young Tom Morris at St. Andrews. He thrilled the crowd with his descriptions of the clubhouse, the holes and the other sites. He was a dynamic and charismatic man who charmed those around him. He even convinced the upcoming Olympic games to award Glen Echo the golf matches even before the site was completed!

Sounds similar to an event almost ninety years later when the Ryder Cup would award Kiawah the 1991 matches before the Ocean Course was completed by Pete Dye!

A few months later another group, headed by John Lowry, William Plant, Walter Gilliam and Dr. William Hall were planning the *Normandie* course, also on the Lucas farm. As the crow flies, these clubs are only about two par 5's apart. But when it comes to which came first, they might as well be on other sides of the coast!

Both clubs planned eighteen holes, something that was uncommon in the area at the time, as all previous clubs, except

Three of the five Foulis Brothers; (l-r) Robert, Jim and Dave.

Jimmy Manion and his wife Gladys. He would have a successful Insurance career and Gladys would found a successful Clayton-based Real Estate company.

Charles McGrew Founder of Glen Echo CC

Gene Sarazen He was one of many prominent players who visited St. Louis. Here is at Sunset CC in 1927.

Albert Bond Lambert Winner of the Paris 1900 Olympic Golf Matches

for Triple A were nine holes. If newspaper accounts are any indication, Glen Echo also had the better press agent! The opening of the course was in the paper for months before the opening day event in 1901, and when they opened the second season in 1902, you would have sworn the club was new!

Normandie on the other hand, got fewer columns in the local papers. Tradition has stated for years that Normandie CC is *"the oldest golf club at its present site west of the Mississippi"* and this legacy has sustained itself through the years. The Del Monte course in California (at Pebble Beach) has also laid claim that it is the oldest course west of the Mississippi, though it is known that the club moved at one point. We also know that Glen Echo has been at it's present site since it's opening. What does all this mean? Does the establishment of the "club" mark the date? Or is it when the course construction begins, or when it's completed? Or is it when it is opened for play? Whichever standard you care to use, I hope to clarify the situation with the following information.

Based on articles from the Globe-Democrat and the Post-Dispatch, the **Glen Echo** course was opened first, on May 25, 1901, and was in play during that summer, first with nine holes and by mid-summer the entire eighteen.

An article in the Globe-Democrat on September 29, 1901 announced the formation of the **Normandie Park Club** and a week later on October 6, both the Post and Globe announced that a temporary course with 9 holes was available for play by the members. Given the fact that there was a course

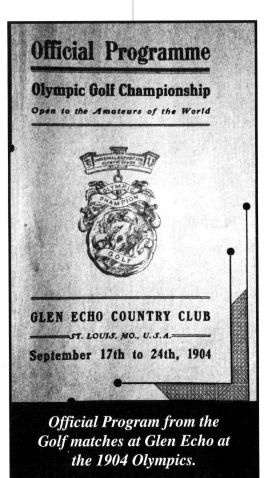

Official Programme

Olympic Golf Championship

Open to the Amateurs of the World

GLEN ECHO COUNTRY CLUB

ST. LOUIS, MO., U.S.A.

September 17th to 24th, 1904

Official Program from the Golf matches at Glen Echo at the 1904 Olympics.

available for play within a week of the club's founding lays credence that some construction must have taken place prior to the formation of the club! Also, in April 1902, the full 18 holes and clubhouse were opened for use. To assume that all this took place between October 1901 and April 1902, during a St. Louis winter, would not be practical, though it is conceivable. To further confuse the issue, from the book *"Architects of Golf"* authors Ron Whitten & Geoffrey Cornish credit Robert Foulis as the designer of both courses along with his brother Jim at Glen Echo, with the dates of Normandie as 1901 and Glen Echo as 1902, dates which are obviously inaccurate. Whatever the case, Glen Echo was definitely organized prior to Normandie, as a golf club and was opened for play first.

Since Robert Foulis was the architect on both courses, with his brother Jim assisting on Glen Echo, one story suggests that Normandie may have been partially constructed and then the crew moved to Glen Echo to complete that layout for the May opening before moving back to Normandie to complete their work. However, there is no documentation for this theory. The actual events may never be known for the records have long since been misplaced and the courses as envisioned by the brothers remain a long-lost image on the retina of their eyes!

Glen Echo CC

Located *"...1 3/4 miles NW of St. Louis on the Wabash RR Lines..."* sat *Glen Echo CC.* Originally conceived as the Mound City Golf Club, the name was not considered "pretty enough" so the Glen Echo name was adopted prior to the opening of the course.

The original Glen Echo clubhouse was an enormous Victorian style facility with a large awning-covered porch that members would sit to view the grounds. As noted earlier, the Glen Echo club officially opened on May 25, 1901. It was one minute past three when St. Louis Mayor Rolla Wells stepped to the speakers' position under the flagstaff to make his remarks to the gathering of 500 anxious guests. He congratulated the management on the success of carrying out such an enormous project, noting that as a boy he had played on the grounds nearby. Club President McGrew then had the honor of hitting the first shot off the tee. He hit his first shot poorly, half-topped his second, then finally hit a good drive to christen the course. McGrew, a member of the Western Golf Associations' Board of Directors, as well as the force behind the Glen Echo Club, could not contain his enjoyment as Willie Smith of the Midlothian Club and James Foulis from the Chicago Golf Club, would battle in

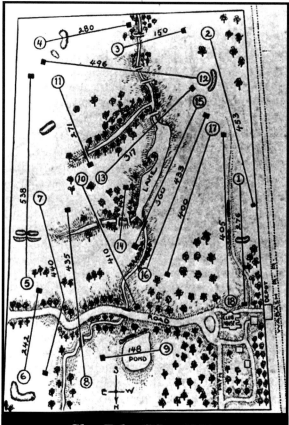

Glen Echo CC c. 1902.
Lucas & Hunt Road is to the left with the RR tracks on the right, parallel to the 1st & 2nd fairway. Sixteen holes remains essentially with the same layout today.

the opening match. Smith would win the match 3 and 2, with medal scores of 87 to Foulis' 92. The paper comments on the bad luck had by Foulis, who was 1-up at the end of nine, but it was mostly due to the strong winds that played havoc with his shots. A friendly match played that morning between Smith and James and Robert Foulis saw quite a different outcome as James shot a 41 to 44's by the other two. This original match was the first played in St. Louis between two professional golfers, the exhibition at the Jockey Club not considered a true match!

1901 had been a bad spring in St. Louis and as a result only nine holes were open for play, with the other nine being delayed for approximately six weeks. *"...while the full eighteen-hole course has been completed, the backward spring has resulted in the failure of the grass to grow sufficiently to justify the use of the full course..."* from an April 28, 1901 Globe-Democrat article.

As the club prepared for the 1902 season, many changes had been made. The course had been lengthened to almost 6,200 yards and the greens re-worked. Members surveying the new grounds were cautioned not to step on the new greens or risk the wrath of Colonel McGrew.

In 1904 the course had 27 holes, including a 9 hole putting course which was lighted! This was used as the site of a putting contest during the Olympics of that year which was won by Burt

McKinnie, under the lights. According to reports *"...putting courses are rare in this country, and the idea of illuminating the course is absolutely original..."* The article goes on to state that a putting course *"...is a regular part of every golf course [in Scotland] ...and will cover an area of 300 feet by 100 feet"*. We think of this as our traditional putting green today, though it was fairly large for the day, and of course somewhat unusual.

An interesting aspect is the course and it's rating. The yardage was 6,148 yards and had *"...a bogey of 79"*. The holes were as follows with the layout shown on page 22. Note the par 6 on the 5th hole and the "bogey or par" of 79. The reference to the "bogey" of the day was the score before recording a bogey on the hole, as opposed to our noting of "Par" today!

The clubhouse has changed through the years, but the routing and location of most of the holes are essentially the same.

Despite the caliber of the membership, by 1915 the club found itself with serious financial problems, having incurred debts of approximately $84,000. Early in 1916 the club went into bankruptcy. It was reorganized under the name Ridgedale CC the same year and kept the that name until 1921 when it reverted back to Glen Echo CC.

Normandie CC

The course of 1902 at Normandie would bear some resemblance to todays layout - 13 of the holes are on the same grounds - but the routing would bear little similarity. Holes 13-17 were located across Nor- mandie drive on what is today the Incarnate Word Academy grounds. The 18th hole is roughly where it is today, but was originally a par 4. The first hole ran where the 10th is today and the 12th would today be the 17th. However, once you left the clubhouse you did not return until the end of the match.

In the April 27, 1902 edition of the Globe-Democrat the following article was noted;

"The golf season is now in full swing and the prospects seem to be very good indeed. The links are in good condition and the players even more enthusiastic than at this time last year. The opening at Field Club was very auspicious, and yesterday a good game was played at Country Club, the two teams being captained by Mr. C.W. Scudder and Mr. Stewart G. Stickney." and later in the article *"Out in Normandie Park everything is progressing finely ...and the house is approaching completion"*.

Descriptions of the holes are as follows; #1, carry a ditch at 110 yards, the ground is gently rolling; #2 & #3, both are easy par 4's; #4, is down a hill and over a ravine at 120 yards makes good playing for 3; #5, 150 yards are through a beautiful oak, elm and hickory grove, then over undulating turf, and another 4 will halve the hole; #6, is rather uphill, over fine sod to an inverted saucer green, which makes a 5 interesting; #7 is an easy 4; #8, is through a grove, requiring an iron shot for a lie,

Original layout for Normandie in 1901. Note 5 holes (#13-17) across road from present location. #1 is where present #10 is situated. St. Charles Rock Road is at bottom, with Normandie Drive dividing the holes.

before crossing a ditch and hillside. Then a brassie or spoon will assist you in getting a 5; #9, over a pond for a 3; #10, a 140 yard carry is necessary to negotiate a ravine, but beware of a slice into the lake; #11, #12 & #13, should be easy 4's; #14, another lake requiring a 110 yard carry then a brassie or spoon and an iron to drop over a ditch "dead" on the green; #15, good playing is required here for a 5; #16, same play as 15 required here, except minus the lake for a five; #17, the ground rolls beautifully uphill for a splendid view of the country. A good drive, a brassie and an iron is glad to get a 5; #18, home in four well-placed shots.

Cup won by Albert Lambert at the 1900 Paris Exposition Games

And once again from the Globe-Democrat article; "*The course is only 6005 yards long and 76 is bogie. Nine of the holes are over sod which never had a plow to it. There are three water jumps, and several ditches to cross, but there are no artificial hazards.*"

Another article appeared in the Post-Dispatch recording the details of the new clubhouse on April 27, 1902 with an accompanying picture, course diagram and a complete description of the interior. The club also announced that they had extended the lease from ten to fifteen years from the J.B.C. Lucas family and looked for a prosperous and long life. The Post-Dispatch article went on to add; "*The clubhouse is conveniently located, if not more so, than any other country*

Ralph McKittrick

clubhouse in the vicinity of St. Louis. It can be reached in fifty to fifty-five minutes from Fourth Street by any one of the three lines of cars to Wellston, namely the Olive Street "through" car, the Suburban Railroad, or the Easton avenue line, and from Wellston to the clubhouse door in eight minutes via the St. L., St. C., and W. railroad" and *"...during the golf season it is expected that cars (streetcar or trolley's) will run from Wellston to the clubhouse as frequently as every fifteen minutes.*"

The first matches of 1902 at Normandie took place on May 3. This tournament was to decide the club championship and to select a team to represent the club in the local inter-club matches. Prominent players from 1901 at the course were Walter Gilliam, Willis Hall, Edgar Floyd-Jones, A.C. Vickery, Arthur Meyer, Dr. Short, Dr. Dorchester, J.S. Lowry, Charles Allen and William Saunders, and from this group would undoubtedly come the club's representatives to the matches.

The officers of the club in 1902 were listed as John S. Lowry, president; William Saunders, vice president; J. Stewart Walker, treasurer and Mr. Walter Gilliam as chairman of the golf committee.

In 1919, the club was able to secure additional land from the Lucas Estate, and the 118 acres needed to move all the holes to the same side of Normandy Drive was completed. To fund the $700 per acre purchase price, members were required to purchased one share in the newly created Normandy Investment Company at $250 per share. The present 18 hole re-design was then completed.

Westwood CC

As is the case today, success by one group leads others to try their luck. So it was with another group who formed **Westwood CC** in Glendale in 1907. Members of the group included Frederick Arnold, Louis Aloe, Irvin Bettman, Dr. Hanau Loeb, Henry Ittleson, Charles Rice, David Sommers, Dr. Sidney Schwab, Edwin Schiele, Moses Shoenberg, Charles Stix and Charles Schwartz. They entered into a lease for the George S. Myers property and created their new course in 1908 as they hired architect Tom Bendelow to lay-out the course. The grand opening was a spectacular affair as a private rail car was rented for the occasion for the members to arrive at the club. By 1911 the club had grown to 191 regular members.

There are those of you who are reading this that would suggest that this must be in error. Today that site is occupied by Westborough with Westwood on Conway Road! You are correct. The Westwood club did abandon the Westborough site in 1927 as they built their new club, keeping the same "Club" name. So the Westwood Club goes back to 1908 while their course dates only from 1927, just the reverse for Westborough.

Stuart Stickney

At the Olympics

At the Olympic Golf contest in 1904 played over the Glen Echo links, George S. Lyon of Toronto defeated Chicagoan H. Chandler Egan of Exmoor Club 4 and 3. Stuart G. Stickney from St. Louis CC led all qualifiers with a 163 over the track. Other St. Louisans in the competition were; Albert Bond Lambert (Glen Echo), Ralph McKittrick (St. Louis), Fred W. Semple (St. Louis), S.T. Price (Normandie), A.C. Vickery (Glen Echo), Burt McKinnie (Normandie), H. Potter (St. Louis), Jesse Carleton (Glen Echo), W. Arthur Stickney (St. Louis), Sim T. Price (St. Louis), Bernie Edmunds (Glen Echo), C.W. Scudder (St. Louis), Bart Adams (St. Louis), W. H. Hersey (St. Louis), E.M. Davis (Normandie), S.J. Harbaugh (St. Louis), J.J. Howard (St. Louis), J.T. Watson (Glen Echo), E.M. Gould (St. Louis), A.H. Annan (St. Louis), W.W. Grossclothes (St. Louis), G.F. Powell (St. Louis), M. Carleton (Glen Echo), F.E. Newberry (St. Louis) and Harry W. Allen (St. Louis).

There was also a team contest held between the Trans-Mississippi Association, the Western Association and a "picked" team. With most of the St. Louisans playing for the Trans-Miss team they lost to the Western Golf squad. This followed a special match team between the Trans-Miss and the Western where the Trans-Miss won by 5 points.

The demise of the Olympic Golf matches seemed destined

1904 Olympic Golf Medal

from the very beginning. In 1900, Englishmen did not want to play with Scots and no Englishmen entered the 1904 Event at Glen Echo. When the British clubs were asked to open their facilities for the games in 1908, and all refused, the event eventually had to be canceled.

Early Players

Stuart Stickney was one of the early talented St. Louis golfers. In 1902 he faced H. Chandler Egan in the finals of the Western Amateur and lost 1-up. At the Olympics he would lose to the eventual winner, Lyon, in the second round. *Burt McKinnie* would last to the semi-finals where he would also fall to Egan 4 and 3. Egan was one of the early stars in the Chicago area, and he won several early Western Opens.

Albert Lambert was also an excellent player, having won the amateur championship of France in 1900 and also the Olympic championship played in Paris. He would return and capture the 1907 Missouri Amateur crown as well, as would fellow Country Club members Ralph McKittrick (1910) and Stickney (1912).

Lambert was a left-handed player, remarkable for the time as left-handed clubs were scarce. When he traveled to Europe for the 1900 Olympics he entered the golf competition, which was a handicap tournament. With his 10 handicap he shot a net 73 to capture the title. The trophy he won was donated to the USGA museum by his grandson, Donaldson Lambert.

James Foulis Architect of many early St. Louis courses, winner of the 2nd US Open, (1896) & one of the countries top Professionals. He was head pro at St. Louis CC 1912-15.

The Foulis'

When **Robert Foulis** came from Scotland via Chicago to the area he brought with him his experiences from his days as an assistant in Tom Morris' Shop at St. Andrews and the "Old Course" there. So while the land presented to him for the course at Glen Echo and Normandie did not match the seaside contours he remembered from St. Andrews, he gave the course as much of the feel as he recalled from those early days.

Jim Foulis arrived in the area in 1896 when he completed the initial 9 holes for *St. Louis CC*. Two years later, as noted previously, he laid out the 9 holes at *The Jockey Club*.

Robert arrived in the US in 1895 and was head professional at Lake Forest CC, then Onwentsia CC before moving to Minnesota. In 1900 he traveled to St. Louis where he was to do Glen Echo and Normandie. After acquired these contracts he called upon his brother James to join him in St. Louis to assist with Glen Echo.

James was already recognized as one of the finest players in the country, having won the second US Open in 1896, and was already renowned as a designer. [Amazingly, none of the Foulis brothers ever played in a British Open or Amateur, yet James won the US Open in only his 2nd year here!] James served as the first professional at Chicago GC, the countries first 18 hole club, from 1895 to 1905. Having been privy to watching C.B. Macdonald at work at the Chicago club, he gained first-hand knowledge about course architecture in America, and began to apply that throughout the midwest. In

The 13th Fairway (then called the Fair Green) in 1904 at Glen Echo. The entire course was termed the "green" with the Fair Green being the area between the teeing ground and the "putting" green; the place where the ball was "put"!

Foursome on the green at Triple A c. 1908

Early ladies on the course at Sunset Hill CC, now Sunset CC.

Scotland he undoubtedly gleaned much from Tom Morris at St. Andrews and this influenced him greatly in his later design, though it was Robert who actually had formal training from Old Tom Morris in course design!

Their work was so exceptional that within three years Glen Echo was host to the first Olympic golf matches, and not a single written word notes a negative comment on the course, in fact the level of praise for the condition of the greens was noteworthy.

While Robert Foulis was becoming a force in the area, Jim and Dave assisted him with the design of Glen Echo, Bellerive and Sunset Hill. Robert would design one of the midwest's top courses, Minikahda Club in Minnesota, while James went on to design Denver CC and the original Milwaukee CC along with several others no longer in existence.

Jim Foulis was also a club-maker of some renown. While at the Chicago GC he designed many clubs similar to his days at St. Andrews. Some of his clubs are on display in Chicago, with his name *"James Foulis - Wheaton, IL"* stamped on the back of each club. In fact he and Dave held several patents on clubs, including the first concave "wedge" type club used to stop a ball on the rock-hard greens from a distance of 60 yards. They called it their mashie-niblick.

Typical of many early pros, they were also skilled in golf ball construction. The early rubber-Haskell balls were smooth and would not go very far, yet they were more durable than the old gutties. When Dave and Jim applied the "bramble" pattern to the original Haskell, they had a winner. They made quite a bit of money buying Haskells, modifying them, and re-selling them,

Forest Park Golf Course c. 1916

Tom Bendelow

much to the displeasure of Coburn Haskell.

Current St. Louisan William Gahlberg, one of the founders of Butler National and a member of Chicago GC has donated many of Foulis' clubs from his collection to Butler National to be put on display.

While James returned to Chicago, Robert went on to layout Algonquin CC (1904), Bogey Club (1912), Log Cabin (1909), Sunset CC (1917 with James), Forest Park GC (1913), Triple A (remodeled), the original Bellerive (1910), along with Midland Valley (1911) and Riverview/North Shore (1916). Robert also ventured to Jefferson City where he designed the original 9 holes for the Country Club there in 1922. One of Robert's last layouts was the design of Ruth Park in 1931 with Robert Bruce Harris.

Robert was the pro/greenkeeper at Glen Echo in 1902, moved to Normandie for a time before moving to Bellerive in 1910, where he became the their first pro/greenkeeper and remained there until he retired in 1942, being pro emeritus the last 12 years.

As we all know, growing grasses in this area can be very trying. Zoysia seems to do the best, while the warm nights do not bode well for bent fairways. Several early District clubs had members who attempted to study the effects of various chemicals on grasses. The information gained from one series of tests was shared among all the clubs.

We know from minutes of the St. Louis District Golf Association that when Robert Foulis arrived in St. Louis in 1899 he soon went to work as greenkeeper for area clubs, though which specific clubs are not known. In 1904 he was listed as the greenkeeper and professional at Glen Echo CC during the Olympic Golf

Matches that year. Still other accounts show him as professional and greenkeeper at Normandie and Glen Echo at the same time. While still later newspaper accounts indicate he was the professional at Normandie in 1909, before moving to Bellerive the following year.

The following statement from Robert Foulis was from the minutes of the St. Louis District Golf Association in 1927. *"When I came to St. Louis in 1891 [1898] I there were no greens, nor any fairways, just cow pastures. The clubs didn't want to spend any money. I brought seed from Europe, experimented with them until I found what was right for St. Louis. The greens we have at Bellerive have not been out of play since 1912. Fungicide treatments have brought our greens through the summers without a brown patch."*

In researching the Foulis' I had an occasion to speak with his grandson and among his possessions is a large box that was given to him by his mother [Elinora Foulis Miller, Robert's daughter] with various types of seeds that Robert Foulis had kept over the years.

Foulis also worked with courses to maintain their grasses and greens, in particular Algonquin, Glen Echo and Normandie. He was instrumental in the organizing of the Greens Section for the District, whose members met along with the regular District representatives. This group was important in the early days as courses were continually experimenting with grasses and methods to eradicate the various weeds, fungus and other diseases that plagued area

The Train station was used as the clubhouse at Algonquin around 1900. Players would change inside and then walk to the course.

courses. Today's modern superintendent follows a long line of early pioneers. Some of these were Colonel Goetz from Algonquin, Foulis from Bellerive, Montgomery from Normandie, Johnson from Midland Valley, Eberhard Anheuser at Sunset and Roy Flesh from Kirkwood CC. Christian Kenny from Sunset CC, president of the District in 1927 made the following comments, *"...I have followed and watched the work of Robert Foulis for a good many years and I believe there would now be no Sunset, Algonquin, Bellerive or Glen Echo if it wasn't for him and the work he has done..."*. Foulis also spent time at Normandie in 1927 to assist them with their greens, which had been incorrectly fertilized and were suffering from fungus. One of the other individuals who was singled-out for his work with the courses was Eberhard Anheuser. Not a greenkeeper by design or experience, he worked tirelessly to learn as much as possible about improving the course at Sunset. His comments about the steps being taken to insure a quality facility, indicate the high level of knowledge he acquired about course management. Perhaps this experimentation explains the numerous grasses that have existed at Sunset over the years!

Another interesting fact involves the Foulis brothers and the early organization of the PGA of America in 1916. They were partners and investors in the P.G. Golf company and this became the foundation of the PGA. David, head professional at Hinsdale and instructor at Chicago Golf, was one of the early pioneers and served as Illinois PGA

President.

The Foulis brothers were not the only architects active in the area. Scotsman *Tom Bendelow*, who is credited with designing or laying-out over 400 courses, toured the midwest working his trade for those eager to test their skill on the links. (Only Donald Ross, who is said to have designed or remodeled over 600 courses, can count this many to his credit) Bendelow worked for the A.G. Spalding & Bros. Sporting goods company and he performed for clients who sought assistance from Spalding for their courses. Known by many as designing "eighteen-stakes-on-a-sunday-afternoon", Bendelow did the original layout at Westwood [Westborough] in 1908. Ironically, Bendelow was a very religious man and he never did stake a course or play golf on a Sunday!

He also spent time in Alton, where he designed Rock Springs in 1912. Another dozen or more layouts in the outstate area, along with others in Illinois and Indiana, are among his creations. Some of his more famous designs are French Lick in Indiana, Medinah CC (#1, 2 & 3) and Skokie CC in the Chicago area, and in Kansas City, Kansas City CC and Mission Hills CC. While his reputation as a designer may not pass muster by some of todays standards, staking a course in those days was a simple, albeit unsophisticated method. Starting at the first tee and pacing-off to a bunker, then to the green, then a tee and so-on until completed. The fee for this

Burt McKinnie
Early member of the Algonquins, he would later play out of Normandie. A perennial runner-up, he would compete against Bart Adams, Stuart Stickney, Charles Scudder and the like during his entire career.

was a mere $25! Surprisingly, not all clubs opted for a professional opinion, as courses such as Forest Park in 1913 were initially done by committee. Bendelow was not alone in this method, as many others laid-out a course in the same method, including Alex Findley, Robert White and, on occasion, Donald Ross. Still, there were few to challenge his expertise and with the number of quality courses that are still around, few to doubt his method of picking a good routing. Such was his reputation that in his later years he wrote and lectured at the University of Illinois on course architecture.

Sunset Hill CC

In 1910 still another new facility was being planned in southwest county, this one even further south. The Sunset Hill CC began as a fine restaurant created by Anheuser-Busch to sell its products. Unsuccessful just as a restaurant, in 1917 it was turned into a Country Club, complete with a new Robert and James Foulis-designed course. The course continued with a strong membership until the depression hit the area. Head Professional Johnny Manion, tried several ideas to help the club, including opening the doors to the public for two years in an effort to keep the club solvent. When this proved unsuccessful, it reverted back to a members-only facility. During the early 40's the course was sold to members and a new clubhouse was constructed in 1957, regrettably removing a large stained-glass of a Hohenzollern eagle which was a centerpiece of the facility.

Chick Evans and Jimmy Manion in 1929
Jimmy beat Chick in the Trans-Miss, one of his biggest victories.
Chick was the first amateur to win both the US Open and US Amateur
in the same year(1916); and the only person other than
Bobby Jones (1930) to have done so

Midland Valley CC

Just north of Page Avenue on Ashby in
Overland, the Midland Valley Club was formed in
1910 with the course being completed in 1911. Led
by businessmen Frank Canter, Lee Grant, Rudolph
Kilgren, Albert Hitchings and Percy DuBois, the
club was an immediate success and grew to 150
members in just a few years. Early golfing great
Jimmy Manion was one player who made Midland
Valley his home course, though he would also call
several courses "home" during the years. The club
would be home to many early champions as it was a
magnificent layout. The club suffered on hard times
during the depression and in 1932 declared bank-
ruptcy. William Berberich (of the newspaper
delivery company) bought the club, renamed it
Meadow Brook and took it public. Following a

particularly bad run of business, he decided to sell it
and in 1934 a group of businessmen, brought to the
club by then-member Bob Cochran, negotiated the
sale of the club, The club would continue until 1958
when it was being negotiated to move to the present
location on Clayton Road. The clubhouse burned in
'58 and the club operated out of a hotel for over a
year. The club was completed in late '59, with the
course opening in 1960.

Midland Valley & Donald Ross

Historical evidence points to Midland Valley
CC being remodeled in 1919 and again in 1928. It is
these projects that lend a footnote to the history of the
course.

Donald Ross is said to have been an architect in
the redesign of the club in 1919. If this is true, it

would make it only the second course he worked-on in Missouri, the other being Hillcrest CC in Kansas City which he designed in 1917. Perhaps the most well known of all architects of the day (and maybe still today) his courses are classic in design while simplistic in style. Courses such as Pinehurst #2, perhaps his best known, The Broadmoor in Colorado, Seminole CC in Florida, Oakland Hills in Michigan, Pine Needles in North Carolina, Scioto in Columbus, OH, Aronimink in Pennsylvania, Beverly CC in Chicago and Banff Resort in Alberta.

Ross was brought to Pinehurst by the Tufts family as their architect, and he made it his winter home from 1901 to 1948. At one time during the 1920's & 1930's his company had over 3,000 men working on his projects around the country.

The reference to Midland Valley comes from records at the Tufts Pinehurst Museum & Library and from notes made by Ross relating to a possible design. If Midland Valley was indeed one of his designs or redesigns, its loss to the area is unfortunate.

St. Clair CC

On the Illinois side of the river, the St. Clair CC course was in the planning phases. A nine hole course existed on the bluffs above the Mississippi river at Signal Hill Boulevard and Bluff Road, near Belleville in 1908 and some of the men who played there began to envision a larger facility. For two years they worked to organize the new club. Led by Alonzo Vickers, T.D. Watkins, Edmond Goedde, Stephen LaPage and W.E. Trautmann, they opened their new clubhouse on July 4, 1910. A year later, August 1911, they purchased 63 acres for a new course and golf began at St. Clair. Years later, in 1927, the present front nine would be created as they hired William Langford to design them.

Elliott Whitbread

C.B. Macdonald

St. Louis CC finally developed its new 18 holes in 1913 at the Ladue site, having brought **Charles Blair Macdonald** and Seth Raynor to town.

Having completed two courses for Chicago CC over a 3 year period from 1892-1895, the first being a 9 holer located in an area called Belmont (today it is the Downers Grove GC), and when the Chicago club moved to Wheaton in 1895, he designed the present course.

It is an interesting fact that despite the number of courses James Foulis designed throughout the country, he did not attempt any changes to Chicago GC. This is a credit to two circumstances; first the members recognized the beauty of the course and the only change made to it was suggested by Macdonald himself in 1913. The second was the dominating personality of Macdonald. He was such a taskmaster and looming figure that it would be inconceivable that Foulis would have touched the layout without the approval of Macdonald. [James Foulis would also become the first professional at the new St. Louis CC in 1912 and he stayed until 1915. To what extent Macdonald influenced this decision is unknown].

Macdonald had won the initial US Amateur in 1896 and as a result enjoyed a national reputation, both for his golf and design capabilities. (In reality, he won the third tournament, but it was the first "Official" Amateur sanctioned by the newly formed USGA. The two previous were won by others, also in 1895, but Macdonald claimed that they could not be considered true "National" championships, since they were sponsored only by individual clubs! Had he would have won either of the two earlier events, his response might be different, since the same players were in all three events!)

Course design was not a profession for Macdonald, only an avocation, and he never accepted a fee for any of his courses. So when the members at St. Louis CC saw the growth of other Country Club courses it became only logical that when they decided to move and build 18 holes that someone of his stature would be selected. Selecting Macdonald was undoubtedly done not just to insure a quality design, but to remove themselves from the "also-ran" label that could have been given had they selected a designer who was already doing work in the area. New Yorker Seth Raynor, Macdonald's associate on this project, had been hired by Macdonald in 1908 to help survey the over 100 courses that appear with his name. Becoming a partner with him in a few years, Raynor was the technician, and oversaw all of the projects they undertook. Macdonald, on the other hand, concentrated mainly on his "pet projects" and left much of the detail work to Raynor. Other designs of theirs included the Old White Course at the Greenbrier, Mid Ocean in Bermuda, Fox Chapel in Pennsylvania, Sleepy Hollow, Fishers Island, Piping Rock all in New York, and Yale University GC.

One characteristic of Macdonald's courses, and to some extent all courses of the day, was the incorporation of famous holes from Scotland; in particular Redan, Cape and High holes. The Cape hole is a dogleg par 4 across a bay where a player could cut off as much as they wished. At St. Louis, this is the #8 hole. The Redan hole is a par 3 that offers a variety of shot selections. This is the 16th at St. Louis CC. Typical of older, Scottish style courses, all the holes at St. Louis are named. From

Dwight Davis

the 1st "Preparatory" to the 3rd "Eden", to the 7th "Shorty", the 11th "Valley", the 14th "Dome" and the 18th "Oasis" they all reflect the character of the hole.

An author traveling to see all the Macdonald-Raynor courses as part of a book he was writing, came to St. Louis and pronounced it one of the finest works he had seen. Another Macdonald-aficionado, architect Brian Silva, who specializes in restoring Macdonald courses, recently came to review the course, and pronounced it a wonderful example of Macdonalds work - and remarkably well maintained over the years in the traditional style. The all-bent grass course is unlike almost any other course in the area as it features rolling terrain with large trees and medium size greens. It was a favorite of the USGA for many years hosting 5 championships including US Opens and Amateurs.

Bogey Club

As noted earlier, the Bogey Club was formed by gentlemen who sought to acquire the land adjacent to the Log Cabin Club. The course was constructed in 1912 and struck an agreement with the Log Cabin Club to share the two courses, making a full 18 holes. If you examine the scorecard for each club, you will find that they are different. Depending where you begin, you take a different route! The membership here is usually limited to CEO's of the major St. Louis companies. Several early members held memberships at St. Louis CC as well. The stately clubhouse burned in 1971 and a new facility, while not near as grand, reflects the personality of the members. With no Professional or pro shop, members just sign-in and play.

Forest Park GC & Dwight Davis

The birth of public golf was not an easy one. Despite the rise in private clubs, public courses were still being shut-out, that is until 1912. A young man in his mid-thirties, Dwight Davis had supported the current Mayor of St. Louis Frederick H. Kreinmann, and to reward him Davis was appointed Park Commissioner. Thankfully for St. Louis, this would mark the watershed event for public golf. Davis immediately contacted some of the founders of area private clubs, in particular C. Norman Jones of Log Cabin and Jesse Carleton of Glen Echo, to ask their support in developing a public course in the city. Henry W. Allen, secretary of Bellerive, tried to get the group to hire a professional to "stake out the course", but to no avail. Instead a small group toured several clubs in NY, Pennsylvania, Chicago and Kansas City and then settled on the design. Construction was begun and in 1912 the first 9 holes was opened.

An article in the Post Dispatch in 1912 recounted opening day with this account of the first tee shot by one of the participants; "...*Mrs. E.N. Farar, an athletic young woman, bareheaded and dressed in white, walked to a tee...whirled a golf stick through the air and sent a ball soaring.*"

The following year, 1913, another 9 holes were added to the layout and shortly thereafter another 9 holes, bringing the total to 27. By

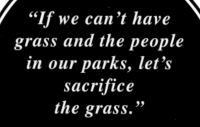

"If we can't have grass and the people in our parks, let's sacrifice the grass."

... Dwight Davis (1911)

1915 an article appeared in the Globe Democrat that stated "*...golfers often had to wait their turn to play the 18 hole course which was regarded as the best - meaning the most difficult - course in the St. Louis District*". The course was open every day and though golfers had to get a permit to play, it was free, however the player had to supply their own equipment! By 1924 only 10 of the 140 municipal courses in the country were free, including the two in Forest Park. The following year, 1925, the first green fees were implemented; a golfer could purchase a $10 annual permit, or pay single round fees; fifty cents for 18 holes and twenty-five cents for 9. Dwight Davis continued to serve as Park Commissioner under Henry Kiel and Victor Miller. Golfers who have played the Forest Park courses should give a brief moment of thanks to Davis, for it is his dedication to the growth of athletic facilities in the cities parks, both for golf and tennis, that give us what we have today.

The sport was gaining ground in the public arena, but the private courses still held the reins tightly on the championships, and control of the sport on the national and local level was controlled by organizations organized by and for the private clubs. It took a lot of effort on the part of many country club players to push for greater public facilities and championship events, and without the efforts of men like Stuart Stickney, Chris Kenney, Harry Allen, Jesse Carleton and of course Dwight Davis, public golf would have lagged further behind.

Francis Ouimet

The 2nd hole at
Forest Park.
From a 1916 picture above,
and as it looks today. The
tree-lined hole made for a
narrow tee shot to the
200 yard par 3.

Kirkwood CC c. 1925
Another of the early clubs
that gave way to housing
developments. Renamed
Woodlawn CC in the 20's,
this course sat on Woodlawn
just south of Manchester.
There were a total of three
clubs within a 2 sq. mile
area; Algonquin, Westwood
(Westborough) and
Kirkwood,

The year is 1920. The only semi-majors played in St. Louis thus far had been the 1908 Western Open at Normandie, won by Willie Anderson and three Trans-Miss events, 1905, 1913 and 1919. On the horizon would be the *1921 US Amateur* and the *1925 US Women's Amateur* both to be held at St. Louis CC and the *1929 US Publinks* would be held at Forest Park. But with the "Roaring Twenties" approaching, there are only 11 golf courses in the area, with all but 2 being private. Only Forest Park and Rock Springs were open to the public. But the situation was about to change.

There was very little activity from 1914-1921 as the first World War consumed everyone's attention, and to many golf was essentially a rich-mans activity. But following the return of the doughboys, the early 1920's brought new vigor and new courses began to appear.

Tom Bendelow was already a presence and designers Joseph Roseman, Wayne Stiles, William Langford, Harold Paddock and others came to our area and brought their experience and ideas.

Robert Foulis continued to build courses as he remodeled Triple A. North Hills CC (renamed Norwood Hills in 1933) developed it's two courses with Stiles, the West in 1922 and the East a year later. Grand Marias hired Joseph Roseman around 1935 though it was called Lake Park GC at the time, the original Greenview was staked by Bendelow in 1922, St. Clair hired Langford in 1927 to add nine holes while Westwood contracted with Harold Paddock and their 27 hole course became a reality in 1928 as the club moved from Glendale to the Conway Road site. Creve Coeur CC developed it's original 18 hole layout in 1924 on the rolling farmland at Craig and Olive. The original 18 holes extended up to Olive in those days, and it was one of the better public layouts up until the early 1960's when an Office Park was deemed more important than public golf. Five years later, in 1929,

Dick Bockenkamp

William Diddel designed Crystal Lake CC in what was then, far west county, off of Bopp Road between Manchester and Clayton Roads. It was one of the best public facilities in the area for years, and one of the authors' favorites.

According to the minutes of the St. Louis District Golf Association of 1928, a committee was formed to "investigate and consider the advisability of establishing additional municipal golf courses in the St. Louis District" and reported that he had contacted Park Commissioner Pape and would wait until they could meet with St. Louis Mayor Victor J. Miller. The papers advocated links being built in at least three parks, but no record can be found of this occurring. When the depression hit in October 1929, the thought of diverting money for golf would be unthinkable. So public players would have to wait for better times.

During this period, a publication was started, the *"Nineteenth Hole"*, which was to be a monthly magazine devoted exclusively to St. Louis Golf and country club activities. Another magazine begun during this era was *"The St. Louis Athlete"*. Both of these existed for a few years, but like many such publications their existence would be short lived. National magazines promoting golf were rare --more likely the occasional article about an event or player. Local tabloids existed for a time but they too were very transitional.

Exactly what sparked the rise of golf in the early 1900's will probably never be known. However, many attribute Francis Ouimets' victory in the 1913 US Open at The Country Club in Brookline, Massachusetts as a logical beginning. When Ouimet won, there were approximately 350,000 golfers throughout the country. By 1920 there were over 2 million golfers. Ouimets' victory over Ted Ray and Harry Vardon, like Arnie in the '60's, Nicklaus in the '70's, Norman in the '80's and perhaps, Couples or Pavin in the 90's, became the model for modern golfers. Whatever the event or inspiration, it brought more golfers to the first tee to test their skill and courage.

On the national scene, celebrities such as Babe Ruth would be seen playing golf and sportswriters such as Grantland Rice gave more attention to golf, not just football and baseball. Men such as writer O.B. Keeler followed Bobby Jones around the world, document-ing his exploits, before joining with him in docu-menting them in, perhaps the best golf book written, *"Down the Fairway".* Following his 1926 victories in the US and British Open Jones was a National hero. Four years later, following his Grand Slam wins of 1930, your average sports enthusi-ast could not get enough of Jones as he appeared on magazine covers, newsreels and instructional films. More American-born players created a bond between the game and the golfing public, never mind that most professionals still had Scottish-ties. The Roaring 20's were in full swing, and it seemed like nothing could stop the spread of golf, or for that matter, the easy-going, fun loving spirit that was the centerpiece of the post-war days. But as we all know, it would end all too quickly.

During this early period of expansion, there were groups and individuals whose desire was to bring golf on a national level to the area, and in some cases internationally. Like Abner Doubleday or James Naismith, we should be more concerned with the individuals who promoted and placed their reputations on the line to see these events occur—

Early magazine featuring the top golfers of the day; Wolff, Manion and Held.

rather than focus on the events themselves—for they were the true pioneers of the game and the reason why we can still play today.

As noted earlier there were several early players (pre-1910) who gave golf in the area it's first boost. *Stuart Stickney*, from St. Louis CC, was the first area amateur who competed in the National Championships as he competed in the 1899 US Amateur and again in 1900, 1902, 1907 and 1911. He was also a player of note in the local competitions as he won the 1912 Missouri Amateur and the 1917 District title. He was joined by another area champion, *Ralph McKittrick* at the Amateur in 1902 and in 1903 *Albert Lambert* competed as well. But it was Stickney who was the early representative to the Nationals from St. Louis as he traveled to competitions from Illinois to Ohio and New York, not an easy task in those days.

As players from St. Louis competed more and more in regional and national events, they were recognized whenever they traveled to distant cities. But while some cities could boast of one or two, St. Louis had several. Few were the equal of Eddie Held, Jim Manion, Clarence Wolff or Rich Bocken-kamp and while not given as much credit for their ability, Elliott Whitbread and Clarke Morse also ranked among the best during this period. But the most colorful player of the pack would be "little dynamite" *Jimmy Manion*.

At 5'6" and 110 pounds he was, pound for pound, the greatest golfer of all. This is not idle speculation. These comments came from Walter

Hagen who nominated Jimmy for this title. Jimmy beat most of the best local players (and frequently nationally ranked players as well), and it often took their best when they did get the better of him. He defeated Chick Evans in 1926 at the Western Amateur 8 and 7 in what was perhaps his most cherished victory, for Chick had reigned supreme at the Western for many years (Chick would win the Western Amateur a total of 8 times). Jimmy qualified for the US Amateur four times, but each time the draw went against him. George Von Elm beat Jimmy at Flosmoor in 1923 and again at Oakmont in 1925. In 1919 he won the medal but lost in the first round to Bobby Jones again at Oakmont. Finally in 1921 at St. Louis CC he lost to Willie Hunter in the second round [who then proceeded to thump Bobby Jones in the next match before bowing to Robert Gardner in the semi's]. Jimmy would win the Trans-Miss title in 1924 by an 11-10 margin over an out-manned Lawson Watts from Joplin, and was ranked as the fourth best amateur in the country in 1921, quite a feat with men like Bobby Jones, Francis Ouimet, Jess Sweetser and Robert Lewis as competitors.

Jimmy represented several clubs over the years, Midland Valley, Riverview and Normandie; but it was his exploits at Normandie that were legendary. Never one to "turn the other cheek" he was as tough off the course as he was on.

Eddie Held was perhaps more prominent at the national events than Manion, for he had won the first US Public Links Championship in 1922, but in their head-to-head matches, it was Manion who came out on top more often. Eddie was ranked among the top 10 amateurs in the country and was the low amateur in the Western Open in 1927.

He won the Trans-Miss twice and qualified for the Amateur four times as well as winning District and state titles. Eddie was also the Canadian Amateur Champion in 1929 and won the Colorado Amateur in 1939.

When he burst on the scene at the Publinks, it gave us our first USGA National Champion. Although at the time, it wasn't considered a significant accomplishment since most players belonged to clubs. But as the number of public players and courses grew, the USGA could not ignore this group and the tournament has continued until today. Eddie though, would not defend his title. Following his victory, Held came back and joined Algonquin CC.

But Held, like Manion, was a tough competitor. At the Western Amateur in 1926 Held arrived early for practice rounds, and a few days later he developed acute appendicitis. Despite doctors advice to undergo immediate surgery, Held shrugged it off. He was in the semi-finals, 2,000 miles from home, and was determined to win the event. Despite a high blood count and sterner warnings, Held slept the night and had the doctor accompany him to the match. He played slowly, taking his time between shots, not his normal routine. The result was a 6 and 5 loss.

Despite

> **Many hundreds of people pass each day inside a building dedicated to Mr. Mahlon Wallace, husband of Audrey Wallace. It is the St. Louis County Library on Lindbergh, of which Mr. Wallace served as president for many years.**

Golfers at Triple A - 1899

losing in the final to Bon Stein, Held did not use the illness as an excuse. He merely stated that his game was just not up to Stein's that day. But those who know him, and his game, were convinced that had he not been sick, the trophy would have been his. *"The exhibition displayed by the Algonquin lad was one of the finest exhibitions of nerve, and displayed that admirable quality called courage than we have seen in all the annals of our sports competition in St. Louis"* wrote the St. Louis Athlete in August, 1927. The article goes on to state that *"...it would be an immeasurable injustice to say that Eddie Held failed in Seattle. True, he didn't win the Western Open golf championship. But he did something far more important. He proved himself a man of courage and determination. He proved that he knows what fidelity of purpose means and the mere fact that he did not win the championship takes away none of the glory of his real achievement."*

Clarence Wolff, who doubled as secretary to the St. Louis District Association for many years, was a very stylish player, capable of brilliant rounds. When he and Manion met in the finals of the city championship they both displayed their excellence; Manion went out in 33, and Wolff came right back on the inside for a 33 as they finished the first 18 of their 36 hole final. Wolff then threw another 33 back at Jimmy on the next 9 and eventually had the better of Jimmy this day. That is rare golf indeed!

But Wolff, a perennial qualifier for both amateur and open events, had about the same luck as Manion as he ran into the big names early in the battle. One of Wolff's best achievements came in the finals of the Western Amateur in 1920 when he faced Chick Evans. Chick had just eliminated Bobby Jones

"Wild Bill" Mehlhorn Head Pro at North Hills (Norwood Hills) 1922 Played the PGA tour during the 20's. Called so not for his erratic game, but for his ability to shoot some "wild scores" from time-to-time!

in the semi-finals, a match that Jones later recalled as one of the high spots in his brilliant career. Though Chick would win, Clarence gave him a tough battle. Clarence did win the Trans-Miss Amateur, one of the premier events of the day in 1925. In fact, the Trans-Miss would be dominated by St. Louisans from 1923-26 as Eddie Held, then Manion, Wolff and Held again would win in consecutive years. Years later Jim Jackson would win back-to-back Trans-Miss in 1954 & 1955 a feat Jack Nicklaus would duplicate three years later.

The final member of this group was **Dick Bockenkamp** who for years challenged the former trio in most area events. But while his game slipped in the late 20's, his record in District and State events is excellent, claiming two of each. He would compete one last time in 1930 in the Missouri Amateur and come away victorious, but business pressures continued to reduce his practice time and he never regained his earlier form.

Whitbread came on later; from 1928 through 1936 he would win two District titles and a like number of State crowns. He would battle Jimmy Manion in several finals and though Jimmy would win most, "Cotton" as he was known, fared well enough. In 1928 and 1929 he would win back-to-back state amateur titles with the 1929 victory being wire-to-wire. At the 1928 finals at Riverview CC he defeated Chester O'Brien of Forest Park GC in the finals 4 & 3 and prevented the second public course player in a row from tasting victory as Harold "Monk" Wilson of Swope park had won the 1927 title. A year later Elliott would beat Frank Aylward playing out of Swope Park to capture the title.

Another player whose roots began in St. Louis

and then spread was *Jess Sweetser*, 1922 Amateur Champion and runner-up in 1923. Jess began competing at Normandie CC prior to 1920 before he moved on to Siwanoy Club and national acclaim. Jess also was a member of the first five Walker Cup teams in 1922, 1923, 1924, 1926, 1928 and then came back for a finale in 1932. His six selections places him behind only the likes of William Campbell, Jay Sigel and Francis Ouimet in number of times he has represented the US. [Brit Joe Carr, who would defeat Bob Cochran in the 1960 British Amateur has competed in 10 Walker Cups, the all time record] Like others, before and after, St. Louis would be but a stop in Jess' lifetime, a footnote to his biography. But we may claim him none-the-less as a former St. Louisan.

Golf during these early days tended to be dominated by the same players year in and year out. Each city had their players, and team matches between cities were common. The first such matches appear to be in 1901 between the Field Club and the Kansas City CC in Kansas City. KC won handily over a fairly good team. A re-match the following year turned the tables as the KC team lost to both the Field Club and St. Louis CC when venturing here.

The minutes of the District from 1927 note another match between St. Louis and Chicago as well, and team competition at the US Publinks was quite intense. But in reality, the same players tended to win the "big tournaments"; and outsiders were generally not welcome. The St. Louisans

Audrey Faust Wallace
5-time District Champion

Virginia Pepp
5-time District
Champion &
1st Female
Professional
in Missouri

included in this list are noted earlier, and the names of other champions are sprinkled throughout. Bobby Jones was clearly the best amateur in this period while Walter Hagen and Gene Sarazen dominated the Professional ranks.

For example, in the Publinks, Carl Kauffmann, often referred to as the "*public Courses Bobby Jones*" due to his victories in this event, won three times prior to 1930, including the 1929 played in St. Louis, and as we all know, Jones won four Opens from 1923-1930, with the likes of Sarazen, the great British golfer Cyril Walker, Tommy Armour, Johnny Farrell, Hagen and Willie Macfarlane being the other contenders in the Open. The Amateur was even more interesting. While Jones dominated with five wins in the 20's, Chick Evans, Jess Guilford, Jess Sweetser, George Von Elm, Francis Ouimet and Robert Gardner were winning what he did not. These were the same names that appeared in the Trans-Miss, the Western and as amateurs in the Open.

While players like Jimmy Manion won local and regional tournaments and competed well in national events, it was victories over those name players that gave one the national recognition so important to the players. This is why Jimmy's win over Chick Evans was so significant, and why losing to Jones only 2 and 1, or 3 and 2, gave you excellent credentials for future events.

Ladies on the Links

The first area women competing on the national scene were Miss Edith Collins and Mrs. Lilburn G. McNair, both from St. Louis Country Club, who ventured to Chicago to compete in the 1903 Amateur at the Chicago Club of C.B. Macdonald. But the early woman who dominated from the area was Grace Semple. She not only won the inaugural Missouri Women's Amateur, but she competed in the US Womens Amateur 9 times from 1906 to 1915, reaching as far as the semi-finals. These early days of Women's golf were dominated by three ladies; Beatrice Hoyt and sisters Margaret and Harriot Curtis. Between this trio, from 1895 to 1912, they won seven times and were medalists thirteen times, including the famous 1907 matches when Margaret beat sister Harriot for the title, the only time this has ever occurred.

Among the Ladies however, the number of quality players, locally and nationally, was even smaller. The Amateur was the only national tournament (the Open would not begin until 1946) and Glenna Collett and Alexa Stirling were the dominant players, following in the footsteps of Beatrice Hoyt and Margaret and Harriot Curtis earlier in the century. Collett was so good that from 1921 to 1930 she won five times, was runner-up once and was medalist four times, She would win her sixth title in 1935, breaking all marks for a USGA event. Stirling was from the East Lake Club in Atlanta, and she was tutored by Stewart Maiden, as was Bobby Jones. She won just about everything Collett did not. From 1916 to 1927 three was her number; she won three times and was runner-up three times and she claimed three medals. Other ladies of note were Margaret Gavin, Maureen Orcutt, Dorothy

Ed McNamara - Golf Professional turned Policeman

Campbell, Virginia Van Wie (who would win three times in the early thirties).

The St. Louis Ladies were well represented; not necessarily in the USGA events, but particularly in the Trans-Miss, Women's Western and local District events. One of the best was Virginia Pepp. From 1922 to 1930 she won five Women's District titles. She might have won state titles but from 1922 to 1934 the Women's State Championship was not held. So, after winning everything in sight, and after a little convincing from Triple A head pro Benny Richter, Virginia turned pro in 1931 and became the first woman pro in the state, and perhaps the first in the country. She played numerous exhibitions with Helen Hicks, Women's Amateur Champ, and men professionals as they visited St. Louis. Joining Benny Richter as in instructor at Triple A was a thrill for Virginia, at first. But a few years later, with no time to play, and few professional events open to women, she applied for amateur reinstatement but could never attain her original form.

Another outstanding player in this period was Audrey Faust (Mrs. Mahlon Wallace). Audrey won 5 District titles from 1924-1932, several against here good friend Virginia Pepp. There were, of course, fewer women playing and ladies such as Babe Zaharias, Mickey Wright and Patty Berg would not come into their own until the late 30's and 40's. But you can only play against your competition, not against might-have-been, and these two bested those who did show up on the first tee for almost 15 years.

These two ladies were so dominating that from

1922 to 1932 only one lady apart from Virginia or Audrey, Mrs. I.S. Hynes, would win a District event. Their skills were such that Audrey was in the finals nine times between 1924 and 1932 and Virginia six times between 1922 and 1930, They met in the finals four times, each player winning twice. Each would also win back-to-back titles twice. They also met in the semi-finals another two times during this period.

Early Professionals

In the history of the US Open, only four players have won back-to-back Championships. Two of these have served for a time as head professional at St. Louis CC. They are **Willie Anderson** and **Ralph Guldahl**. The other two are Ben Hogan and Curtis Strange.

The US Open prior to 1910 was considered mainly for professionals, though amateurs were welcome, since their presence elevated the stature of the event. The stories about professionals not being allowed into the locker room are true, as the private clubs regarded them merely as employees, brought in to teach them the game and manage the shop, with a little repair work on the side. As noted from the Oscar winning movie about the 1908 English Olympic team Chariots of Fire... *"the way of the Amateur is the correct path"* and professionalism in traditional amateur

David Ogilvie

Willie Anderson 4-time US Open winner & Head Pro at St. Louis CC in 1909

sports was severely frowned upon in athletics prior to the 20's. But as more pro's ventured across from Scotland, England and Ireland, they brought with them not only their clubs but also their outstanding skills; the professional gradually became more accepted, though for years, tolerated would better describe the relationship.

The earliest St. Louis pro to play in a US Open appears to have been Club Pro **Robert Simpson** in 1900 at Chicago Golf Club, where he would finish 14th behind winner Harry Vardon, and again in 1901 at Myopia Hunt Club [a site that would draw *Jim Fogertey* away from St. Louis some 34 years later], where he would again end up 14th behind eventual winner, Willie Anderson. [In both of these Opens *Jim Foulis, Robert Foulis, Willie Anderson, Gilbert Nicholls* and *C.B. Macdonald* would also be among the competitors.

As one of the early area professionals, Simpson was at the Field Club in 1900 before moving to the Country Club in 1901. Simpson was quite a good player, playing not only in several Opens but also the Western Open, which he won in 1907 and again in 1911. The young Scot who succeeded Simpson at the Field Club was **David Ogilvie**. He had come to America in 1897 from Levanlief, near St. Andrews Scotland. He had his first head pro position in 1898 after arriving, but he stayed for only two seasons in St. Louis before moving on to Baltimore. What is interesting about Ogilvie is what happened after he left St. Louis.

He was the head pro at the Augusta CC for 40 years from 1908-1948. He was asked by Bobby Jones to become the first professional at Augusta National, but he turned him down, though he did play in the inaugural Masters in 1934 and would set the pins for each Masters until 1950. His son was born on the 2nd floor of the Augusta GC in 1907 and he went on to become the head pro at Oakwood CC in Cleveland. His grandson, Dave, is currently head pro at Flosmoor CC in Chicago. The current Dave was honored in 1986 as the Club professional of the year. 1998 will mark the 100th consecutive year that an Ogilvie has been a head professional, a most remarkable achievement.

A few years later more St. Louisans competed in Opens; 1903 saw *William Braid* and *Gilbert Nicholls* at Baltusrol and Nicholls would return a year later at Glen View in Chicago and finish second to *Willie Anderson*. Anderson would win his third consecutive title and 4th overall in 1905 and then would use his St. Louis contacts a few years later to become the head pro at St. Louis CC in 1909. He would compete in the Open that year and finish fourth. Though only 30, Anderson would die in 1911 from heart problems. Quite the player, he won his first Open with the old "gutty" and could post only a 331 total. His last three were with the "Haskell" ball and he would shoot US Open record rounds of 73 & 72 with the new ball.

1908 would bring a national title to a future St. Louis Pro as *Fred McLeod* would defeat Willie Smith in a playoff at Myopia CC. Fred would play in three others, 1910, 1911 and 1912 while head Pro at Sunset Hill CC, and would finish 4th in 1910 and

Jim Barnes Winner of the first two PGA Championships & a US & British Open. Was head Pro at Sunset CC 1917-20 & St. Louis CC 1921-22

again in 1911 and in 1912 he would tie for 13th in his last year in St. Louis before leaving for Columbia CC. Another area pro, *David Patrick* would compete in 1911 as well, but without as much success. He would compete again in 1921 but would tie for second with Walter Hagen as *Jim Barnes* would wear the crown.

While Barnes won the PGA in 1916 and again in 1919 (technically back-to-back wins, since no event was held in 1917 or 1918) he represented two different clubs. But he was at Sunset Hill when he won his 1919 PGA (defeating Fred McLeod) and also finished 11th in the Open at Brae Burn. So it would appear the first National Crown to be awarded to a St. Louis player, while living here, would be *Jim Barnes* in 1919!

Another highly successful pro came to St. Louis in 1919, not because of the money, but because of a promise. *Stewart Maiden*, the David Leadbetter of the day, was the mentor to Alexa Stirling and Bobby Jones when he was head pro at Atlanta's East Lake CC. He made a promise to come to St. Louis CC if it was awarded the *1921 Amateur*, and when the USGA gave the nod, Maiden arrived here and stayed for two years. One of his students during this time was *Audrey Faust Wallace*, which probably accounts for her rapid success.

Because of his presence here, his most prominent student made frequent trips to Ladue to sharpen his game. A few Country Club members recall Jones on the practice area, driving balls with a long flowing draw towards the end of the range. Having fulfilled his promise, he went back to Atlanta in 1921 at the conclusion of the Amateur.

As with many pro's of the day, McLeod, Jim

Barnes, Anderson and others came to where the clubs offered the best jobs. Anderson, for example, teamed with Nicholls in several events so in coming here he did have some ties. In later years McLeod would represent almost every major golfing state from Florida to New York as he competed well into the 70's in Senior events. The life of the pro was that of nomads as they traveled across the country looking for the best opportunity. The situation is not much different today. The longevity has changed as they look to settle with their families, but the younger pro's continue to wander from club-to-club in search of the right spot.

It appears that no St. Louisans were in the field to witness first-hand *Francis Ouimet's* Open victory in 1913; the win which captured the hearts of golfers everywhere, and catapulted golf onto the front pages. To say that his victory was an upset is an understatement. It is comparable to a high school golfer winning the US Open today. Ouimet had not had much championship experience, the Massachusetts amateur being the one exception, and had not competed well in other national championships. Still, he accomplished that remarkable feat and claims his place in golf annals forever. Ironically he entered the Open only because the USGA wanted more amateurs in the field - only 5 of the 49 finalists were amateurs. Many are under the impression that Ouimet just entered the Open in 1913, won the tournament, then dropped out of sight. Nothing could be further from the truth. He would win the US Amateur in 1914 and again in 1931 and finished 2nd in 1920 to *Chick Evans*. In 1920 he would defeat a 18 year old Bobby Jones in the semi-finals. He served on nine consecutive Walker Cup teams from 1922-1949, four as a non-playing captain. But more importantly he would

remain a lifelong amateur, culminating with his being elected as Captain of the R&A in 1951, the first American so honored.

As the 20's began, new faces began to appear, mixed-in with the veterans. *Tommy Armour* would compete as an amateur for a few years before turning pro. Hagen and Sarazen will still among the best around, while **Alex Ayton** and **Jess Sweetser** and *Leo Diegel* and **Bill Mehlhorn** were among the upstarts.

Mehlhorn began first in Tulsa then moved to *North Hills* (Norwood Hills) in 1923 where he would come to the forefront. His record in the Open during the 20's and early 30's is enviable; tie for 55th, 49th, 35th, 27th, 4th, 8th, 3rd, 15th, 3rd, 5th, 9th, 4th. As the head pro at North Hills CC "Wild Bill" would win the *1924 Western Open* over the Calumet CC course, where he had been an assistant years earlier, taking the lead after the second round and never relinquishing the advantage. Unfortunately he competed during the 20's, and even the best pro's could not compete successfully against Bobby Jones. Macdonald Smith, Al Espinosa, Joe Turnesa and Bobby Cruickshank all share a common legacy. But for Jones they all would have won US Opens. In fact Macdonald Smith also lost the 1930 British Open to Jones, depriving Smith of two crowns in one season, making him perhaps the best player to never win a major, with the record to prove it.

Bobby Jones

And so as the era comes to a close, all would admit that the 20's was something special in sport throughout the country. Fortunately for golf it had a genuine hero in Jones who fit well in the mix, if not on top of, stars such as Dempsey, Gehrig, Ruth and Grange. In an era of heroes, Jones was perhaps the most shining star.

Traditional Club Names	
Woods	
1	Driver
2	Brassie
3	Spoon
4	Cleek
5	Baffy
Irons	
1	Driving Iron
2	Mid-iron
3	Mid-mashie
4	Mashie iron
5	Mashie
6	Spade mashie
7	Mashie niblic
8	Pitcher/lofter
9	Niblick
W	Pitching wedge

There are few golfers who have not heard of Bobby Jones. There are many who have read ***"Down the Fairway"*** and have an even greater sense of admiration for his skills, both on and off the links. To some he is an icon; to others he is associated solely with the Masters; and to others just another golfer. As a composite figure he was the Ben Hogan, Byron Nelson, Sam Snead, Greg Norman, Jack Nicklaus, Arnold Palmer, Hale Irwin, Fred Couples, Cory Pavin, Tiger Woods of his era. In short, he had few if any weaknesses on the course.

Long drawing tee shots, accurate iron play and a deadly putter made him the favorite at each venue. Plaques on courses throughout the world commemorate his most significant shotmaking skills in major championships in Britain and the US.

To fully appreciate his dominance I offer the following testament. He was a lifelong amateur who played in only 52 tournaments in his career, from 1914 to 1930. (Today the average touring pro will compete in 25-30 in one year) In the 12 US Amateur competitions from 1919 to 1930 he would win 5 times, finish 2nd twice and be medalist six times. As good as this is, his performance in the US Open was even better. From 1922 to 1930, he was in the finals every year except 1927. He won 4 Open titles and finished second 4 times as he bested the likes of Sarazen,

Robert Tyre 'Bobby' Jones

The Greatest Amateur of them all.

Hagen and Armour. Of those 52 tournaments, (he retired in 1930 at the age of 28) he won a remarkable 27. He played in a total of 27 "major championships" in his career and once again, won a remarkable 13 of these, while finishing second an additional 6 times. All this from a young man with an engineering degree from Georgia Tech, a Harvard graduate degree in literature and a law degree from Emory University.

Bill Upthegrove, a St. Louis CC member and a 9-time club champion, recalled seeing Jones at St. Louis in the 1920's when he was a caddie. Jones traveled to St. Louis to see Stewart Maiden, his long-time instructor who had taken the position at the Country Club prior to the 1921 US Amateur. On the practice range, he routinely drove the ball through the end of the range, a length of just under 300 yards, with hickory-shafted clubs.

His record in the Walker Cup was equally outstanding. He played in only 5 (he missed 1923 as he was attending Harvard at the time) and he was undefeated with no ties, winning all five of his singles matches. He hold the record for the two largest "routs" as he won 13 & 12 and 12&11 on two 36 hole matches., the latter over Cyril Tolley the two-time British Amateur Champion.

Jones so dominated in the sport at both the pro and amateur level, that Walter Hagen chastised the Pro's during one Open for allowing Jones to show them up. This coming from a man who would win two Opens, four British Opens and five PGA titles from 1914 to 1929, but he would never win a major tournament when Jones was entered!. The same was true for Gene Sarazen who, following his 1922 US Open win, would not defeat Jones in any Open Championship from 1923-1930.

"I never learned anything from a match I won" was a phrase Jones would use frequently as he used the lessons learned from his losses to build the character that would carry him through his life, the last few years of which were spent in a wheel-chair, crippled by a spinal disease. Fortunately his mind was not affected, and those who met him in those later years, found the man as gracious, charming and witty as ever. Following his departure from golf in 1930, the sport suffered a letdown since it was his charisma and skill that attracted many to those matches. Sarazen or Hagen or Denny Shute could not fill the void. But when he opened his little course in Augusta in 1934, some of the glamour would return as the Masters association with Jones would carry it forward to today, as his character would rub-off on the event, in sharp contrast to the event making the person today.

Bobby Jones would cease to compete in 1930, much to the pleasure of amateur and pro alike. He participated in numerous charity events during the war years for his fans still loved to see that smooth swing.

In Europe in 1936 to view the Olympics, he could not leave without a visit back to the course he loved, St. Andrews. When his name was placed on

James Foulis Sr. (third from left) in front of Tom Morris' Golf Shop at St. Andrews. Old Tom Morris sits in the middle (fourth from left) Young Robert Foulis is in the back row on the right end. Jim Foulis Sr.' father also worked at St. Andrews prior to the War of 1812 and used to herd sheep around the course to keep the grass down.

Caddies at Glen Echo CC - 1910.
In the middle with the arrow pointing toward him is Jimmy Manion. He led the caddies on a strike for better pay.
To dramatize the situation they literally walked through the gates onto Lucas & Hunt Road and marched toward Natural Bridge en masse! They got their raise!

the ballot for a tee time, it simply stated "*R.T. Jones, Jr.*" While having lunch he saw the crowd lining the first fairway, he thought a match was taking place over the Old Course. Word had spread that "Bobby's back" and practically the entire town closed-up as they came to see him play one last time.

Following birdies on #2, #5 with the rest pars, Bobby hit a high fading 4-iron on the par 3 8th which stopped 9 feet from the pin for birdie 2. As he put his club back into his bag his caddie spoke the words they all felt "*My, but you're a wonder, sir.*"

When he died in 1971 the flags at St. Andrews were lowered to half staff. On September 10, 1972, the 10th hole at St. Andrews was named the Bobby Jones hole. The only other hole named after a player is the 18th, the Tom Morris hole!

The early 30's also saw a sort of "changing of the guard", both locally and nationally as youngsters like Bob Cochran made their first entrance. Though he would not win until 1940, Bob would reach the finals in 1934 and 1938 and the semi-finals in 1936 and 1939. Patty Berg was on the horizon as was

Lawson Little and Johnny Goodman. In 1930, Snead, Hogan and Nelson were all only 18 years old. There mark would come years later. Sarazen and Hagen were still the top players in the world, but Ralph Guldahl and Jimmy Demaret would soon earn their stripes. Glenna Collett Vare and Virginia Van Wie would continue their fine play, but the opportunities for women would continue to be limited.

The 30's also saw the first decline in golf as the world economic events took their toll on players as well as the courses.

Golf without Jones would leave the national amateur events in a void until the 50's when a new young lion named Palmer came out of Pennsylvania, followed shortly by the Golden Bear in the early 60's.

Golf would experience significant changes during the 30's, but it would survive, and in many ways become even stronger, as though fighting the Depression was just one more course they had to conquer.

*Ad in the 1904 Olympic Program for
Golf Clubs by Jim & Dave Foulis
with a testimonial from
Willie Smith of Nassau CC*

"When I play with him he speaks to me on every green. He turns to me and says, 'you're away.'"

...Jimmy Demaret speaking about playing with Ben Hogan

The depression effectively stopped golf in its tracks. The wealthy had lost much and were having to cut some extras and golf would be one of them. But for most of America, it was more serious than just giving up a round or two a week. Many would struggle just for food. As a result, hundreds of courses went bankrupt or just fell into dis-repair during this period. Many would never come back.

The Tour continued, but with fewer events. Despite the desperate situation which existed, we still needed our heroes and golf provided us with a few. Winning a $500 top prize during 1933 would go a long way. Many regular stops were canceled from 1935-38 while others ceased from 1932 through the end of World War II. Many of the tournaments that are part of today's tour began immediately following the War, and still more began in the 1960's. Few from the 20's or 30's remain, The LA Open, Western Open, Pebble Beach, Greater Greensboro Open, USF&G and Phoenix Open being the exceptions. Touring professionals would seek jobs at courses to pay the bills, and hopefully still give them time to pursue their dreams. *Ralph Guldahl*, back-to-back US Open winner, was a pro at St. Louis CC in 1933, before winning the Opens in 1937 & 38. Guldahl would finish 2nd to Johnny Goodman for the '33 Open while at St. Louis, and after leaving our

Ralph Guldahl
Pro at St. Louis CC
1932-33

town he would win the 1939 Masters before hanging up his competitive clubs for good.

In 1934 as St. Louis CC was about to pick a new head professional. Springfield Missouri native Horton Smith, who would be the 1934 & 1936 Masters winner, had applied for the job and most thought he had a lock on it. But the board gave it to another, Alex Ayton. A good player in his own right, Alex held the course record of 62 at St. Louis for many years and was a favorite among area players during his stay here.

During World War II, the US Open championship was also halted. Chicago Businessman George May began a series of events at Tam O'Shanter CC, which offered the richest prizes in golf. May attempted to make his event the highlight of the year with prize money double that of any other event. But for this honor, he asked the pro's to parade around like jockeys with numbers on their backs. Many balked at this unseemly concept, but the money was too big a temptation and while the numbering never caught on, the pro's flocked to Chicago for the $50,000 top prize.

Another tournament which took place during the war years was called the Hale American Tournament. Ben Hogan won this event in 1943, in what would have been his 5th US Open crown. A medal almost identical to those given by the USGA was his prize and all the top pro's were present. The USGA has steadfastly refused to recognize this victory, so a 5th Open crown remains unclaimed by any male competitor.

Golf here followed the national trend. A few courses were built in the late 20's and early 30's (Belleville CC (Westhaven) in 1926, Cloverleaf GC, Alton and Ruth Park in 1931), but after that only Joachim opened during this period. Greenbriar Hills did come into existence in 1937, but it was only a name change from the recently bankrupt Osage CC. This short spurt was brought on in large part by the WPA projects in the mid-30's. The federal program allowed many municipalities to hire course architects to design and build public courses. Donald Ross was particularly active in this period as each course required about 200 men to create the layout, and any project that put people to work was looked upon very favorably! Most of the WPA courses were built with limited earth moving equipment, and the WPA courses were literally hand-built by men using only hand tools and wheelbarrows.

Another aspect of the period was the presence of Albert Warren Tillinghast, creator of such courses as San Francisco CC, Indian Hills in KC, Winged Foot GC, Baltusrol GC and Bethpage GC. He was hired by the PGA in the mid-30's to tour the country and make recommendations to clubs that would improve the courses and in the hope save money. Courses merely trying to avoid foreclosure could seldom take advantage of his ideas, but he performed this task for almost three years. He claimed that over this period he eliminated over 7,000 useless bunkers that were either used as cross-bunkers or as penal fairway bunkers. The effects of this was dramatic, both on

Bob Cochran (1946)
President of the St. Louis
District Golf Association

course maintenance and player enjoyment. While there is no record of what changes courses made here due to his recommendations during this time, he is known to have spent the majority of his efforts on the east coast. There are two exceptions. Notes from Tillinghast at Wingfoot list Westwood CC as one of the courses he did work for in the 1930's as well as Kansas City's Swope Park which he redesigned in 1934. "Tillie" as he was called, is also given credit with coining the term "birdie" as the shot holed in one less stroke than par, a term not used previously. Area courses may have adopted some of the principles advocated by the PGA without having Tillinghast present. If your favorite course dates back to the depression days, look around to see grass bunkers instead of sand. This could be the result of such recommendations.

Surprisingly, though the depression was world-wide, many new courses were built outside of the US. In Britain alone, almost 40 courses a year were built. Just as it seemed that the golf boom might continue as the US began to dig itself out of the depression, the Second World War erupted and those plans were altered.

World War II had a much greater effect on golf than the depression. While people were put back to work on war-related activities, golf was the last thing on most of their minds till 1945. Courses in major areas had access to some gas and oil products, though limited by the rationing. Still, only a few courses in the area closed; most just scaled back and tried to ride out the storm. Even clubs that had no financial difficulties found things difficult. Without sufficient oil, fertilizer or man-power their fairways soon became pastures. Even Augusta National fell into dis-repair during this

1947 Ryder Cup Team; (Front l-r) Ed "Porky" Oliver, Jimmy Demaret, Craig Wood, Ed Dudley, Walter Hagen, Sam Snead, Byron Nelson. Back row; Herman Barron, Herman Kaiser, Ben Hogan (Captain) E.J. "Dutch" Harrison, Lloyd Mangrum, Lew Worsham.
Photo courtesy Forest Hills CC

Bob Hope and Bing Crosby visited the area in 1942 as part of the drive to raise money for the War effort. This event was held at the old Meadowbrook CC in Overland. At left is Eastern Missouri PGA President Homer Herpel.

1930-1950 - The Expansion

period. Course construction would effectively come to a standstill in the area until almost 1950.

From 1941 till 1945, only about 25 courses were built nationally, and most of them were finished in 1944 or 1945. The Pro tours had gone from events to exhibitions for War Bonds. Byron Nelson traveled the country giving such exhibitions and raising money for the war effort with his pal and fellow "Gold-Dust Twin" Jug McSpadden from Kansas City. Many celebrities did likewise in their sport; Joe Louis and Joe Dimaggio are two examples, as well as many actors and musicians. The District Golf Association still held tournaments, but they were to raise money for the

Bryan Winter
He captured two District and a
State crown during 1931-32.

Red Cross. Trophy presentations were deferred during this time as well. As one reads the minutes of the District Golf Association during this period you get the feeling that you are being thrust back into time. On occasions, a moment of silence was in order as members such as Cornelius "Corny" Schnecko were remembered following their death in service.

The Hale America weekend tournaments were advocated by the USGA as a way of showing support and cooperation of the member clubs across the country for the war effort. Prizes that were given were also in the form of war bonds and stamps. The second St. Louis Victory Open tournament held in 1943 reportedly raised

The "Big Three" in area golf from 1920-1930;
Clarence Wolff, Jim Manion, Eddie Held.

Juniors at Osage CC c. 1930

(l-r) Sara Caughey(Greenbriar), Audrey Faust Wallace (St. Louis), Mrs.Carl Daniel (Algonquin) and Mrs. I.S. Hynes (Westborough).

1930-1950 - The Expansion

Jim Fogertey c. 1930

$1,650 for the USO of St. Louis. These events helped provide a degree of normalcy to the time. Walking the fairways to watch Bob Hope and Bing Crosby at Meadowbrook in 1942 made your day a little brighter. Watching Frank Moore or Clarke Morse compete took your mind off events half a world away.

When the war finally did conclude in 1945, the soldiers returned to find that much of the life they had left had changed dramatically. The post-war baby boom began and the 45+ year old group today reflects that growth. From 1946 to 1949 over 150 courses were constructed. Many of these were constructed by the military on their facilities as much space was freed-up. Architects like Billy Bell, Dick Wilson, William Diddel, Robert Trent Jones, Joe Finger, Perry Maxwell and Donald Ross

(until his death in 1948) were active during this period. This period is also significant for beginning of major golf course development in Hawaii. Prior to the War, only a handful of courses were present, but several courses were completed just prior to 1950 which, as we all know, would mark the start of Hawaii as a great golfing destination.

In the early 1930's, the holdovers from the roaring 20's were still competing, with most playing well. Elliott Whitbread, Bryan Winter, Ted Adams and Eddie Held were still competitive as was Chester O'Brien, who won the 1938 District and two State titles. On the Kansas City side, players like Walter Blevins and Warren Riepen were formidable as they claimed state titles. Held would capture the 1937 District title, his second, as he continued to be a solid competitor. He would turn professional in 1940 as he operated his driving range on Manchester. He also had an indoor "range" -- at least it was indoors -- at the Warson Woods shopping center he had a store front that allowed you to come in and hit balls into a mat! Bryan Winter had moved into the area in the late 20's and would immediately challenge Jim

Frank Fogertey
He would become head pro at Osage CC in 1936 and, as the club became Greenbriar Hills, stay on as head professional for 37 years, until he retired in 1973. Along with his wife Billie, they mentored to hundreds of families and had one of the strongest junior programs in the area.

Manion as the top player. But he would have to wait until 1931 before claiming his initial District championship, the same year he would win his State crown. The *1938 Western Open*, the only major event held locally during the 30's, saw Ralph Guldahl take the top spot at Westwood CC. Other events would have to wait till after the War years. Beginning with the *1946 Western Open* at Sunset CC, we would host the *1947 US Open* at St. Louis CC and the *1948 PGA* at Norwood Hills. The latter two would be significant, one for who didn't win and the other for who did!

During the 30's and 40's the balance among the men was remarkable as only Chester O'Brien would win multiple state titles. As a consequence, St. Louis golfers would lose their dominance in the Missouri Amateur winning only eight of the seventeen crowns available. This was in sharp contrast to the earlier decades when the Manion's, Wolff's, Bockenkamp's and Held's

Chester O'Brien

dominated the scene.

Bob Cochran made his first move on the scene during the early 30's. winning back-to-back District titles in 1933-34 and his first state title in 1940. Then came December 1941, and sport in general took a back-seat to more important interests - like freedom. Like others in sport, Ted Williams for example, players at their prime during the war years suffered the fate of losing some of their best productive years, and their careers should be noted with an asterisk. With most tournaments during this period canceled, or severely curtailed, professional and amateur alike were relegated to scrambling to keep their careers on track.

Cochran was in this mode, as were Nelson, Hogan, Snead and others, as the various Opens were canceled until 1946. Bob won what events were played in the area, winning the *St. Louis Open* in 1942, '43, '45 and added the 1946 for good measure.

Osage Clubhouse c. 1930

Frank Fogertey in the Pro Shop at Osage CC

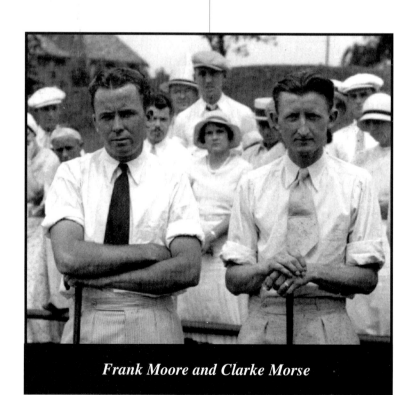

Frank Moore and Clarke Morse

Homer Herpel with his daughters. Jackie (3 1/2) and Marilyn (7). The disinterested caddie in background usually caddied for Marilyn. Note the number of clubs in her bag. She usually played with only 4 at this age.

He had won three District titles prior to 1942 and would win three consecutive from 1946-48, then come back in 1961 and 1965 for his 7th and 8th. But it was definitely Cochran who was feared. In the war years, the area players he competed against in the St. Louis Open, for example, were area professionals such as Benny Richter and Frank Moore. Other local events saw Bob Cochran win the 1942, 1943 and 1945 St. Louis Victory Opens, with Benny Richter claiming the 1944 title. The St. Louis Metro Open and Amateur began prior to the War and continued through the 40's but timing and support gradually let these events fade away. But not before Jim Fogertey, Frank Moore, Tom Draper and others captured their share of the awards.

When Cochran tired of competing locally, he packed his bags and joined the Tour on their weekly stops throughout the midwest. During 1945 and 1946 he competed from Memphis to Chicago against the likes of Nelson, Hogan, Harrison and Snead. Their names alone would send fear through most players. But to a cocky and confident Cochran, they were just targets he would take aim at.

As an amateur Bob was not alone in competing on the Tour. Freddie Haas, Frank Stranahan, Bud Ward and Dale Morey were among not just the top amateurs, but the top players during this period. Haas and Stranahan join Cochran as amateurs who won Pro events during the 40's, though Bob may well be the ONLY amateur to have won a pro tour event who did not later turn professional!

In 1948 another player came onto the scene,

1930-1950 - The Expansion

A few of the Area Pro's in 1941
(l-r) Clarke Morse (Normandie), Homer Herpel(Crystal Lake) , Alex Ayton (St. Louis), Johnny Manion (Meadowbrook), Clarence Norsworthy (University City) , Bob Morse (Pro Tee Range), Bob Jessiman (Bellerive), and Benny Richter (Triple A).

and he would make a mark like no other. Like Cochran, his career would span several decades and their head-to-head battles are the stories of legends. His name was Jim Jackson. He began by capturing the 1939 High School State title. In 1941, as a 19 year old, he lost a 36 hole playoff to St. Clair pro Frank Moore for the Metro Open title, after being tied in regulation and at the end of the first 18 hole playoff. His major accomplishments were in the later years and are covered in greater detail in the following sections.

The ladies faced the same dilemma, but the number of players who were competitive were much fewer. Kansas Citian Opal Hill, a great champion and USGA board member, dominated the ladies state events in the mid-to-late 30's. Audrey Wallace was winning her last two district titles early in the era, but there were no State titles for the ladies to claim from

1924 to 1934 as all events were canceled.

Sara Guth won a single state title in 1938 following three District titles in 1934, '35 and '36 and she was an extraordinary player.

But perhaps the dominant lady of the era was Betty Jane Haemerle-Broz. Following the war she won three of the four state titles and all four of the District crowns! It seemed that nothing could stop her. But, like many ladies of other eras, her career was brilliant, but short, for she would not continue to compete following her marriage. Her main competition had come from ladies from Triple A and Normandie; Mrs. R.I. Caughey, Georgia Dexheimer Schwartz and Jeannine Dobbin-Lewis. Marilyn Herpel would be on the rise as Betty Jane stopped competing, but Marilyn would never defeat Betty Jane for a major title. Caughey and Dexheimer would claim the last three District crowns of the 30's

Peggy Hartenbach (r) from Normandie CC in the 1946 Junior District Finals against Marilyn Herpel (l)

and the opening 1940 event with Georgia capturing the 1939 title and Caughey taking the rest. Jeannine Dobbin would begin the 50's with two victories in the District having fought Betty Jane for titles in the late 40's.

As the 40's ended the problems of course access continued; only one course had been constructed following the war, Indian Meadows, bringing the total of courses in the area to 34, having lost 4 courses. However, only 14 of these were public access facilities (8 in Missouri and 6 in Illinois) with only 18 holes existing at Forest Park, Indian Meadows, Crystal Lake, Lake Park (Grand Marias) and Creve Coeur, as private clubs continued to dominate the landscape. But no new private facilities had been constructed since Westwood in 1928 and not until Old Warson in 1954 would there be another.

However, on the drawing board were fourteen courses that would come in the next decade as we began to savor golf for our free time. Of the new courses, eleven would be public, though only five

would have 18 holes! It appeared that, at last, the worldwide events of the last 20 years were behind us and we were about to experience a resurgence in sport.

Paramount Golf Club

Another Golf organization would begin in 1930 that continues to the present. It does not receive much notoriety, and you would be hard pressed to find information about it in the papers. It is the Paramount Golf Club, the oldest black club in the area and one of the oldest in the midwest. Since Forest Park was one of the few public courses in the area, their annual tournaments were held here. There events were held on Mondays; weekends were reserved for the "other" events. The story goes that the Paramount, or other black sponsored events, had to conclude by noon as a bell was rung in the Forest Park pavilion signaling an end to the Paramount event and opening the course up to whites. If you were in your backswing, you had better stop!

1930-1950 - The Expansion

Segregation and lack of access to the facilities was a major factor in the lack of early black golfers. The opportunities open to them, other than as caddies, were almost non-existent. It took real determination and love of golf to continue despite these hardships. Some of the early champions from the Paramount group included Sam Shephard Jr. and Julia Siler. Ms. Siler was a 9 time winner and Mr. Shephard won at least twice. Another prominent player during the 40's was Mrs. Isadore Channels and Dr. William Smiley, who won the 1942 title.

During this period, and much of the time prior to the present, most minorities were politely excluded from most Private clubs and were effectively banned from many Semi-Private clubs. The white players knew what questions to ask, such as *"...is there a dress code?"* and the person on the other end of the phone would act accordingly. Still at other courses, you had to pay a fee to "join" the Semi-Private club, and minorities or other undesirables, would be told that memberships for the day (or week or month) were sold out.

Forest Park was the exception. And for years it was the center of Black golf throughout the area. The powers that be among the private clubs at times differed on the role of the public players. Many persisted in their position that public players should not be excluded from golf activities and favored area-wide championships. Still others were vehemently opposed to any public players being included. (A trend that unfortunately, continues to this day) Whether this opposition had any basis other than the

traditional public vs. private battles can never be truly known. As in other sports, most minorities would be excluded from professional play until the post war period, but during the 60's, "the Park" was the center of area golf for many public players, regardless of race or color. And many future champions would rise from the dust of the Park to compete at the national level in select events. Among them was professional Earl Parham who would win several St. Louis Publinx and would compete in two US Senior Opens in later years. But he grew up playing the Park, and learned the game over those hills. He was just one of many black golfers who competed throughout the midwest during this era.

Dutch Harrison at the 1946 Western Open

"I would rather open on Broadway in Hamlet with no rehearsals than tee off at Pebble Beach."

...Jack Lemmon

During the Ike years, America was in a kind of "funk". Apart from the Cold War sometimes scaring us into our basements or under our classroom desks, although I never did understand how that 1/2" of pine would protect me from nuclear fallout, we were in your traditional post-war boom. Business was good, and with occasional photos of Ike at Augusta with Bobby Jones and Clifford Roberts, golf began to grow as we had more leisure time. Television brought us the first pictures of the US Open a few years earlier (here in St. Louis from KSD-TV) at the 1947 Open at St. Louis CC where Lew Worsham continued Sam Snead's frustration at attempting to capture the US Open. So as we saw Arnie hiking his pants, puffing on the cigarette and sinking those wonderful putts, we became excited about the game. We couldn't see the green at Augusta or Cherry Hills CC or Oakmont, everything was black and white (or more accurately, 16 shades of grey). But we went to Famous Barr or Stix, Baer and Fuller and bought ourselves those Izod-style golf shirts (remember Ban-Lon?) that seemed to fit the pro's very well and we watched the Black Knight, Gary Player play those strange looking Shakespeare fiberglass clubs that were in some respects, the forerunner to today's modern graphite. We marveled at this kid named Nicklaus as he vanquished Arnie in the 1962 Open at Oakmont and then again in 1967 at Baltusrol. We saw Hubert

Bob Cochran
The best amateur
of the day

Green win the '77 Open and told ourselves that if that swing could win the Open then maybe we could win the weekly nassau. We envisioned ourselves doing the same to Joe Next-Door and bought a set of clubs, often used, or a set your dad or uncle had placed in the basement years earlier, and headed for the golf range. Actually we may have first gone to the garage for a "shag bag" of used balls. Today, it seems nobody has a "shag bag" any more, another bygone relic of yesteryear. It's just easier to go to a range. But back then, we went to an open field and hit wedges from one end and then back again, honing our skills, as best we could envision, and imagined performing in front of 10,000 as we marched up the 18th to accept our trophy.

Golf in the Bi-State area, as it was now becoming known, saw over 50 courses spring to life. We had completed the Gateway Arch in 1966 and felt a new emergence of pride. The downtown area began a small revival that would culminate in the 1980's. Old Warson (1954), Bellerive (1960), Lockhaven (1955), Meadowbrook (1961), Cherry Hills (1964) and Forest Hills (1965) became the places where the new-found Country Club golfers could be found. All but one of them, Lock-haven, are located in west St. Louis county, noting the growing change in demographics as people moved from the city to the county as they looked for greater safety, more room and better schools for their kids. Corporations used the

The Growth - 1950-1980

membership lure to keep employees from jumping ship (downsizing was not even a word we recognized then) and playing "client golf" became a recognized business practice. Memberships were reasonably priced, $2-5,000 for many courses, slightly more for the top layouts, even less for "junior memberships" that were snatched-up by eager "palmer-types".

But public golf was still languishing far behind. By 1970 the top public courses were not found just in Missouri; many ventured across the Mississippi to play the Illinois venues. The 18 hole public courses on the West side of the Mississippi were Paddock, Forest Park, Crystal Lake, Green Trails, St. Charles, Riverside, Southmoor, Paradise Valley, Bogey Hills, North Shore (27) and Creve Coeur. There were several good nine hole layouts in the area; Triple A, St. Charles (9), Ruth Park, Ballwin, St. Ann, Forest Park (9), West Par, Pebble Creek, GolfMohr, Parkwood Oaks, and Duwe GC and a few in the outlying areas. The East side also had a number of good courses; Columbia, Clinton Hills, Belk Park, Triple Lakes, Tamarack and Locust Hills. We lost some good layouts, but that trend would continue as long as land for homes outpaces green fees, such as what occurred at Green Trails, West Par, Crystal Lake, Pebble Creek, Parkwood Oaks and others. Other courses, such as Glenwood closed and remains an empty lot today.

I have vivid memories of getting up at 6:00am to make a 7:00 tee time at St. Charles or St. Andrews or Paradise Valley or Forest Park. My golfing

Jay Haas
This 1975 photo of the future PGA Pro marked the end of his amateur career. He accumulated three District titles, a Walker Cup, a NCAA Individual title and the Fred Haskins Award as the outstanding college player of the year. Two Ryder Cup teams, a Presidents Cup and 9 tour wins would be in his future.

buddies, Jerry and Tom Hennenhoefer, were early risers! Waiting to hit on the first tee at St. Charles, the long par 3, was definitely not on anyone's top 10 list! But these were the public courses we all played in the early-mid 70's. You couldn't get on Crystal Lake on the weekend, unless you were a regular.

Municipalities began to get into the golf business to attract homeowners to their communities, and as a way of increasing their tax base. St. Ann, Ballwin and St. Peters got into the golf business, and found that it was not always smooth sailing. Municipal courses provide a great benefit to their communities and to area golfers.

Your traditional courses, closer to the city, were still doing well. Bob Riley was holding down the fort at Forest Park, where he would be followed by Ken Sample and later Steve Sebastian. Ageless Henry Christman was fulfilling the same role at venerable Ruth Park while Ken Sample got things started at Paddock before moving to Forest Park with partner Zeke Seeger in 1969. Movement among area pros would continue as they progressively searched for the "right" opportunity. More courses began to employ PGA Professionals as their professionalism, teaching ability and management skills allowed the courses to more effectively compete for the consumer dollar. The Pro's lent stability to a facility, and though the assistants seemed to move from course to course quicker than you could pick up a conceded "gimme three-footer", the head professional was the mainstay. But perhaps of equal importance was the hiring of green superintendents. Not just someone to cut the fairways and greens, but

Pro's attempting to Qualify for the 1953 PGA
Kneeling: Ted Neist [St. Louis] Bob Greene [Triple A]
Standing: George Quelch [Westwood] Ray Schwartz Don
Clarkson [Glen Echo] Frank Moore [Southmoor]
Tony Henschel [Westborough] Walter Ambo [Meadowbrook]

Bob Cochran (r) with partner Gene Andrews as they prepare to face-off against Ronald Shade (l) and Michael Bonallack at the 1961 Walker Cup in Seattle. They pulled off perhaps the biggest upset of the matches, defeating the talented British duo 4 and 3. Bonallack is current Secretary of the R&A at St. Andrews.

The Growth - 1950-1980

a professional; someone who knew how to spot a problem and provide the correct solution quickly. Too frequently we have seen the result of the ineptitude of poorly trained individuals as greens must be replaced and tees are closed. Fortunately this is becoming uncommon as the USGA and the Golf Course Superintendents Association increased their base of knowledge and training.

This was the era of Nicklaus and Palmer, of Player and Floyd and TV golf and the Shell Wide World of Golf matches. The Masters became a media event because of TV and we first discovered the British Open despite the poor BBC pictures.

At the 1956 Carling Open, held at Sunset CC, many nationally known

***Mary Gail Dalton
c. 1970***

pro's came to compete. One of them was an aging Tommy Armour. Having come over as an amateur in 1921, Armour was still a contender. Leading the tournament going into the last round, the Scotsman was seen downing at least two shots of Scotch prior to teeing off. His caddie, hoping to make a few dollars should Armour win, remarked that that might not be such a good idea, to which Armour retorted in his thick brogue *"Laddie, 'afta a few o' these, that $2,500 first prize'll seem like 25 cents!"*

The St. Louis Publinks began in 1960 under the direction of Milton Frank and it's continued growth has been tremendous under his successor, Bart Collida. Golf as a means of promoting charity events began and

***Jim Cockburn and Ed Furgol at Westwood
Furgol won the 1954 US Open while at Westwood,
having succeeded the popular Cockburn upon his retirement***

seems to be over-saturated as almost every charity, school and worthwhile organization (and sometimes not-so-worthwhile) hold their outing. But mostly golf just grew. TV allowed us to dream of being like our heroes, and despite never taking a lesson, we approached the first tee with par on our minds. We played clubs with names like Northwestern, Sam Snead, Hogan, Wilson K-28 and Staff, PGA, Shakespeare, Haig Ultra and MacGregor. Walking was common, sometimes with pull-carts, and carts were used infrequently, usually on weekends. Country Club life continued as we all had more

Marcella Rose

free time as the 80's brought us a different way of conducting business - on the golf course - and businessmen took advantage of it.

From 1950 to 1980 the trio of Jackson, Blair and Cochran were the names most often mentioned when you wondered who won what event on the men's side. These three were perhaps as good as any threesome anywhere in the country. For one of them not to reach the finals of a local event was something of an upset, and a bit of humiliation. While Jim Tom played more outside the area, Jackson and

1950 picture of area pro's: (Front) Frank Moore (Meadowbrook) and Benny Richter (Bellerive);Back (l-r) Clarence Norsworthy Sr. (Ruth Park) Ray Schwartz (Norwood) Paul Norsworthy (Ruth Park), Bob Morse (Normandie), Bob Green (Triple A), Walter Ambo (Westborough) Jim Cockburn (Westwood)

The Growth - 1950-1980

Eastern Missouri Gateway Pros in 1951: (l-r kneeling): Front: Frank Fogertey [Greenbriar], Henry Christman [Ruth Park], Ed Komlose, Joe Switzer, Elliott Whitbread, Hord Hardin [advisory Committee], Ben Richter [Bellerive], Dave Sutherland [Triple A]. Back: Walter Ambo [Westborough], Don Duwe [Forest Park] Clarke Morse [St. Clair], Alex Bopp [Crystal Lake], Clyde Webb [Centralia], Frank Moore [Meadow Brook], Bob Green [Triple A], Fred Clarkson [Glen Echo], Jim Cockburn [Westwood], Jim Fogertey [Sunset], Fred Bolton [St. Louis], Ray Schwartz [Norwood], Homer Herpel [Indian Meadows], Lou Miller [Rock Springs], John Manion [Normandie]

Cochran were just about everywhere. Both had sales positions and they frequently played in tournaments throughout southern Illinois and Missouri as their clients called to "show them off" [while making a few dollars on the side with various wagers] and Jimmy and Bob won numerous tournaments in this format.

This was also an era when a young Tom Watson began to win frequently as did a slightly older Jim Colbert. In the State Amateur Bill Stewart of Springfield was one of the outsiders who would occasionally break through as did Scott Bess from Mizzou and Columbia CC. Others coming to prominence included Jay Haas and Jim Holtgrieve.

At the *1961 US Amateur* at Pebble Beach, St. Louis had quite a contingent. Besides Jackson, Cochran and Blair, newer faces ventured west; Tom

Hulverson from Sunset, Vince Greene from Meadowbrook and Les Slattery from Normandie.

Marilyn Herpel, Judy Torluemke, Mary Gail Dalton, Barbara Bubany Berkmeyer, Kathy Severson and Marcella Rose would lead the ladies events more than others in the state events, while Jeanne Dobbin Lewis, Ellen Conant, Susie Driscoll and Doris Phillips would add their names to those above in competing for the local titles. All of these ladies are great champions and most had their nemesis. Marilyn Herpel for years had a tough time beating Betty Jane Haemerle, while Marcella Rose and Doris Phillips went head-to-head so many times it was probably a draw! Barbara Berkmeyer was perhaps the most outstanding as she captured five district titles and four state crowns in this period. Of the

Judy Torluemke at age 16 on the 1961 cover of SI. After a poor showing at the British Amateur that summer she almost hung up her clubs. This spurred her on and she became the low Amateur at the 1961 US Women's Open. A year later she was on the LPGA Tour.

The Growth - 1950-1980

thirty-one District titles up for grabs in this era, one of the ten above lay claim to it 28 times!

This era was also different in that the combination of Pro and Amateur was probably at it's highest in years. The money on tour, prior to the mid-80's was fairly reasonable, and Club pro's were able to qualify for Tour events, at least until the days of the TPC/PGA rift. Amateurs like Bob Cochran, Jim Tom Blair, Jim Jackson and others routinely went to Tour events to compete. Competition was keen. Players had to play well or they were quickly ousted.

On many a Monday a crowd would gather at local courses - Triple A, Normandie, Forest Hills, Crystal Lake - and the games would begin. It was rather informal; names would go into a hat, as they were drawn teams were formed. But that was just the beginning. The real fun began when the bets were announced. The usual games were present; skins, nassau's, the occasional calcutta. But the side bets made it most interesting. When it came to the "presses" (when, how, automatic) the money began to mount, The matches were intense as the level of play was outstanding. Dutch Harrison was a frequent entrant as was Dick Shaiper, Jim Offer, Gene Webb, Cal Tanner, Bob Cochran, Jim Jackson and others.

Bob Green and seven year old Judy Torluemke at Triple A

Forest Park was still one of the main spots for a game. "The Park" also affectionately known as "FOPO", was so busy, and unfortunately so slow, that six hour rounds were common on weekends.

The city owned the course and despite the work of Ken Sample, Ed Duwe and others, the money for maintenance was seldom enough. Rock hard fairways gave you that extra roll and experience rather than skill was often more important on the greens.

The Park was where players such as Earl Parham, Fleming Cody, Booker Ford, Pepper Moore, Bob Terrell and others congregated. Area politicians such as Leroy Tyus lent his support and name to events as the city was going through a revival during this era. But their play was not limited to the Park. Paddock, St. Andrews, Paradise Valley and later Crystal Highlands and Eagle Springs all served as sites for the various events. *The Lambs Golf Association* held a series of tournaments where Dutch Harrison, Bob Rosburg, Charlie Sifford, Walter Morgan, Lee Elder, Chuck Thorpe (Jim's brother), the legendary Ted Rhoades, Fred Carter and others would compete. The *Paramount Golf Association* continued to hold their events, as they had since 1930, but they were no longer limited to just Forest Park, and as a result more participants came from throughout the area.

Patty Berg in an exhibition at
Triple A in 1952with
7year old Judy Torluemke

Jim Jackson (l.) and Jim Tom Blair in
1966 at Twin Hills in Joplin.

Ellen Conant
Won 3 consecutive District titles
in the late 50's

Boxing legend Joe Louis was a frequent visitor to our town, and he always brought his clubs. I recall one day playing behind him at St. Andrews. Walking up to meet him and shake his hand, it was more like his hand engulfed yours, such was its' size and expanse; you could almost feel the impact it would make, and any thoughts you had of boxing died immediately!

But some of the larger breakthroughs would not occur until the 80's and into the 90's, when more public courses would be built and greater access would be available.

Bob Goalby following his 1955 St. Louis District Championship. The runner-up, Joe Switzer is on the left, with Les Slattery on the right.

Jim Tom with his mother following his 1955 win over Ed Loeffler (l) at Indian Hills

Bob Cochran with his "gimme" birdie on the first hole in the 1958 State Amateur at Kansas City CC.

Barbara Berkmeyer with her trophies from her 1975 victories

The Growth - 1950-1980

"Bipp" Fogertey (as Frank was known) on the left with Jim Benson, St. Louis District Secretary (center) and Jimmy Jackson at a barbecue at the Fogertey's in the mid-70's.

Front (l-r);Tim O'Connell, Clarke Morse, Tony Henschel, Walter Ambo. Back; Don Duwe, Henry Christman, Gene Webb, Dick Lotz, Bob Green, Lee McClain, Jim Fogertey, Ed Duwe, Frank Fogertey, Al Oulds.

Ky Lafoon
Head Pro at Meadow
Brook from 1956-57.

Frank Keller
Head Pro at Normandie 1959-65

Greenbriar Juniors - 1967
Front (l-r); Doug Sproule, Deb Wetzig, Frank Fogertey, Paula Eger, Christy Brandt
(Mrs. Tom Kite), Jim Mason. Back;Jim Larimore, John McConnell, Brad
Moore,Phil Marx, Bodie Marks, Bob Mason, Stu Johnston, Chuck Patrick

Bob Cochran at the 1960 British Amateur at Royal Portrush. In his only trip to England Bob had a great week,

Jim Holtgrieve and Bob Goalby at a presentation honoring Jim in 1978.

HOLE	MINIMUM YARDS	MAXIMUM YARDS	PAR	HANDICAP RATING			HOLE	MINIMUM YARDS	MAXIMUM YARDS	PAR	HANDICAP RATING		
	HANDICAP							HANDICAP					
1	365	400	4	9	190 *sp top rt*		10	445	485	4	6	157 *2nd sp left flat*	40
2	475	555	5	1	114 128 *big tree left 3rd tree rt.*		11	345	445	4	12	160 *sp top center*	
3	340	360	4	11	102 108 *sp left center*		12	130	155	3	16		
4	170	220	3	15			13	455	485	5	4	180 200 *sp left center*	
5	410	450	4	5	300 *sp center to lump*		14	390	420	4	8	164 *tree left to lump*	
6	160	190	3	17			15	465	520	5	2	100-105 *rt sp*	
7	315	365	4	13	115 *sp rt center*		16	125	190	3	18		
8	465	530	5	3	85 *sp rt 2nd tree right*		17	345	400	4	14	138 *start left trap ropes on right*	
9	380	440	4	7	150 *sp rt center on flat* 100 *bottom of hill*		18	380	420	4	10	150 *sp center top*	35
OUT	3080	3510	36				IN	3080	3520	36			
							TO'L	6160	7030	72			

SCORER

ATTEST   DATE   NET SCORES

Minimum distances as shown represent yardage from front of tees to nearest pin locations. Average playing length from members tees is approximately 6300 yards.
Maximum distances represent measurements from back of tees to the farthest pin locations. Average playing length from championship tees is approximately 6850 yards.

Bob Goalby's personal yardage scorecard from his final round at the 1968 Masters. He is not keeping his score here, but using the references from a practice round to help determine club selection, etc. At the Masters during this era there were no Pin location sheets handed to the players as there are today. Also note the term "SP" on the card. There was only a single row of "sprinklers" on the course (yardage was not marked on them), usually about 40 yards apart. Bob used the card to help determine his clubs, but he, like most players of the day, did not play by yardage exclusively, rather it helped him determine the "type" of shot to play.

Bob Goalby with his nephew Jay Haas at age 10 in 1963

DISTANCE-YDS.	444	382	330	400	355	144	484	440	381	3360	163	429	189	432	337	473	494	164	328	3009	6369	Men's Course	
PAR	4	4	4	4	4	3	5	4	4	36	3	4	3	4	4	5	5	3	4	35	71		
																						Women's Course	
PAR	5	4	4	5	4	3	5	5	4	39	3	5	3	5	4	5	5	3	4	37	76		
HANDICAP	④	⑨	⑬	⑧	⑪	⑱	②	⑤	⑩	TOTAL-OUT	⑰	⑦	⑮	⑥	⑫	③	①	⑯	⑭	TOTAL-IN	TOTAL-18	HANDICAP	NET
HOLES	1	2	3	4	5	6	7	8	9		10	11	12	13	14	15	16	17	18				

WON+LOST—HALVED O   DAVENPORT ProCARD   SELF_____

DATE_____   ATTESTED_____
Kindly refrain from bringing Beer or Food onto any part of Club Grounds. Food and Drinks can be had in Club House.

The best lady pro to come out of the area; Judy Rankin.

Judy is shown here in 1968 on her way to capturing her first pro title, the Corpus Christi Open. Her real pro achievements would come during the 70's as she won 25 events during that decade.

Above, a scorecard from Crystal Lake CC. This was one of the areas top public venues for almost 50 years. The skin games held there over the years were legendary, as the areas top players met on the first tee, threw their money in the hat and teed it up. They included; Eddie Held, Jimmy Jackson, Dick Shaiper and Jimmy Manion, Bob Cochran, and many more.

*One of the defining moments in sport. Raymond Floyd and Bob Goalby
(at left) going over their scorecards at a patio table just off the 18th green.
Behind them Tommy Aaron speaks with an official about his error.
To the right sits a dejected Roberto Devicenzo, painfully aware of the mistake
he committed that cost him a chance at a playoff for the 1968 Masters.*

*This incident led to several changes in the post-round scorecard routine.
Perhaps the most important was setting up a tent away from the congestion
where players could review their cards in a quieter situation.*

You learn very soon, I think, in tournament golf, that your most formidable adversary is yourself. You win or lose according to your own ability to withstand pressure. You must learn to keep on playing your game despite all the disturbing thoughts that may keep crowding in upon your consciousness, and, above all, you must keep fighting the awful pressure, no matter how much you would like to give in to it."

...Bobby Jones in *Golf Is My Game*

No one can quite put their finger on exactly when the "golf boom" hit. Was it the first TPC course in 1981? Or was it when Hilton Head was first developed in 1969? Or perhaps it was when Airfares started getting cheaper which enabled golfers to travel to resort destinations? Many believe in the Arnie-Eisenhower-TV theory and golf just continued to grow from the mid-60's to today.

Nevertheless, the period from 1980 to the present has seen not just a boom in terms of number of courses, but the quality of courses as well. This is not to say that the early courses were not good; quite to the contrary, they are among the very best. But with equipment changes, the rise of Palmer, Nicklaus, Player, Trevino and the like, more players took up the game and the demand for courses grew with that surge. Many did not succeed, while others saw their fairways plowed-under as the value of the land outpaced green fees. Courses such as Crystal Lake turned into Barrington. Parkwood Oaks in Maryland Heights begot condominiums while Southmoor [alias Bahnfyre] and Green Trails begot homes on the 14th fairway.

During this period not only did public golf grow, but private courses began a revival. Union Hills (1982), The Players Club (1983), Boone Valley (1992), Fox Run (1993), Country Club at the Legends (1989), St. Albans (1992) and Whitmoor (1988) all are private, though The Players Club began public.

Architects who had not been in St. Louis before, nationally recognized names, were designing area courses. We saw Weiskopf-Morrish at St. Albans and P.B. Dye at Boone Valley. Robert Trent Jones returned to design the Legends while Karl Litton did the 36 at Whitmoor, and Lawrence and then Roger Packard completed the 27 holes at the Players Club. St. Louisan Gary Kern continued his excellent work at Fox Run, Quail Creek, Fox Creek and Union Hills.

Ellen Port
The best woman Amateur
in the Area
with the Trans-Miss
Championship Trophy

1980-Present - The Boom

The Country Club lure itself was not what brought these men and their considerable skills to the area. Often it was through old friendships as was the case between Spencer Olin and Arnold Palmer who met years earlier at a pro-am. So it was only natural when Olin decided to build a course for the community, that Arnie and Ed Seay would be selected. Tom Fazio, the hottest architect nationally, designed the *Missouri Bluffs* in 1994, while Dr. Michael Hurdzan completed *Crystal Highlands* in 1988 and just completed the 2nd 18 holes at St. Albans. 1965 Open champ Gary Player returned and *Tapawingo* opened in 1994. Jack Nicklaus designed one of his very few public courses for Jack Wolfner as *Stonewolf* welcomed golfers in September 1996.

Lesser known architects brought us some quality courses, many times on a par with their more famous counterparts, but often at a much lower price. *Hawk Ridge* by Larry Flatt opened in 1995 as the city of Lake St. Louis responded to their residents requests. Senior Player Jim Cochran did some negotiations with the Pipefitters Union and developed *Emerald Greens* in 1994. Jim is perhaps best known for his two courses in south county, *Paradise Valley* and the *Players Club*. Masters' Champ Bob Goalby did not forsake his Belleville roots and developed *The Orchards* in 1991 and is currently developing *Champions Trail GC* in Fairview Heights, due to open in 1997. Originally this was in conjunction with tennis great Jimmy Connors, US Open winner Curtis Strange and nephew Jay Haas, but

**Jim Holtgrieve
St. Louis' Premier
Amateur**

**Don Bliss
4-time State Champ &
1996 Metro
Player of the Year**

they have now bowed out of the deal as new owners have taken over.

Other new layouts are *Pevely Farms* by Arthur Hills, the Art Kerckhoff dream facility near the Players Club; *Persimmon Ridge*, a tribute to the hard work of Jeff Whitfield, which has brought this to the final stages. The Walters group has also begun design on a new layout adjoining the St. Louis International raceway in Illinois, the *Gateway National Golf Links*. The latter two are being designed by the most recent settler to St. Louis via Phoenix, Keith Foster.

Perhaps the most overlooked area architect, probably because he is local, is Gary Kern. Gary has designed or remodeled some of the best layouts in the area including Quail Creek, Fox Run, Fox Creek (Edwardsville), Sun Valley, Fourche Valley and Eagle Lake. He is also designing the third nine at the Legends for new owner Pat McEvoy. Trying to temper his own creativity to make it blend with the original RTJ-designed eighteen is a tribute to his talent and abilities. It is often said that *"a prophet in his own land has no honor"* and for Gary, the fact that he resides on Clayton Road clouds the issue that he is an excellent golf course designer. His son Ron has collaborated with many designs and is fast developing into a fine designer in his own right as he works out of Indianapolis.

Hale Irwin, who is enjoying unbridled success on the Senior Tour, began a design business as his career on the regular Tour seemed to be declining—he obviously had no idea how successful his Senior career would be—as he and Gary Kern initially collaborated on Quail Creek in 1986. Today he has projects working all over the world, as his reputation and ability provide him with opportunities. Locally, he has been retained to re-work the proposed changes to the Forest Park golf course, as the powers-that-be attempt to re-route off Art Hill. Let's hope they don't force Hale to destroy the character of the layout in the name of improvement.

Other "celebrities" have gotten into the design business; Weatherman Dave Murray designed Tree Court (now Family Golf Centers) and Indian Mounds GC at Tee-Up Golf while Ned Storey, owner of the areas Golf Discounts, laid out his Mid-Rivers Course.

Still other courses were completed by amateur architects or course owners searching to make their mark in golf. One such facility is Deer Creek, in House Springs, designed by owner Brooks McCarthy. The former-Sunset member completely sodded the course as he cut the fairways through the wooded acreage near Hillsboro.

Despite the availability of top-notch architects there continue to be courses developed that for a variety of reasons are plagued by water problems, poor greens, infestations and other ills. Our initial reaction might be to condemn these as poor layouts ...and they may well be. But each course serves a purpose. No one would want to play Bellerive from the "tips" all the time (no...really you wouldn't!), just as the scratch player would shy away from a Riverside or Legacy to challenge his game. But for an individual golfer a course serves a purpose or it goes out of business. St. Ann, Ballwin, Alton, Ruth Park, Creve Coeur or Berry Hill do not survive just because they are municipal courses, they do so

Roger Null
Missouri Seniors Champ
in 1996

because golfers enjoy playing them. For each golfer, finding the layout best suited to your game is the challenge, for that is the tract you will re-visit over and over again.

The number of golfers continues to grow by staggering proportions. Unfortunately, the number taking lessons has not. The five hour round has become famous (or infamous!) and etiquette is sometimes hard to find between the beer cans and un-repaired ball-marks. Course marshals are often little more than retirees trying to fill their shag bag and seldom is course management their biggest concern, though at a few courses this is changing. Almost every survey indicates that this is the biggest hurdle golf faces in the future, since the number of rounds dictates the survival rate of a course!

During these two decades we have seen a number of top quality players appear on the scene. Derre Owsley has made his impact felt, while the Barry brothers, Tom and Dan, have, at times, been so dominant you wonder why they don't win everything in sight! Bob Beckmann, Scott Thomas, David Lucks and Mark Boya-jian were brilliant as it seemed like a horserace with the thoroughbreds continually bumping for position down the home stretch.

I would be remiss in not noting the play in the early 80's of two players who moved elsewhere for competition -- not out of the area -- but to the Pro tours -- Jay Delsing and Jerry Haas. Had they remained amateurs they undoubtedly would have been extremely successful. But they had other goals in life, and they continue on that track today.

A group of players from Normandie in particular, have made their mark on area championships, while Norwood Hills continues its dominance among

1980-Present - The Boom

the private clubs with several players winning titles. However players from St. Clair CC, The Players Club, Algonquin and recently St. Albans have also risen to the top.

But through the years, a few names continually rose to the top, not in every event, but enough to let others know that they still have that competitive drive, with the game to match. These individuals would be none other that Jim Holtgrieve and Don Bliss.

Nine State titles were claimed by seven St. Louisans since 1980, as Don Bliss captured three crowns and was the only repeat winner during this stretch. Don had moved to California for business during the late 70's, but would return and win the '83, '86 and '88 titles. With his close second in '96, Don proved he can still duel with the best and he has reaffirmed his role as the premier area player today.

Jim Holtgrieve won his second state title in 1981 and then John Hayes culminated the '82 season with his victory. David Lucks had a spectacular year in 1987 with his win as did Scott Thomas in 1992 with his thrilling 38-hole victory. Bob Beckmann would win his trophy in 1993, making him the last St.

Louisan to capture State as more golfers from Kansas City, Springfield and Columbia made their mark.

Holtgrieve would compete more throughout the world through the mid-80's than in local events as he would play in two Walker Cups and several Masters. His goals were fixed on the national titles, and as we all are aware, he would win the inaugural 1981 USGA Mid-Am crown at Bellerive.

Several single-year winners were among the titleholders, most from outstate, as few dominant players were present throughout Missouri, Bliss being the notable exception, though Holtgrieve can never be discounted.

As the *Metro Championship* began in 1991, Bliss once again roared to the front with the initial win and repeated in 1993. Derre Owsley, a former pro, regained his amateur status and became a factor in any tournament, winning the '92 Metro. Craig Schnurbusch would capture the '95 Metro and continue his excellent career while Jim Holtgrieve would regroup and defeat all comers in the '94 Metro. Perhaps the recently completed '96 Metro was a fitting conclusion as Bellerive fought back against the onslaught and only Tom Barry was able to

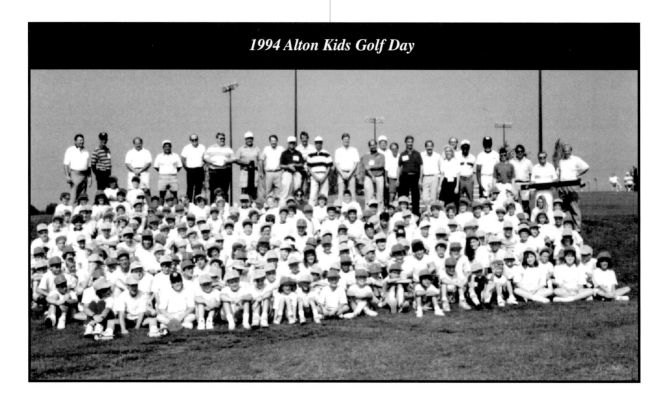

1994 Alton Kids Golf Day

Participants in the 1988 Wilson Cup Matches
Front (l-r) Phil Hewitt, Paul Hooser, Ron Akin, Joe Schwent, Roger Null,
Ben Godwin, Craig Schnurbusch, John Valuck, Bob Jones
Back; Dave Levine, Joe Rotarius, Scott Oulds, Lynn Roseley, Jerry Waitulivich,
Terry Carpenter, Scott Bess, Alex Vandiver, Don Brozio, Bob Beckmann, Don Bliss,
Dee Sanders, Craig Hardcastle, Bobby Godwin.

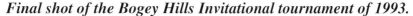

Final shot of the Bogey Hills Invitational tournament of 1993.

1980-Present - The Boom

Tom Wargo tee's off in the Blue Cross shoot-out at Bogey Hills.

Below: East team members of the Missouri Cup Matches for 1996.
(l-r) Bobby Godwin, Craig Schnurbush, Brian Kennedy, Andy Frost, Phil Keim,
Tom Barry, David Rhoads, Don Bliss, Roger Null, David Estes, Jim Holtgrieve.
Missing: Scott Thomas.

Don Clarkson
Glen Echo and Old Warson Pro.
Loved by all who knew him.

Joe Jiminez
Senior Tour Member, Head Pro at
Jefferson City CC and member of the
Gateway PGA Hall of Fame.

Contestants at the District Senior
Championship.

One of the many treasures in the collection of Bob Goalby

solve the greens, though David Estes gave him quite a run.

The *Jimmy Jackson tournament* was born in 1985 following his untimely death in 1983 and its champion is always one of the areas best. The Triple A *"Champion of Champions"* title is still sought after as it concludes the season, though the number of eligible players is quite small.

The new *Missouri Mid-Amateur* was begun in 1995, and Scott Thomas and then Don Bliss came

away winners, two fitting titleholders, and representatives of lifetime amateurs.

The *Missouri Cup* and *Wilson Cup* continued strong as East vs. West battled it out in the amateur ranks, then took their shots at the Pro's, doing quite well at times. The Wilson Cup in particular traces it's roots back to the early 1900's when Manion, Held, Wolff and the like battled the Pro's.

In the Men's District Jerry Haas, Mark Boyajian and Bob Beckmann would all be multiple winners, with Delsing, Highlander, Holtgrieve,

The Board of Governors
of the
Augusta National Golf Club
cordially invites you
to participate in the
Nineteen Hundred and Eighty-Five
Masters Tournament
to be held at
Augusta, Georgia
the eleventh, twelfth, thirteenth and
fourteenth of April

Hord W. Hardin
Chairman

R.S.V.P.

Receiving one of these in the mail would most likely make your day!

Ellen Port and husband-caddy Andy.

1980-Present - The Boom

Bobby Stroble
Two-time winner of the
Lou Fusz St. Louis Open and
current Senior Tour Member

Jerry Waitulivich
Top amateur and Ping Sales Rep.

Terry Houser
Winner of 6 Publinks Champion-
ships, two St. Louis Open's, &
Director of Golf at "The Falls"

Don Bliss (l) and Scott Thomas at
the recent Missouri Cup Matches at
St. Albans CC

Jerry Haas being congratulated for his individual title in the 1981 Illinois High School Championships. His Belleville West team would finish third overall. Others in the picture are;
Front (l-r): Scott Moore and Kye Goalby;
Back; Jerry Haas, Troy Henard, Coach Gene Maurer, Scott Martens, Andy Mulconnery.

Thomas, Ed Schwent, Sam Scheibal and Jeff Johnson winning single titles. Dustin Ashby, the 1996 winner, would be unique in that he is a true Publinks player, and may be the first Publinks player to win the District, for when Manion won in 1923 he had just joined a club after having played public courses for years, as did Eddie Held in 1924.

The Women's District would record several back-to-back winners since 1980; Barb Beuckman, Jill Bertram and Maria Palozola along with Barb Berkmeyer's two titles in '94 and '96. Jeannine Dobbin Lewis had last won a District in 1953, but she came back to capture the 1985 trophy. Mary Gail Dalton would dominate the Senior Women's events, capturing five titles as Betty Von Rump and Alice Sampson each would win two.

1980-Present - The Boom

Cindy Mueller-Riess
Another of Belleville's great players;
Illinois Junior Champ and two-time
Illinois State Champion (1985 & 1987)
Most recently an instructor at St. Louis
Country Club

The 14th hole at
Spencer T. Olin.

The 6th hole at
venerable Triple A links

BOONE VALLEY
CLASSIC

September 2 - September 8, 1996

**BOONE VALLEY
GOLF CLUB**

On the state level, Ellen Port would capture two titles as would Lindsey Murfin. Barb Berkmeyer would win her fifth title in '84, second only to Karen MacGee's seven wins. Conspicuous by her absence was Marcella Rose who won two state and a district title in the 60's. She, like Ellen Port, would concentrate more on regional and national events.

Ellens' two state crowns would be only warm-ups for her national competitions, and this is where she concentrated her efforts, and had her greatest success!

Though few National Tournaments have started recently, at least one began in St. Louis. With the growth of Seniors in the country the National Senior Olympics came to St. Louis in 1987 to crown the national champion. Two St. Louisans, Harris Frank and Ken Marshall, active in the St. Louis Senior Olympics for 8 years, decided the time had come to organize a national tournament at which local medal winners could vie for national recognition. So in late June the seniors arrived to shoot for par. Held over the site of the 1904 Olympic Golf matches, Glen Echo presented the perfect venue for the inaugural tournament. John Jacob of Cedar Rapids, Florida shot a 148 to defeat Pete Dye (of architect fame) by a stroke. His wife, Alice Dye, won the Ladies championship flight with a 5 stroke win, shooting 169 total.

1980-Present - The Boom

As the decade draws one year closer, the area's craving for golf seems to becoming more satisfied: a Nike event at the Missouri Bluffs, the newly named Michelob Light LPGA Classic remains at Forest Hills, The Boone Valley Classic gets a three year contract with increased purse and TV for '97, and Old Warson has captured the 1999 Mid-Amateur, the first true championship held there since the Ryder Cup in 1971. Bellerive is on the prowl for another championship, but undecided as to which one. Spencer T. Olin is close to announcing the news that they will also have an event in 1999, the US Amateur Publinks!

What's the downside to all this? There remains pressure on the clubs to contribute their courses for the ever-growing demand for tournaments. Most clubs have set limits -- the rule is two at many -- and when you have the District, Metro and State knocking at your door for Men, Women, Senior and Junior, it does get overwhelming. Couple this with the desire of some clubs to seek-out national events, and the number of days available continues to shrink.

The upside is the new public courses which are more than capable of hosting some of these events. Sure, it won't be the same as playing Sunset or Bellerive, or Forest Hills, but who says it won't be better!

Golf has some significant choices that will guide its future. Equipment is outstripping the courses in many communities to such an extent that any layout under 6800 is in jeopardy of not being long enough to handle quality amateur events, much less pro stops.

And as the number of players grows, we run the risk of rounds growing even longer and more frustrating. Course management must develop

Veteran Pro - T.D. Morris

policies, and enforce them, that allow all of us to enjoy the sport in a timely fashion. Clocks on tee's and marshals who actually marshal (and eject those who won't or can't comply) are essential to the future success of area golf.

The St. Louis area has suffered from a variety of ills through the years when it comes to crowning a champion. The District has always been limited to primarily the private clubs, and they have made no pretense about who their champion represented, though select public players are now invited to take part.

During the 1920's there were three events; the District, the Municipal and the City championship, and the winner of these (at least the City and District) was often the same. The cream did rise to the top!

The 40's saw the Metro Open and Amateur, but they were short lived, as Bob Cochran captured half of the events played, once again showing that no matter what you call it, the top players will find the victory circle.

The early St. Louis Opens were generally open to all, but in the 30's through 50's, pro's played for the purses, so the amateurs were left fighting for low amateur and little more than bragging rights.

The Michelob Match Play of the 70's was the closest to an area wide event, but it too suffered from lack of sponsorship. The various other amateur events (Normandie Amateur for example) had most of the better players present, and it continues to flourish.

However, with the rise of the Metro tournament in 1991 we appear to have a single Amateur event that is bringing it all together. It's champions have been among the elite. The fields have been tremendous, and the golf outstanding. The air at the

Dale Douglas works on his game prior to the opening round at Boone Valley

tournament is heavy with the concentration and anticipation that is evident at a major event -- the players know it, the officials know it and the spectators know it.

If the Metro can continue the momentum into the next decade, then we will have something special to recall in later years. However, we cannot let the task rest on the shoulders of just a few to keep it alive. The area must draw together to support an event such as this which benefits us all.

Perhaps the other reason to support the Metro is that it may finally be able to bring the Ladies events together. Certain groups within the Women's events have tried hard, sometimes with success, to keep good, young players out of their events, even those that were qualified. Various challenges were used, skirt-length or handicap became the favored manner, to eliminate the competition. Accusing them of cheating was a harsher indictment at times. Most of these accusations were untrue, but sadly for Ladies golf, it cast a pall over their competitions.

On occasions, the situation was so bad that reporters assigned to cover the ladies refused to do so, such was their frustration with the situation.

As the 100th anniversary of golf in the area is being celebrated, we should be thankful for the many

Hale Irwin
As one of the stars of the Senior Tour, Hale's time is in demand. Here a local broadcaster tries to get a few "sound bites" for the evening sports.

1980-Present - The Boom

Earl Parham (2nd from left) with fellow competitors; Gordon Schoby, E. Heffner and Bob Hay at the recently remodeled Grand Marias GC

wonderful courses and events we do have throughout the area.

But like the early pioneers of 1896 who built the first area course, and organized the first tournaments, what we do in the coming months and years will impact future players. Today the youngsters who dream of being a Tiger Woods just want the chance to compete. For that we must provide the courses, the instructors and the events. Those who"beat balls" at local ranges in search of "the zone", and who walk the fairways enjoying the peace and contentment the game offers are the up-and-coming players who will decide how we did when our generation held the torch.

Let's hope we make the most of our opportunity.

Golf is a game passed on from father to son or daughter (as well as mother to child). Here we have a father and son (above) at Triple A enjoying a casual round, while below, in a more intense competition, young Steve Irwin attempts to qualify for the US Amateur as father-caddie Hale, helps read the line.

"Imagine showing up on the first tee attempting to qualify for the US Amateur and the caddie for your playing partner has won the US Open three times! No pressure there!!"

...comment heard at the 1996 Amateur Qualifying at Fox Run

A few familiar faces; (l-r) Stan Musial, Governor Warren Hearnes, Bob Goalby, Bob Cochran and Red Schoendiest. Stan is among the most active in assisting Charity Golf events, and is honorary chairman for several.

Memphis-native Bobby Cochran won the Amateur title at the Lou Fusz St. Louis Open in 1990. Currently the Florida State grad is playing on the Hooters and Nike Tour. Grandson of our own Bob Cochran, Bobby is sooting to make his own career in golf as he moves toward joining the "big show" in the near future.

A few of the Ladies District Champions; (l-r) Seated; Marcella Rose, Jeannine Dobbin Lewis, Mary Gail Dalton. (Standing) Susie Driscoll, Barb Beuckman, Lynette Chrenka, Kathy Welsh, Jill Bertram, Lisa Minnihan, Barb Berkmeyer. This group of 10 accounted for 30 titles since 1950!

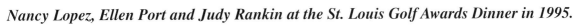

Nancy Lopez, Ellen Port and Judy Rankin at the St. Louis Golf Awards Dinner in 1995.

1980-Present - The Boom

The Gateway Golfing Society celebrates the traditions of golf with traditional Scottish costumes. Just one of the many groups which are founded to promote golf.

The Clubhouse for the CC at St. Albans

A gathering of former St. Louis District Champions in 1995

Back row; Richard Jarrett, Ed Schwent, Ken Highlander, Jim Mason, Jim Holtgrieve
Middle; Jeff Johnson, Mark Boyajian, Bob Beckmann
Front; Newell Baker, Jonas Weiss, Bob Cochran, Les Slattery.

At the birth of the Country Club at the Legends Don Breckenridge (l) was all smiles as he had contracted with legendary Robert Trent Jones to design the course. A few years later, plagued by membership problems and housing delays, Breckenridge would sell the club.

1980-Present - The Boom

Crystal Highlands GC. This Michael Hurdzan design, about a 30 minute drive south in Crystal City/Festus, is an outstanding public facility. This is the view from the clubhouse down the 16th fairway (left) with the 18th green at the lower center.

"Doc" (l) and Denny Walters. They built four courses through the years (Bogey Hills, Whitmoor (2) and Missouri Bluffs, the last three within the past 15 years, and they have one more on the drawing board! They hosted the Bogey Hills Invitational, the Gateway Masters and in 1997 will host the Nike Gateway Classic event at the Missouri Bluffs.

St. Louis District Golf Association

Formed on June 3, 1916 the SLDGA was founded to provide an association of private clubs throughout the area. The member clubs today are; Algonquin, Bellerive, Bogey Hills, Forest Hills, Fox Run, Glen Echo, Greenbriar, Lake Forest, Lockhaven, Meadowbrook, Norwood Hills, Old Warson, Players Club, CC at St. Albans, St. Clair, St. Louis, Sunset, Sunset Hills, The Legends, Westborough, Westwood and Whitmoor. Today the 22 member clubs hold a championship each summer to determine the best player that year from among their members. In 1929 Sunset CC donated the "Ben Langan Trophy" as emblematic of the Amateur Golf Championship of the District. Today, the Arthur Griesedick trophy is awarded the District Match Play Men's champion.

The forerunner to the SLDGA was the St. Louis Golf Association which was founded in 1901, but had never been a formally organized body. The first SLGA President was none other than Glen Echo's Colonel Charles McGrew. Since 1992, they have added some of the top public golfers to their tournament format, and it has increased the participation and level of play. To participate as a public golfer you must qualify for one of the USGA, Missouri Amateur or other events. Larry Etzkorn, Executive Secretary for the past 12 years, administers the tournaments and handles other administrative duties for the clubs. Each club sends a representative to the District and officers are elected from this group. Tim Crowley, from Bellerive CC, is the 1996 President.

Tournaments sponsored, in addition to the District Championship, include a Pro/3 man, Father & Son, Jim Jackson Memorial, Jim Benson Memorial and the District Senior tournament. (Jim Benson was secretary of the SLDGA for 35 years from 1946-1981) A total of 9 tournaments are sponsored by the District each year. Other Secretaries of the Association have been, Sterling E. Edmunds (1916-17), William F. Fahey (1918-19), Frank B. Nall (1920-1924) Clarence Wolff (1924-1945), Jim Benson (1946-81) and Bob Mason (1981-84).

The 22 member clubs have a great deal of loyalty to the District, while recognizing the concerns of each club in attempting to satisfy their members.

St. Louis District Women's Golf Association

Founded in 1915, the organization has held competitions since 1920 to find the top female amateur in the area. Similar to the Men's organization, the Ladies have documented their history in great detail. Their first district championship was held at Algonquin in 1920 as Mrs. E. Lansing Ray captured the trophy There have been many multiple champions during their 76 year history and as a result, only 32 ladies have worn the champions crown. In the early years the women were more of a subsidary to the Men's group, as even their funding came from the Men's District, but today they run their events independently of the men. Membership is open to all ladies who are members of District clubs.

St. Louis Seniors Golf Association

This group, headed by Bill Gill, is for golfers over 55 who wish to continue their competitive efforts. The Group holds 3 tournaments each year, and the popularity

Organizations

grows each season. The initial tournament goes back to 1954 and some of the best senior players lay claim to the title. There is a 5 year waiting list for new members to participate in tournaments as those wishing to join far-outnumber the ability of the organization to handle their number.

Metropolitan Amateur Golf Association

Tom O'Toole

This organization was founded in 1991 with the goal of providing a promotional and regulatory body for St. Louis area amateurs. Headed by

attorney Tom O'Toole, who serves as the executive director, the association fosters amateur competitions throughout the area. Several USGA events are sponsored by Metropolitan Amateur Golf Association (MAGA) each season, in particular the Taylor Cup, which pits top amateurs against pro's. Local Qualifying for the US Open, the US Senior Open, US Junior, US Women's Amateur and the US Amateur, US Senior Amateur and the US Mid-Amateur are also under their direction. The concluding events are the Men's Metro Championship, the Women's Metro and the Senior Metro, in which the best amateurs go head-to-head.

One significant obstacle which over the years has prohibited non-club association from achieving success in area-wide competitions, was access to the better area courses for their championships. The MAGA appears to have solved this with their most recent championship held at Bellerive CC. While limiting the field based on available tee times, this gives the MAGA a good start on future events in developing a true area-wide championship.

Among those who volunteer their time to making the MAGA a success, some of which were the original founders of the association, are; Rick Meier, George Meyer, Mike Corry, Jim Holtgrieve and Jim Tom Blair. Tom O'Toole is recognized, along with Stan Grossman, as the two finest tournament directors in the area. When they run an event, it is run well and the course is set-up competitively, but fairly. This trend should continue.

One early obstacle in getting MAGA off-and-running was friction between the Metro and the Missouri Golf Association. To the members of the Metro, the Bi-State area has been largely ignored by the MGA. Another thorn was the resignation of Mike Corry as MGA president, as he helped found the Metro. A more serious issue that separated the groups, though this was recently resolved through mediation with the USGA, is the handicapping services offered by both groups and the fees paid by the participating clubs. Currently there are over 50 clubs that are members of the Metro and almost 30 using the GHIN service. Members of the Metro believe that there is room for both organizations, since as they serve different interests; one of local competitions or national qualifying, and the other for statewide play.

As noted earlier, access to championship layouts will, in all probability, determine the long-term success of the Metro as a true championship organization. With the District, Ladies District, Junior, Senior, Missouri Golf and Metro all vying for tee times, many clubs are opting to reduce their availability. This would result in a sad state of affairs for the area, for the clubs would ultimately only hurt area golf if this continues. A method must be addressed to allow championship competitions to be played on the best available courses. To this end the MAGA, MGA and District must work together in the best interests of area golf.

Gateway PGA

(l-r) Executive Director Jeff Smith, Junior Director Shannon Miller, and Assistant Executive Director Patty Sturgis.

The Gateway PGA is one of 41 geographical "sections" throughout the country. Each section operates within the framework of the PGA Constitution. The Gateway PGA is headed by Executive Director Jeff Smith (through 1996) and is comprised of member clubs in Southern Illinois and Eastern Missouri. The local Organization has two divisions, a Regular and a Senior group with over 150 facilities and 400 club professionals involved. In addition various committees are established to fulfill a variety of objectives. The officers, elected on an annual basis, maintain close ties to the PGA of America staff in Florida, along with a very competent local staff. A full complement of tournaments for Head Pro's and Assistants is featured. Points are awarded based on finishes and the end of the season winner is crowned for both the overall and Senior player. The Gateway grew out of the Eastern Missouri PGA which was founded in the 1920's by Pro's like Homer Herpel, Clarke Morse, Clarence Norsworthy and Ed Duwe.

The ongoing education of the golf professional is essential and to this end the PGA provides nation-wide seminars, workshops and programs on everything from merchandising, to cart control, to player movement around the course. An aggressive apprentice program assists new PGA members with the necessary information to move forward in their careers. The Section works with local charities and social agencies to sponsor a variety of activities. The Hale Irwin "Clubs for Kids Day" is one such event as are various golfing events at area clubs.

Missouri Golf Association

While concentrating mainly on their Amateur Championship, the MGA also provides competition for Juniors and Seniors. The organization continues to add new events to meet the needs of Missouri golfers. From its headquarters in Jefferson City, under the direction of William Wells, the MGA coordinates golf throughout the state with competitions from May through October. The premier events are the Men's Amateur, the Ladies, the Senior Amateur, the Mid-Amateur matches and the Missouri Cup

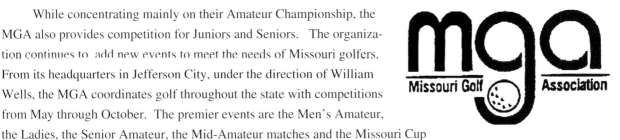

matches. The present Cup matches are only three years old, but the honor of playing and the level of competition has made these outstanding attractions for player and fan alike. Attempting to work with golf associations across the state can be challenging at times. The MGA, like other state and regional groups, must continue to adapt as course access and the number of competitors strains many resources. With an executive board represented by the various regions of the state, the MGA reflects the growing legions of new golfers that swell the courses each year with demands for better and better events.

Organizations

Women's Golf Associations & Groups

Since 1985, more women than men have taken up golf. Like the thousands of men who have played the game over the past century, women find the game challenging and exciting. As society has changed, women have better access to many country clubs, though many argue that it should be even more open. In business, women want the same kind of access to clients that a round of golf offers. However, when women taken up the game, unlike many of their male counterparts, they actually take lessons before heading to the first tee to avoid the embarrassment that could occur. Also more couples are finding that the time spent together on the links is actually very enjoyable. Golf vacations, retirement living and golf communities have encour-

aged women to join their spouse, or friends, on the links. Local groups include; **Missouri Women's Golf Association**, **St. Louis Women's Golf Association, St. Louis Professional Businesswomen's Golf Association** and **Senior Women's Missouri Golf Association.**

The **St. Louis Women's Golf Association** (SLWGA) is perhaps the largest local group with between 230-250 members. All members must play at public courses and their competitions alternate years between Match play and Medal play. Having begun in 1976 it provides a very competitive environment not always available for public course players. Pam Rothfuss Whalen was the founder of this group, when she organized the ladies from most of the areas public facilities under a common banner. There are 31 public course members and they conduct several levels of competition each season. These include a Match Play or Medal Play (in alternating years), low net and low gross events, Senior events and team competitions.. The original Women's Metro was begun in 1980 under the direction of the SLWGA and continued until 1986. In their support of National Golf events, the sectional chairman of the USGA Publinks has been a member of the SLWGA since 1977. Local standout Ellen Port played in one of her first competitions with this group in 1986!

Local USGA Representatives

- Bart Collida, USGA US Publinks Championship Committee
- Larry Etzkorn, Local USGA Committeeman
- Dan LeGear, Sectional USGA Committeeman
- Tom O'Toole, Sectional USGA Committeeman
- Stan Grossman, USGA Junior Championship Committee
- Mrs. Jane Watson, USGA Women's Regional Affairs Committee, Missouri
- Mrs. Waldo W. Forsan, USGA Senior Women's Amateur Championship Committee
- Mrs. Pat Will, USGA Women's Publinks Committee
- Mr. George Meyer, Senior Amateur Championship Committee
- Jim Holtgrieve, USGA Mid-Amateur Championship Committee
- Mrs. Barbara Berkmeyer, USGA Women's Mid-Amateur Championship Committee
- Hale Irwin, USGA Implements and Ball Committee
- G. Randall Martin, USGA Green Section Committee
- Carol Fromuth, USGA Girls' Junior Championship Committee

Miscellaneous Groups & Tournaments

While it is hard to determine when golf became so closely tied to charity outings, it cannot be denied that each Monday (and often Tuesday, Wednesday, Thursday & Friday) an outing for some charity or another can be found. At last count almost 200 charity events are held from April to October. This is in addition to the 70 odd tournaments and dozens of smaller events held at clubs throughout the area. The events are held at almost all private courses and the majority of the public facilities. The entry fees range from $50 to $500 per player. In the late 80's, the number of events was closer to 50. Golf has become better at raising money than selling cookies!

courses, it hosts 30-35 tournaments during the summer, raising almost $1.5 million for various charities. Played mostly in a scramble format, which allows golfers at all levels to ride the coattails of their "A" player, a good time can be had by all. Whitmoor has recently become a "major factor" in the outing business as they have their 36 holes, and frequently move excess players to the Missouri Bluffs, further increasing the popularity of Whitmoor as site.

Local celebrities dot the scorecards as their presence ups-the-ante for the entry fee. Frequently a tournament needs to be tied to a celebrity to fully realize its potential. Personalities such as Jack Buck, Dan Dierdorf, Hale Irwin, Pat Leahy, Lou Brock, Ozzie Smith, Mike Shannon and a host of others lend their name to worthwhile events. There are many groups who sponsor these weekly events, but perhaps none more than Kim Tucci of the Pasta House Company who is an active supporter of area charities. Another favorite of ours is Dr. Bill Droege. Regardless of who is in his foursome, you can count on Bill winning several events

Perhaps the first such tournament in the area was the Bob Goalby tournament to benefit the Cystic Fibrosis foundation.

One of the first to involve the Pro's was the LPGA events held at Glen Echo in 1964 to benefit Monsignor Behrmann and his St. Mary's Special Home. Today Hale Irwin and Children's Hospital team up to promote one of the best and most generous events at Old Warson.

The course that dominates the "Charity Opens" is definitely Norwood Hills. With two

each season!

The bottom line is that from a skin game, to a major charity or corporate function, almost every week at some course throughout the area an event can be found. Some of the tournaments which have provided substantial benefits to area charities and institutions, provide outstanding gifts for the participants, and are widely recognized as contributing greatly to the betterment of the area are on the listed on the following page.

Organizations

Academy of the Sacred Heart
Almost Home
Alton Marquette High
American Cancer Society
American Diabetes Assn.
American Heart Association
American Lung Association
American Red Cross
Annie Malone Home
Aquinas Alumni
Arthritis Foundation
Billiken Tip-off
Blues/March of Dimes
Boys & Girls Town of Mo.
Boys Club of St. Louis
Busch Tiger Pro-Am
Camp Nedtez
Camp Sunnyhill
Camp Wyman
Cancer Support Center
Cardinal Glennon Charity
Caring for Children
Catholic Children's Home
CBC Mike Shannon Tour.
Celebrity Scramble/Diabetes
Chaminade High School
Charlie Gitto Invit.
Charlie Gitto Italian Open
Chesterfield Rotary
Child Center of Our Lady
Childhaven
Children with Disabilities
Collinsville Lions Club
Cystic Fibrosis
Dakota Boys Ranch
Dan Dierdorf Classic
Dan Kelly Classic
Dan Kelly Tournament
Deaconess Nurses College
Eagle Scout Association
Early Intervention Center
Emmaus Homes Benefit
Epworth Children & Family
Family Resource Center
Florissant Rotary
Fr. Dunne's Newsboy Home
Guardian Angel
Guide Dogs of America
Habitat for Humanity
Hale Irwin Children's Hosp.
Hampton Lions Club
Hardly Able
Hellenic Spirit Charities
Hillsboro High School

IMA/Make A Wish Found.
Incarnate Word/Alzheimers
Jerry Clinton AMC Pro-Am
Jerry Clinton/AMC Pro-Am
Ken Boyer Memorial
Ken Reitz/Harris House
Kidney Foundation
Kilo Foundation
Kingdom House Benefit
Kirkwood/Webster YMCA
Lifecrisis Tournament
Lou Brock/ECHO
Lou Fusz/Edgewood Home
Lupus Foundation Pro-Am
Lutheran Altenheim Assn.
Lutheran Golf Benefit
Make A Wish Foundation
Marine Corp. Scholarship
Maryville U. Benefit
Masonic Home Benefit
McBride Alumni
Met Life/Jack Buck
Metro Ministry
Mid County YMCA
Mike Shannahan/Pepsi Classic
Missouri Head Injury Assn.
Missouri Special Olympics
Mizzou Tiger Tournament
Muscular Dystrophy Classic
Navy League Charity
NF Celebrity
NFL Alumni
Northwest YMCA
Olivette Chamber of Comm.
Operation Food Search
Operation Liftoff
Our Lady of Angels
Ozzie Smith Invitational
Paralyzed American Veterans
Parkway Education Fund
Pride Inc.
Priory Alumni
Queen of Peace Inv.
Region II Special Olympics
Ron Bohley Memorial
Ronald McDonald House
Rosary High School
Rotary Club of Ferguson
Scholars Caddies to College
Shamrock Open
Shelter the Children
SLAHU/Asthma & Alergy
South County YMCA
St. John's High School

St. John Police/DARE
St. Joseph's Academy
St. Joseph Institute
St. Louis Ambassadors
St. Louis Blues Alumni
St. Louis Children's Classic
St. Louis Hemophilia Assn.
St. Louis U. High
St.Joseph's Carmelite Home
St.Joseph's Medical Center
Stan Musial/Deaconess
Together For Kids
UMSL Red and Gold
VFW Scholarship Fund
Washington U Athletics
Webster University Open
Wheelchair Athletic Assn.
Whitey Herzog Foundation
Wings of Hope
Womens/Cardinal Glennon

Golf is 20 percent mechanics and technique. The other 80 percent is philosophy, humor, tragedy, romance, melodrama, companionship, camaraderie, cussedness and conversation."
...Grantlant Rice (1920)

While the majority of us who play the game are classified as amateurs, there are many levels that can be defined in this category. There are the infrequent players, the *"once a year at the company outing"* type, the *"I have my regular tee-time"* weekend player, the *"sneak out and play during the week"* player, and the *"taking a client for a round"* player.

Then we have the group of outstanding players who, while the names change from era to era, dominate local play with their excellent shotmaking. This is the group that has the time, effort, access and ability to take their talent to the next level. Some may have attempted to compete at the Professional level, and were beaten back by the travel, family demands and often sheer talent of their competition. The annual reinstatement by the USGA of 400-500 amateurs each year reflects this. Then there is a group, one that seems to grow smaller each year, of the lifelong amateur. They never attempted to turn professional. They were satisfied with the amateur competition. Their lives are just a fulfilled, their talent just as great. All these guys can really play!

Golfers on the 1st tee at Forest Park

We do tend to have better "short-term" memories as we invariably claim that the latest "greatest" player would have bested all comers, regardless of era. It is the media-types that attempt to anoint them as the next Jones-Palmer-Nicklaus-Mickelson or whoever! It is unfair to all to do this. Would Nicklaus have won the grand-slam in 1930 against the same competition? Would Hogan have won more titles had Nelson not been around? How would Jones fare today? The questions are all moot. The answer lies in long covered-over divots!

Players such as Eddie Held, Jimmy Manion, Clarence Wolff and Richard Bockenkamp, Bryan Winter and the ageless Bob Cochran, all won titles prior to 1940, while Gene Fehlig, Jack Geiss and Jonas Weiss won several prior to 1960. Christian Kenney, Elliott Whitbread, Chester O'Brien were successful at the Missouri Amateur prior to 1940 as well as National events. Their ability and efforts are not questioned.

The trap we often fall into - attempting to compare athletes from one era with another - will never adequately address the "who-is-better" question. It is safe to say that there are four male golfers who were definitely the best in their era. In the 1910-1930 period, few were better than Eddie Held and Jimmy Manion in the state, local and in representing St. Louis in national competitions, From the 1915 City Championship to the 1930 St. Louis Open, they battled with the best and their record speaks for itself. From 1930-1970 it was Bob Cochran. Winning his first District title in 1933 and his last in 1965, with 4 state titles Bob continued to win State Senior titles up until 1978. Finally from 1977 to the present it would be Jim Holtgrieve. Once again, it is not the mere number of titles, but the length of his career and the importance of the titles that stake his claim. With Jim's imminent move to the Senior Tour later in 1997, Don Bliss is more than capable of picking up the torch and carrying it forward.

Among the women the list is shorter, but is no less brilliant. Many of these champions had shorter careers, often achieving their successes in a three to five year career. Others managed to continue over decades, winning continuously, to the dismay of their competitors. During the early 1900's Grace Semple was perhaps the leading area female as she competed in 9 US Women's Amateurs prior to 1915. From 1915-1930 there were two; Audrey Faust and Virginia Pepp. These two dominated all others, winning a combined ten District titles in this period, all while being the best of friends throughout their lifetime.

Marilyn Herpel, Betty Jane Haemerle and Jeannine Dobbin Lewis were the dominant triumvirate during the 40's and 50's as they won a combined 12 district and five State titles. Georgia Dexheimer Schwartz and Sara Caughey captured several events during the late 30's and early 40's as well, making a case for their talent. Toward the end of the 50's Ellen Conant and Judy Torluemke burst on the scene and were dominant in their own right, winning state and district titles and competing in national events.

Group enjoying the day at Ruth Park

The period from 1960-85 could be properly termed the Berkmeyer era. While Doris Phillips would play brilliantly and win four District and three Illinois state titles in a seven year span, it must take a silver to Barb Berkmeyer's five district and five state titles. Marcella Rose would settle for the bronze in this group as she managed two District and two Missouri titles, although Marcella did not play in many area events as she concentrated on the national championships. All three competed in the national events at the Women's Open and Amateur during this era while Barbara would also play in three LPGA events.

While Barbara Berkmeyer would win still more titles in the 90's including two more District crowns and the St. Louis Metro, the 1985 to 1996 era belongs to Ellen Port. When she came to St. Louis in the mid-80's no one, especially not Ellen, could even imagine what the next 10 years would bring. She has crammed into these few short years a lifetime of memories and successes.

For the ladies, their chances for recognition were limited prior to the 1950's. Surely Ellen Port would be recognized in any era for her accomplishments, as would Betty Jane Haemerle, Barbara Berkmeyer, Barbara Beuckman, Marilyn Herpel, Marcella Rose, Audrey Faust Wallace and Virginia Pepp. So too would be the accomplishments of Mary Gail Dalton on the Senior level or Paula Eger had she stayed in the area. Many of these ladies are better known within their locker rooms than by the golfing public. But once again, the level of championship play and national recognition must, in the end, be one of the yardsticks used.

That being said, the individuals listed on the following pages are generally considered, regardless of the standard used, to be among the area's best Amateurs, and in some cases have been so for almost many years. The group below consists mainly of those who chose to forsake the pro route (with a few exceptions) and have competed primarily as amateurs most of their career. The list is definitely weighted toward modern players - we simply know more about them - but those listed whose names are not as familiar to you should not be overlooked. In their day, against the best competition around, they were champions.

Barbara Berkmeyer

The term used to describe Barbara today is "veteran player", but to those competing against her it would be more appropriate to equate her with Hale Irwin than Miller Barber. Veteran, in her situation, means that she has won more events than she cares to remember - 5 Missouri Amateurs and 7 District titles (the last being in 1996). She has competed in the Trans-Miss Championship, the US Women's Amateur, the US Mid-Am and more recently the District Senior Women. Barb has played in 4 LPGA events and was low amateur in two of these.

Barb began winning at age 13 in her home state of Iowa as she won junior events in the Hawkeye state. She got an early beginning with golf as her father was a Pro at several courses in northern Missouri and Iowa and had won the Iowa PGA tournament, beating Jack Fleck for the title. They moved to St. Louis when Barb was 16 and she continued her winning ways here.

In 1962 Barb won her first Junior event in the area, then won her first Amateur in 1965 as Barbara Bubany. Marriage did not stop her from continuing her wonderful career as she won three times in six years in the early 70's. No other player in the St. Louis area and only one other Missourian, Karen Shull McGee, has won the Amateur more times. All the more remarkable is that she did this not in a few short years, but over a twenty year span!

In 1964 Barb was invited to play in the *LPGA St. Louis Squirt Open* at Glen Echo. When the pairings came out, she was to play with legendary Mickey Wright. Upon hearing this, Barb was intent on making a good impression. She went out and hit balls for almost a week to groove her swing. She practiced so much that her hands hurt, and she was afraid that she couldn't play in the tournament. But play she did and ended up low amateur. Playing with Mickey was one of the two highlights of her career.

The second was the *1969 US Amateur* at Las Colinas CC in Dallas [today the TPC course at the Woodlands]. In her first round she played well and shot a 73. Her playing partner did not fare as well, and the next day with an early tee time, her fellow-competitor failed to show. The committee considered moving Barb back to a later tee-time, one that would be in the heat of the day. Barb countered that this wasn't fair and that the heat could be a factor in the outcome. By coincidence, JoAnne Gunderson Carner's playing partner was ill and did not show, so Barb was paired with JoAnne instead. Despite her initial fears, she played well, and in the end was tied for the final playoff spot. Barb remembers that when the playoff began, JoAnne and her husband came out to cheer Barb on. Barb birdied the second hole and won the final spot.

In another year, she met Jane Bastanchury [Booth] who, at the time, held a record for the most matches won in the US Amateur But this day she would fall to Barb. In her role as a USGA official, Barb will see Jane at matches throughout the country as Jane's daughter, Kellee Booth, is among one of the top amateurs in the country and competed with Ellen Port on the recent Curtis Cup team.

The US Amateur holds another special moment for Barb. Her first attempt came in 1964 at Prairie Dunes, that magnificent Perry Maxwell links course in the sand dunes of Hutchinson, Kansas. She set a goal to return when the 1991 Amateur returned there, and she did. Like bookends to a wonderful national Amateur career, the 27 year lapse did not lessen her love of the layout. Recently, for their family vacation, they traveled the central US playing some of the terrific layouts over which she has had the pleasure of competing.

The Amateurs

Barb also holds another distinction; before title IX, scholarships for ladies, in any sport were very rare. Barb was the first woman to receive a golf scholarship to the University of Missouri [and maybe the first female scholarship overall] as Don Faurot recognized her talent and awarded her the grant.

Another key figure in St. Louis golf, and a significant sponsor for the Publinx, was "Spinny" Gould. Spinny was always trying to give Barb money to attend tournaments, but her father had always taught her not to be beholden to anyone, so she consistently refused. While at Mizzou, the team traveled to many tournaments, sometimes flying, other times going for extended events. Only after graduation did she learn that it was Spinny who was financing the team, as a way of indirectly financing Barb.

At other times she played exhibitions with Sam Snead, Patty Berg, Marilyn Smith and Cary Middlecoff. Her smooth, rhythmical swing matched those of the pro's, and her ability to beat par frequently made her presence a requirement. But unlike others, Barb does not think of golf as an end in itself. She enjoys the camaraderie, the exercise and the challenges. But she is not the stereotype steely-eyed opponent. Rather she goes about her business in a matter-of-fact manner, usually with outstanding results. She notes that her husband Rick and son Skip fall into the "avid lover of golf" category!

**Barbara
Bubany
Berkmeyer
1970**

In 1996 she captured the Missouri Women's Metro Championship, marking the fourth decade Barbara has captured a major title. Perhaps a sixth State title would look good alongside that mark, or an eighth District crown!

- Missouri Women's Amateur Champion
  (1965, 1970, 1974, 1975, 1984)
- St. Louis Women's District Champion
  (1967, 1968, 1971, 1976, 1978, 1994, 1996)
- US Women's Amateur
  (1964, 1969, 1972, 1977, 1991)

- Trans-Miss Amateur (1991)
- District Junior Girls Champion (1962)
- St. Louis Metro Champion (1996)
- US Women's Mid-Amateur (1991)
- District Senior Women's Amateur (1995)
- LPGA Events (1964, 1967, 1969, 1970)

Jim Tom Blair

Competing in an era with some of the best amateurs Missouri has known, namely Jimmy Jackson and Bob Cochran, Jim Tom did more than just hold his own, in many competitions he owned the field. In the nine finals from 1951 to 1959, he won or made the finals in the Missouri Amateur six times. Competing in New Orleans while a student at LSU, he won their Invitational tournament and then the Hardscrabble in Fort Smith, Arkansas. He qualified for 11 US Amateurs and 8 US Open's and was runner-up in the Western Amateur. He also came within a stroke of winning a PGA Tour event in 1956 at the Phoenix Open.

Perhaps the event most indicative of his level of skill occurred in 1965. Following the death of his parents in 1962, he barely touched a club in almost three years. His wife encouraged him to get back into competition and he focused on qualifying for one of the two spots open to amateurs at the US Open at Bel-lerive. He spent a month in Florida preparing for the qualifying, struggling to get his game back into competitive form. To do this he would have to conquer two of the area's toughest courses in the qualifying rounds — St. Louis and Westwood — not exactly "user friendly" courses! As he stood on the first tee at St. Louis CC, he could barely control the nervous shaking of his hands. Paired with Jim Fogertey in the round, Fogertey never tired of telling Sunset members of the incredible round. So sharp was his game that day that Jim Tom got the ball up and down from spots that, given a hundred chances, he is certain he could not do it again. He shot even par at Westwood during the afternoon round and won one of the spots.

One of his most remarkable feats came as an amateur on the PGA tour as he finished 3rd at the 1956 Phoenix Open. Jim Tom led after 36 holes, and the next day was paired with Cary Middlecoff, who would be the eventual winner. During the 3rd round, they came to the 16th hole at Phoenix CC, a dogleg left par 4. Jim Tom hit a good tee shot, but a lady crossing the fairway was hit by the ball and it caromed into an unplayable lie. Not what you need at that stage of a tournament. At the beginning of the final round, Jim Tom was still one-up on the field. On the opening hole, he knocked it on the par 5 in three but his birdie putt lipped out, while Middlecoff drained his to tie for the lead. Middlecoff would be ahead by one as they came to the 15th, a par-3 with the pin tucked in the front right, just over the water. Going for the win, *"I wasn't going to get any more money finishing first or second or third"*, Jim Tom shot at the pin, and when it came up short it fell into the water. When the round was over, Jim Tom was sitting in front of his locker as his coach, Leland Gibson of Kansas City walked by. He had walked the last 36 with Jim to see how he would perform under the pressure. *"Well junior"* said Leland, *"when you quit feeling sorry for yourself, remember you went out there with the last foursome on Sunday and you put 70 on the board. Most amateurs I know would have shot 80! So you've got nothing to be ashamed of"*. Years later sportswriters would act amazed that an amateur could compete with the Pro's, but Jim Tom bested most of them over 40 years ago.

The fact that Jackson, Cochran and Blair competed against each other probably helps account for their greatness as they fed off each other. Cochran was the "aging veteran" that Jim Tom and Jimmy had to beat to claim their place as the top amateur in the area, no easy task! During this period their records against each other are quite remarkable. Depending on the event, at any given time, one would have the upper-hand -- but only for a while —

then the die would turn. Jim Tom wins District, Bob wins North & South, Jimmy wins State, and then they would reverse rolls during the next series of events. Their level of play, particularly in match play was marked by fierce competition, and the utmost respect. In medal play it was different. You had to shoot "lights-out" to insure the top spot. Jim Tom did just that as he claimed more than his share of titles in the 50's and early 60's.

Jim believes he focused more on the national events; the Open and the Amateur, than the local events. While they all performed well in each, and all qualified many times for the Amateur and the Open, he believes that Cochran and Jackson focused a bit more on the State and District titles. His mark of competing in eight US Opens definitely indicates his success in that event.

Most would state that his length was his biggest strength, but Jim states rather firmly that it was his putting.

When this is mentioned to some rather prominent players who knew Jim Tom, many look with amazement, for they don't recall his play on the greens as that spectacular. But when reminded that in 1951 he played a total of 1,281 holes of competitive golf and only three-putted eight times, the eyebrows go up, and a quiet nod occurs, denoting that perhaps Jim Tom was pretty good with the blade after all!

An avid storyteller, one of his favorites is of a round he and his father played with Sam Snead at the Greenbriar in West Virginia. Sam was his fathers idol and Jim Tom had arranged a round with him. Sam, as is his nature, set a "friendly wager" on the match. Jim Tom and Sam played well, both coming to the 18th as the sun was setting needing par's to shoot 63 and 62 respectively. Sam was on in two and as Jim Tom prepared to hit, darkness prevented him from being certain of the yardage and he asked his caddie, who gave him a questionable distance. Jim Tom flew the green into a bush and took a 6. As he went to settle the bet, Sam told him to keep his money. It seems Jim Tom's caddie had bet against him and this was his chance to make certain he would lose. Sam went and got the caddie fired. [The caddie master later told Jim Tom he had never seen Sam so mad]. When they met in the grill, Jim Tom's father, playing to a 15 that day, had shot a 73! In his best backwoods drawl, Sam commented, *"Well, Governor, I don't know much about politics, but if your handicap is any indication, I'll stay away from Missouri!"*

When Jim Tom joined the tour, it was quite different from today. Many amateurs competed, depending on where the tournaments were held. They were there mostly for "local color". But the tour allowed the top 10 amateurs each week to play the entire tournament and play the following week. Jim Tom always finished in the top ten, usually in the top 2-3, so he played 72 holes each week. As an amateur he was not playing for the money, but he did want to learn —learn how to play golf. This does not mean he didn't make any money. Weekly calcutta's were common (until outlawed by the tour in the late 50's). But the weekly money matches were where some of the big money was earned. And sometimes the pro's would pair up with the amateur and gamblers who followed the tour would bet on the pair. Frequently totals of $1,000 per hole or more were on the line - only the pro knew for sure. Besides, the pro's didn't make that much money from the tournament itself. The top money winner made maybe $40,000, with a top ten player making about $10,000 per season. This is why they needed club jobs. In Curt Sampson's book, "Hogan" he notes that Hogan, Nelson, Picard, Demaret and many more (all perhaps except Walter

Hagen) had club pro jobs to pay the bills while on tour. Sometimes there were playing pro's, but in many cases they actually worked the counter and gave lessons.

At the 1950 US Open in Dallas, after finishing his practice round, Jimmy Demaret walked up to Jim Tom in the locker room. Jim Tom played at a rather hefty 220 pounds, and occasionally took some ribbing for it. *"Hey fatboy,"* yelled Demaret, *"I hear your pretty good, I've got a match for us."* Well the chance to play with Demaret was exciting so Jim Tom changed his shoes and went back out. Demaret was waiting on the tee as a crowd gathered. Jim Tom was certain they were not there to see him, and Demaret was past his prime. The third member was a talented club pro, Bill Trombley, so it wasn't him. Just then the crowd parted and Ben Hogan walked through. Jim Tom walked over to Demaret and quietly inquired as to the sanity of Demaret's plan! *"Why, you can beat Trombley, can't you, and I can take Hogan!"* As Jim Tom prepared to tee off, he took out his 1-iron and hit the biggest boomerang hook he had ever seen. Jim Tom glanced back at the other members of the group, and Hogan uttered his only comment of the day. *"Well, if I were you, I'd hit another one!"* Despite this poor start, he and Demaret won the match.

Outspoken, Jim Tom has for years advocated an improvement in the management of golf, not only in St. Louis but throughout the state. Jim was one of the organizers of the Metropolitan Amateur Golf Association and has gone head-to-head with the Missouri Golf Association in attempting promote the MAGA.

He is also on the Western Amateur Board which promotes amateur golf and in particular the Evans Scholar program. Jim is one of the few on the Board, maybe the only member, who competed against it's namesake, legendary Chick Evans!

Despite coming from one of the first-families of Missouri — his father was governor and his grandfather a state supreme court justice — Jim Tom wanted to establish a name for himself on his own merits. With a successful insurance business and a terrific golfing career, unfortunately cut short by multiple sclerosis, Jim Tom will remain one of the greats of Missouri golf. He plans to keep playing as long as possible despite his infirmity. Strong and determined, I wouldn't bet against him shooting in the 70's soon!

- Missouri Amateur (1952) 1st
- Missouri Amateur (1955) 1st
- St. Louis District (1958) 1st
- St. Louis District (1969) 1st
- St. Louis District (1970) 1st
- Western Open (1951) Low Amateur
- Missouri Amateur (1951) 2nd
- US Amateur (1951) 5th round
- US Amateur (1950, '51, '55, '56, '57, '59, '60, 62, '63, '65)
- US Open - 8 times - (1950, 1951, 1965)
- British Amateur (1972, 1974, 1975)
- New Orleans Invitational - 1st
- Hardscrabble Invitational - 1st
- Canadian Amateur (QF)
- Phoenix Open (PGA Tour) (1956) 3rd
- California State Fair 1st
- Trans-Miss (6 times)

The Amateurs

Don Bliss

What more needs to be said about Mr. Bliss that his record does not. He grew up caddying at Glen Echo where he got his first taste of golf. Later, on the fairways of Norwood Hills he competed as a youngster against John Johnson and Frank Furlong for nickels. In 1966, when just a freshman in high school and only years after he started playing, he won the St. Louis Junior District title. He continued to play well through school and then in the summer of 1969, following his graduation from Normandy High School, he qualified for the US Amateur at Oakmont. While he didn't qualify for the weekend, his confidence grew to the point where he turned down scholarships from area colleges to attend Oklahoma State and learn under the tutelage of legendary OSU coach Labron Harris.

Don was not on scholarship, and even though he finished 4th in the trials, Labron red-shirted Don his freshman season. While at OSU his roommate was fifteen-year PGA Tour player Danny Edwards. Danny was an All-American and gave Don a real insight into what it took to excel at college golf. Later as a Pro Danny would win 5 times on tour and when he retired would continue his success in business. Don continued to improve and following his junior year he won the Missouri Amateur in 1972. He qualified for the US Amateur that summer where he made the cut and finished in the top 40. The next year displayed even greater success for him, as he won the Big Eight Individual Championship. In his senior year a new coach came to OSU, Mike Holder, and that year saw Don as an honorable mention All-American as he finished 8th in the NCAA individual competition against the likes of Ben Crenshaw, Jay Haas and Tom Kite.

His career could have been more successful but for an unfortunate event in the summer of 1972. He was invited to play in a Scratch Pro-Am event at Westborough with area pro's. While he did not win any prizes, unknown to Don the NCAA prohibited such events, and he lost his eligibility for a semester. He did appeal this to the NCAA and it was eventually overturned, and his eligibility was restored. Following graduation Don knew that while he loved golf, and for a time considered a career as a club pro, but he decided that as an amateur he would be most content

From 1975 to 1980, Don continued to play in the US Amateur, but he kept running into some pretty good players in match play; 1975 it was Curtis Strange who stopped his march and in 1980 it was Fred Couples. Work took Don to Kansas City for a year, where he met his wife, and then for five years to California from 1977 to 1981. While in the "Golden State" he ran up against some very good players, but still managed to finish among the top 16 in 1980 and 1981 in the California Amateur. He also competed in the 1978 LA Open on the PGA Tour and, though he was not playing particularly well, he still made the cut.

Don returned to the area in 1982 and continued winning as the 1983 State Amateur went his way. As one of only 5 players to have won four State Amateur titles, with the fifth barely eluding him this past June, Don ranks as one of the all-time best players from the area.

At 44, Don believes that he still has many more years of good competitive golf ahead. The goals that have eluded him have been a national title and playing on a Walker Cup squad. He competes in only about 12 tournaments a year as work and family take precedence. He recently joined St. Albans where Terry Grosch is working with Don to refine his technique. He has a few goals in mind, one of which is to win that fifth Amateur crown.

There have been many individuals who have influenced Don's career. Danny Edwards was mentioned earlier and Bob Cochran, who always took an interest in the young players at Norwood. Others include Stan Utley with whom Don has had some terrific matches, not the least of which was the 1983 Amateur final at Jefferson City CC where Don won 2&1 but it took a 5-under round to best Utley's 3-under! Another who had an impact on Don was Al Chandler, legendary golf coach at Mizzou. He showed Don that despite the "style" of your game, there can be many ways to win. The last individual would be Jim Holtgrieve. He set the standard by which all golfers competing throughout the area today are judged and Don has tremendous respect for Jim.

Slight of build and mild-mannered, Don does not present an imposing sight on the course. But three important attributes are present; confidence in his game, desire to win, and an intense competitive nature. The combination of these make Don the champion he is.

- Missouri Amateur Champion 4 times (1972, 1983, 1986, 1988)
- St. Louis Metro Champion (1991, 1993)
- St. Louis Publinx Champion (1993)
- Leadbelt Open winner (1991)
- US Open (1982)
- US Mid-Amateur (1987, 1989, 1991, 1994, 1995)
- Missouri State Amateur (1996) 2nd
- US Amateur (15 years)
- LA Open (1978) made-cut
- California Amateur (1980) Semi-finals
- California Amateur (1981) Quarterfinals
- Southern California Tour of Champ (1980)
- US Mid-Amateur (1995) 2nd low qualifier
- Missouri Amateur Medalist (6 times) *record
- St. Louis Open (1985) 2nd
- Missouri Mid-Amateur (1996) 1st

The Amateurs

Mark Boyajian

With the build of a stocky Corey Pavin, and the competitive fire to match, Mark was a standout in area and national competitions during the 70's and 80's. One of only a handful of players to win back-to-back District Titles, the St. Clair CC member also performed well in national events, particularly the US Mid-Am.

In 1983, while playing in the Mid-Amateur in Denver at Cherry Hills, Mark opened with a spectacular 29 on the front, breaking the 20 year record of Arnold Palmer in the 1960 Open. While his back side was shot in 38, his opening 67 was good enough to keep him in the hunt. Thanks to the presence of Jim Holtgrieve to assist, the USGA was able to research this and determine that it is the lowest 9-hole score ever in a USGA Championship event!

Mark probably holds another record, though this is quite unique, and will certainly never be broken. He is perhaps the only player to have lost to Curtis Strange and his twin brother Allen in US Amateur events. Curtis got the better of Mark at the 1974 Amateur (4 and 3) and in 1976 he would fall to Allen 3 and 2. Ironically Curtis Strange would also oust Don Bliss in the 4th round at the 1975 Amateur.

At the 1975 Amateur, Mark was particularly "on his game". Having qualified well, he drew a Bye in the first round before facing Bruce Ziemski who had just defeated amateur-great Dick Siderowf in their 2nd round match. Mark would win 6 & 5 and then face Steve Mayo in the 4th round and would win this, 3 and 1. Facing Bill Mitchell in the 5th round, Mark would ease to a 3 and 2 win, setting up a quarter-final match against Henri deLozier of Maryland. deLozier would win 3 and 2 to oust Mark, but not before letting everyone know that Belleville had a successor to Goalby and Haas.

Oddly, Mark almost didn't play in the District in 1981. His love at that time was roller hockey...actually it was more of a passion! His team traveled across the country competing in tournaments. The same week as the District was the National Hockey tournament, so he usually opted for hockey. But in '81 his team hosted the event in Spanish Lake so Mark decided to play in both. Thursday the District was rained out so he played 4 games that day. Friday he won two matches and played in 2 hockey games. He got a fly in his eye on Saturday and had to go to the doctor it was so painful. During the finals his eye was red and swollen, but he was 3-up and playing well when he got the "Yips". He lost the next 6 holes and was suddenly 3-down with 3 to go! *"Luckily I won the last 3 holes in the pouring rain and then won the 1st hole in sudden death; we also won the National Hockey Tournament! What a great week!"* During 1976 both he and Jim Mason made it to the Semi-finals of the US Amateur.

In 1976 he was first alternate for the Open when the USGA called and told him that Larry Ziegler had to withdraw, so Mark hurried to the Atlanta Athletic Club where he was paired with Miller Barber and Bob Gilder. Though he missed the cut with rounds of 83 & 84, he had a great week.

Mark doesn't compete much these days, but with such great memories not much could top what he has done.

- St. Louis District Championship (1981) 1st
- St. Louis District Championship (1986) 1st
- St. Louis District Championship (1987) 1st
- St. Louis District Championship (1985) 2nd
- US Mid-Amateur (1983, 1984)
- US Amateur (1969, 1974, 1975, 1976, 1980)
- US Open (1976)

Bob Cochran

Like Jim Holtgrieve of the 70's and 80's, Bob Cochran was among the best amateurs of his era; not just in St. Louis but throughout the country. Beginning in 1931 when he won the Western Junior, Bob went on to win several City Amateur titles and at least two Metro Amateur crowns. He is probably the finest area golfer when it came to winning events at the state or district level.

He competed frequently against the Pro's in Open events and on several occasions, he came away the victor. In 1945 and 1946, having proved himself against all comers in local events he began to compete against the Pro's, particularly in the Western Open, The Tam O'Shanter and midwest Pro Tour Events. In July 1945 he

Bob being congratulated by a young Jack Nicklaus after Jack defeated him at the North & South in 1959

competed in Memphis at a very memorable PGA event. Byron Nelson had won 11 tournaments in a row coming into Memphis but this is where the streak would end. Bob played well and finished third (ahead of Byron Nelson who finished 4th) that broke his streak. Oddly, another amateur, Fred Haas, would be the tournament winner!

During much of 1945 Bob played every other week on the PGA tour. At Nashville he had a memorable match against Ben Hogan. On the opening hole, a long par 5, Bob recorded a rare Double Eagle, while Hogan could only manage a birdie. Bob went out in 30 and had Hogan on the ropes. Bob closed with a 35 on the back, but Hogan, the tenacious competitor, birdied the last five holes and shot a 64 to claim the title. Bob also competed at Southern Hills and finished 3rd as Sam Snead topped all comers. Later, Hogan would reward Bob for his efforts in their earlier matches and give him an invitation to his Colonial Tournament. Once again, against the Pro's, Bob made the cut and competed well. His real mark came at a tournament in Decatur at Southside CC in 1943 where Bob shot a 198 over 54 holes (65-66-67) - an average of 66 per round - and won the tournament. He played at Decatur again in 1945, and this time he shot a 209 but Dutch Harrison would take the title with a 196 total.

In 1946, none other than Bobby Jones called Cochran the Top Amateur in the country, and honored him with an invitation to the Masters. Many of his friends knew of the invitation and on the weekend prior to his leaving for Augusta Bob received what he thought was a prank phone call. *"Mr. Cochran"* the conversation started, *"this is Bob Jones, I would like for you to come down to Augusta for an afternoon round with me on Wednesday"*, stated the caller. Bob, thinking this was one of his buddies responded, *"...well, Mr. Jones, if this really is Mr. Jones, I will be most happy to come and in fact I would even walk to Augusta for the opportunity to play a round with you!"* To which the caller replied, *"well then Mr. Cochran I suggest you start walking!"* It indeed was Bob Jones! When Cochran arrived, not only was Jones present but also Byron Nelson and Herman Kaiser. It was to be just the four of them as the course had been closed for this exhibition. Bob was slightly terrified at the thought. When he approached the first tee, his name was announced as having the honors. As he stepped forward to tee his ball, his hand was trembling. Nelson noticed this and jokingly offered to tee the ball for Bob! Regaining his composure, his tee shot sailed over the corner bunker, and he ultimately shot a 70! During the event Bob shot two rounds in the 70's and made the cut.

The Amateurs

Bob also competed in the 1960 and 1961 Masters, as well as being selected to the 1961 Walker Cup team. At the 1961 Masters the opening round was contested in freezing rain and sleet. It was so cold that you could barely hold the club, but Bob was able to put together an 80 that round. The next day was even going into the 18th, when Joe Dye walked out to the green and told Bob he needed a birdie to make the cut. Bob lipped the putt out and with his par missed the cut by one.

Following the 1960 Masters, Bob went to Ireland to compete in the British Amateur. This was his first trip to the Amateur and like the great players who preceded him, he made the most of it. Bob made it to the finals of the Amateur at Royal Portrush before losing to Englishman Joe Carr. Carr, who would go on to win 3 titles, was one of the best in British golf history and was awarded the Bob Jones award for outstanding sportsmanship for his career. Bob had played a terrific match in the semi-finals, playing perhaps his best golf (he often related that if that had been the final round, he would have been the Amateur Champion) before winning on the 38th hole. In the finals, Carr was just too much as Bob lost 8 and 7 on the 30th hole.

The ultimate amateur, his record below speaks for itself. His victories in the Missouri Amateur were over the best players of the day, including Jim Colbert in 1962 and Buddy Godwin in 1965. Against players such as Senior Tour great Jim Colbert, Cochran was equal to the task, defeating him soundly three times. From 1931 till he joined the Senior division in 1973, he reached the third round or better 15 times where he compiled a record 78-27 mark. As good as this record is, it almost pales in comparison to his feats in the District Championship. His eight victories are five more than anyone else. His victories came over former titleholders like Tom Draper, Jack Geiss, Jonas Weiss, Dick Bockenkamp, Les Slattery and Elliott Whitbread.

At the 1961 Walker Cup, which the US squad won by the lopsided score of 11-1, Bob teamed with Gene

- Walker Cup team (1961)
- City Amateur Champion (1935)
- Metropolitan Amateur Champion (1947 & 1948)
- Metropolitan Open Champion (1949 & 1950)
- The Masters (1946, 1960, 1961)
- Tournament of Champions (10 victories)
- St. Clair Open Champion (10 times)
- Missouri State Amateur Champion 4 times (1940, 1958, 1962, 1965)
- St. Louis Open Champion (1942,'43, '45, '46)
- St. Louis District Champion 8 times (1933, 1934, 1941, 1946, 1947, 1948, 1961, 1965)

- Missouri Senior Amateur Champion 3 times (1971, 1972, 1978)
- North & South Senior Champion (1967, 1970)
- Western Junior Champion (1931)
- St. Louis District Junior Champion (1931)
- Decatur Open Champion (PGA Tour) (1943)
- World Amateur Match Play (1945) 2nd
- Ranked #3 Amateur in country in 1960 and 4th in 1961.
- Ranked #3 nationally among Seniors in 1968 and 4th in 1970.

Andrews to defeat Michael Bonallack (present Secretary of the R&A) and Ronald Shade 4 and 3. Bob and Gene were playing so well that they had the Brits seven down after 27 holes. An interesting note about Gene Andrews, who today lives in California, is that he was one of the first players to play by yardage, and he first developed the yardage books which are so common today. During the Walker Cup, Gene constantly tried to get Bob to play by yardage, hoping they could help club each other. On one hole during a practice round, after getting help from Gene (reluctantly), Bob's approach flew the green! He never again took advice on club selection from Gene!

Among the highlights of individual rounds he has had, Bob remembers one special round at Pinehurst during the North & South where, on the #2 Donald Ross gem, he shot a 29 on the front side, including an ace on #9!

Today, Bob is in his eighties and you might think he is slowing down. Well, a little maybe. He no longer shoots below par, "...*usually between 70 and 77*" says Bob.

Bob was a past President of the St. Louis District, three time President of the Missouri Golf Association, a 50 year member of the Missouri State Amateur Board and the USGA Board. He was inducted into the Missouri Hall of Fame, the St. Louis University Hall of Fame (where he was also a standout basketball player) and McBride High School. He has been honored by the Elks as athlete of the year among numerous honors. His active career spanned 46 years (1931-1978) and throughout it all, he is among the most respected and feared golfers in any match.

To sit and speak with Bob is to sit was a legend in St. Louis sports history. Outgoing and affable, the years have not dampened his competitive spirit. He speaks about the golf swing like describing a beautiful woman, for in many ways golf has been his mistress. But Bob is also a true and loyal friend. When Jim Jackson was ill, and many would be surprised at this, Bob visited him almost every day. Despite their rivalry, Bob cared greatly for Jackson and was devastated at his passing He spoke of Hord Hardin's recent death as well as that of long-time friend Howard Zachritz. He recalled competing against Jimmy Manion, Eddie Held, Benny Richter, Orville White, Ralph Guldahl, Frank Moore, Clarke Morse, Elliott Whitbread, Dick Bockenkamp, Clarence Wolff and almost every other St. Louis golfing legend, amateur and pro alike. His memory is sharp and he recalls shots made in 1945 like they were made yesterday!

Today there appear to be three things for which Bob has deep passions...his wife, his children and his grandchildren. He speaks about the chances for his grandson Bob, to make it on the Tour someday. The walls of his home are filled with memorabilia of his career, the Masters buttons, the US Open medals, the State and District trophies and plaques (only a small portion of these) and numerous pictures of his family.

At his best, Bob was the steely-eyed competitor who would let nothing deter him from victory. To have had the opportunity to visit with Bob would be a cherished memory for any avid golfer.

The Amateurs

Hord Hardin

Hord falls into a category almost without equal. As an amateur he won the club championship at Bellerive 22 times and was runner-up in the Missouri Amateur in 1946 at St. Louis CC when he lost to Jonas Weiss 1-up on the 37th hole.

As a member of the USGA and chairman of the Championship Committee he worked to celebrate golf throughout the country. In 1968 Hord was selected as President of the USGA, succeeding William Forshay. Hord served the USGA in many capacities starting in 1951 and he was treasurer in 1962 and 1963. He was also president of the District Golf Association in 1950-51 and a former director of the Western Golf Association and a member of the Advisory Committee of the PGA.

He qualified for the US Amateur seven times and for the US Open in 1952. As a retired chairman of Augusta National Golf Club, he had the honor of presiding over perhaps the most prestigious tournament in the land. Described by many as rather tyrannical at times, these were the qualities that were needed by someone who would lead not only clubs such as Bellerive and Augusta National, but attempt to reign in the ego's of individuals within the USGA as well. Perhaps because of his dominating presence, and level of intimidation that followed him, that he was able to accomplish what perhaps no other individual of this time would have thought possible; bringing a championship to St. Louis. Hord was single-handedly responsible for bringing the 1965 US Open to Bellerive, which began the revival of golf in St. Louis 30 years ago, when he answered a phone call from then mayor Raymond Tucker. It is for this and his other exploits that he will be remembered.

Hord died at the age of 85 at his summer cottage in Michigan on August 5, 1996.

***One of the legacies of Hord Hardin; the beautiful
12th hole at Augusta National Golf Club.***

Betty Jane Haemerle-Broz

If ever a player "owned" an era, Betty took ownership of the 40's. Playing against the best in the area from 1941-1949 (no events were held between 1942-1945) Betty won ALL the District titles contested. All five of them! And to close out the decade she won the 1946, 1948 and 1949 Missouri Amateur for good measure.

Beginning at age 12 Betty began by going to tournaments with Dorothy Campbell. Having to borrow clubs and a bag, her start was rather inauspicious; a 130 (70-60) in her first effort. After her father got wind of her score he made things very clear. Either you're going to quit or get a whole lot better! Betty decided the latter would be more fun!!

As an only child, she had the competitive drive to be the best. Beginning with lessons at Triple A from Benny Richter and Bob Green, she followed Benny to Bellerive where the two of them could be seen on the range practicing for hours. Benny was a stern taskmaster; when chipping, it wasn't a three-foot circle, it was a two foot circle. When putting you didn't make four out of five, it was five for five. Betty soon learned the routine and she not only fell in line, but grew to love it!

Walking from her home in Pasadena Hills to Bellerive, or sometimes taking her bike, Betty left Visitation, hurried home and went out to practice, play and talk golf with Benny. Hord Hardin, the ruling czar of Bellerive at the time, tolerated her presence on the course, mainly because she was under the eye of Benny, who Hord admired, and she could play very well!

Her parents kept a close eye on her, so the only events she traveled to play in were usually with them. In fact she only played in three events ever without her parents present. At age 18 in 1944, she traveled to the Women's Western Open in Chicago at Park Ridge GC. In the first round Betty defeated Barbara Cain of Michigan. She would then face the defending champion, Patty Berg, fresh from the military, and defeated her in their quarterfinal match, 1-up in 19 holes. In the semi-finals she would face the legendary Mildred "Babe" Zaharias. As most know, Babe was the 1932 Olympic javelin champion and perhaps the greatest female athlete of all time. She took up golf at the urging of sportswriter Grantland Rice and almost immediately became a scratch player. Betty had Babe 1-down at the 14th hole. After halving 15, Babe birdied 16 and 17 as Betty could only manage two pars. When they halved the 18th with par's, Babe had her 1-up victory and she would go on to win the title over Dorothy Germain.

Betty would marry Allen Broz in 1949, win the state and District titles and then settle into marriage, having her first child in 1950. She played sparingly in the following years, but never regained her former dominance nor attempted to make another run at the top. Today at 71, Betty still plays, though usually with Allen and friends at their home at the Lodge of the Four Seasons

- Missouri Women's Amateur (1946) 1st
- Missouri Women's Amateur (1948) 1st
- Missouri Women's Amateur (1949) 1st
- St. Louis Women's Junior District (1940) 1st
- Women's Western Open (1944) Semifinals

- St. Louis Women's District (1942) 1st
- St. Louis Women's District (1946) 1st
- St. Louis Women's District (1947) 1st
- St. Louis Women's District (1948) 1st
- St. Louis Women's District (1949) 1st

Eddie Held

The first USGA National Champion from St. Louis, Eddie was among the early great players in the area. Like Jim Holtgrieve who would follow him some 59 years later, Eddie would also win an inaugural USGA event, the 1922 USGA Publinks which was contested in Toledo. Immediately following his win he would join Algonquin and could thus not defend his title. But it was perhaps his rivalries with Jimmy Manion, Clarence Wolff, Dick Bockenkamp and a host of other early champions that he will be best remembered for.

Eddie was among the top three golfers in the area for almost 15 years. But he was also a national presence, similar to his friend and rival Jim Manion. Determining who was the better player is a task best left to others. Each had their moments of glory and from time to time, bested each other.

As a national competitor, Eddie was undoubtedly the more accomplished and recognized player. Besides the US Publinks, he became the first United States player to win the Canadian Amateur when he did this in 1929. Then in 1939 he won the match play championship of the Colorado Amateur, a title Hale Irwin would hold 27 years later.

He was runner-up in the 1927 Western Amateur, losing to little-known Bon Stein. Eddie also reached the quarterfinals of the US Amateur in 1926, 1927 and 1933. In 1935 he would reach the round of 16 before falling to Walter Emery from Oklahoma 5 and 3. Emery would go on to the finals where Lawson Little, the defending champion, would dispatch him 4 and 2.

He would capture two district titles, and a state title in addition to his national wins. At every event of the day, from 1920 to 1930, when Manion and Held entered, they were carrying not only their own personal pride, but the pride of the area with them as they fought for the crowns.

Eddie would turn professional in 1940 and at his driving range, he would give lessons for years. Clarence Norsworthy Jr. recalls caddying for his father in matches with Held, Benny Richter and Clarke Morse. The winning scores would frequently be in the low 60's for best ball, such was their talent! All who knew Eddie recalled what a gentlemen he was as well as an outstanding golfer.

Eddie died in October, 1981 at the age of 78.

- Canadian Amateur Championship (1929) 1st
- US Publinks Championship (1922) 1st
- Trans-Miss Championship (1923 & 1926) 1st
- Missouri State Amateur Championship (1925) 1st
- US Amateur (1921, 1923, 1924, 1925, 1926, 1927, 1933, 1935)
- US Open (1923, 1926, 1927, 1929)
- St. Louis District Golf Association Championship (1924) 1st
- St. Louis District Golf Association Championship (1927) 1st

Marilyn Herpel Conroy

Like many of her era, Marilyn began competing at a relatively young age. Daughter of area pro Homer Herpel, Marilyn took to the game quickly and was the area Junior champ from 1946-48. At age 19 she captured the 1950 Missouri Women's Amateur, and then again with back-to-back wins in 1953 & 1954. She would also capture the 1954 & 1955 Women's District crown.

The dominance of a group of women in the District was significant. From 1942 until 1959 (No tournament was held from 1943-45) only five ladies won District crowns, Betty Jane Haemerle (5), Marilyn Herpel (2), Jeannine Dobbin (3), Susie Driscol (2) and Ellen Conant (3), but of this group only Betty Jane and Marilyn would capture state crowns, each with three.

Marilyn competed against Betty Jane in the late 40's, but Betty Jane was such a dominant player that during this stretch she lost a state title only once; that to Kansas City's Jean Hutto in 1947. When Betty Jane married in 1950, all the women saw the door swing open, but only Marilyn stepped through immediately.

Marilyn competed in the Western Open, the Trans-Miss and other area events as she, Betty Jane, Dorothy Campbell, Peggy Hartenbach, and Jeanie Dobbin challenged the competition.

During the 1954 finals she played brilliantly and defeated Mrs. Roy Diefenbach 5&4 as Marilyn had six birdies in the morning 18. She had won the medal at the 1954 state with a 78, and she was co-medalist with Jeanie Dobbin in 1955 with 77's. In the semi-finals Marilyn defeated Susie Driscoll then faced 16 year old Kate Richards in the finals. Miss Richards was no match for the two-time champ as she was routed 9&8. Marilyn set many women's records for the day including the record at Westwood, Algonquin and Meadowbrook. At the 1954 Westborough round robin, which included Arnold Palmer in one of his last Amateur events, Marilyn finished 3rd behind US Amateur champ Mary Lena Faulk and future pro Joyce Ziske. Barbara McIntire future Amateur champ finished 5th. Marilyn also competed in the 1956 LPGA Norwood Open. She stopped competing in the late 50's. She was the first woman inducted into the St. Louis Sports Hall of Fame in the 1960's. She died in June 1994 at age 64.

- Missouri Women's Amateur (1950) 1st
- Missouri Women's Amateur (1953) 1st
- Missouri Women's Amateur (1954) 1st

- St. Louis Women's District (1954) 1st
- St. Louis Women's District (1955) 1st
- St. Louis Women's Junior District (1946) 1st
- St. Louis Women's Junior District (1947) 1st
- St. Louis Women's Junior District (1948) 1st

The Amateurs

Jim Holtgrieve

Perhaps no other from St. Louis has achieved the status of which Jim may claim. He has not been in the top 10 on the PGA tour, nor has he won a "Modern Major" title. But on a national level, the Webster Groves natives' name and reputation are well known. He has competed against professionals from the US, England, Scotland, and the rest of Europe. The Westborough member holds the course record at 59 (along with Club Pro Phil Hewitt on the par 69 course) and is a major contender anytime he enters a tournament.

Growing up, his father put a club in his hands at age 4, though Jim can't remember much of the result! The pro at Sunset was Jim Fogertey and he gave Jim his first lessons. By age 6 they had joined Westborough where he fell under the tutelage of Tony Henschel and later Phil Hewitt, both of whom made impacts on his game. Today Jim travels to St. Albans where he is under the watchful eye of Terry Grosch, one of the premier teachers in the area. Jim is trying to recapture his swing of the early 80's when everything seemed to be in sync, and when his 1-iron was like a lightening bolt.

In the Missouri State Amateur Jim has been Medalist three times, and second or third another seven. His average score is 72.3 and he has compiled a 30-11 mark in match play, and along the way he has managed to win the event twice. He has also captured four District titles and the same number of Ozark Invitationals. He has competed in 9 PGA Tour events and has made the cut in 6 of these. His presence in a competition elevates it's importance to the other competitors.

Like many of us that grew up in the 50's and 60's, Jim's hero was Arnold Palmer. Who can forget "The King" in those days; tossing his cigarette on the fairway, hitching his pants and then with the swing that looked as if it were not-quite-finished, launch the ball toward the green as his head moved from side to side and he grimaced waiting for the result! But unlike most of us, Jim had the opportunity of playing with Arnie in the first round at the 1981 Masters. Jim couldn't miss that day as his famous 1-iron was red-hot. Going into 18 Jim was 2-under par and he let loose with a bomb, over 270 yards. Arnie yanked the club from his hands and said "what is this thing? Do you know how far you just hit it?" To which Jim replied, *"Arnie, I'm playing at Augusta, I'm playing with my idol, and I'm two-under par. I'm just a little pumped!"*.

Two of his idols he was never able to meet; Bobby Jones and Ben Hogan; men whose record and legacy he great!y admires. When the subject turned to Nicklaus all he could remember is the tremendous concentration he exhibited in a pairing at Muirfield Village, and despite a round in which Jack appeared to not be on his game, he still managed to circle the course in a 1-under 71!

One of his most memorable moments came in the Walker Cup matches at Cypress Point in 1981. He was playing Ronan Rafferty, who was and still is, a quality player. Corey Pavin, Jay Sigel and others had gone off early in the match and Jim was right in the middle. They were both playing well; Jim was 1-up when Rafferty drained a 25-footer for birdie on the 139 yard par 3 15th. Not to be outdone, Jim, putting from 20 feet, dropped his birdie on top of Rafferty's, effectively silencing any comeback. But, like all great courses, the 16th at Cypress, the picturesque 233 yard par 3 would provide it's own share of drama. Ronan had the honors and, going for the green, pushed his shot into the white-capped cove. Jim initially pulled out his 4-iron. He had two options; play safe to the left knowing Ronan had to hit a career shot just to tie, or go for the green and chance the water. With all the confidence of the champion he is, he replaced the 4-iron with his 2-iron and his tee shot ended 4-feet from the hole. He closed Rafferty out on the next hole with a par. Such are the legends of champions!

In his office on Brentwood you see the pieces of his business - steel components and castings - and also the tools of his avocation. Pictures of Augusta National, Walker Cup memorabilia, various cups, plates, pictures, plaques, balls and clubs, a picture of Pine Valley and finally a Pine Valley flag, celebrating a 1993 hole-in-one. Scattered amid the steel and golf are pictures of his family.

Jim could see himself competing on the Senior Tour, and will probably attempt to qualify this coming December at the Senior Q-school when he turns 50. He thoroughly enjoys the amateur competitions, though he has scaled back these last few years since his son's are at an age he wants to be home and enjoy them growing up.

When Jim talks about golf, it is almost with a reverence reserved for someone or something that has earned that right. Golf has allowed him to represent his country, of which he is justly proud. He has traveled and met friends all over the country. He has played in every major tournament open to him except the British Open. He has earned the respect of other people's hero's - among them Fred Couples, Corey Pavin, Hale Irwin, Arnold Palmer and Jack Nicklaus - and does so quietly and modestly.

When the subject turned to competitiveness, Jim just pointed to three places; your heart, your gut and your head. He admires Tom Wargo who he believes has that internal toughness that has allowed him to go from a "good club pro", to one of the best on the Senior Tour. He feels the same way about how Jay Williamson has competed successfully on the Tour, without the classic amateur background you would expect.

The younger players coming up look to beat Jim, to add his notch to their gun. But although Jim nears 50, if the competitive juices flow once again and he gets back into the "zone" for competitive golf, I would not want to be the player who stood between Jim and his next championship.

- 3 Walker Cup teams (1979, 1981, 1983)
- The Masters (1980, ''81, ''82, ''83, ''84)
- The Masters (1980) 2nd low amateur
- The Masters (1981, '1982) made-cut
- US Amateur (12 times)
- US Amateur (1980) Semi-finals
- US Amateur (1982) Quarter-finals
- US Open (1978) made-cut
- British Amateur (1983) 2nd
- Won 2 State Amateurs (1978, 1981)
- Won 4 District Titles (1977, ''78, ''79, ''89)

- Won inaugural USGA Mid-Amateur (1981)
- Won 4 Ozark Invitatational. (1983, '1984, '1985, '1988)
- Memorial Tournaments (1982, 1983, 1984) made-cut in 1982 & 1984
- Quarterfinals of US Mid-Amateur (1988)
- World Cup Amateur Championship (Twice)
- US Junior Nationals (1964)
- Jimmy Jackson Memorial Champion (1990, 1992, 1994)

The Amateurs

Jim Jackson

When all the scores are tallied, and the roll of champions is called, Jim Jackson will surely be toward the front of the line. In the history of St. Louis Golf, perhaps no individual commanded more respect and was more widely loved than Jim. From the 1950's to the early 70's, Jim was almost unbeatable as he, Cochran and Blair literally owned every event.

From his initial win in 1948 at the St. Louis Open till his death in 1983, he captured 18 "major amateur titles" and countless opens, classics and invitational prizes. In the State he captured his first and last titles 25 years apart,

in the Publinx it was only 20 years, such was the quality of his game. His two Walker Cup appearances trail only Holtgrieve in area representation, and his five Masters is the equal. He competed in 18 US Amateurs and a US Open in 1952 where he was low Amateur. In 1970, after being medalist, he lost in the finals of the Missouri Amateur to a young Kansas Citian, Tom Watson, 2 & 1. Besides losing to Watson, Jim Colbert defeated him in the finals in 1963, again 2 & 1 at Hickory Hills. In all he was in the finals of the Missouri Amateur 8 times, winning four. His victory in the 1976 Missouri Amateur at age 53 made him the oldest champion to date, a full 25 years after his first crown in 1951. Jimmy was also the only amateur to win the Missouri Open (1977) when he defeated a young Jim Mason in his first pro event.

When it came to competing against the best, Jim was at his. In the State for example, he defeated Jim Tom Blair in 1951 and again in 1959 for the title. He and Bob Cochran never met in the finals, but Jim won in the semi-finals in 1954 and 1963 while losing to Bob in 1965. The very nature of Match play makes the outcome hard to predict. Shooting a low number does not insure a win, only winning more holes!

Jimmy's son, Beau, was also an fine player. In 1974 Beau had perhaps the week of his life. He qualified for match play where he defeated Bob Enger from Kansas City, Jack McClain from Kirksville, Payne Stewart from Springfield and Bill Daniels from Kirksville before falling to Dale Jutz from Kansas City 1 up at the 42nd hole in the finals, to date still a record for the longest final match in State Amateur history. Beau was never the player his father was - very few were or ever would be - but for that week, it was Beau that captivated the crowds with his fine play. This was the same year that Don Bliss set the record for the lowest qualifying round in state history with a 135 over the Twin Hills Joplin course, a feat he would duplicate in 1986 at Kansas City's Oakwood CC.

Jimmy was very proud that he had won Missouri state titles in six decades! Beginning with his 1939 State High School championship from Kirkwood to his 1980 and 1981 Missouri Senior Amateur crowns, his longevity will be hard to surpass.

Jim played in countless tournaments, both amateur and open events through the years. He played with the likes of Demaret, Hogan, Snead, Nelson, Oliver, Keiser, McSpadden, Mangrum, Middlecoff, Finsterwald and a host of others. One of his biggest thrills was meeting Bobby Jones on his many trips to the Masters.

One story he liked to tell was of a round he played with Lloyd Mangrum at the Western Open at Westwood in 1952. Mangrum would be the eventual winner and after their round Jimmy went to Lloyd and asked him if he could give him any comments on his play, anything that he could use to improve his game. To which Mangrum retorted, *"...son, I didn't watch you hit a shot all day."*

Described by many as a magician around the green, Bob Cochran believes Jimmy was perhaps the best long putter [35-40 feet] he has ever seen. This is echoed by Jim Tom Blair who believes that in 1951 Jimmy was perhaps the best amateur in the country! Even Bob's son, Bob Jr., who would occasionally caddie for Jimmy in tournaments told his dad, *"...you know, pop, you've got a good short game, but this guy Jackson is terrific!"*

Despite his remarkable skills, Jim was a very erratic driver, often playing army golf, left then right, with his tee shots. One incident at Greenbriar though illustrates his remarkable skill. Playing with Jim Benson and Ken Heilman, perhaps the best ball-striker of the day [though easily psyched on the greens], Jimmy hit his drive far right on the opening hole, with Ken in his usual position, down the middle. Jim was forced to maneuver over and around several large trees. His recovery shot sailed a bit long and ended on the back fringe, 20 feet away. Heilman was safely on 15 feet away. Jim walked up and drained the putt for a birdie. Heilman, who had seen this occur numerous times before, leaned over and picked up his ball. Under his breath mumbled something about *"...never again playing with that S-O-B..."* he walked back to the clubhouse!

Perhaps more important than all the titles was the character of the man, and this is why Jimmy is so fondly remembered. His record below is not just impressive; it reflects the accomplishments of a man who enjoyed golf and could play it like few others.

Jim died on September 23, 1983 from complications from a brain tumor. He was 62.

- British Amateur (1955)
- Missouri Open (1977) 1st
- Missouri Senior Amateur (1980) 1st
- Missouri Senior Amateur (1981) 1st
- Missouri State Amateur Champion (1951, 1954, 1959, 1976)
- Missouri State Amateur Runner-up (1950, 1960, 1963, 1970)
- Missouri State High School Champion (1939)
- Ozark Open Champion (1954)
- St. Louis District Champion 3 times (1963, 1966, 1971)
- St. Louis Open Champion (1948, 1949)
- St. Louis Publinx Champion (1962, 1963, 1967, 1976, 1982)
- The Masters (1953, 1954, 1955, 1956, 1957)
- The Walker Cup teams in 1953 & 1955
- Tournament of Champions (12 times) (1957,
- Trans-Miss Amateur winner (1954, 1955)
- US Amateur (18 times) (1948, '49, '50, '51, '52, '53, '54, '55, '60, '61, '62, '63, '64, '66, '67, '76)
- US Open (1952) Low amateur
- US Open (1976)
- US Senior Amateur (1980)

The Amateurs

David Lucks

Born in St. Louis and raised in Webster Groves, Dave has a family tradition of great golf. His uncle played against Jimmy Manion during the 20's while his aunt, Betty Von Rump, has won several Senior Women's events. His collection of clubs is noteworthy but it is his book case, which houses over 100 golf titles, that shows where his passions lie.

Playing in high school several years behind Holtgrieve, David did well in area competitions, but was not outstanding. A freak leg injury while playing intramurals ended his golf aspirations while at SMU, so he never competed in college, though he did play several local courses including the Tennison Park track, where Lee Trevino legends abound.

Returning to St. Louis, Dave met Steve Lotz from Tower Tee who introduced him to Jim Jackson. It was this meeting which propelled Dave to his present status today. Dave went to work for Jackson at Chase Bag company and the two traveled to customer sites together, with Dave prodding Jim constantly for stories about his golf. As a result, probably no one outside of Jackson's family, knows as much about him as Dave. Leaving time for "client golf" the two played together weekly for over three years, often playing four to five times a week. The bag business was good!

When Jimmy fell ill in 1983, things changed dramatically and in October he succumbed to the brain tumors. David stayed at Chase for another three years, and in 1987 had his most successful season to date; winning the Missouri Amateur and qualifying for the US Amateur. Dave moved to Nashville for three years, where he won one tournament and was runner-up in a couple more, before returning to St. Louis in 1991. He did return in 1989, first to play in the Jimmy Jackson tournament, which he won that year, and to qualify for the Amateur. He also returned to defend his State title in 1988, but lost in the semi-finals to eventual winner Don Bliss, 1 up in 21 holes.

There is no doubt that Jackson's influence on Dave had a significant impact on his career. Working and playing with a legend cannot help but give you a new perspective on the game.

David continues to be one of the area's more formidable players. Not a long hitter, Dave relies on positioning and consistency to wear his fellow-competitors down. After having the "yips" for much of the 80's, David seems to have found the putting stroke that will serve him well under pressure. It may look a little strange, his left hand turned almost parallel to the target line with his palm facing out, but it succeeded in getting his game back on track. To follow Dave in a round is to watch a tactician at work. Like many of today's better area players, his mistakes are few and risks are taken only when the rewards are great, and generally achievable.

Capturing another state title and winning the District are some of his goals, as well as competing more successfully on the national scene. But like most of us "weekend-warriors" work and family make finding the time to practice a challenge.

- Missouri State Amateur (1987) 1st
- St. Louis Publinx (1992) 1st
- St. Louis Publinx (1993) 1st
- US Mid-Amateur (1983, 1989, 1995)
- British Amateur (1996)
- US Amateur (1987, 1991, 1995)
- Jimmy Jackson Memorial (1989) 1st
- St. Louis District Golf Association (1993) 2nd
- Metropolitan Amateur Championship (1993) 2nd
- Missouri 4-ball championship (1995) 2nd

Jim Manion

Jimmy Manion was among a group of early St. Louis amateurs who excelled, not only locally but were well-known on the national level. As the winner of the Missouri Amateur in 1917, Jim soon went national with his game, and at the 1919 US Amateur at Oakmont CC he was Co-Medalist along with the ultimate winner Davey Herron and Paul Tewkesbury at 158.   The course was playing extremely difficult and Bobby Jones was the only other player under 160, and the high qualifier was 172 or 86 per round average. Jim played well in the first round of match play, but lost to Bobby Jones 3 and 2.

In 1921 Grantland Rice, legendary sportswriter, probably best known for his naming of the Notre Dame Four Horseman under Knute Rockne, ranked Manion as the fourth best amateur in the nation. At one point in his career his scores over some of the best area courses are astonishing; a 63 at Sunset, a 65 at St. Louis (which he believed was his best round ever), a 66 at Algonquin, a 67 over the old Bellerive CC and a 66 on the West course at Norwood. All of this, prior to 1932, when the quality of the courses and equipment was far from what we know today.

In the 1929 St. Louis Open, Jimmy won by 10 shots over the tough Bellerive CC course, shooting a 7-under 135. In 1930 he played the final round in a foursome with Walter Hagen, Gene Sarazen and shot the low round of the day, a 66 over the Sunset CC track. The $10,000 purse attracted most of the nations best as Leo Diegel, Ralph Guldahl, Paul Runyan and Horton Smith also joined the competition.

Ultimately Tommy Armour, legendary Scottish professional, would win the purse.

A lifelong amateur, his brother Johnny, went the professional route, and was head pro at Sunset, Meadowbrook and Normandie until his retirement in 1958. Often the two would be confused as to who shot the better score, such was the quality of the golf during this period.

Jimmy's wife, Gladys, remarked in one event that Jimmy won he received a pin for his prize, while Walter Hagen, the runner-up got the cash prize, that it hardly seemed fair. To which Jimmy countered, *"I'll have this pin forever, Walter will have that check only until he finds the first track!"* Gladys Manion would go on to found one of the

The Amateurs

areas most successful Real Estate Agencies in 1935 that today resides on Forsyth Blvd. in Clayton. Their son, Jimmy, was one of the founders of Boone Valley and has been a member of Bellerive for many years, as has their grandson, Stafford.

In 1963 at a banquet held in his honor, the question was poised, *"What has golf done for you?"*, to which he replied *"What has golf done for me? I just couldn't begin to tell you. It has given me my health, my life, my friends and by business. Right now, it's the source of my greatest pleasure. What else is there?"* Jimmy died at age 87 in 1984. We are fortunate that his children have preserved the events of his career for all of us to enjoy and marvel at his successes.

- Missouri Amateur Champion (1917, 1921, 1923, 1926)
- St. Louis District Champion (1923, 1925, 1927, 1928)
- St. Louis Open Champion (1928, 1929)
- St. Louis Open runner-up (1930)
- US Amateur (1919) Medalist
- St. Louis Municipal Champion (1915, 1917, 1919)
- Trans-Miss Amateur Champion (1924)
- Trans-Miss Amateur runner-up (1930)
- Trans-Miss Amateur Medalist (1922 & 1925)
- Missouri State Senior Amateur Champion (1959)

Bob Mason

Bob has had an outstanding amateur career in the area. As a member of Greenbriar he, and his brother Jim, were two of the best around. Bob still holds the course record at Greenbriar (on the course prior to the present remodeling) of a 61. When he later joined Bellerive his level of play improved significantly. Never one to practice much, Bob would be seen running to the first tee from the locker room with shoes untied and scrambling to find tees and balls in his bag. He would then proceed to shoot a 70-something. At times he was brilliant shooting consecutive rounds in the 60's.

A rather odd-event occurred in 1972 in the Mason family.   Bob was playing the 4th hole at Bellerive and made a double-eagle on the long par 5. When he finished his round, he was preparing to call his brother Jim to tell him the news. As Jim answered he was just as excited; he was about to call Bob to tell him that he had made a double-eagle on the 3rd hole at Greenbriar! Later they would both belong to Bellerive and one would hold the Club Champion crown 9 of the 12 years between 1979-1990.

He lost two significant matches in the finals of the District, launching careers of two area stars; Jay Haas and Jim Holtgrieve. In 1972 Haas was a 19 year old fresh from his first year at Wake Forest and his 1-up win on the 36th hole over Bob helped launch is career. Five years later almost the same circumstances occurred against Holtgrieve. In 1977 Bob once again lost in the finals 1-down at the 36th hole in the District. This also helped launch Holtgrieve's career as this was one of his first major wins. When Bob qualified for Match Play at the 1986 US Amateur he faced a strong player, Nolan Henke, fresh out of Florida State University. Bob shot a 38 on the front...but was 5 down!

There are three other significant events worth noting in Bob's career...and none involve his playing. In 1972 Bill Stewart, the great Amateur champion from Springfield, called Bob and asked him to come down and play a round with him at Hickory Hills. Bob was joined by Bill's 15 year old son Payne. Bob shot a 71 over the tough track but was outdone by young Payne who shot a 66. When Bob went back to school and told his golf coach about young Payne, the coach followed his career, and eventually gave him a scholarship to SMU, one of the few schools to make Payne an offer!

The second involves the 1981 US Mid-Amateur coming to St. Louis. Jim Holtgrieve had been approached by the USGA about such a championship for the career amateur. The USGA felt that a central location was important to jump-start the championship and allow players from all over the country to come.   Jim then approached Bob, who gathered support from Tim Crowley and John Stupp. They approached the Board at Bellerive about hosting the event and so was born the Mid-Amateur.

Finally, Bob was one of the driving forces within Bellerive to bring the 1992 PGA here. He worked tirelessly with Hale Irwin, Sandy McDonnell, August Busch III, Chuck Knight and other local businessmen as they prepared a video presentation to the PGA back in 1986, concluding with Hale playing all 18 holes as Jay Randolph narrated. As club champion, Bob was among the contingent that made the final pitch to the PGA at Inverness in 1986. The contracts were signed the following year and the 1992 PGA was Bellerive's.

The Amateurs

Bob also served as Secretary of the District Golf Association for 4 years, succeeding Jim Benson. Bob's efforts behind the scenes are what makes him such a respected person. He has never looked for glory in his actions...only the satisfaction of having done his best.

A true gentlemen, husband and father, Bob has been one of the outstanding amateurs in the area, both on and off the course, for the past 25 years. Others may have won more awards and titles, but few have done so with such honor.

- All Southwest Conference at Southwest Methodist University (SMU)
- Club Champion at Bellerive 7 times (1979, '80, '82, '83, '85, '86, '89)
- Qualified for US Amateur 8 times (1975, '77, '78, '79, '86, '87, '88, '89)
- Reached match play in US Amateur in 1986
- Played in the US Junior (1968)
- US Mid-Amateur (1981, 1982, 1991)
- District Junior Champion (1968)
- St. Louis Open Low Amateur (1981)

Jim Mason

When Jim graduated from the University of Texas, it appeared as though he would embark on a successful pro career. He would win the District title in 1976 and at the US Amateur that year at Bel Air CC would lose in the semi-finals to the eventual winner, Bill Sander. Along the way he would defeat Dennis Goettel, Fred Ridley, Wesley Adcock and John Fought. Others in his bracket included Vinny Giles, Clayton Haefner, Jimmy Jackson, David Ogrin, Lennie Clements and Dan Forsman. He had competed in 1975 and won his first match so he knew what to expect and the pressures that were present. Having seen his teammates from Texas, Tom Kite and Ben Crenshaw move on to the tour, he knew what was needed to compete at the highest level.

But things don't always go as planned and after a year on tour and a stint on the Asian Tour - he finished third in one tournament to Isao Aoki where he played in the last group on Sunday - he finally returned to St. Louis to begin a new career, and regain his amateur status. Today Jim represents Bridgestone/Precept in the area and spends his time visiting pro shops, and playing an occasional round or two. One of the best ball strikers in the area, it has been his putting that has left him frustrated recently.

Jim was involved in the creation of the Fox Run course and was Director of Marketing when the club first opened. He was instrumental in helping it gain the Tommy Armour Tour event and the recently played Women's Western Amateur.

Still one of the best amateurs around, Jim has competed in the Taylor Cup matches against area Pro's and in the Missouri Cup matches against the Western side of the state. Together with his brother Bob, they are a formidable twosome. During the 1980's they each won the club championship at Bellerive, meeting in the finals several times.

Like many outstanding players, his self-criticism is more harsh than anyone else could bestow. He continues to compete, and in many cases qualify for, state and national events. But it is his own level of expectations that he must measure up-to, not that of others.

- All-American at the University of Texas
- St. Louis District Champion (1976)
- US Amateur (1975, 1976 (Semi-finals), 1994)
- US Mid-Amateur (1989, 1990, 1994)
- US Junior Boys (1972)
- Taylor Cup (1996)
- Missouri Cup (1994, 1995)

The Amateurs

Virginia Pepp

Born in St. Louis in 1904, one of seven children, Virginia was an avid lover of golf, the beauty of the courses and the good companionship of fellow golfers. Her brothers, Johnny and Frank Pepp (their real name was Peplausky) were both Pro's in the area and Frank Pepp teamed with Jimmy Manion and Clarence Wolff in team matches against Chicago in 1916, while Johnny taught golf at the YWHA and YWMA (Young Men/Women Hebrew Association) for many years. He was also an assistant at St. Louis CC and Meadowbrook. During World War I, with her brothers away in France, Virginia, then only 14 picked up their clubs from the basement and began her career.

In 1920, at the age of 15, she won the Municipal Golf Championship and in 1922, at only 18 years of age, she won the Women's District Championship. She went on to win a total of five District Titles during this era, the last being in 1930.

In 1931 Virginia became the first woman golf professional in Missouri and was later inducted into the St. Louis Hall of Fame. According to an article by Melvin Shelvin in the Globe-Democrat in 1937, he credits Virginia with being the VERY FIRST female professional in the country, at least three years before Helen Hicks is credited with the title. This may be due to the tremendous amateur record that Ms. Hicks had, winning the US Amateur and playing on the first Curtis Cup team. Nevertheless, Virginia was, in all probability, the very first lady pro in the country.

She worked alongside Benny Richter at Triple A giving lessons to men, something not done at all in those days (and still not as much as could be, given the number of women teaching pro's) and later worked with Eddie Held at his driving ranges teaching promising students.

One of the more interesting events occurred as Virginia was attempting to compete in the Women's Western Amateur of 1923 at Glen Echo. As is the case today, you must belong to a member club to play in this event and Virginia, clearly the area's best player, belonged only to Forest Park Club, while the Triple A club was a Western Member. The morning of the event, Frank went to Triple A and joined, thus allowing his little sister a chance to compete. The situation was not downplayed, rather it was the lead headline in an article about the event,

- St. Louis Women's District (1922) 1st
- St. Louis Women's District (1923) 1st
- St. Louis Women's District (1925) 1st
- St. Louis Women's District (1926) 1st
- St. Louis Women's District (1930) 1st
- Trans-Miss (1922, 1925)

- St. Louis Municipal Golf Championship (1920) 1st
- Competed in 2 Western Golf Championships
- US Women's Amateur Championship (1925)
- Finished 2nd in the 1927 St. Louis District
- Semi-finalist in the 1928 District Championship

such was her status as a player. While Virginia did not win the event, she did finish as the low St. Louisan, but she lost in the quarterfinals to the defending champion, Mrs. Lee Mida from Chicago. The Triple A team did win the Maschmeyer Trophy as the low Team, finishing ahead of the Olympia Fields team.

One of Virginia's best friends was also one of her chief competitors, Audrey Faust Wallace. While Virginia struggled to squeeze golf into her busy schedule, Audrey, a member of St. Louis CC, helped to get her friend the practice and playing time needed to compete at the championship level. Audrey would frequently send a car to Virginia's home to pick her up for the trip to the club. Such was their friendship that Virginia's niece Audrey Hatlan, former President of the Women's District, is named after Mrs. Wallace!

In 1934 Virginia was faced with a serious decision about her pro career. With very few events for women, and the fact that teaching actually hampered her ability to play, she petitioned the USGA to reinstate her amateur status. She remained a professional until 1939 and was then reinstated.

If there had been a LPGA at this time, there is no doubt Virginia would have been one of the early players. But with the Ladies Tour not on the horizon (it would not begin until 1948) Virginia had little choice if she wanted to play competitive golf.

Virginia was inducted into the St. Louis Sports Hall of Fame in the 1960's.

Virginia and Ralph Guldahl in an exhibition match. She would compete against many men pro's, including Johnny Bulla, Frank Moore, Benny Richter, Jim Fogertey, Orville White and Eddie Held. She also competed in exhibitions with Helen Hicks, the first female Professional with National Open victories to her credentials, and the legendary Babe Zaharias, winner of the 1946 US Amateur, the 1947 British Ladies Amateur and a founder of the LPGA.

The Amateurs

Ellen Port

Ellen has been one of the brightest stars in golf in the St. Louis area, man or woman, over the past 6 years. A Kansas City native, she arrived in St. Louis in 1983 and within a few years made her presence felt in the Women's events. Her accomplishments on the local, national and international level are second to none as an amateur. While many of her contemporaries have moved on to the Pro ranks, Ellen remains competing for medals not money. As a teacher-coach at John Burroughs she brings an enthusiasm to her work uncommon among most nationally ranked players.

Ellen Port at the 1996 Curtis Cup

Like most amateurs, she must squeeze most of her play in between her real work. During 1996 Ellen will have ventured to Ireland for the Curtis Cup, North Carolina for the US Women's Open and sites in-between for matches, lessons and charity events. She culminated the season by defending her US Mid-Amateur title with a 2&1 win in Rancho Mirage, CA. Her husband Andy, caddies for her and provides the support when the shot, or round, doesn't go as planned. All this and she has only been playing golf for 10 years!

But before we say to ourselves, *"Yeah, but she was probably some kid who grew up at the country club"*, let's put that to rest. Ellen is, above all, a very good athlete. She competed in basketball, swimming and tennis in high school in Kansas City, claiming state honors in hoops. Golf was the furthest thing on her mind. She would occasionally tag along with her father, but she really didn't get "the bug" until her marriage to Andy Port. She proudly admits that without his support, and that of her whole family, all she has accomplished, would never have occurred.

Her first victory would hardly seem that significant; the ladies match at Bahnfyre, where she was so nervous she hit several tee shots OB! But following this 1983 win she began to take lessons, first from Phil Hewitt at Westborough and later from Terry Houser, then at Sunset Tee. Terry was very influential in Ellen's career growth. It was Terry who first mentioned to Ellen, as they were sitting following a practice session at Paradise Valley, that one of the greatest accomplishments of any golfers career, even bigger than winning a major, was to play for your country! Ellen, at the time, had never heard of the Curtis Cup! Ellen never forgot that seemingly off-handed comment. And as she was selected for the Curtis Cup in 1994 it all came back to her.

In 1987 she would win the District Ladies Match Play title and though she would compete in the Publinx and the Western, it would be as much a learning experience as it was shooting for honors. "*I didn't know enough that I wasn't supposed to reach that high*" Ellen noted, "*I hadn't been playing long enough to know what I could and couldn't do.*"

Ellen really made a run at almost every area title and national qualifications in 1991. It all seemed to come together for her. She was medalist for the US Women's Mid-Amateur and advanced to the quarterfinals. She qualified for the US Women's Amateur and made the quarterfinals of the North and South at Pinehurst. She finished 5th in the Missouri State Women's Amateur and made it to the third round of the Western Amateur. So the stage was set for 1992 when she hit paydirt; winning the State Amateur and advancing to the final eight in the Amateur, Mid-Am, Broadmoor Invitational and Western Amateur where she was medalist. Ellen also was a finalist in the District Match Play championship and won the 3-day stroke play tournament. She has been off and running ever since.

In 1996 since June, Ellen has played in the US Open, US Amateur, Curtis Cup, British Ladies Amateur and the LPGA Titleholders Classic and recently lost a playoff for the State Amateur on the third extra hole. She remains ranked #7 in the country prior to her

Ellen with the trophy from her first "major" win, the 1994 Trans-Miss.

- Ladies British Amateur (1996)
- Won Women's US Mid-Amateur (1995)
- Won Women's US Mid-Amateur (1996)
- Won Women's Metropolitan Championship (1993 & 1994)
- Won Trans-Miss National Championship (1994)
- Won Missouri Women's Amateur (1992 &1995)
- Women's Western Amateur (1992) Medalist
- Women's Western Amateur (1992(QF), 1993(QF), 1995, 1996)
- US Women's Open (1993, 1994, 1996)
- Top 8 in the US Mid-Amateur (1992)
- Top 8 at the US Amateur (1992)
- US Women's Amateur (1989, 1991, 1992 (QF), 1993, 1994, 1995, 1996)
- US Women's Mid Amateur (1991(QF), 1992, 1994 (QF), 1995)
- St. Louis District Women's Stroke Play Championship (1992, '93, '94, '95)
- Reached 3rd round of North & South (1995)
- Reached 1st round of Western, Trans National and US Amateur (1995).
- Ranked #9 nationally among women amateurs (1995)
- Ranked #7 nationally among women amateurs (1992)
- Ranked #6 nationally among women amateurs (1996)
- Quarterfinals of US Mid-Amateur (1994)
- Broadmoor Invitational (1996) Medalist
- Broadmoor Invitational (1993) Quarterfinalist
- Canadian Amateur (1993) 10th
- Missouri Amateur (1996) 2nd
- World Team (1994) Alternate
- Post Dispatch Player of the Year (1992)
- Member of 1994 & 1996 Curtis Cup Teams
- First Woman to play in the St. Louis Publinx Championship
- 2nd round of Western Amateur (1994)
- 2nd round of US Amateur (1994)
- 2nd round North & South Amateur (1992)
- 2nd round North & South (1994)
- LPGA Rail Classic (1993)
- Sprint Titleholders LPGA event (1996)

victory in the Mid-Am, so her stock should soar.

As she reminisces she realizes how lucky she has been. Not the kind of luck that allowed her to win, but rather that which coincides with timing. Taking up the game at the right time, finding the right teachers, the right jobs that allowed her to compete, and finally the right city to settle. *"St. Louis has been great to me. The area golfers, men and women have been very supportive, and the recognition I have received has been wonderful"*.

Ellen also has a good deal of faith. She understands that she has been blessed with the talent, some would call it a gift, and that she takes advantage of the opportunity to make the most of it. It is now time for she and Andy to have a family, and with their first child expected in March, 1997 she knows that this may curtail some of her play. So while she has spent the last 6 years searching for, and finding the golden ring on the national level, perhaps it is now time to focus on area events a bit more. But her 2nd consecutive Mid-Am title will be defended next fall so she has a goal to shoot for in the 1997 season.

She acknowledged that the careers of many Lady linksters are rather short, as they focused on family and then golf. Perhaps she will be more in the mold of others, more well rounded individuals, who recognized when it was time to pursue other interests. Perhaps it is because her idol, Bobby Jones, first set this standard, that Ellen decided that it was time to pursue other interests in her life. Not to put the club aside, but to look at golf from a different perspective, and with different goals.

Ellen being honored as the 1995 Golfer of the Year

Marcella Rose

Born in St. Louis, Marcella has been an educator for almost 25 years. But since the late-50's it has been the love of competitive golf that has provided her with the challenges. An exceptional athlete, Marcella played softball, tennis, basketball and just about every other sport around until her "Aunt Lou" took Marcella over to the Forest Park 9-hole course, after a little instruction in the back yard, and she proceeded to shoot a 35. Still she wasn't hooked - that would take about 10 rounds. She competed in her first District in 1957 at age 16 and the following year won the "C" flight in the state meet at Westwood CC.

Marcella was an exceptional player; long off the tee, averaging about 240 yards, she ate-up the shorter courses and even moving to the men's tees did not stop her talent from shining through. But as the win's began to pile up, a certain resentment began to occur within the Ladies District. Marcella won the 1962 District, and after playing in the Invitational in 1963, she was quietly discouraged from competing in the Ladies District. Forced to go elsewhere, Marcella began to compete nationally and she was a regular in events such as the Trans-Miss, the Ladies Amateur, the Western and several US Opens. It was here that she would mingle with the cream-of-the-crop of the ladies professionals; Patty Berg, Mickey Wright, Kathy Whitworth and top Amateurs such as Carol Sorenson and Barbara McIntire.

It has been 40 years since she first picked up a club, but the competitive fire still burns. She is now making more time to practice and looks forward to competing more in the 1997 season; not as a senior golfer, but against the best in the championship flight.

- Missouri Women's Amateur (1963) 1st
- Missouri Women's Amateur (1969) 1st
- Missouri Women's Amateur (1961) 2nd to Judy Torluemke
- Missouri Amateur Medalist (1962,1963,1971)
- Broadmoor Invitational (1968, 1977)
- Cosmopolitan Open (1963, 1965)
- Heart of America Open (KC) (1961) 2nd low amateur
- LPGA Clayton Federal Open (1966) 2nd low amateur
- Missouri Intercollegiate Champion (1971)
- North & South Amateur (1968)
- Norwood Hills Club Champion (1990, 1991, 1993, 1996)
- Tournament of Champions (1990, '95, '96) 1st

- St. Louis Women's District Champion (1960 & 1962)
- St. Louis Women's District Medalist (1962 & 1965)
- Titleholders Championship (1965, 1966)
- Trans Mississippi (1959) Quarterfinalist
- Trans Mississippi (1965) Quarterfinalist
- Trans Mississippi National (1959, '60, '62, '65, '66, '67 (2nd), '68, '69, '70, '71, '72, '73, '74, '75, '76, '77, '91, '93, '94, '95, '96)
- US Women's Amateur (1963, '64, '65, '66, '67, '69)
- US Women's Open (1960, '61, '63, '65, '66)
- Western Amateur (1960, '61, '63, '64, '65, '66, '67, '68, '69, '73, '91, '93, '94, '95, '96)
- Western Amateur - Marion Miley Award- 1965 & 1966 as Low amateur in Western Amateur & Open
- Western Amateur Medalist (1965, 1967)
- Western Open (1960, 1963, 1965, 1966)

The Amateurs

Scott Thomas

A native of Minnesota, Scott has been in the St. Louis area for the past dozen years, and has made a significant impact on area golf. Growing up playing and caddying at Midland CC in Minneapolis, Scott spent time in Hawaii before ending up in St. Louis. Playing out of Normandie initially, Scott played in several US Amateurs in the 80's, and the US Mid-Am in the early 90's. He played in the British Amateur in 1990 and 1992, having pre-qualified by his showing in the Mid-Am, and qualified for the US Publinks in 1992. Scott joined Norwood Hills in 1993 and promptly won the District Title that year.

Tall and slender, his appearance might easily fool an over-confident adversary. His mild manner beshadows a champions concentration and his long, albeit jerky-looking swing, not only serves him well, but continues to pressure opponents into taking risks that usually prove fatal.

Not a long hitter, his consistency and all-around play make him a contender on almost any layout. His play in five British Amateur's have enabled him to develop a variety of shots in all conditions. During the 1992 Ozark Invitational, a cold, rainy day greeted the competitors. And while most were donning rain-suits and cursing the gods, Scott was already developing his game play from lessons learned in Great Britain. The outcome was almost inevitable.

Perhaps his most satisfying victory came in the 1992 Missouri Amateur. Five down at the turn and 6 down later, he rallied for a tie at the end of 36 holes. Played over the CC at the Legends, the playoff began on #1, a relatively short par 5, reachable by many in two. Scott was on the fringe in two, though with a testy down hill try. Rollie Hurst, the Southwest Missouri star - with his coach and former Missouri Amateur winner Bruce Hollowell as his caddie - continued to battle and he nearly holed his pitch over the front bunkers. The hole was halved with birdies and they moved on to two, a tough dogleg right requiring a lay-up in front of a creek and a mid to long-iron to the green. Scott hit a perfect three-wood, while Rollie hit an iron, leaving him a longer shot into the elevated, well-bunkered green. He found the front right bunker while Scott was on the green, though facing another fast downhiller. With a poor lie in the sand, Rollie blasted out, but he would not need to strike the ball again as Scott eased his putt into the cup for the title. The realization sunk in hours later, and the real celebration took place later that evening.

Scott is like many of today's better amateurs; he plays a couple times a week and tries to practice a few more. But early in the season, when the qualifying for the Open and other events take place, his game is still not strong. The late season outings are his focus as the period from July to October he tends to shine. He is among the list of perhaps ten current players who, at any time, are capable of winning every event they enter.

- St. Louis District Golf Association (1993) 1st
- Missouri State Amateur (1992) 1st
- Ozark Invitational (1992) 1st
- US Amateur (1984, 1989, 1996)
- Normandie Amateur (1989) 1st
- Normandie / Ping Amateur (1995) 1st

- US Amateur Publinks (1992)
- British Amateur (1990, '92, '94, '96)
- US Mid-Amateur (1990, 1991, 1994)
- Missouri Mid-Amateur (1995) 1st
- Southern Illinois Amateur (1991) 1st
- Jimmy Jackson Invitational (1995) 1st

Audrey Faust Wallace

In an era of outstanding lady golfers, Audrey was one of the best. As noted earlier, Virginia Pepp was one of her best friends, and most ardent competitors. As Audrey Faust she won the 1924 District crown. Virginia Pepp had won the two previous titles and would win the next two, before Audrey would return, this time as Mrs. Mahlon B. Wallace to claim the 1927 and 1928 titles. The following year a very odd event occurred; someone other than Pepp or Wallace triumphed in District. That was short lived, as Pepp captured the 1930 event and then Mrs. Wallace was victorious in 1931 and 1932. Her five District titles puts her in the rarest of air — only Barb Berkmeyer has more — and ties her with Virginia Pepp, Betty Haemerle, and Barbara Beuckman. Of interest is that the Pepp-Wallace battles were very reminiscent of the Berkmeyer-Beuckman rivalry; both good friends and competitors.

As a member of St. Louis CC her life was in sharp contrast to Pepp, the public player from Triple A-Forest Park, but their games were well matched. They competed together in the Women's Western Amateur and the Trans-Miss tournaments, where they frequently were usually the low St. Louisans.

The opportunities for women to compete were limited, as no Missouri Women's State event was held from 1922-1934. Had this event taken place, one of the pair would have undoubtedly captured one or more.

The 1924 match was related in the Globe-Democrat as *"one of if not the most grueling final matches that has ever attended a women's tournament in St. Louis"*. Ms. Faust had Ms. Pepp dormie two after halving the sixteenth at Glen Echo. *"Miss Pepp's performance at the last two holes will go down in golf annals as the most brilliant and plucky that has ever been bared by a feminine player on a local links"* wrote the Globe that day, *"...any hope that*

the biggest gallery that has ever trailed a women's match in St. Louis obtained for a Pep triumph must have faded when the principals left the sixteenth green....Miss Faust was playing remarkable golf... there was slight chance of her losing them both when by halving even one she would clinch the match". Miss Faust hit a poor drive on seventeen and Miss Pepp hit a long straight drive on the par 5. A poor pitch from the rough made matters worse and when Virginia hit her second dead at the pin the crowd of about 300 cheered. After a poor run-up, Audrey conceded Virginia her eagle putt. They then moved to the eighteenth with Audrey one up. Miss Pepp drove long and straight as Miss Faust pushed her tee shot. Her second was short of the green while Miss Pepp's approach also came up short. Miss Pep made an excellent chip, while Miss Faust did not match as she had a 12 footer to win. When she missed and Miss Pepp dropped her 5 footer, the match was square. On the first extra hole both played nervously and the hole was halved with 5's. The next hole, a par 5, had a temporary green. Both hit poor second shots, but Virginia was on in three while Audrey chipped over. Virginia had a tough downhill-sidehill putt, and while tapping it lightly, it rolled five feet past. She then missed the come-backer, but left a half stymie for Miss Faust. Audrey calmly rolled-in the putt and claimed the crown.

Mrs. Wallace continued to play in selective District Championships, with the last documented in 1950, where she defeated the medalist Mrs. Clyde Webb in what was termed a major upset.

Mrs. Wallace was also a member of the USGA "Golf House" committee which was formed in 1950 to raise funds so the USGA could "purchase a modest

The Amateurs

building in New York City to house the USGA Golf Museum and Library and the executive office of the body".
Today that site is in Far Hills, NJ, home of the USGA. Other members from St. Louis on the committee with Mrs.
Wallace were Paul B. Jamison Jr. and Hord Hardin.

The granddaughter of Adolphus Busch, Audrey was a gracious lady whose charm and talent put those around
her at ease. Whether it was working the scoring tent at the LPGA event at Norwood or a casual round at St. Louis,
Audrey retained the qualities that made her a champion on and off the course.

- St. Louis Women's District Championship (1924) 1st
- St. Louis Women's District Championship (1927) 1st
- St. Louis Women's District Championship (1928) 1st
- St. Louis Women's District Championship (1931) 1st
- St. Louis Women's District Championship (1932) 1st
- Trans-Miss (1925, 1930, 1931)
- Women's Western Amateur (1922, 1925, 1926)
- US Women's Amateur (1922, 1923, 1924, 1925, 1937)
- British Ladies Amateur (1923)

Other Prominent Amateurs

Don Anderson

Tom Barry

Bob Beckmann

Jill Bertram

Barbara Beuckmann

Jo D Blosch

Dick Bockenkamp

Sara Caughey

Lynette Chrenka

Ellen Conant

Mary Gail Dalton

Tom Draper

Susie Driscol

Don Dupske

Scott Edwards

Paula Eger

David Estes

Jack Geiss

Jill Gromic

Sara Louise Guth

Craig Hardcastle

E.D. Imboden

Christian Kenney

Jeannine Dobbin Lewis

Dottie Linsin

Cindy Mueller Reiss

Lindsey Murfin

Roger Null

Chester O'Brien

Doris Phillips

Jack Powers

Spencer Sappington

Craig Schnurbusch

Georgia Dexheimer Schwartz

Grace Semple

W. Arthur Stickney

Stuart Stickney

Betty Von Rump

Elliott Whitbread

Jonas Weiss

Clarence Wolff

The Amateurs

*St. Clair CC members Mark Boyajian (l) and Jerry Haas
battled for the 1985 District crown on their home course.
Haas would emerge the winner.*

Craig Schnurbusch

Doris Phillips

Amateur
Champions

Championships Won by Amateurs

Aboussie, Jonathan	• US Publinks (1993)
Adams, Bart	• City Championship (1900) 1st
Adams, Ted Meadowbrook	• Canadian Amateur Championship (1938) 1st • US Open (1938) • Missouri State Amateur (1939) 1st
Anderson, Barbara Sunset Hills	• St. Louis Women's District (1995) 1st • St. Louis Women's District Junior (1979) 1st • St. Louis Women's District Junior (1977) 1st
Bahn, Bill	• St. Louis Publinx (1994) 1st • US Mid-Amateur (1981, 1989) • Normandie Amateur (1994) 1st
Bair, Bill	• St. Louis Publinx (1985) 1st
Baker, Newell Algonquin	• St. Louis District Golf Association (1967) 1st • Champion of Champions (1965) 1st • Trans-Miss (1962)
Ballman, Mrs. Edward Lockhaven	• US Senior Women (1970, 1973, 1974)
Barnard, Cindy Greenbriar	• St. Louis Women's District Junior (1972) 1st • St. Louis Women's District Junior (1971) 1st
Barry, Dan Normandie	• US Amateur (1994) Local medalist • US Amateur (1995)
Barry, Tom Normandie	• St. Louis Metropolitan Championship (1996) 1st • US Publinks (1987, 1996) • US Amateur (1994) • US Mid Amateur (1994, 1996)
Baur, Adele Glen Echo	• St. Louis Women's District Junior (1936) 1st
Beckmann, Bob Norwood Hills	• US Amateur (1992) • St. Louis District Golf Association (1995) 1st • St. Louis District Golf Association (1994) 1st • Missouri State Amateur (1993) 1st • US Mid-Amateur (1991)
Begley, Tim	• Champion of Champions (1996) 1st
Benbrook, Brad	• US Amateur (1987, 1989)
Bender, Billy	• US Mid-Amateur (1989)
Benson, Jim Greenbriar Hills	• Champion of Champions (2) • Western Open (1953)
Berkley, W.J. Algonquin	• US Amateur (1947)

Berkmeyer, Barbara Bubany Norwood Hills	• Missouri Women's Amateur (1965) 1st • Missouri Women's Amateur (1970) 1st • Missouri Women's Amateur (1974) 1st • Missouri Women's Amateur (1975) 1st • Missouri Women's Amateur (1984) 1st • St. Louis Women's District (1967) 1st • St. Louis Women's District (1968) 1st • St. Louis Women's District (1971) 1st • St. Louis Women's District (1976) 1st • St. Louis Women's District (1978) 1st • St. Louis Women's District (1994) 1st • St. Louis Women's District (1996) 1st • St. Louis Women's District Junior (1962) 1st • US Women's Amateur (1964, '69, '72, '77, '91) • St. Louis District Senior (1995) 1st • US Women's Mid-Amateur (1989, 1995) • St. Louis Metro Women's (1996) 1st • LPGA Events (1964, 1967, 1969, 1970) • US Senior Women's Championship (1994)
Berkmeyer, Richard (Skip) Norwood Hills	• US Amateur (1995) • British Amateur (1996)
Bernard, J.K. Westborough	• British Amateur (1955)
Bernsen, Virgil Greenbriar Hills	• St. Louis District Golf Association (1968) 1st
Bertram, Jill Norwood Hills	• St. Louis Women's District (1987) 1st • St. Louis Women's District (1986) 1st • St. Louis Women's District Junior (1982) 1st • St. Louis Women's District Junior (1981) 1st • Women's Western Amateur (1988)

Beuckman, Barbara
  St. Clair
  Norwood Hills
	• St. Louis Women's District (1961) 1st
	• St. Louis Women's District (1979) 1st
	• St. Louis Women's District (1981) 1st
	• St. Louis Women's District (1982) 1st
	• St. Louis Women's District (1984) 1st
	• St. Louis Women's District Junior (1955) 1st
	• St. Louis Women's District Junior (1956) 1st
	• St. Louis Women's District Junior (1957) 1st
	• Missouri Women's Senior Golf Association (1993) 1st
	• US Junior Girls (1957)

Championships Won by Amateurs

Blair, Jim Tom
    Jefferson City CC
    Old Warson
    Meadowbrook
    Greenbriar
	• US Amateur (1951) semi-finals
	• US Amateur (1950, '51, '55, '56, '57, '59, '60, '62, '63, '64, '65)
	• US Open (8 years) (1951)
	• British Amateur (1972, 1974, 1975)
	• Phoenix Open - PGA Event (1956) 3rd
	• Missouri State Amateur (1952)1st
	• Missouri State Amateur (1955)1st
	• Missouri State Amateur Medalist (1951, '52, '57, '59)
	• Missouri State Amateur (1951(Medalist), '56, '57, '59) 2nd
	• St. Louis District Golf Association (1958)1st
	• St. Louis District Golf Association (1969)1st
	• St. Louis District Golf Association (1970)1st
	• Western Amateur (1951) Low Amateur
	• Western Amateur (1951) runner-up
	• Western Open (1951)
	• US Junior Boys (1948)
	• New Orleans Invitational (1951) 1st
	• Hardscrabble Open (1952) 1st
	• Canadian Amateur (1956)Quarterfinals

Bliss, Don
    Norwood Hills
    St. Albans
	• Missouri State Amateur (1972)1st
	• Missouri State Amateur (1983)1st
	• Missouri State Amateur (1986)1st
	• Missouri State Amateur (1988)1st
	• Missouri State Amateur Medalist (1972, '74, 82, 83, '86, '96)
	• St. Louis Metro Championship (1991) 1st
	• St. Louis Metro Championship (1993) 1st
	• St. Louis Publinx (1993) 1st
	• US Amateur (15) 1972, '75, '79, '80, '82, '85, '89, '90, '93;
	• Advanced to Match play 5 times
	• US Mid-Amateur 5 times (1987, 1991, 1995)
	• Missouri Mid-Amateur (1996) 1st
	• Big Eight Champion (1973)
	• LA Open (1978) made-cut
	• LA Open (1981) made-cut
	• US Open (1982, 1991)
	• California Amateur (1980) semifinals
	• California Amateur (1981) quarterfinals
	• Southern California Tournament of Champions (1980) 1st
	• Missouri Cup Team (1994, 1995, 1996 Captain)
	• Normandie Amateur (1989) 1st

Blosch, Jo D	• US Women's Amateur Publinks (1995, 1994)
Bockenkamp, Richard Sunset	• US Amateur (1919, 1921) • St. Louis District Golf Association (1921) 1st • St. Louis District Golf Association (1920) 1st
Boyajian, Mark St. Clair	• St. Louis District (1981) 1st • St. Louis District (1986) 1st • St. Louis District (1987) 1st • US Amateur (1969, 1974, 1975, 1976, 1980) • US Mid-Amateur (1983, 1984) • US Open (1976)
Bradford, Sarah	• US Women's Amateur Publinks (1991, 1993, 1994)

Brewer, Ron	• US Amateur (1978)
Brown, Barry	• St. Louis Publinx (1986) 1st
Brumm, E.J. Old Warson	• US Junior Boys (1988)
Buck, Robin Sunset Hills	• St. Louis Women's District Junior (1989) 1st • St. Louis Women's District Junior (1988) 1st • US Junior Girls Championship (1991) • US Women"s Open (1994)
Burchfiel, Hugh Old Warson	• US Amateur (1960)
Burns, Earl	• St. Louis Publinx (1978) 1st
Butler, Marci Cherry Hills	• St. Louis Women's District (1989) 1st
Cameron, R.E. Mrs.	• US Senior Women's Amateur (1963)
Campbell, Dorothy Jane Norwood Hills	• St. Louis Women's District Junior (1941) 1st • St. Louis Women's District Junior (1939) 1st • St. Louis Women's District Junior (1938) 1st • Western Women's Junior Championship (1941) 2nd
Caravia, Phillip St. Clair CC	• US Junior Boys (1995)
Carnivale, Tony	• US Junior Boys (1989)
Caughey, Sara Triple A	• St. Louis Women's District (1940) 1st • St. Louis Women's District (1938) 1st • St. Louis Women's District (1937) 1st
Chaney, Michael	• US Amateur Publinks (1992)

Chrenka, Lynette
    Glen Echo
    Greenbriar Hills
	• St. Louis Women's District (1983) 1st
	• St. Louis Women's District (1977) 1st

Crowd watches as Audrey Wallace hits her tee shot on the 12th hole at St. Louis CC in the 1930 finals. Virginia Pepp would defeat Mrs. Wallace for the title.

Championships Won by Amateurs

Cochran, Bob
  Norwood Hills
  Meadowbrook
	• Missouri State Amateur (1940)1st
	• Missouri State Amateur (1958)1st
	• Missouri State Amateur (1962)1st
	• Missouri State Amateur (1965)1st
	• Missouri State Amateur Medalist (1937, '38, '54, '64)
	• St. Louis District Golf Association (1933)1st
	• St. Louis District Golf Association (1934)1st
	• St. Louis District Golf Association (1941)1st
	• St. Louis District Golf Association (1946)1st
	• St. Louis District Golf Association (1947)1st
	• St. Louis District Golf Association (1948)1st
	• St. Louis District Golf Association (1961)1st
	• St. Louis District Golf Association (1965)1st
	• St. Louis Victory Open (1942, 1943, 1945, 1946) 1st
	• Hale America National Open (1942)
	• Missouri Senior Amateur (1969, 1971, 1972, 1977, 1978) 1st
	• St. Louis District Senior Championship (1982) 1st
	• St. Louis District Senior Championship (1980) 1st
	• St. Louis District Senior Championship (1978) 1st
	• St. Louis District Senior Championship (1974) 1st
	• St. Louis District Senior Championship (1972) 1st
	• St. Louis District Senior Championship (1967) 1st
	• St. Louis District Senior Championship (1965) 1st
	• St. Louis District Senior Championship (1963) 1st
	• North & South Senior (1968 & 1970) 1st
	• The Masters (1946, 1960 and 1961) Made cut in 1946.
	• St. Louis City Amateur (1935) 1st
	• St. Louis Metro Amateur (1944, 1947, 1948) 1st
	• St. Louis Metro Open Championship (1944, 1948, 1949) 1st
	• St. Louis Open (1936, 1942, 1943, 1945, 1946) 1st
	• Walker Cup Team (1961)
	• British Amateur (1960) 2nd
	• US Amateur (1939, '40, '41, '47, '49, '53, '55, '56, '57, '58, '61, '63, '66, '69)
	• US Open (1935, 1940, 1942, 1946, 1947, 1960)
	• US Senior Open (1980)
	• US Senior Amateur (1969, '70, '71(Medalist), '75, '76, '85)
	• Carling Cup Matches - US-Canadian Match Play Championships
	• Colonial Open -PGA event (1956)
	• Great Lakes Amateur (1945) 1st
	• Memphis Open - PGA event (1946) 2nd
	• Nashville Open - PGA event (1946) 3rd
	• Peoria Open - PGA event (1946) 2nd
	• Decatur Open - PGA event (1943) 1st
	• Western Golf Association Amateur (1945, 1960) 2nd
	• Western Open (1938, 1946, 1953)
	• Tam O'Shanter World Amateur (1945) 1st
	• Tam O'Shanter World Amateur (1946) 2nd
	• USGA Pro-Amateur National Champion (1945) 1st
	• Chicago Victory America Tournament (1945) 1st
	• Tournament of Champs (1942, '43, '49, '50, '51, '53, '58, '61, '64, '67) 1st
	• Western Junior Championship (1931) 1st
	• St. Louis Junior District Championship (1931) 1st

Coe, Brian	• US Junior Amateur (1994)
Colgate, John	• US Senior Amateur (1990)
Collins, Miss E. St. Louis	• US Women's Amateur (1903)
Combs, Tom	• US Senior Amateur (1988)
Conant, Ellen St. Louis	• St. Louis Women's District (1959) 1st • St. Louis Women's District (1958) 1st • St. Louis Women's District (1957) 1st • US Women's Amateur (1956, 1958)
Connelly, Harold Normandie	• US Amateur (1948)
Cowie, Matt	• US Junior Boys (1989)
Crider, Michael	• US Mid-Amateur (1991) • US Junior Boys (1965)
Curran, James B.	• US Publinks (1922, '23)
D'Antoni, Vince Greenbriar	• St. Louis District Golf Association (1952) 1st • NCAA Individual Champion - Tulane (1939)
Dalton, Mary Gail Westwood	• Missouri Women's Amateur (1966) 1st • Missouri Senior Women's (1987) 1st • Missouri Senior Women's (1988) 1st • Missouri Senior Women's (1989) 1st • Missouri Senior Women's (1991) 1st • Missouri Senior Women's (1993) 1st • Missouri Senior Women's (1995) 1st • Missouri Women's Golf Association Senior (1994) 1st • St. Louis Women's District (1975) 1st • St. Louis Women's District (1969) 1st • St. Louis Women's District (1966) 1st • St. Louis Women's District Senior (1993) 1st • St. Louis Women's District Senior (1992) 1st • St. Louis Women's District Senior (1991) 1st • St. Louis Women's District Senior (1990) 1st • St. Louis Women's District Senior (1989) 1st • Tournament of Champions (1990) 1st
Dalton, Richard Westwood	• US Senior Amateur (1989, 1991, 1994)
Davis, I.R., Dr.	• US Publinks (1927, '29, '30)
Dexheimer, Georgia Schwartz, Mrs. Ray	• St. Louis Women's District (1939) 1st • US Women's Amateur (1956) • US Senior Women (1970)
Dillon, Grover	• US Amateur (1946)
Dixon, Brad	• US Publinks (1986)

Championships Won by Amateurs

Dobbin Lewis, Jeannine Normandie Lockhaven	• St. Louis Women's District (1985) 1st • St. Louis Women's District (1953) 1st • St. Louis Women's District (1951) 1st • St. Louis Women's District (1950) 1st • Senior Women's Missouri Golf Association (1982) 1st • LPGA St. Louis Open (1954) Low Amateur
Doiron, Craig	• US Mid-Amateur (1994)
Dolan, Charles J. (Joe)	• US Amateur (1955)
Donohoo, Dan	• St. Louis Publinx (1996) 1st
Donohue, Eddie Father Forest Park	• US Publinks (1935, 1932, 1928)
Doyel, Raymond Norwood Hills	• US Publinks (1948)
Draper, Tom Sunset	• US Amateur (1938, '36, '35, '34) • St. Louis District Golf Association (1935) 1st • Western Seniors Champion (1971, 1973, 1976) • British Amateur (1968) • Western Open (1953)
Driscoll, Susie Glen Echo	• St. Louis Women's District (1956) 1st • St. Louis Women's District (1952) 1st • St. Louis Women's District Junior (1951) 1st • St. Louis Women's District Junior (1950) 1st • St. Louis Women's District Junior (1949) 1st
Dunn, Jim	• St. Louis Publinx (1995) 1st • US Publinks (1979)
Dupske, Don	• St. Louis Publinx (1988) 1st • St. Louis Publinx (1971) 1st • St. Louis Publinx (1968) 1st • US Senior Amateur (1994, 1996) • St. Louis District Senior (1995) 1st • Metropolitan Senior (1996) 1st
Edwards, Scott	• US Mid-Amateur (1992, 1995, 1996)
Eger, Paula Greenbriar	• St. Louis Women's District Junior (1970) 1st • St. Louis Women's District Junior (1969) 1st • St. Louis Women's District Junior (1968) 1st • St. Louis Women's District Junior (1967) 1st • St. Louis Women's District Junior (1966) 1st • Missouri Women's Amateur (1971) 1st and Medalist • US Women's Mid-Amateur (1989, 1990, 1991) • US Women's Amateur (1972, 1973) • US Women's Publinks (1991) • US Junior Girls (1968, 1969, 1970) • Women's Western (1972, 1973) • Broadmoor Invitational (1971, 1973) • Trans-Miss (1972) • Southeast Iowa Womens Amateur (1969, 1970, 1973) 1st • Missouri Junior Girls (1967, 1968, 1969, 1970) 1st • National PeeWee Championship (under-12) (1965) 1st • National Senior PeeWee Championship (under-15) (1968) 1st • Fred Waring Invitational (1966) 1st • US Girls ranking 12th in 1968, 9th in 1969 and 10th 1970.

Eihausen, Jay	• US Amateur Publinks (1993)
Eisenbeis, Jack	• US Mid-Amateur (1994)
Elbrecht, Karl	• US Publinks (1993, 1983)
English, Frank	• US Senior Men's Amateur (1955)
Ervastu, Edward	• US Amateur (1951)
Estes, David Norwood Hills	• US Amateur (1988, 1995, 1996) • US Mid-Amateur (1990) • Missouri Cup Team (1995, 1996) • Jimmy Jackson Tournament (1996) 1st
Evans, Joe	• US Publinks (1954, '53)
Faulkner, Mark	• US Mid-Amateur (1989)
Faust, Audrey Wallace, Mrs. Mahlon B. St. Louis	• St. Louis Women's District (1932) 1st • St. Louis Women's District (1931) 1st • St. Louis Women's District (1928) 1st • St. Louis Women's District (1927) 1st • St. Louis Women's District (1924) 1st • Women's Western Amateur (1922, 1939) • US Women's Amateur (1922, 1923, 1924, 1925, 1937) • British Women's Amateur (1930)
Fawcett, Charles Norwood Hills	• US Junior Boys (1951, 1952) • US Senior Amateur (1991) • US Amateur (1956)
Fawcett, Nancy Norwood Hills	• St. Louis Women's District Junior (1961) 1st • St. Louis Women's District Junior (1960) 1st • St. Louis Women's District Junior (1956) 1st • US Women's Amateur (1958) • US Junior Girls (1956, 1960)
Fehlig, Gene Westborough	• US Amateur (1960) • St. Louis District Golf Association (1960) 1st • St. Louis District Golf Association (1964) 1st
Finders, Linda	• US Women's Publinks (1979)
Findley (Mrs.), Thomas	• St. Louis Women's District (1941) 1st • Michigan State Amateur (1940) 1st • Women's Western Amateur (2 years)
Forsman, Mrs. W.W.	• US Senior Women (191976, 1977, 1979, 1981)
Fox, Barbara	• US Senior Women (1990)
Frank (Miss), Allyn Greenbriar	• St. Louis Women's District Junior (1973) 1st
Frank, Milton	• US Publinks (1955, '54, '52, '50, '49, '48) • US Senior Men's Amateur (1967)
Freeland, Jerry Old Warson	• US Amateur (1973) • US Mid-Amateur (1982)
Friedlein, Michael	• US Publinks (1929)
Fromuth, Michael Forest Hills	• St. Louis District Junior Championship (1976) 1st • US Amateur (1973, 1980) • St. Louis Publinx (1990) 1st
Fromuth, Susan Forest Hills	• St. Louis Women's District Junior (1980) 1st • St. Louis Women's District Junior (1976) 1st • US Women's Amateur (1979, 1982, 1983) • US Junior Girls (1979, 1980) • US Women's Open (1983)

Championships Won by Amateurs

Frost, Andy	• US Amateur (1990, 1992, 1994) • Missouri Cup Team (1994, 1995, 1996)
Furlong, Frank Norwood Hills	• St. Louis Publinx (1970) 1st • US Amateur (1959) • US Senior Amateur (1990, 1991)
Gallaway, Matt C.	• US Senior Men's Amateur (1959, 1963)
Gates, Ray	• US Publinks (1931, 1936)
Geiss, Jack Norwood Hills	• US Amateur (1949, 1953) • St. Louis District Golf Association (1956) 1st • St. Louis District Golf Association (1950) 1st • Western Open (1946)
Gill, Greg	• Missouri Amateur (1989) 1st
Gioia, Diane Greenbriar	• US Women's Open (1990) • US Junior Girls (1980) • Women's Western Amateur (1988, 1989)
Goalby, Kye St. Clair	• US Mid-Amateur (1995) • US Junior Amateur (1987)
Godwin, Buddy	• St. Louis Publinx (1969) 1st • US Amateur (1976)
Green, Dennis	• US Amateur (1973, 1974)
Greenberg, Joan Meadowbrook	• St. Louis Women's District Junior (1954) 1st
Greene, Vince Meadowbrook	• US Amateur (1961)
Gromic, Jill St. Clair	• US Women's Publinx (1996) • US Women's Publinx Qualifying Medalist (1996) • Illinois State HS Tournament (1996) 2nd overall • among boys & girls in individual competition • LPGA Michelob Light Heartland Classic (1996)
Guariglia Donald Normandie	• US Amateur (1951) • US Junior Boys (1950) • St. Louis District Golf Association (1953) 1st
Guariglia Ron Normandie	• US Junior Boys (1950)
Guth, Sara Louise Algonquin	• Missouri Women's Amateur (1938) 1st • St. Louis Women's District (1936) 1st • St. Louis Women's District (1935) 1st • St. Louis Women's District (1934) 1st

Haemerle, Betty Jane
   (Broz, Mrs. Allen)
   Glen Echo
   Norwood Hills
   Triple A
	• Missouri Women's Amateur (1946) 1st
	• Missouri Women's Amateur (1948) 1st
	• Missouri Women's Amateur (1949) 1st
	• St. Louis Women's District (1949) 1st
	• St. Louis Women's District (1948) 1st
	• St. Louis Women's District (1947) 1st
	• St. Louis Women's District (1946) 1st
	• St. Louis Women's District (1942) 1st
	• St. Louis Women's District Junior (1940) 1st
	• Women's Western Open (1944) 2nd
	• Trans-Miss (1947, 1948)

Hagen, Glen	• US Publinks (1953, '50, '49)
Hamamoto, Togo	• US Publinks (1929)

Hand, John	• US Publinks (1954, 1975)
Hardcastle, Craig	• St. Louis Publinx (1989) 1st • Phil Cotton Invitational (1991) 1st • US Amateur (1988, 1989) • US Mid-Amateur (1990) • US Publinks (1988, 1991) • Southern Illinois Amateur (1988) 1st
Hardcastle, Dick	• US Publinks (1965)
Hardin, Hord Bellerive	• US Amateur (1953, '54, '56, '58, '59, '63) • US Open (1952) • Western Open (1953)
Hartman, Mike	• St. Louis Publinx (1995) 1st • US Publinks (1988)
Hatlan, Audrey Cherry Hills/St. Albans	• St. Louis Women's District Senior (1986) 1st • US Senior Women (1979) • Missouri Senior Women's (1984) 1st
Heilman, Ken Greenbriar	• St. Louis District Golf Association (1949) 1st

Held, Eddie
   Forest Park
   Algonquin
	• Canadian Amateur (1929) 1st
	• Colorado Amateur (1939) 1st
	• Trans-Miss Championship (1923) 1st
	• Trans-Miss Championship (1926) 1st
	US Amateur (1921, '23, '24, '25, '26, '27, '29, '32, '33, '34, '36, '39)
	• US Publinks (1922) 1st
	• US Open (1923, 1926, 1927, 1929)
	• St. Louis District Golf Association (1924) 1st
	• St. Louis District Golf Association (1937) 1st
	• Western Open (1924 (3rd), '25, '26, '27, '40, '46, '52, '53)

Helmbacher, Bill	• US Junior Boys (1973)
Hemker, Roger	• St. Louis Publinx (1960) 1st
Hepler, Jay	• US Junior Boys (1988)
Hepler, Sara Sunset Hills	• St. Louis Women's District Junior (1986) 1st
Herold, Paul	• US Junior Boys (1958)

Herpel Conroy, Marilyn
   Indian Meadows
   Crystal Lake
   Algonquin
	• Missouri Women's Amateur (1950) 1st
	• Missouri Women's Amateur (1953) 1st
	• Missouri Women's Amateur (1954) 1st
	• St. Louis Women's District (1954) 1st
	• St. Louis Women's District (1955) 1st
	• St. Louis Women's District Junior (1948) 1st
	• St. Louis Women's District Junior (1947) 1st
	• St. Louis Women's District Junior (1946) 1st
	• Trans-Miss Championships (1950, 1951, 1952)
	• Women's Western Open (1941, 1944, 1945)

Herpel, Jacqueline
   Indian Meadows
   Crystal Lake
	• St. Louis Women's District Junior (1953) 1st
	• St. Louis Women's District Junior (1952) 1st
	• Colorado Women's Amateur (1958) 1st

Higginbotham, Jerry	• US Senior Amateur (1990, 1991, 1993)
Highlander, Ken Sunset Hills	• St. Louis District Golf Association (1988) 1st

Championships Won by Amateurs

Holtgrieve, Jim Westborough	• US Amateur (1975, '77, '78, '80, '81, '82, '83, '84, '85, '86, '88, '89, '90, '93, '94, '95) • US Amateur (1980) semifinals • US Mid-Amateur (1981) 1st • US Mid-Amateur (1982, '83, '84, '86, '88, '89, '94, '95) • US Open (1978) made-cut • The Masters (5) (1980, 1981, 1982, 1983, 1984) • The Masters (made cut -1980, 1981, 1982) • British Amateur (1983) 2nd • British Amateur (1979) 4th Round • Walker Cup Team (1979, 1981, 1983) • Missouri State Amateur Medalist (1976, 1978, 1984) • Missouri State Amateur (1978)1st • Missouri State Amateur (1981)1st • St. Louis District Golf Association (1977)1st • St. Louis District Golf Association (1978)1st • St. Louis District Golf Association (1979)1st • St. Louis District Golf Association (1989)1st • Ozark Invitational (1983, '84, '85, '88) 1st • International Four Ball Championship (1989) 1st • St. Louis Publinx (1975) 1st • Missouri Cup Team (1996) • World Amateur Match Play Team Championship (1980) 1st
Holthaus, Julie Bellerive	• St. Louis Women's District Senior (1995) 1st
Hulverson, Tom Sunset CC	• US Amateur (1960, 1961) • British Open (1954)
Hynes (Mrs.), I.S. Normandie	• St. Louis Women's District (1929) 1st • Trans-Miss Championship (1931) 2nd
Imboden, I.M.	• US Publinks (1955)
Irwin, Steve Old Warson	• US Junior Amateur (1992) • Normandie Ping Amateur (1993) 1st
Isherwood, Robert	• US Publinks (1931)

Don Bliss (left) and Wayne Fredrick enjoy a quiet moment prior to their 1996 Missouri Cup match

Jackson, Jim
   Greenbriar Hills
   Algonquin
	• The Masters (1953, 1954, 1955, 1956, 1957)
	• US Amateur (18 times) (1948, '49, '50, '51, '52, '53, '54, '55, '60, '61, '62, '63, 64, '66, '67, '76)
	• US Open (1952) Low Amateur
	• US Open Qualifying (1976) 1st
	• Missouri Open (1977) 1st
	• US Senior Amateur (1980) 2nd round match play
	• British Amateur (1955)
	• Missouri Senior Amateur (1980) 1st
	• Missouri Senior Amateur (1981) 1st
	• Missouri State Amateur (1951)1st
	• Missouri State Amateur (1954)1st
	• Missouri State Amateur (1959)1st
	• Missouri State Amateur (1976)1st
	• Missouri State Amateur Medalist (1950, '58, '61, '70)
	• St. Louis Open (1948)1st
	• St. Louis Open (1949)1st
	• St. Louis District Golf Association (1963)1st
	• St. Louis District Golf Association (1966)1st
	• St. Louis District Golf Association (1971)1st
	• St. Louis Publinx (1962) 1st
	• St. Louis Publinx (1963) 1st
	• St. Louis Publinx (1967) 1st
	• St. Louis Publinx (1976) 1st
	• St. Louis Publinx (1982) 1st
	• Walker Cup Team (1953 & 1955)
	• Trans Miss Amateur (1954) 1st
	• Trans Miss Amateur (1955) 1st
	• Champion of Champions Winner (1947, '52, '54, 59, '66, '71, 72, '73, 75, 77, '81)
	• Western Open (1952, 1953)
	• St. Louis District Junior (1940) 1st
	• St. Clair Invitational (1959) Low Amateur

Jarrett, Richard Lockhaven	• US Mid-Amateur (1992) • St. Louis District Golf Association (1991) 1st • US Amateur Publinks (1992)
Jennemann, Arthur	• US Publinks (1954, '51, '50, '49, '48, '47)
Johnson, James M. Algonquin	• US Senior Men's Amateur (1962, 1963, 1964)
Johnson, Jeff Norwood Hills	• St. Louis District Golf Association (1982) 1st • Normandy/Ping Championship (1991) 1st
Johnson, Jim	• St. Louis Publinx (1966) 1st
Johnson, John Norwood Hills	• St. Louis District Golf Association (1974) 1st
Jones, Pete	• St. Louis Publinx (1965) 1st
Karcher, Dan	• US Junior Boys (1980)
Keeley, Patrick J. St. Clair	• US Senior Amateur (1987)
Kell, Fred	• US Junior Boys (1962)

Championships Won by Amateurs

Kenny, Christian Algonquin	• St. Louis District Golf Association (1918) 1st • Missouri Amateur (1908) 1st • Missouri Amateur (1909) 1st • St. Louis Open (1910) 1st
Keim, Phil St. Albans	• US Mid-Amateur (1985, 1996) • Missouri Cup Team (1994, 1995, 1996) • Western Amateur (1986)
Kioski, Jim	• US Publinks (1974, 1975)
Kiplinger, Gail Algonquin	• St. Louis Women's District Junior (1975) 1st
Knoesel, Jim	• US Publinks (1985) • US Junior Amateur (1984) • US Amateur (1988)
Kohlman, Richard Normandie	• US Amateur (1947, '50, '58, '59) • St. Louis District Golf Association (1959) 1st
Kohn (Mrs.), R.J. Norwood Hills	• St. Louis Women's District (1933) 1st
Kolda, Mary Ann	• US Women's Publinks (1993)
Kootman, Michael	• US Mid-Amateur (1994)
Kopolow Hitch, Audrey Meadowbrook	• St. Louis Women's District (1973) 1st • St. Louis Women's District (1980) 1st
Kreikemeier, Ken	• St. Louis Publinx (1961) 1st
Kueper, John	• US Publinks (1990, 1993)
Kurtzborn, Jim	• US Publinks (1981)
Lambert, Albert Bond St. Louis Glen Echo	• US Amateur (1903, '05) • Missouri Amateur (1907) 1st • France Amateur Championship (1900) 1st • Paris Olympic Golf Champion (1900)
Lambert, Don	• US Senior Men's Amateur (1955)
Lanning, Ken	• St. Louis District Golf Association (1962) 1st
LaRiviere, Pete	• US Junior Boys (1951, 1952)
LeBeau, Harry	• US Publinks (1953, '52, '51, '49, '48) • US Senior Amateur (1991)
Lehr, Barbara	• St. Louis Women's Metro Tournament (1985, 1986) 1st • St. Louis Women's Match/Stroke Play (1979, 1980, 1982, 1983) 1st
Lewis, Randy	• US Mid-Amateur (1989)

Linsin, Dottie (Mrs. Roger)	• US Senior Women (1977, 1978, 1979, 1982) • Senior Women's Missouri Golf Association (1975) 1st • Senior Women's Missouri Golf Association (1977) 1st • Senior Women's Missouri Golf Association (1978) 1st • Missouri Senior Women's Amateur (1981) 1st • Missouri Senior Women's Amateur (1982) 1st • Missouri Senior Women's Amateur (1983) 1st
Lord, Roger Algonquin	• US Amateur (1921) • St. Louis District Golf Association (1916) 1st

Lucks, David
   Algonquin
   Players Club
	• Missouri State Amateur (1987) 1st
	• St. Louis Publinx (1992) 1st
	• St. Louis Publinx (1993) 1st
	• US Mid-Amateur (1983, 1989, 1995)
	• British Amateur (1996)
	• US Amateur (1987, 1991, 1995)
	• Missouri Cup Team (1994, 1995)

Malench, Joe	• US Amateur (1978)
Malley, Thomas	• US Publinks (1922)
Maloney, Frank	• US Publinks (1950)

Manion, Jim
   Midland Valley
   Riverview
   Forest Park
   Normandie
   Norwood Hills
	• Trans-Miss Amateur Championship (1924) 1st
	• St. Louis Open (1924) 1st
	• St. Louis Open (1928) 1st
	• St. Louis Open (1929) 1st
	• St. Louis Municipal Championship (1915) 1st
	• St. Louis Municipal Championship (1917) 1st
	• St. Louis Municipal Championship (1919) 1st
	• Missouri State Amateur (1917) 1st
	• Missouri State Amateur (1921) 1st
	• Missouri State Amateur (1923) 1st
	• Missouri State Amateur (1926) 1st
	• St. Louis District Golf Association (1923) 1st
	• St. Louis District Golf Association (1925) 1st
	• St. Louis District Golf Association (1927) 1st
	• St. Louis District Golf Association (1928) 1st
	• US Amateur (1919) Medalist
	• US Amateur (1919, 1921, 1923, 1925, 1932)
	• US Senior Men's Amateur (1956)
	• Selected 4th best Amateur in the country (1921)

Mankowski, Glen	• St. Louis Publinx (1964) 1st

Mason, Bob
   Greenbriar Hills
   Bellerive
	• US Amateur (1972, 1977, 1978, 1979, 1987, 1988, 1989, '90)
	• Reached Match Play in US Amateur (1987)
	• US Mid-Amateur (1981, 1982, 1991)
	• St. Louis District Golf Association (1972, 1977, 1986) 2nd
	• St.Clair Invitational (1980) Low Amateur
	• Missouri Cup Team (1980)

Mason, Jim
   Greenbriar Hills
   Bellerive
	• St. Louis District Golf Association (1976) 1st
	• US Amateur (1975, 1976 (Semi-finals), 1994)
	• US Mid-Amateur (1989, 1990, 1994)
	• US Junior Boys (1972)
	• Missouri Cup Team (1994, 1995)

Championships Won by Amateurs

Matthews, Bill	• St. Louis Publinx (1973) 1st • US Publinks (1974, '73, '70, '68, '67)
McCabe, Linda Norwood	• St. Louis Women's District Junior (1974) 1st
McCoy, Fred	• US Publinks (1928)
McKinley, Marcia St. Clair	• St. Louis Women's District Junior (1978) 1st

McKinnie, Bert
    Algonquin
    Normandie
	• US Amateur (1904)
	• Western Open (1904)
	• St. Louis Open (1901, 1904) 1st

McKittrick, Ralph St. Louis	• US Amateur (1902) • Missouri Amateur (1910) 1st • St. Louis Open (1905, 1906) 1st • City Championship (1898) 1st
McNair, L.G. Mrs.	• US Women's Amateur (1903)
Medart, Mrs. James R. Glen Echo	• US Senior Women's Amateur (1962, 1963, 1965, 1969)
Medart, W.S. Sunset Hill	• US Open (1928)
Meeh, Bob	• St. Louis Publinx (1992) 1st • Missouri Cup Team (1994)
Michaelis, John	• St. Louis Publinx (1988) 1st
Miles, Stacia Forest Hills	• St. Louis Women's District Junior (1993) 1st
Miller, Candy	• US Women's Publinks (1989)
Minnihan (Mrs.), James Bogey Hills	• St. Louis Women's District (1990) 1st
Montgomery, Brian	• US Amateur (1989)
Mooney, Libby Algonquin	• St. Louis Women's District Junior (1992) 1st • St. Louis Women's District Junior (1991) 1st
Moore, C. Alex	• US Junior Boys (1976)
Moore, Dennis	• US Mid-Amateur (1993) • US Junior Boys (1962, 1963) • US Amateur (1990)
Moretti, Bill	• St. Louis Publinx (1981) 1st • St. Louis Publinx (1975) 1st • St. Louis Publinx (1974) 1st • US Publinks (1975, 1977)
Morgan, Charles	• US Senior Amateur (1982, 1988, 1992)
Morris, Chris	• US Women's Publinks (1988)
Morrison, Alan	• US Junior Boys (1953)
Mueller-Riess, Cindy	• US Women's Publinks (1983) • US Junior Girls (1982, 1983) • US Women's Open (1988, 1991) • Women's Western Amateur (1988) • Illinois State Amateur Championship (1985) 1st • Illinois State Amateur Championship (1987) 1st
Murfin, Lindsey Bogey Hills	• St. Louis Women's District (1988) 1st • Missouri Women's Amateur (1988) 1st • Missouri Women's Amateur (1987) 1st

Murphy, Gary	• US Amateur (1989)
Murray, Walter	• US Publinks (1925)
Naes, Mark	• Tournament of Champions (1990) 1st
Norsworthy, Clarence Jr. 　Lake Forest	• US Amateur (1960) • Tournament of Champions (1957, 1969, 1970) 1st • District Junior Championship (1946) 1st
Nowicki, Alex	• US Senior Amateur (1992)
Nieberding, Sr. , Bob 　Norwood Hills	• St. Louis Seniors (1988) 1st
Null, Roger 　Norwood Hills	• Ozark Invitational Championship (1982) 1st • US Mid-Amateur (1981, 1993) • Missouri Senior Amateur (1996)1st • Missouri Cup Team (1994, 1995, 1996)
O'Brien, Chester 　Westborough	• US Amateur (1934, '35, '52) • St. Louis District Golf Association (1938) 1st • Missouri State Amateur (1933, 1934) 1st
O'Hare, Tom	• US Junior Boys (1961, 1963)
Osborne, Dennis	• St. Louis Publinx (1980) 1st
Owsley, Derre	• US Mid-Amateur (1992) Reached Quarterfinals • US Publinks (1994) • Missouri Cup Team (1995)
Pailer, Harry	• US Amateur (1947, '50) • St. Louis Metro Amateur (1945) 1st
Palozola, Maria 　Forest Hills	• St. Louis Women's District (1993) 1st • St. Louis Women's District (1992) 1st • Missouri Women's Amateur (1993) 1st
Parnell, Jackson	• US Junior Boys (1951)
Pass, Jeffrey	• US Junior Boys (1959)
Pearce, Richard	• US Junior Boys (1961)
Penberthy, Jack	• US Publinks (1949, '48)
Pepp, Virginia 　Forest Park 　Triple A	• St. Louis Women's District (1930) 1st • St. Louis Women's District (1926) 1st • St. Louis Women's District (1925) 1st • St. Louis Women's District (1923) 1st • St. Louis Women's District (1922) 1st • St. Louis Ladies City Golf Championship (1920, 1922, 1923) 1st • Women's Western Amateur (1922, 1939)
Phillips, Doris 　St. Clair 　Norwood Hills	• US Women's Open (1961, 1962, 1963) • US Women's Amateur (1965, 1963, 1961, 1960, 1959) • St. Louis Women's District (1970) 1st • St. Louis Women's District (1965) 1st • St. Louis Women's District (1964) 1st • St. Louis Women's District (1963) 1st • Illinois Women's State Amateur (1967) 1st • Illinois Women's State Amateur (1965) 1st • Illinois Women's State Amateur (1963) 1st • Women's Western Amateur (1958) • Trans-Miss Amateur (1958) • US Women's Amateur (1958, 1959)
Placke, Don 　Sunset	• US Amateur (1962)

Championships Won by Amateurs

Plummer, Jim 　Lake Forest	• Missouri Senior Amateur (1992, 1993) 1st
Polk II, Charles M.	• US Amateur (1963)
Port, Ellen 　Sunset CC 　Fox Run GC	• US Women's Mid-Amateur (1995) 1st • US Women's Mid-Amateur (1996) 1st • US Women's Amateur (1989, 1991, '92 (QF), '93, '94, '95, '96) • US Women's Mid-Amateur (1991(QF), '92, '93, '94(QF), '95, '96) • US Women's Open (1993, 1994, 1996) • US Women's Publinks (1987, 1988, 1989) • US Curtis Cup Teams (1994 & 1996) • Broadmoor Championship (1996) Medalist • Ladies British Amateur (1996) • Trans-Miss National Championship (1994) 1st • LPGA GHP Heartland Classic (1994) • LPGA Rail Classic (1993) • LPGA Sprint Titleholders (1996) • Missouri Women's Amateur (1992 & 1995) 1st • North & South Amateur (1987, 1991(QF), 1992, 1995 (3rd)) • St. Louis Women's District Match Play (1991 & 1992) 2nd • St. Louis Women's District Stroke Play (1992, '93, '94, '95) 1st • St. Louis Women's Golf Association Match Play (1987) 1st • St. Louis Metropolitan Championship (1993 & 1994) 1st • Women's Western Amateur (1987, '89, '91, '92 (QF), '93(QF), '94, '95, '96) • Women's Western Amateur (1992) Medalist
Powers, Jack 　Glen Echo	• US Senior Amateur (1988, 1991, 1994) • District Senior Amateur (1993, 1994, 1996) 1st • Metropolitan Senior (1995) 1st
Pruett, Richard	• St. Louis Publinx (1985) 1st
Purdum, Jack	• US Amateur (1950, '48)
Quick, Lyman (Smiley)	• Walker Cup (1947) • US Amateur Public Links (1946) 1st • US Open (1946) Low Amateur • US Amateur (1946) 2nd
Ray (Mrs.), E. Lansing 　St. Louis	• St. Louis Women's District (1920) 1st • Missouri Women's Amateur (1917) 1st
Redman, Ruth	• US Women's Publinks (1988)
Reynolds, Bob	• St. Louis Publinx (1972) 1st • US Publinks (1966, '61)
Rhoades, David	• US Amateur (1989, 1992) • US Amateur Publinks (1991) • Missouri Cup Team (1995, 1996)
Roney, Richard	• US Senior Men's Amateur (1959)

Rose, Marcella Forest Park Normandie Crystal Lake Norwood Hills	• Missouri Women's Amateur (1963) 1st • Missouri Women's Amateur (1969) 1st • US Women's Amateur (1963, 1964, 1965, 1966, 1967, 1968, 1969) • US Women's Amateur (1965) Co-Medalist • US Women's Open (1964) 2nd low amateur • US Women's Open (1965) low qualifier • US Women's Open (1960, '61, '63, '65, '66) • St. Louis Women's District (1960) 1st • St. Louis Women's District (1962) 1st • Women's Western Amateur (1965, 1967) Medalist • Marion Miley Award Winner (1965 & 1966) • - Award for being Low amateur in Western Open and Western Amateur. • Trans-Miss National Tournament (1959, '60, '62, '65, '66, '67, '68, '69, '70, '71, '72, '73, '74, '75, '76, '77, '91, '94, '95) • Missouri Intercollegiate Championship (1971) 1st • Tournament of Champions (1990, 1995, 1996) 1st • LPGA Clayton Federal Open (1961) • LPGA Heart of America Open (1961)
Ryan, Dave	• US Mid-Amateur (1991) • US Amateur (1989)
Sabo, Michael	• St. Louis District Junior (1996) 1st
Sampson, Alice Greenbriar	• St. Louis Women's District Senior (1994) 1st • St. Louis Women's District Senior (1988) 1st • US Senior Women (1988, 1989)
Sappington, Spencer	• St. Louis Publinx (1979) 1st • St. Louis Publinx (1975) 1st • St. Louis Publinx (1974) 1st • US Publinks (1973, '74, '75, '76, '77, '81) • US Mid-Amateur (1984)
Scharnhorst, Grant	• US Senior Amateur (1996)
Scheibal, Sam Sunset Hills	• St. Louis District Golf Association (1990) 1st • US Junior Boys (1989)
Schirmer, Raymond	• US Open (1936)
Schlude, Mark	• St. Louis District Golf Association (1940) 1st
Schnurbush, Craig	• US Amateur (1988, 1991, 1992, 1993) • US Mid-Amateur (1986) • US Open (1991)
Schoenberg, Russ	• US Junior Boys (1953)
Scudder, Charles W.	• City Championship (1899) 1st
Schuelin, Ben Westwood	• US Amateur (1962)
Schuette, Lawrence	• US Publinks(1926)
Schwent, Ed Bogey Hills	• US Mid-Amateur (1991, 1992) • St. Louis District Golf Association (1992) 1st
Semple, Grace St. Louis	• US Women's Amateur (1906, '07, '08, '09, '10, '11, '12 (SF), '14, '15) • Missouri Women's Amateur (1915) 1st
Sertl, Susan Sunset	• St. Louis Women's District Junior (1965) 1st
Severson, Kathy	• (See Welsh, Kathy)
Shannahan, Dave	• US Senior Amateur (1990, 1992)

Championships Won by Amateurs

Shepherd, Sam Jr.	• Paramount Golf Champinship (1943) 1st
Sher, James Westwood	• US Amateur (1962) • US Junior Boys (1963)
Sheridan, Mary Rosalie Forest Park	• St. Louis Women's District Junior (1937) 1st
Siegel, Rose Meadowbrook	• Trans-Miss (1972) • US Senior Women (1973, 1974, 1975, 1976, 1977) • LPGA Sears Women's World (1972) • LPGA St. Louis Squirt Open (1965)
Siler, Julia	• Paramount Golf Championship (1943, 1945) 1st (Won a total of 9 Paramount championships)
Slattery Jr., Les Sunset	• St. Louis District Golf Association (1954) 1st • US Amateur (1953, '57, '61) • Western Open (1953)
Slattery, Les Normandie	• US Open (1928)
Smiley, William Dr.	• Paramount Golf Championship (1942) 1st
Smith, Bo	• St. Louis Publinx (1992) 1st
Smith, Mike	• St. Louis Publinx (1982) 1st • St. Louis Publinx (1984) 1st
Smith, Paul	• US Publinks (1976)
Smith, Paula	• St. Louis Women's District Junior (1964) 1st • St. Louis Women's District Junior (1963) 1st
Solomon, Sid Westwood	• Chicago District Championship (1938) 1st
Spencer, James	• US Publinks (1955, '50, '49, '48)
Spilkes, Eugene	• US Junior Boys (1949)
Staats, Richard	• US Junior Boys (1957)
Stahlschmidt, John Old Warson	• US Amateur (1996) • US Junior Amateur (1991)
Stamer, Earl Normandie	• US Amateur (1962)
Stanford, Jerry	• US Publinks (1929)
Steedman, E.E.	• City Championship (1897) 1st
Steedman, E.H. Mrs.	• US Women's Amateur (1914)
Stickney, Stuart St. Louis	• US Amateur (1899, 1900, '02, '07, '11) • Missouri Amateur (1912) 1st • St. Louis Olympic Golf (1904) • British Amateur (1920) • Trans-Miss (1913) 1st • St. Louis District Golf Association (1918) 1st • Western Open (1908) • St. Louis Open (1902, 1903, 1908) 1st
Stickney, W. Arthur St. Louis	• US Amateur (1907) • Western Open (1908) • St. Louis Open (1907, 1909, 1911, 1912) 1st
Story, Ned	• US Junior Boys (1963)
Strickfaden, Gary	• St. Louis Publinx (1974) 1st • St. Louis Publinx (1977) 1st
Sutton, Bill	• US Junior Boys (1961)

Sweetser, Jess Normandie Yale Univ.	• US Amateur (1922) 1st • US Amateur (1920, '21, '22, '23, '25, '28, '29, '30, '34, '36, '38, '40) • US Open (1921) • British Amateur (1926) 1st • NCAA Championship (1920) 1st
Switzer, Joe Sunset Old Warson	• US Amateur (1949, '50, '55, '56, '59, '60, '63) • Western Open (1939) • St. Louis District Junior (1932) 1st
Terrell, Robert	• Paramount Golf Championship (1945) 1st
Tessary, Susan	• US Junior Girls (1995)
Tessary, Terry	• St. Louis Publinx (1992) 1st • St. Louis Publinx (1979) 1st • British Amateur (1973) • US Publinks (1981, 1987, 1989)
Thomas, Scott Normandie Norwood Hills	• St. Louis District Golf Association (1993) 1st • Missouri State Amateur (1992) 1st • Ozark Invitational (1992) 1st • US Amateur (1989, 1984, 1996) • Normandie Amateur (1988) 1st • Normandie Amateur (1992) 1st • Ping Amateur (1995) 1st • US Amateur Publinks (1992) • British Amateur (1990, 1992, 1994, 1996) • US Mid-Amateur (1990, 1991, 1994) • Missouri Mid-Amateur (1995) 1st • Jim Jackson Memorial (1992) 1st • Trans-Miss (1988) • Southern Illinois Amateur (1991) 1st • Missouri Cup Team (1994, 1995, 1996)
Todorovich, Mike Bellerive	• US Junior Boys (1991)
Toney, Richard	• US Senior Men's Amateur (1959)
Tumminia, Todd	• US Junior Boys (1983)
Uthoff, Lizzie Norwood Hills	• St. Louis Women's District Junior (1995) 1st
Vandiver, Alex	• US Amateur (1988)
Van Diver, Lee Sunset Hills	• St. Louis Women's District (1991) 1st • St. Louis Women's District Junior (1987) 1st
Voigt, Cece St. Clair	• St. Louis Women's District Junior (1985) 1st • St. Louis Women's District Junior (1984) 1st • St. Louis Women's District Junior (1983) 1st
Von Rump, Betty Westborough	• St. Louis Women's District Senior (1987) 1st • St. Louis Women's District Senior (1985) 1st • US Senior Women (1986, 1988, 1989) • Missouri Senior Women's (1986) 1st • Missouri Women's Golf Association Senior (1996) 1st

Championships Won by Amateurs

Waitulavich, Jerry	• St. Louis Publinx Champion (1991) • US Publinks (1990) Quarterfinals • US Mid-Amateur (1988, 1993) • US Amateur (1988) • Western Amateur (1988) • British Amateur (1988) • Trans-Miss (1988)
Wasson, Lynn Glen Echo	• St. Louis Women's District (1921) 1st
Watts, Lawson	• US Amateur (1924)
Weiss, Jonas Meadowbrook	• Missouri Valley Conference Championship (1938) 1st • St. Louis District Golf Association (1939) 1st • St. Louis District Golf Association (1951) 1st • Missouri State Amateur (1946) 1st
Welch, Kathy Severson, Kathy Cherry Hills	• St. Louis Women's District (1972) 1st • St. Louis Women's District (1974) 1st • Missouri Women's Amateur (1977)1st • Senior Women's Missouri Golf Association (1995) 1st
Wening, Lisa Norwood Hills	• St. Louis Women's District Junior (1990) 1st

Whitbread, Elliott
   Osage CC
   Sunset CC
	• St. Louis District Golf Association (1930) 1st
	• St. Louis District Golf Association (1936) 1st
	• US Open (1928)
	• Westrn Open (1938)

White, D.K.	• US Open (1906)
White, Patrick	• US Junior Amateur (1995)
Wickenhauser, Tim	• US Amateur (1973) • US Publinks (1989)
Wilke, Mel Greenbriar	• St. Louis District Golf Association (1957) 1st
Willingham, W.M.	• US Senior Men's Amateur (1956)
Winter, Bryan Westborough	• St. Louis District Golf Association (1931) 1st • St. Louis District Golf Association (1932) 1st
Wohlford, Brent	• US Mid-Amateur (1990)
Wolff, Clarence Sunset	• St. Louis District Golf Association (1919) 1st • St. Louis District Golf Association (1922) 1st • St. Louis District Golf Association (1926) 1st • St. Louis District Golf Association (1929) 1st • Western Amateur (1920) 2nd • US Amateur (1921, '25) • US Open (1926, 1927, 1928)
Wright, Jacqueline	• US Women's Amateur Publinks (1993)
Wright, Tom Algonquin	• US Amateur (1988)
Wyman, Hermann	• US Publinks (1951, '48)
Yahling, Barry	• US Amateur Publinks (1994)
Yonney, John R.	• US Amateur (1961)
Zachritz, Howard Algonquin	• US Amateur (1948)

Note: Those events listed with the year(s) following indicate the individual qualified for the event in that year. Their participation in the actual event, in some cases, may or may not have taken place.

"I'm only afraid of three things, lightning, a sidehill putt and Hogan."

...Sam Snead

Amateur Champions

This section deals with those individuals from the area who competed in the various national events and deserve special recognition. These are the amateur players who won National Championships, or who performed exceptionally in these events. There is a second category for players who have represented the United States on the Walker Cup or Curtis cup teams.

There have been three long-time St. Louisans who won USGA Amateur Championships; *Eddie Held*, *Jim Holtgrieve* and *Ellen Port*. A footnote must be added here for a fourth and a fifth, *Jess Sweetser*, who captured the 1922 US Amateur at the Country Club in Brookline, MA over Chick Evans and *Smiley Quick*.

Eddie Held
Winner of 1st US Publinks in
1922 in Toledo, Ohio

At the time of his Amateur victory, Sweetser was playing out of Siwanoy Club in Bronxville, NY. However he lived in St. Louis prior to 1918 and learned his golf over the Normandie links. From German-ancestry, his parents changed their name to Sweetser due to the anti-German sentiment during the War and moved to New York.

Smiley Quick was born in Centralia, IL, but made his mark while living in Los Angeles in the mid-40's as an amateur before turning pro in 1948.

In addition, there are other National championships that St. Louisans have won that are documented here. This includes the *Trans-Miss National championship* and the *North & South Senior*.

Among other National events, two St. Louisans have captured the *Canadian Open*, Eddie Held in 1929 and Ted Adams in 1938. Bob Cochran captured several events in the 40's, among them are the *Decatur Open* on the PGA Tour in 1943 and the *Tam O'Shanter World Amateur* and *the Great Lakes Amateur* in the same year.

Holtgrieve and Cochran also share another common honor; both finished 2nd in the *British Amateur*, Cochran in 1961 and Holtgrieve in 1983. Cochran also finished 2nd in three other events in 1945, the *Western Open*, the *World Amateur* title and the *Memphis Open*. Jim Tom Blair finished 3rd in 1951 at the PGA *Tour Phoenix Open* (after leading at the halfway mark) and 2nd at the *Western Amateur*. In the *Women's Western Open*, Betty Jane Haemerle-Broz finished 2nd in 1944.

US Publinks

Unknown to many St. Louisans is the story of Edmund S. (Eddie) Held. The 1925 District winner had a true championship career. When the first Publinks was held in 1922, there had been no

The Champions

The 1961 Walker Cup Team (l-r); Bob Cochran, Frank Taylor, Charles Coe, Deane Beman, Gene Andrews, Jack Westland (Capt), Bill Hyndman, Don Cherry, Robert Gardner, Jack Nicklaus, Charles Smith

national tournaments held for public players. James D. Standish was the prime mover behind convincing the USGA that such a competition was needed. The ranks of public golfers had swelled greatly since the end of World War I, and the number of municipal and public courses had growth in proportion. His conviction swayed the committee and Standish donated the permanent Championship Cup. The USGA had one big concern; they had no way of knowing how many players would show up. They were greatly satisfied when 140 players entered, even though less than half showed up with golf shoes. Among the group was nineteen-year-old Eddie Held. Played at Ottawa Park Golf Course in Toledo, his 6&5 victory over Richard Walsh allowed him to take the James Standish championship trophy home to St.

Louis. Shortly after he returned, Held joined Algonquin CC, and thus could not defend his title.. In later years, Eddie Held owned and managed the Held Driving Range which was located on Manchester Road near the present West County Shopping Center.. He would later move his facility and locate it further west on Manchester across from the McGraw-Hill company near Wideman Road.

Lyman 'Smiley' Quick from Centralia would capture the 1946 US Publinks title. A relative of Smiley's still resides in Centralia but he remains somewhat of a mystery to many golf enthusiasts. Following his runner-up spot in the 1947 US Amateur, and his finish as low amateur in the 1947 US Open, he turned pro in 1948.

US Mid Amateur Championship

No history of St. Louis would be complete without the classic fairy-tale ending. *"The Walker Cup player, state champion, lifelong amateur, Jim Holtgrieve, playing in the first US Mid-Amateur at Bellerive CC in his hometown of St. Louis"*. The stage is set, right out of "The Natural". And, like Roy Hobbs (the movie not the book), Jim delivers with a 2-up victory over his former Walker Cup team-mate Bob Lewis Jr. 1981 was a great season for Jim; winning the Missouri State Amateur over the summer for the second time and the Mid-Amateur in October.

Jim also holds a few marks for his play at the Mid-Am. He has 21 victories at match play, second only to Jay Sigel's 28. He also had 9 consecutive match play victories during 1981-82 play. This mark is also second only to Jim Stuart's 12 consecutive wins.

Jim also played a role in bringing the Mid-Amateur to St. Louis. While at the 1980 amateurs dinner preceding the Masters, Jim was approached by Jim Gabrielsen of the USGA. He was considering a proposal to begin a new championship, one for the over-25 businessman-amateur to compete in over their career. He had garnered support from this effort from other amateurs; Jay Sigel, Buddy Marucci, and Vinny Giles, and wanted Jim's angle on the idea. There was one note of concern however, would this event detract from the US Amateur? Would these amateurs stop competing in favor of the Mid-Amateur? Jim assured Gabrielsen that to win an national title was still the objective and the US Amateur would always be a goal. Once the executive committee agreed to the competition, it was up to finding a site. Jim proposed Bellerive. As a former US Open site, it had the USGA approval and it was centrally located, ideal for getting a large field for the initial event. Jim contacted Bob Mason and with the help of Tim Crowley and John Stupp, the Mid-Amateur began in 1981.

Jim Holtgrieve
1981 US Mid-Amateur
Champion

There have been other memorable events by area players in the Mid-Amateur. In 1987 at Brook Hollow club in Dallas, ***Don Bliss*** began his round on the 10th hole and promptly aced it. When he came to his 17th hole (the 8th), he promptly aced that as well, for his 2nd hole-in-one in a single round, becoming the first player to score two holes-in-one in the same round in a USGA championship.

Belleville's ***Mark Boyajian*** had a memorable round at the Mid-Am at Cherry Hills CC in Denver in 1983. Mark shot a 67 for the 2nd lowest round played in the Mid-Am to date, which included a 29 on the front side, breaking Arnold Palmers record of 30 (30-35=65), set in the final round of the 1960 US Open. This is believed to be the lowest nine holes in the history of USGA competitions. Mark went on to defeat the defending champion, Bill Hoffer 4&3 in the 2nd round and then Richard Sucher fell 4&3. He next faced Craig Scheibert in the quarterfinals and lost 1-up in 19 holes. Scheibert would lose in the semi's to eventual champion Jay Sigel.

The Champions

U.S. WOMEN'S MID-AMATEUR CHAMPIONSHIP

Sept. 24-29
Mission Hills
Rancho Mirage, Calif.

Brenda Kuehne (145) / Jo-Ann Lindsay (162) — Kuehne, 3 and 2
Patricia Cornett (158) / Linda Pearson (158) — Cornett, 1-up
Cornett, 19 holes
Andrea Kraus (160) / Margaret Watson (155) — Kraus, 6 and 5
Kerry Postillion (155) / Aileen Robertson (160) — Postillion, 3 and 1
Postillion, 21 holes
Postillion 3 and 2
K. Hartwiger (150) / Elizabeth Haines (161) — Hartwiger, 2 and 1
Lorie McCabe (157) / Peggy Kirby (159) — McCabe, 4 and 2
Hartwiger, 2-up
Mina Hardin (150) / Cathy Schaefer (161) — Hardin, 6 and 5
Victoria Abens (157) / Gail Flanagan (159) — Abens, 4 and 3
Hardin, 2 and 1
Hartwiger, 20 holes
Postillion, 2 and 1
Caryn Wilson (147) / Diane Staats (162) — Wilson, 19 holes
Lancy Smith (157) / Leland Beckel (158) — Beckel, 2 and 1
Wilson, 2 and 1
Cindy Carroll (154) / Patrice Cooper (160) — Carroll, 3 and 2
Robin Burke (156) / Colette Rosenberg (159) — Burke, 4 and 2
Burke, 3 and 2
Wilson, 5 and 3
Carol Thompson (148) / Cynthia Navis (162) — Thompson, 7 and 5
Missy Farr-Kaye (157) / Martha Leach (158) — Farr-Kaye, 19 holes
Thompson, 5 and 4
Carolyn Creekmore (154) / Kelli Rinker (160) — Creekmore, 2 and 1
Robin Weiss (156) / Martha Dement (159) — Weiss, 1-up
Creekmore, 8 and 7
Thompson, 1-up
Thompson, 19 holes
Postillion, 1-up

Port, 3 and 2 — Ellen Port (146) / Leslie Shannon (162)
Carmichael, 3 and 2 — Julie Carmichael (158) / Claudia Pilot (158)
Port, 7 and 6
Slobodnik, 2-up — Leigh Klass (155) / Stacy Slobodnik (160)
Ewart, 1-up — M.J. Anderson (155) / Sue Ewart (160)
Ewart, 4 and 3
Port, 3 and 2
Wiesner, 7 and 6 — Toni Wiesner (149) / Theresa Wanek (162)
Moore, 3 and 2 — Lisa Griffin (157) / Patty Moore (159)
Moore, 2-up
Lang, 4 and 2 — Sherry Houser (152) / Martha Lang (161)
Schriber, 5 and 4 — K. Bhaedhayiibh (157) / Selby Schriber (159)
Lang, 5 and 3
Lang, 3 and 2
Port, 2 and 1
Jemsek, 3 and 2 — Marla Jemsek (147) / Reva Kamins (162)
Lane, 1-up — Debbie Lane (158) / Tish Preuss (158)
Lane, 3 and 2
Monisteri, 20 holes — Eva Monisteri (154) / Sarah Ingram (160)
Cowan, 2-up — Karla Kalian (155) / Lynne Cowan (159)
Monisteri, 1-up
Monisteri, 6 and 5
Harrity, 2 and 1 — Virginia Grims (149) / Dana Harrity (162)
Kim, 2 and 1 — Jennifer Ederer (157) / Sylvia Kim (158)
Kim, 23 holes
Gysin, 5 and 3 — Amy Bubon (153) / Karen Gysin (161)
Brower, 1-up — Taffy Brower (156) / Lee Burton (159)
Gysin, 3 and 2
Gysin, 3 and 1
Monisteri, 4 and 3
Port, 1-up

THE USGA

The pairings sheet for the 1996 Mid-Amateur Championship, this was Ellen Port's second consecutive Mid-Am win.

US Women's Mid-Amateur

There is also a **USGA Women's Mid-Amateur Championship,** though like most women's events it would be hard at times to find the results, or that it took place. Begun in 1987, 1996 marked the 10th anniversary. But for St. Louisan Ellen Port nine was her lucky number. The John Burroughs teacher won the **1995 Women's Mid-Amateur** to become the first USGA lady champion from the area.

Some may call winning one "major" a lucky streak, you get on a roll, have a hot putter and suddenly your the winner. After all it has happened several times. But to successfully defend your title denotes a true Champion. Ellen accomplished just that as she defended her title in the **1996 US Women's Mid-Amateur** on Sunday, September 29

beating Kerry Postillion of Burr Ridge, Ill., 2 and 1.

Ellen took control of the match early, hitting a 6-iron approach to within 18 inches on the 405-yard third hole for her second consecutive birdie to take a 3-up advantage. Postillion, who is a reinstated amateur, was within a hole of squaring the match after Ellen bogeyed the par-4 13th. But the two-time U.S. Curtis Cup player, countered with a 20-foot birdie putt on the par-3 14th to keep Postillion at bay. The match ended with a two-putt par on the par-3 17th.

"Last year I won it with my putter, this year I wasn't putting as well," said Ellen, who was 3 1/2 months pregnant with her first child. *"But I still felt that I could win because the rest of my game was so strong."*

"One of my goals was to come out early and to play really aggressive," Ellen said. "I had been

sitting back a little in my other matches, thinking that I had a lot of holes to win.''

Ellen became only the second player in the history of the Mid-Amateur to repeat as winner. Three-time winner Sarah LeBrun Ingram of Nashville, Tenn., also won consecutive titles in 1993 and 1994. Ellen also became the fourth USGA champion this year to successfully defend a title, joining Annika Sorenstam in the Women's Open, Kelli Kuehne in the Women's Amateur and Tiger Woods in the U.S. Amateur.

Walker Cup

St. Louis has been well represented in the Walker Cup competitions, as the Cup itself is named for the St. Louisan whose idea it was, George Herbert Walker. Born in St. Louis, and a member of St. Louis CC, George H. Walker was elected president of the USGA in 1920. During a trip to Great Britain that year, the idea of an international competition came to him. There had been attempts at this, most notably between the US and Canada, but nothing had succeeded over time. He presented the idea to the Executive Committee upon his return and it was finally approved. Originally conceived by Walker as the ***International Challenge Cup,*** the committee dubbed it the Walker Cup and the media picked up on it, though Walker himself was not fond of the idea.

Jim Jackson with the Walker Cup. Jim would play on the 1953 and 1955 squads.

The first event was in 1922 at Walkers home club of the National Golf Links (by this time he was traveling between St. Louis and New York for his investment & banking firm. St. Louis would be the "Home" office, whereas New York was the "Head" office of G.H. Walker & Company). The competition hoped to foster relations between the US and Great Britain on the amateur level. The matches were held each year for the first three, then in 1924 it was agreed to hold them every other year, beginning in 1926. After a hiatus during WW2, they began again in 1947. The following individuals have competed for the United States in this premier amateur event.

Jim Jackson was the first from the area to be chosen for a spot on a Walker Cup team as he was on the 1953 and the 1955 squads. In 1953 at Kittansett Club in Massachusetts, Jim paired with Gene Littler where they defeated James Wilson and Roy MacGregor 3&2. Two years later, at St. Andrews, he paired with Bruce Cudd to defeat David Blair and J. Robert Carter 5&4 in foursomes competition. Jim also won his singles match in 1955 defeating R. Cecil Weing 6&4 to keep his record perfect. An interesting incident involving Jackson occurred in 1953. He and Littler had completed the first hole and were walking up the 2nd fairway at Kittansett CC in Massachusetts, when he discovered that he had 16 clubs in his bag. He went to an official, and while the rules called for

The Champions

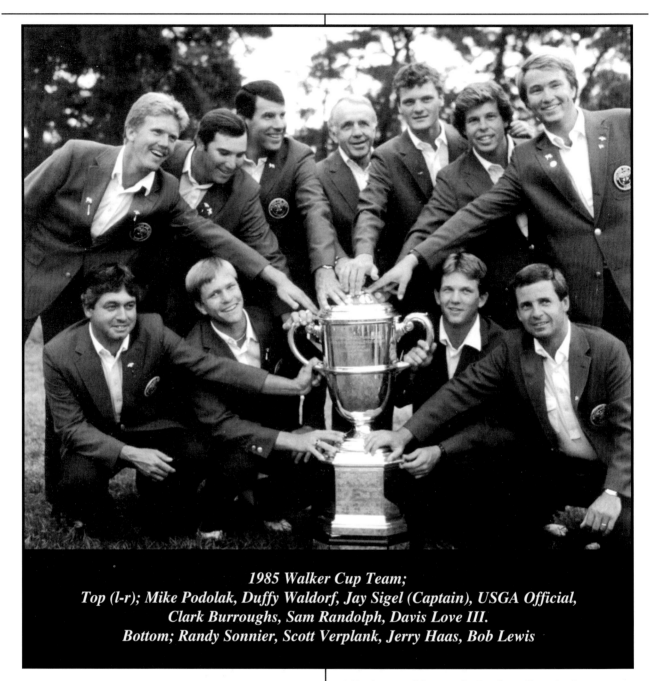

1985 Walker Cup Team;
Top (l-r); Mike Podolak, Duffy Waldorf, Jay Sigel (Captain), USGA Official,
Clark Burroughs, Sam Randolph, Davis Love III.
Bottom; Randy Sonnier, Scott Verplank, Jerry Haas, Bob Lewis

disqualification, and the committee was initially inclined to accept this ruling, the British asserted their desire to win their points on the play of the game. The committee yielded and modified the penalty to two holes, the number which Jackson had played. Despite this 2-down situation, Jackson and Littler won their match 3 and 2.

Bob Cochran was a member of the 1961 team that competed at Seattle GC. This was one of the most lopsided victories as the US won 11-1 with

Cochran and former St. Louisan Gene Andrews defeating 6 time British Amateur Champion and current R&A Secretary Michael Bonallack and Ronald Shade 4&3.

This was an upset of amazing proportions since Bonallack was one of the all time great amateurs in British history and Shade was having a career year. This was the day when the teams "flipped" to pick their opponents and the Brits picked the "two old Americans" (Cochran was at the time 48) expecting a

easy victory.

Jay Haas was a member in 1975 at St. Andrews where he won his singles match against Richard Eyles 2&1 and then teamed with Curtis Strange for two victories, first over Charles Green and Hugh Stuart 2&1 and then over Peter Hedges and John Davies 3&2.

Jay recalled the thrill of initially seeing St. Andrews. Walking the fairways where golf has been played for hundreds of years, sent shivers up his spine.

Jim Holtgrieve was a member in 1979 at Muirfield, 1981 at Cypress Point and 1983 and Hoylake. Jim's record in his three appearances was 6-2, which included a 3-1 record in singles. (Just to your information, Bobby Jones holds the record for won-lost percentage in single matches. He won a total of 5 matches without a loss) Along the way Holtgrieve defeated Ronan Rafferty 2&1 and Lindsey Mann 6&5 in his singles matches. Jim still holds a Walker Cup record along with

his playing partner, Bob Lewis in which they defeated Malcolm Lewis and Martin Thompson 7&6 at Royal Liverpool Club at Hoylake, England in 1983. This is the largest margin of victory in a foursomes match over 18 holes.

Jerry Haas competed in 1985 at Pine Valley where he lost his singles match, then returned with Sam Randolph to win their foursome match 3&2.

Centralia, IL native *Lyman 'Smiley' Quick* as a member of the 1947 Walker Cup team that won their matches 8 - 4 over the GBI Team. Smiley would win his singles over James Wilson 8 & 6, but would fall with Marvin H. Ward to Leonard Crawley and Percy Lucas 5&4. Born Lyman, he had his name legally changed as an adult to Smiley L. Quick due to his ever-present grin!

To be chosen to play on the Walker Cup is perhaps the highest honor an amateur can receive.

Curtis Cup

Most golfers are not as

The Champions

*Above: 1994 Curtis Cup Team (l-r) Standing; Carol Semple Thompson,
Jill McGill, Lenoy Smith (Captain) Wendy Kaup, Sarah Ingram.
Seated; Emilee Klein, Stephanie Sparks, Ellen Port, Wendy Ward.*

*Below: 1996 Curtis Cup Team(l-r) Seated; Carol Semple Thompson,
Sarah Ingram,Martha Lang (Captain),Marla Jemsek, Brenda Corrie-Kuehn,
Standing; Kelli Kuehne, Ellen Port, Kellee Booth, Christie Kerr.*

familiar with the Curtis Cup as they are with the other amateur Championships. But this Women's version of the Walker Cup has been competed for since 1932. Originally donated in 1927 by sisters Margaret and Harriot Curtis, two outstanding amateurs in the early 1900's, the Cup's first matches were held at Wentworth, England and were dominated by the legendary Joyce Wethered and Glenna Collett Vare.

The matches have never been held in the area, and until 1994, no lady from St. Louis had been honored with a selection. In 1994 *Ellen Port* represented the US on the Curtis Cup squad held at the Honors Course in Tennessee and was again chosen in 1996 for the matches at Killarney, Ireland.

In 1994 Ellen teamed with Wendy Kaupp in the foursomes but would fall 6&5. However this would be sandwiched between wins in both her singles matches, the first 2&1 over Mhairi McKay and on the final day she would beat McKay again, this time 7&5. Ellen's 2-1 mark for the matches was behind only Emilee Klein and Carol Semple Thompson's 3-1 marks as the best for the team as the matches were tied at 9 points each allowing Britain to retain the Cup.

The 1996 matches were not kind to the US squad as they went down to the GBI team. And for the first time in the history of the Cup, the GBI team took possession of it for the third consecutive time.

Ellen and Kelli Kuehne won their foursome match against Julie Hall and Lisa Educate 1-up as Kelli played brilliantly, holing a 35 footer on the 14th and pitched in on the 16th. The duo finished 2-0 in their foursomes, the only US pair to do so. But Ellen

would fall to Curtis Cup newcomer Alison Rose in the afternoon singles 6&5. Ellen and Kelli Kuehne did not play in the final singles, something that those present remarked about with amazement, and the GBI team won all four matches and claimed their 10th point for victory.

Jess Sweetser

British Amateur

In 1926 *Jess Sweetser* would become the first American to win the British Amateur in defeating A.F. Simpson 6&5. Playing out of the Siwanoy Club, he would defeat Francis Ouimet in the 3rd round before advancing. Jess had to win eight matches to claim victory.

Jess grew up on the fairways at Normandie in the pre-WW1 days before moving on to Yale University and the New York area. As noted previously, Jim Holtgrieve and Bob Cochran would both finish 2nd in the British Amateur in their careers.

Jess was also very prominent in the Walker Cup matches. He played on six of the first seven teams (1930 being the lone exception) and was Captain in 1967 and 1973.

Trans-Miss Championship

The Trans-Miss was one of the "Major" tournaments from 1900 through the 1950's. Local tournaments were few and traveling across the country for the US Amateur was often difficult and expensive. The Trans-Miss was held at various sites including a few times in St. Louis, and usually the top talent throughout the country entered.

Stuart Stickney was the first local winner in

The Champions

1913 at Glen Echo. In 1919 the Trans-Miss came to St. Louis CC where *Dick Bockenkamp* of Sunset lost in a 40-hole match and again in 1923 he lost in the finals, this time to *Eddie Held.* The win by Held in 1923 began a run of four consecutive years when St. Louisans would win the title. *Jimmy Manion* captured the Trans-Miss in 1924 at St. Joseph CC, and *Clarence Wolff* of Sunset and *Eddie Held* took top prizes in 1925 and in 1926 respectively. Held had the privilege of playing the championship in '26 over his home course of Algonquin when he took top honors, his second in four years. Wolff also finished 2nd once, losing in the 1920 finals, while Manion would lose in the 1930 championship match.

Jimmy Jackson was the first back-to-back winner of the Trans-Miss, having accomplished this in 1954-55.

Ellen Port captured the Trans-Miss National in 1994 as her first national crown. This springboarded her to her two USGA titles during the past few years.

More detailed information on the Trans-Miss Championships is listed in the *Championships* section.

College Championships

While not as widely recognized as other national titles, the NCAA's brings the best of the best together for team and individual titles. Five St. Louisans have captured the individual titles in the NCAA and another the NAIA (National Association of Intercollegiate Athletics) crown.

In 1920, Yale student, *Jess Sweetser*, captured the Individual title at Nassau Country Club. Nineteen years later, in 1939, *Vince D'Antoni* from Tulane would capture the same crown over the Wakonda (Des Moines) CC grounds. [Twelve years later, Vince would upset Bob Cochran in the 1952 District Championship]

In 1967 Colorado Buffalo *Hale Irwin* would shoot a 286 to grab the title at Shawnee GC in

Delaware.

Eight years later *Jay Haas*, a Demon Deacon at Wake Forest would follow his teammate, Curtis Strange in back to back titles as they would win team and individual titles in 1974 & 1975. Jay would also capture the Fred Haskins Award as the outstanding college golfer of the year in 1975.

A footnote to this would also show that future Westwood Professional, *Fred Wampler* from Purdue would win the 1950 Individual title.

St. Louis CC pro *Steve Spray* would capture back-to-back individual titles while at Eastern New Mexico in 1962 & 1963 to win the NAIA title.

Professional Champions

With all the respect their ability demands, the Professionals who have won Major or significant Championships who are from the area fall into a separate category, and deserve a separate distinction.

The first of the champions in this category is Bob Goalby. His victory in the *1968 Masters* marked not only a turning point in his career, but also the first Major Professional win for a St. Louis area native.

The second would be the three *US Open* titles won by Hale Irwin. Despite his many professional victories and other titles, it is these which will forever be the cornerstone for his career.

Next would be the Senior Titles won by Hale Irwin and Tom Wargo. Tom would win the *PGA Seniors* in 1993 and Hale would duplicate that in the 1996 edition.

Other national titles on the Professional level were won by Algonquin pro Milon Marusic who won the *Quarter Century* crown in the PGA Club Pro's in 1982. Walter Ambo won the *Senior Stroke Play* title in 1986 while Marusic had accomplished the same feat in 1987 for the 70-89 year old group.

In perhaps his biggest accomplishment, Tom

Bob Goalby waits prior to the presentation of the Green Jacket for his 1968 Masters victory. Runner-up Roberto DeVicenzo can only ponder what would have happened. Bob shot a 66 in the final round including an eagle on #15 to jump into the lead. His 277 total was the 4th lowest up to that point and his final round tied for the lowest final round by the eventual winner until Gary Player's 64 in 1978.

Wargo, at age 49, was chosen as the *PGA Club Professional Player of the Year* in 1992. Tom also won the *1991 Stroke Play* title as well,

Other National Titles

Bob Cochran captured the 1931 *Western Junior* when it was the premier Junior event in the country.

Benny Richter, the outstanding pro at Triple A and Bellerive, would win the 1934 and 1935 *National Left-Handed Championship*, the first two years of the event.

Judy Rankin would win four *National Pee Wee*

titles, her first at age 8 in 1953, then again in 1954, 1955 and 1956. Paula Eger has won two National PeeWee titles as well, one in 1965 and again in 1968. Jay Haas would capture this title in 1960 at age 7.

Eddie Held would become the first American to win the *Canadian Open* when he did so in 1929, a feat Dutch Harrison would duplicate in 1949 as a pro.

The Ryder Cup

When Samuel Ryder donated the cup that bears his name for the professional competitions, there is no way he could have envisioned the "near-hysteria

The Champions

1979 Walker Cup Team
Standing Top (l-r); Jim Holtgrieve, Mike Peck.
(Middle) Hal Sutton, Jay Sigel, Doug Fischesser,
Dick Siderowf (Captain), Mike Gove, Griff Moody
(Front) Marty West, Scott Hoch, Doug Clarke

that would develop over the challenge matches

From the beginning the Americans were the dominant team, with the Great Britain squad hoping to make the matches competitive

But when Jack Nicklaus suggested that they include the whole of Europe in the competitions, it ushered-in a drama that may be un-matched in sport..

From the first matches in 1927, the St. Louis area has been represented with professionals who called St. Louis home during their careers.

In the first matches it was *Bill Mehlhorn*, the former North Hills Pro who helped the US squad to victory By 1935 future Meadowbrook pro *Ky Lafoon* was the selected for the squad. *Ralph Guldahl* was on the 1937 team after spending two seasons at St. Louis CC earlier in the decade.

The matches were suspended during the war years and when they resumed it was *Dutch Harrison* who was on the 1947, 1949 and 1951 teams.

Former Westwood Pro, and US Open champ

Ed Furgol would be on the 1957 team and the 1959 version would have another Westwood representative, this time it was the 1969 professional *Bob Rosburg*.

Bob Goalby would make the 1961 team, but since he had not been a PGA member the required five years (a bylaw that has since been repealed) he would have to wait until 1963 for his berth against the Brits at East Lake CC.

The area would have to wait until 1975 when *Hale Irwin* would be the selection, and again in 1977, 1979 and 1981. 1979 marked the first year of the Europe vs. US matches and the appearance of Seve Ballesteros. Hale would finish this four appearance span by finishing with a record of 11-3-1 including 3-1-1 in singles matches.

In 1983 *Jay Haas* would represent his country at PGA National as the matches were the closest in years with the US winning by a single point.

1991 at the Kiawah Ocean Course, dubbed the "battle by the sea", saw *Hale Irwin* go 3-0-1 as his

The 1963 Ryder Cup Team
(L-R; Bottom) Arnold Palmer (Captain); Julius Boros, Gene Littler, Billy Maxwell, Dow Finsterwald, Dave Ragan. (Top); Johnny Pott, Billy Casper, Bob Goalby, Tony Lema

halve the final day cinched the Cup for the US by a single point.

Jay Haas would return in 1995 as Europe would exact a bit of revenge by gaining a single point victory over the US on American soil at a "US Open-type course" at Oak Hill in Rochester, New York. It marked the finest comeback performance since 1957, and the matches were decided late as five singles matches were won on the 18th hole.

The Presidents Cup

One of the newest international competitions began in 1994 with a Ryder Cup-like competition between the US and the remaining non-European

[read Greg Norman & Company] players.

Selected as captain for this initial team was *Hale Irwin* and one of his Captain's choices was *Jay Haas*. Facing the International team at the Robert Trent Jones Club at Lake Manasas, Virginia, they were no match for the Americans as Fred Couples played brilliantly as the US won handily.

The Championships

*"All I know is that Nicklaus watches Hogan practice, and
I never heard of Hogan watching Nicklaus practice."*

...Tommy Bolt

PGA Championship

Two PGA Championships have been contested in St. Louis, the *1948 PGA Championship* at Norwood Hills and the more recent *1992 Championship* at Bellerive. The 1948 Championship was unique because they were still competing at match play. Ben Hogan, the 36-year old, steely-eyed Texan, came into the tournament having won the PGA two years earlier, and having just won the US Open at Riviera. He seemed to be on a roll that would stop at nothing. Just 1 year later he would lay near death after the near fatal bus accident. But his determination would survive and he would return in 1950 to capture his second US Open defeating Lloyd Mangrum and George Fazio in a playoff at Merion. But the best was yet to come, for in 1953 he would accomplish the near perfect; the modern Grand Slam. 1953 was the year he would win the British Open, the US Open and the Masters. Only the PGA would elude him. In reality he did not even enter the event that year! He would never again attempt the British Open, so the modern Slam would forever be safe from the "Hawk".

The 1948 PGA was contested like the previous 32 since 1916, at Match Play. The event began with a 36 hole stroke play elimination phase in which 63 players would join the previous year's winner in the quest for the title. The defending champion was current senior player Jim Ferrier, who forecasted that a young player would win over the hilly Norwood course. Hogan finished 5th in the qualifying shooting a 6-under 138. Local pro's Frank Moore (Meadowbrook) and Walter Ambo (Westborough) also made the cut. But Moore would run into Snead in the 2nd round and Ambo would fall to 'Porky' Oliver in the 1st.

Play was slightly different in 1948; the stymie was still used—a player had to putt around or over an opponents ball if it was in his line on the green— though it would be abandoned shortly. Odd by todays standards, the tournament did not conclude on a weekend—it began the match play on Saturday and the finals were held on Tuesday.

Hogan won his six matches to claim the victory, but along the way had a few errant shots, including one from the thick rough where he was able to advance the ball only several inches. But keep advancing he did. In his opening match he defeated Jock Hutchinson 1-up (23 holes). Next he dispatched Johnny Palmer - where he finished eagle-par-birdie - to win 1-up. He met Gene Sarazen in the third round and they played even with

WEST COURSE

NORWOOD HILLS COUNTRY CLUB

NORMANDY, MISSOURI

Scorecard from the 1948 PGA at Norwood Hills
Courtesy of Bob Green

Hogan eventually winning 1-up again. In his fourth match he defeated Chick Harbert 2&1 and then Jimmy Demaret 2&1 to reach the final against Turnesa. Reeling off a birdie streak on the 4th, 5th and 6th, Hogan never looked back and finished the match on the 12th hole (30th of the match) with a 7&6 victory.

The "Hawk" would capture his 2nd and last PGA title at Norwood Hills and cash the $3,500 check as champion. He would go on to win over 60 Tour events and 9 Majors including the "Career Slam".

The 74th version of the *PGA* at Bellerive in 1992 was more a circus environment than a golf tournament; not to demean the tournament as a sideshow, but rather like the circus' of old where when the circus arrived at the edge of the city, the whole town shut down and every citizen showed up to see the sights for themselves. Where the performers marched down main street and were greeted with cheers and awe's as they performed their magic. The PGA had the same effect here. A golf 'Major' had

Championship Events held in St. Louis		
1904	Olympic Golf Matches	Glen Echo
1905	Trans-Miss (Men)	Glen Echo
1908	Western Open	Normandie
1913	Trans-Miss (Men)	Glen Echo
1919	Trans-Miss (Men)	St. Louis
1921	US Men's Amateur	St. Louis
1925	US Women's Amateur	St. Louis
1926	Trans-Miss (Men)	Algonquin
1929	US Men's Publinks	Forest Park
1931	Trans-Miss (Ladies)	St. Louis
1937	Western Open	Westwood
1940	Trans-Miss (Ladies)	Glen Echo
1941	Trans-Miss (Men)	Sunset
1946	Western Open	Sunset
1947	US Open	St. Louis
1948	PGA Championship	Norwood Hills
1952	Western Open	Westwood
1953	Western Open	Bellerive
1954	LPGA St. Louis Open	Glen Echo
1955	LPGA St. Louis Open	Norwood Hills
1960	US Men's Amateur	St. Louis
1962	Trans-Miss (Men)	Old Warson
1964	LPGA Squirt Open	Glen Echo
1965	US Open	Bellerive
1965	LPGA St. Louis Open	Norwood Hills
1966	LPGA Clayton S&L Inv.	Norwood Hills
1967	LPGA St. Louis Inv.	Norwood Hills
1968	LPGA Holiday Inn	Norwood Hills
1969	LPGA St. Louis Inv.	Norwood Hills
1970	LPGA Johnny Londoff	Glen Echo
1971	Ryder Cup	Old Warson
1972	PGA St. Louis Open	Norwood Hills
1972	US Women's Amateur	St. Louis
1973	PGA St. Louis Open	Norwood Hills
1981	US Mid-Amateur	Bellerive
1988	PGA Junior	Bellerive
1992	PGA Championship	Bellerive
1994	LPGA Heartland Classic	Forest Hills
1994	Nike Gateway Classic	Lake Forest
1994	Tommy Armour Tour	Fox Run
1995	LPGA Heartland Classic	Forest Hills
1995	Nike Gateway Classic	Lake Forest
1995	Senior Global Series	CC at Legends
1996	US Women's Publinks	Spencer Olin
1996	Women's Western	Fox Run
1996	Nike Gateway Classic	Lake Forest
1996	LPGA Heartland Classic	Forest Hills
1996	Boone Valley Classic	Boone Valley

been missing from St. Louis since the 1965 US Open, and the crowds came out ready to party and enjoy the moment. The practice rounds were filled with overflowing crowds, reminiscent of the Masters. The corporate tents, both on and off the ground, were packed to capacity. The souvenir tents ran out of some items early in the week, such was the tenacity with which St. Louisans took to the event. John Daly was the newly crowned 1991 winner at Crooked Stick and he thrilled the crowds with his awesome drives. Even Jack Nicklaus paid him tribute at the "winners exhibition" where everyone from Gene Sarazen, Byron Nelson, Hubert Green and others were greeted with enthusiasm as their shotmaking skills were demonstrated. (Remember Hubert Green hooking his wedge 30 yards?)

When the tournament started on Thursday, it was almost anti-climatic, so much was the anticipation. Fortunately everything went off as planned. Mother nature cooperated and instead of the 100+ heat everyone expected, the mercury seldom rose near 80. The skies remained clear and a mild breeze kept everyone comfortable. The course was in perfect condition and the play reflected the difficulty that only a Bellerive can display. Putts of 100 feet were common, long iron and wood approaches to par 4's were the norm and the par 5's offered little respite as the deep rough placed more emphasis on accuracy than length, ala US Open territory. It has been a magical PGA season; Couples winning at the Masters, Nick Faldo captured his third British Open and forever put to rest the old "Foldo" lines from the British tabloids, and Tom Kite finally rid himself of the demon with his come-from-behind victory in the winds at Pebble Beach.

Perhaps the player coming into with something to prove was Nick Price. He had withdrawn a year earlier when his wife was expecting, but his caddie, "Squeaky" Medlen had stayed and caddied for Daly, the last entrant into the tournament. "Squeaky" was now back with Price and he was on a roll. 1991 had been a great year for Nick, he had won two tournaments, was listening to Leadbetter's advice longer than anyone, and it appeared to be paying off. He opened with two straight 70's and was only 4 shots off after 36 going into Saturday. He had not won a Major and had only two runner-up finishes to his credit, both at the British Open, and both times he had been shot down, the first time by Watson and the latter by Seve. But the good news for Nick was that they weren't at Bellerive on Saturday.

Tour "grinders" Gene Sauers, Jeff Maggert and Russ Cochran led for most of the first three rounds. Maggert look like a "could-be-winner" when he was up by 2 with 8 to play. But we all know that this is uncharted territory for the non-winner and anything that can happen, usually will. Cochran also challenged briefly, then fell away. Sauers had one of the final rounds that we used to expect only from players like Gene Sauers, at least until the 1996 Masters when Greg Norman shot the unthinkable and lost the Green jacket.

Price won the tournament with some excellent putting and a some saving sand shots that enabled him to shoot 68 on Saturday and then a 1-under 71 on Sunday to walk away with the Wanamaker Trophy by 3 shots. Squeaky was a back-to-back winner and Price had his first major. He would win two more in the next two years, the PGA again in 1994 and the British Open the same year to establish himself as the latest successor to Nicklaus, at least temporarily. Bellerive (and Robert Trent Jones) had been much maligned by the national media all week, no character, too long, greens too big, etc. But in the end, a true Champion won. After all, that's why they play the tournaments, isn't it?

USGA Events

Of all the USGA events held in the Greater St. Louis Area the most notable must be the US Opens. St. Louis CC hosted the 1947 US Open and Bellerive the 1965 US Open. They both were significant in the history of the Open.

The *1947 Open* featured Sam Snead once again striving to capture an Open title. Having fallen short 10 years earlier to Ralph Guldahl, Snead was once again a favorite. Hogan was present, but was not much of a factor and few thought that Lew Worsham would be a contender. Little did Snead realize that this would be the 2nd of 4 times he would fall short in the Open. Little comfort to Sam that it ties him with Jack, Arnie and Bobby Jones as all having finished 2nd four times; except that they all won the Open during their careers.

The Open in '47 also is notable for the lowest round ever by an amateur in an Open, a 65 by James McHale in the third round. This was later tied in 1971 at Merion GC by Jim Simons. It was noted that the rough was very deep and that the fairways were as *"narrow as church aisles"* during the week. The all-bent course at St. Louis was 6484 yards, not nearly long enough for today's players. But in 1947 it defended itself well, the winning total was only 2 under for both Snead and Worsham before Worsham shot 69 to Snead's 70 in the playoff.

A classic case of gamesmanship occurred

during the playoff when Snead was about to putt for his par at the 18th when Worsham called for a ruling as to who was away. A bit shaken by the delay, Snead missed his 30 1/2" putt and as Worsham rolled his 29 1/2" into the cup he took the Open.

The *1965 US Open* at Bellerive was the first of the courses that featured not just heavy rough, but Zoysia fairways and a course over 7,000 yards. In 1965, playing at 7,191 yards, it was by far the longest US Open course to date. It was only surpassed in 1990 by Medinah when it was set up to play at 7,195 yards. The winning total of 280 (+2) by Gary Player as he defeated Kel Nagle of Australia was the beginning of a golf mania in St. Louis. It seemed as though we all knew someone who was there, or who caddied for somebody. Yes, young men from the area caddied during the event for the pros! The USGA had a rule that did not allow tour caddies during the US Open, so Bellerive sent out a call to courses around the area for caddies to fill out their ranks. Player used a local high school student, Frank Pagel, as his caddie all week. In a display of gener- osity he not only tipped him generously, but Player donated most of his winnings to the Cancer fund.

Players' win also is remarkable in that it allowed him to conclude the modern career grand slam. He had won the British Open in 1959, the Masters in 1961 and the PGA in 1962. By winning the '65 Open, he became only the fourth man in history to have won the Career Grand Slam, the others being Gene Sarazen, Ben Hogan and Jack Nicklaus.

In 1965, Bellerive was only 5 years old. The large trees that line the course today were barely above saplings. At first look it appeared ripe for conquest. But being the first Open played on Zoysia, the pro's were mystified by the lack of roll and the thick rough that twisted the club if they ventured off the fairway. Though Jones had re-designed Oakland Hills where the open has been played in 1962 and earlier in 1951, this was the first true Jones design that had been contested for an Open.

Other USGA events that have been held in the area were the *1921 US Amateur* and the *1960 Amateur*, both at St. Louis CC. Along with the *1925* and the *1972 US Women's Amateur*.

The *1921 Men's Amateur* at St. Louis CC was significant in the Amateur history for several reasons. It would mark another of the early events in Bobby Jones' career that he would not win, but which he felt laid the foundation for his later triumphs by teaching him how to win. This would also mark the last of 4 times that Robert A. Gardner would be in the Championship match, having won it in 1909 and 1915. His win in 1909 is the youngest by a player, as he was 19 years and 5 months old. He was also the father of Robert W. Gardner, who almost 40 years later, would also lose the US Amateur title in 1960 to Deane Beman, ironically over the same St. Louis CC layout.

This event was so significant in Jones' career that in his book *"Down the Fairway"* he devotes a full chapter to it. The 19-year old felt that he had enough "experience" under his belt and that the time had come for him to win his first national crown. Legendary Francis Ouimet led all qualifiers as medalist as Jones finished 7 back at 151. His first match was against St. Louisan Clarence Wolff, who suffered the same as many of Jones' foes, falling 12 and 11 (all matches were played at 36 holes at that time). Jones won his second match 9 and 8 and he looked to the third match against former British Champion Willie Hunter. Jones could easily outdrive Hunter, but the Brit stayed close all day and Jones was only 2-up at the break. In the final 18 holes that afternoon, he came to the 8th, the Cape Hole, a dogleg right with a short pitch to the green. Trees blocked the corner and Jones had carried them all week with ease. But today he bit off more than he should have, and his shot nicked the top and fell into the ditch on the right. This marked the beginning of the turn of events for both players. Shaken by the loss, Jones putted poorly and on the 35th hole the match ended. At 19 Jones was only on the verge of

The Championships

what would become the greatest amateur career ever.

During the semifinals, the rains began to fall and this put Hunter at a great disadvantage as he battled Gardner who was a much longer player. The soft ground and pressure of the battle with Jones finally took its toll on Hunter as he fell 6 and 5. Meanwhile Jesse Guilford, known as the Great Excavator, moved into the finals over the rain-soaked course. Jones called the string of holes played by Guilford one of the best he had ever viewed. From the sixth through the ninth Big Jess went 3-2-3-4 to tame par (4-3-4-5) and virtually finished Gardner before falling on the thirteenth 7 and 6.

Champion Jesse Guilford had the unfortunate pleasure of competing all of his career against Bobby Jones. Though he was on the inaugural Walker Cup with Jones in 1922, he would never again contend for a major championship.

St. Louisans in the field for match play included Clarence Wolff, Jimmy Manion, Eddie Held, Dick Bockenkamp and Roger Lord.

In the *1925 Women's Amateur*, Glenna Collett, the Nancy Lopez-Dottie Pepper-Annika Sorenstam of the day, soundly defeated another of the Atlanta East Lake wiz-kids Alexa Stirling 9&8. Alexa competed against Bobby Jones at the East Lake club in casual matches and it is said that she may have been better against the women of the day than Bobby Jones was against the men. Alexa won three consecutive championships and finished runner-up in three more. However in running up against Glenna Collett, she found a champions champion. Glenna, who is the

Carl Kaufmann driving in the 1929 US Publinks at Forest Park. He would win 3 titles in the 1920's

USGA's all-time Women's leader, with 6 titles including three consecutive, was in the final 8 times and was medalist in 6 of those. She also knew how to win, and how to take defeat. In 1928 she defeated a very talented Virginia Van Wie 13&12. 4 years later in 1932, she was on the short end, losing to Ms. Van Wie 10&8.

The only St. Louisan to reach match play was Audrey Faust Wallace. She would shoot an 82 over her home course [low qualifying was only a 77 by Alexa Sterling] as only three scores were better than hers. Audrey would unfortunately lose her opening match in 20 holes to Virginia Wilson of the Onwentsia Club.

In the *1972 Women's Amateur*, Mary Budke defeated Cynthia Hill 5&4. For Budke, this was only her second attempt at the Amateur. In her first attempt in 1971, at age 17, she lost in the second round of match play. Cynthia Hill had been runner up previously, in the 1970 finals, where she lost to Mrs. Martha Kirouac. Ironically, Miss Budke, a native of Dundee, Oregon, barely made the qualifying round. Her score of 160 (79-81) was in the bottom third of the scores, and placed her in the lower bracket with defending champion Laura Baugh. She would defeat Lancy Smith 1-up in her first match and then score a 3&2 win over Phyllis Preuss, a veteran of 5 Curtis Cup teams, in her second round match. Meanwhile, Miss Baugh would fall to Barbara Boodie in their third round match, so after Budke disposed of Mary Bea Porter 1-up in 19 holes, (Porter hit two bunker shots out of bounds on holes, (Porter hit two bunker shots out of bounds on the extra hole) all that stood between her and the finals was Boodie. Mrs. Boodie had been playing well, winning all her matches by a 6&5 outcome. She was 1-up on the 18th hole when she called a penalty on herself as her ball moved as she addressed it in the rough. The match now tied, and on the 19th hole her bogie allowed Budke's par to advance her to the finals.

In the morning finals Budke shot a 75 for a 1-up lead and went 2-up with birdie on #2 and 3-up on the 8th with a birdie. At the twelfth, Ms. Hill had to crawl under a fir tree to play her shot and lost that hole. The match was closed out on the 14th. In the 32 holes of the final match, Budke was only three over par as she claimed the title. St. Louisans advancing to match play included Paula Eger from Greenbriar Hills CC.

In 1960 St. Louis CC hosted the *US Amateur* once again and PGA Tour commissioner-to-be Deane Beman defeated Robert W. Gardner 6&4. Beman was one of the finest amateurs of the day, winning two titles and being in the finals three times. He was the ninth player in history to win both the US and British Amateurs, having won the British in 1959. It was his unfortunate fate to be competing against Jack Nicklaus during most of his career (though the same could be said for many others). But the 1960 championship was only his first in the Amateur. He would repeat in 1963 as he defeated Richard Sikes at the Wakonda Club in Des Moines.

In 1960, Nicklaus was the defending champion, and most expected him to win once more. But he lost in the fourth round to first-timer Charles Lewis of Little Rock, Arkansas, 5&3. Beman defeated John

43RD ANNUAL

Western Open Golf Championship

MAY 24, 25, 26, 1946
Sunset Country Club
ST. LOUIS, MO.

ST. LOUIS DISTRICT GOLF ASSOCIATION
WESTERN GOLF ASSOCIATION
PROFESSIONAL GOLF ASSOCIATION

Farquhar of Amarillo, Texas in the semi's as Gardner downed Lewis. In the finals, Beman got out early and stayed in front. He was 3-up after the morning round and finally closed out the match on the 32nd hole. For the week, Beman was an estimated seven under par for his play.

There were a record 1,737 entries for the amateur that year and 200 qualifiers. St. Louisans in the qualifying rounds included Joe Switzer, Jim Tom Blair, Steve Spray (who would lose to Gardner in the quarterfinals 1down), Gene Fehlig, Clarence Norsworthy, Jim Jackson and Hugh Burchfiel.

The *Mid-Amateur* is one of the newest USGA events. Reserved for players 25 and over, mostly to exclude the recent College grads who want another feather before joining the tour. This was established to give the real amateur another National competitive event. As noted in the *"Champions"* section, the *1981 US Mid-Amateur* was held at Bellerive CC and won by Jim Holtgrieve.

Jim won his opening match 5&4 then a 3&1 triumph over Tom Evans in the 2nd round. Randy Nichols was his next victim, this time by a 6&5 margin. Three more matches and the trophy would be his. He topped Kent Frandsen 4&3 and then in the Semifinals downed Robert Housen, who had just knocked-off Jay Sigel, 4&3 again. He would face-off with Robert Lewis Jr. in the finals for the Robert T. Jones Jr. Trophy. Lewis was a fierce competitor who seldom made mistakes. Jim would have to play his best to win. Both started strong with birdies to keep the match even through 8, when Jim bogeyed to go 1-down, while being at even par for the round. On the 13th Jim two putted while Bob three-putted from the same distance. Then on the 15th they both hit poor shots and bogeys halved the hole. On 16 Jim made a great two putt from 50 feet while Lewis three-putts again. Going into 18 1-up all Jim needed was a halve for the win. Lewis made his par, forcing Jim to step up to the plate. Jim rolled his birdie putt, a little hard he thought, but it caught the right edge of the hole and dived in for a 2-up win. Jim had his National Title and we had a new local champ.

St. Louisans in the field included Bob Mason, Roger Null and Bill Bahn. Bob would win his first round match before falling 3&2 in the second round while Roger would be upset 3&1 in his opening match as would Bill Bahn by a 5&3 total.

Forest Park was host to the First *US Publinks* played West of the Mississippi, when the *1929 US Publinks* was held there. The Forest Park Golf Association was the driving force behind bringing the tournament to town, but it needed the support of the St. Louis District to make it a success and in 1928, Forest Park was an Associate member of the District. The Pavilion in the Park had recently been completed and the course was generally considered to be among the best in the area. From pictures that have survived, you can see trees lining the entire left side of the 2nd hole, the tough 200 yard par 3. Other holes were equally as difficult as there was water on each of the first 4 holes as well as on the final 3 holes. The course would provide enough challenges for all.

Scheduled for the first week of August, the summer heat in town affected many of the contestants as they made their way around the 6,000 yard layout. *Carl Kauffmann* survived the heat, course and all competitors and won the championship, defeating Milton Soncrant 4&3. Locals in the qualifying round included Michael Friedlein who fell

3&1, Togo Hamamoto who won his first match, Jerry Stanford who lost 3&1, and Dr. I.R. Davis who won 3&1 before falling 1-down in 19 holes.

Heather Graff from the University of Arizona captured the *1996 US Women's Publinks Championship* at Spencer T. Olin over Kentucky Wildcat Lauri Berles 5&4 on a hot and muggy Sunday in June. Graff had just come off helping her Arizona team wins the NCAA Championship in May. As the Number 2 player on the Arizona team she finished 6th overall in the individual competition. Her triumph in the Publinks was her first national individual title.

Spencer Olin was an excellent venue for the championship, having been voted the top public course in the area for the past 7 years. For many of the contestants, this marks the final chapter on their amateur careers - many of them will use this as a stepping stone to the LPGA tour - while others see this an opportunity to see how they stack up against some of the best Women amateurs in the country.

Tour Events

The PGA regular tour has not had a regular stop in St. Louis for many years. But regular stops ceased in the early 70's. Beginning in 1994, we saw the beginning of a remarkable stretch of golf as four tours came to St. Louis. The Nike Tour came and tested Lake Forest, the Tommy Armour Tour went to Fox Run, the LPGA found a new home at Forest Hills in the Heartland Classic and the Senior PGA Tour found the Boone Valley Classic to be another very good stop on their million-dollar parade.

Several events have been held here over the years. They include The Western Open which was held at a variety of courses in the area over the years. In its early days, the Western Open was a very democratic open; that is to say it was held in a great many Western states. Beginning in Illinois, it has been played in Ohio, Wisconsin, Michigan, Missouri, Tennessee, Indiana, Texas, Arizona, New York, Minnesota, Oregon, California and Pennsylvania.

For years it was held at the Butler National GC in Oakbrook, IL, but in 1991, the tournament moved to Cog Hill #4 (Dubsdread), located on the southern edge of Chicago, a public facility run by the well-known Joe Jemsek. Consisting of 4 courses, the #4 course is one of the best courses in Chicago (if not the country), in an area filled with great courses. The Western Open came to St. Louis in 1908 when Willie Anderson shot a 299 at Normandie, pocketed $200 of the $500 purse and moved on. Then in 1938 Ralph Guldahl, coming off two consecutive victories in the 1937 Western Open and the 1937 Masters, won his third in a row at Westwood CC. Lloyd Mangrum, one of the best Pro's of the day with over 36 career victories including the 1946 US Open, would battle

Guldahl over the 6,785 yard layout. Guldahl would win by three shots this time, but Mangrum would return to win two Western titles in the early 50's.

Nine years later, in one of the first post-war tournaments of 1946, Ben Hogan won the *Western Open* at Sunset CC, shooting a 271 and winning over perhaps the greatest putter of all time, Bobby Locke, and winning $2,000. Westwood would again host the Western Open in 1952 as Lloyd Mangrum, the 1946 US Open champion, would battle with Ed Furgol and would shoot a 14-under 274 to capture the championship. A year later the *1953 Western Open* would be held at the Original Bellerive in Normandy (today the site of University of Missouri at St. Louis), where local Pro Dutch Harrison would battle Fred Haas, Lloyd Mangrum and Ted Kroll for the title. Dutch would shoot a 6-under 278 and hold on to win as even the Old Bellerive would prove a tough test at over 7,300 years. This would be the last time the Western would be held in the area. It would be another 12 years before men's championship professional golf would return, the 1965 US Open.

Players on the range at Norwood warming up for the
1955 St. Louis Open.
They are from left: Betsy Rawls, Betty Hicks, Peggy Kirk,
Mickey Wright, Joyce Hiske.

The Championships

Opens were the first stop on the fall/winter Pro Tour. Tommy Armour (1930) Jimmy Manion (1931) Walter Hagen (1932) Ralph Guldahl (1933) would claim titles before the event unexpectedly ceased as a stop in 1934.

The Tour would return to St. Louis in 1972, with much help from the members and head Pro at Norwood Hills, Dick Shaiper. They would host the *St. Louis Children's Hospital Open* in 1972 and 1973. The incomparable Lee Trevino, who stormed onto the Tour in 1967 and promptly won the US Open in 1968 and again in 1971, would also capture the first event. A year later in 1973, veteran Gene Littler would take the title. This was quite a win for "The Machine", so known for his smooth tempo, as he had undergone cancer surgery in the spring of 1972 but managed to return to the tour that fall. The 1973 win at Norwood allowed him to not only complete his comeback, but also win the Bob Jones and Ben Hogan awards for '73, signifying his remarkable return.

LPGA

St. Louis was a semi-regular stop of the fledging LPGA tour for a few years during the 1950's, 60's and 70's—events were held, but not necessarily each year, nor at the same site.

The first event was in 1954 when Glen Echo hosted a Ladies event called the *St. Louis Open* (as noted earlier, many events used this name through the years) and was held the week following labor day. During this season the events were quite scattered; the previous one in Chicago had been five weeks earlier. At Glen Echo, the event was sponsored by the Eastern Missouri PGA with proceeds to benefit polio research. Betsy Rawls shot a 211 over 54 holes (which was 17 under par) to claim the title and the $750 first prize as Jeannie Dobbin captured the Amateur crown with her fine play. Reno Hahn, sportswriter for the Globe-Democrat, wrote *"Betsy Rawls 12 shot victory carried her so far from the field, that they might as well have been playing two tournaments!"* In 1955 Norwood opened their doors and the St. Louis Open featured a little higher purse (up $800 to $4,300) as Louise Suggs shot a 4-under 289 on the 72 hole event to out distance Mary Lena Faulk, former Amateur Champion. Quincy native Nan Berry claimed the Amateur crown. The Ladies returned to Norwood in 1956 and this time Fay Crocker shot 288 to win.

The LPGA would return in 1964, and this time around they would have a seven year run. The 1964 event, named the *Squirt Ladies' Open*, was the sixth event of the season, and was held at Glen Echo. Held May 8-10, Louise Suggs, Mickey Wright, Marilyn Smith, Betsy Rawls, Kathy Whitworth and Patty Berg arrived to test Glen Echo, and challenge for the $12,500 prize. Mickey Wright, who had won twice previously in 1964, came through the tournament as the eventual winner with Kathy Whitworth finishing second. Wright would win a total of nine times during 1964, remarkable, but four less than she won in 1963 when she went to the winners circle thirteen times! The 1963 tour could have been renamed the Wright-Whitworth tour as between them they won twenty of the thirty-three events.

The *1965 St. Louis Open* moved to Norwood, and also moved dates, this time to mid-August. Mary Mills would claim the title with Marlene Hagge getting the bridesmaid spot. In 1966 the event had a new sponsor, *Clayton Federal Invitational,* but would remain at Norwood as Kathy Whitworth edged Shirley Englehorn for the crown. The St. Louis Women's Invitational was the 1967 title and Kathy Whitworth shot a 209 over Norwood to repeat as champion, as Carol Mann settled for second. The proceeds for both the 1964 and the 1967 event were to benefit the Monsignor Behrmann School for boys and the tournament chairman both years was none other than the popular north-side car dealer, Johnny Londoff. The *1968 Holiday Inn Classic* was a three-peat for Kathy Whitworth as she shot a 1-under 206 to edge Carol Mann and Judy Kimball. *The St. Louis Women's Invitational* returned in May 1969, and the prize money jumped to $16,000 as Sandra Haynie put a halt to Whitworth' streak as she shot 5-under and forced Whitworth and Peggy Wilson to settle for second. The final event of this run was in 1970 and this time the tournament title sponsor was the long-time chairman Johnny Londoff. The *Johnny Londoff Chevrolet Tournament* moved to Glen Echo for the finale and with the purse upped to $22,000 Shirley Englehorn shot even par to force Carol Mann to settle for second for the third time in the event.

The LPGA would not return for 24 years, not until 1994 when Forest Hills hosted the inaugural *GHP Heartland Classic*, a 72 hole event with a $500,000 purse. Though this was the last regular event of the season, many of the Tour's stars were present as they honed their game for upcoming events such as the Solheim Cup and to solidify their money standing for the year. Liselotte Neumann came out firing, shooting a 10-under 278 and captured the inaugural event, as Elaine Crosby and Pearl Sinn finished second.

The 1995 version of the Heartland Classic would provide less drama; but not less activity. Annika Sorenstam began shooting birdies the first round and midway through the event the question was not so much who, but by how large a margin, she would win. Annika did become the eventual winner as she dominated the field by as much of 11 strokes much of the tournament before winning by 10 shots, despite shooting an even par 72 on the final day. Her 10-shot win would be the largest on tour for the year.

The recently completed *1996 Michelob Light Heartland Classic* which could have been termed the Swedish Open following the first two years winners,

Tony Jacklin (left) and Lee Trevino share a light-hearted moment during the 1971 Ryder Cup at Old Warson

took an unexpected turn as LPGA veteran Vicki Fergon shot a course record 63 on Friday and held a 10 shot lead going into the weekend. She continued her find play on Saturday and tough it had shrunk as others played well, she won by a total of 6 shots.

Ryder Cup

The *1971 Ryder Cup* was contested at Old Warson CC, before it became THE RYDER CUP. The Robert Trent Jones course proved an excellent host for the event, which was won easily by the home squad 181/2 to 131/2. This was, of course, prior to the European team days. Only the English-Scottish-Irish players played in these early Ryder Cups. The US team consisted of Billy Casper, Miller Barber, Arnold Palmer, Gardner Dickinson, Jack Nicklaus, Mason Rudolph, Gene Littler, Dave Stockton, Charles Coody, Lee Trevino, J.C. Snead, and Frank Beard. The British Team consisted of Neil Coles, Christy O'Connor, Peter Townsend, Peter Oosterhuis, Brian Huggett, Tony Jacklin, Maurice Bembridge, Peter Butler, Brian Barnes, John Garner, Harry Bannerman and Bernard Gallacher.

The first day's morning foursomes saw the British take a 3-1 lead as Casper-Barber, Nicklaus-Stockton and Coody-Beard all lost. Only the team of Palmer and Dickinson won. The afternoon foursome matches were won by the US 21/2 - 11/2. The second day saw a swift reversal as the US swept the morning fourballs 4-0 and the afternoon fourballs were won 21/2 to 11/2. This put the US up 10-6 after the third day. Going into the singles matches the

final day the pairings were Trevino-Jacklin, Gallacher-Stockton, Barnes-Rudolph, Oosterhuis-Littler, Nicklaus-Townsend, Dickinson-O'Connor, Bannerman-Palmer and Coles-Beard. The morning matches saw Trevino, Nicklaus and Dickinson winning while Palmer, Beard and Stockton halved. This gave the US a 141/2 to 91/2 lead going into the afternoon matches. The afternoon matches were Trevino-Huggett, Snead-Jacklin, Barnes-Barber, Stockton-Townsend, Gallacher-Coody, Nicklaus-Coles, Oosterhuis-Palmer and Bannerman-Dickinson. With the trophy outcome determined, the matches were tied at 4-4 for each, with Trevino, Snead, Stockton and Nicklaus winning.

The final outcome, 181/2 to 131/2 was decisive. Yet this is one of the reasons that eventually led Nicklaus to suggest that it should be a

Morning Foursome on Day 1 of the matches; Maurice Bembridge, Charles Coody, Frank Beard, Peter Butler

European Team, not just a British team. His suggestion would be enacted and the 1979 matches would be played between the US and Europe. It was most likely a very good decision, one that not only popularized the event tremendously, but may have saved it. From 1927 at the inception to 1979, the US had won 19 lost 3 and tied 1. Since 1979, the matches have been much more competitive. The US won in 1979, '81, 83, '91 and '93 while playing to a draw in '89, which allowed the European team to retain the Cup. The European team has won the Cup outright in '85, '87, and '95, the last two being victories on US courses.

Senior Tour

The Senior PGA Tour made its debut at Boone Valley CC as the *Boone Valley Classic* in September 1996. The P.B. Dye design is set amid a beautiful valley in the Missouri wine country near Augusta, has part of the course cut through thick woods and granite/limestone layers that provide not only great views but also await the errant shot.

The *1996 Boone Valley Classic* on the Senior PGA Tour was one of the highlights of the year. At first many doubted that a venue so distant could successfully host a Tour event. But when the 2nd of September rolled-around, the crowds were large and enthusiastic and the course was in magnificent condition. Many of the top names chose not to compete, but enough of the regulars, plus the local draw of Irwin, Wargo, Ziegler, Conner, Hall and Spray, kept fan interest keen. Boone Valley had played very tough at recent US Open qualifying rounds, and most thought it would give the pro's all they could handle.

US Ryder Cup Team (Top)
Seated (l-r); Gene Littler, Jack Nicklaus, Billy Casper, Arnold Palmer, Lee Trevino, Gardner Dickinson
Back: Mason Rudolph, Dave Stockton, J.C. Snead, Jay Hebert (Captain), Charles Coody, Miller Barber, Frank Beard.

Great Britain Team (Below)
Seated (l-r); John Garner, Christy O'Connor Sr., Neil Coles, Tony Jacklin, Bernard Gallacher, Maurice Bembridge. Back;Brian Huggett,Peter Butler, Brian Barnes, Eric Brown (Captain), Peter Oosterhuis, Harry Bannerman, Peter Townsend

The Championships

The opening rounds followed the Pro-Am, where Irwin shot a team total 9-under and set the tone for the weekend. The opening round of the 54 hole classic on Friday saw the pro's take the course under-their-wings and show it why they are professionals as a course record 65 was set by Vicente Fernandez, with a large portion of the field under par. Saturday brought more drama as Hale Irwin responded with another course record as he carded an 8-under 63, that would vault him in 2nd place, two strokes behind Bunky Henry as Sunday began. Frank Conner and Tom Wargo were each at 137, six strokes back and in position to make a charge, while others lurking nearby were Gibby Gilbert, Isao Aoki, Gary Player, Jim Dent, Jim Colbert, Tom Shaw, Vicente Fernandez and Bob Murphy. There were several highlights; among them a rare double eagle on the 6th hole by Kermit Zarley, the only other one on tour in 1996 was by Jack Nicklaus at the Tradition.

Sunday awoke with all anticipating an Irwin victory. He had won virtually everything else on tour during '96 and there was no indication that this would change. But as we know, golf is a cruel partner. Just as the putts fell on Saturday, they eased past on Sunday. So while he was able to maintain his lead going into 18, he had not slammed the door. Gibby Gilbert birdied the final hole, tying Hale and forcing a playoff. As they began to replay 18 for the final time, the 13,000 plus crowd huddled around the green, expecting Hale to pull off the dramatic win. Instead a mis-hit approach shot sailed off-line to the right and found the lake. As Gibby rolled in his par, Hale was the first to congratulate the 55 year old Tennessee native. Champions are still Champions!

Frank Conner would finish tied for 4th and Tom Wargo would be another stroke back. Larry Ziegler and Steve Spray would finish 13 back of the winner and Bill Hall would not play his best and shoot a 227. Tony Jacklin would provide a thrilling moment for the crowd as he eagled the 18th on Sunday as he holed his approach shot over the water.

Several St. Louisans have had their sites set on a Senior Tour event for years. In the mid-80's Edward Whitacre from Southwestern Bell led a group that had the Seniors all but signed to a contract with Old Warson. But tour guidelines on membership, among other factors, led the membership to vote down the event and instead it moved to Kansas City's Loch Lloyd CC in Belton, MO for the 1987 season.

Other courses, when announcing their anticipated construction, laid claim to efforts to lure a Tour event to St. Louis, in particular the Senior Tour. The CC at the Legends, St. Albans, Fox Run and the Missouri Bluffs all stated their desire to pursue such events. With the success of the Boone Valley Classic, it is doubtful that any additional courses could host another event, especially given the already bulging Senior schedule. Perhaps a rotating event is in the offing? Or maybe a regular Tour event? Whichever direction awaits us, we have begun to be recognized, once again, as a terrific stop on anyone's tour!

Nike Gateway Classic

Held at Lake Forest during the July heat in St. Louis, the Nike has been contested over the 7,150 yard par 72 layout that features creeks, woods, water, sand and undulating greens. With a purse of $200,000 and a first prize of $36,000, most of the Nike Tour's leaders have been present.

In 1994 Brad Fabel, former Tour player, successfully challenged Lake Forest in the inaugural *Nike Gateway Classic* and took home the winners check shooting a 2-under 280 as Chris Perry and Jim Carter finished second.

1995 brought a new group of hopefuls to Lake Forest to claim the top prize, and with it, gain another step toward a possible berth to the PGA Tour. But rain forced the cancellation of Thursday's round and a 54 hole tournament was planned. Though rain came and went over the weekend, Chris Smith shot a course record 65 on Saturday, topping a 66 fired the day before by Mike Sposa. Smith and Glen Hnatiuk battled all day and the third round ended with them tied at 203 (-13). Smith birdied the first extra hole to claim the title. Area Pro's were plentiful on the opening round, but only John Hayes and Jerry Tucker made the cut to play on Sunday.

Smith fit the pattern of what the NIKE player is today...former Tour Player, still wanting to compete, hoping to play on the Senior Tour...Chris was a 45 year-old Floridian who played on the PGA Tour in the 1980's and had two seconds, earning almost 1 million dollars on Tour since 1980.

Our favorite Blues Hockey Player, Brett Hull was honorary Chairman and played in the Nike in 1996, though not as well as he is capable and he missed the cut.

The Nike Tour made a switch for the 1997 season, moving to the *Missouri Bluffs*.

Global Senior Series

Competed for over the Robert Trent Jones-designed CC at the Legends in 1995, this event is part of the **Senior Series**, featuring Senior Tour competitors who are challenging for a spot on the Regular Senior Tour. Former Glen Echo pro Bill Hall fired a course record 64 to capture the 1995 title, and pocketed $15,000 of the $100,000 purse. While this event only had a one year contract, future events may find themselves back in the area, as more Seniors vie for a spot on the Senior Tour.

The Series continued during 1996, though it did not return to St. Louis. Unfortunately some apparent mis-management of funds was to prove the downfall

of these events as the promoter withdrew his support and it appears that 1996 will have been the final season.

Women's Western Golf Association

The purpose of the WWGA is to promote Amateur golf for Women. Today it has grown from the 33 initial clubs to over 500 members. They sponsor three national championships, offering competition to the best amateur players from the US and abroad. Area members are; Forest Hills, Fox Run, Glen Echo, Greenbriar, Norwood Hills, Sunset Hills, Old Warson and Westborough. You must belong to a member club to be eligible for the championships.

Women's Western Amateur

Fox Run hosted the **Women's Western Golf Association Amateur Championship** during the end of June 1996. The finals saw Mary Burkhardt Shields from Birmingham, AL, and Diane Irvin of Los Angeles face off over the tough layout in the hot and muggy heat typical of the area. Battling the fatigue and pressure of winning one of the National Women's Amateur events was draining on both ladies. When Shields rolling a 2-foot par putt on the 38th hole of the day to win the sudden-death playoff, both ladies had a sense of relief.

Shields has been on a roll of sorts, finishing

Women's Western Amateur's played in St. Louis			
Year	Winner	Runner-Up	Site
1908	Mrs. W. France Anderson	Grace Semple	St. Louis CC
1922	Mrs. David Gaut	Mrs. Curtis Sohl	Glen Echo CC
1996	Mary Burkhardt Shields	Diane Irvin	Fox Run CC

Women's Western Open played in St. Louis			
Year	Winner	Runner-Up	Site
1939	Helen Detwiller	Beatrice Barrett	Westwood CC

The Championships

Play during the 1922 Womens Western at Glen Echo CC

2nd in the US Mid-Amateur and the Doherty Cup and being medalist in the North-South at Pinehurst. Irvin, a 31-year old from the exclusive Los Angeles CC, had perhaps her worst day in the final 18 holes. Her medal score would have been an 83, hardly good enough to win, but the heat got to both players as the match was level for much of the final as both players stumbled and let the other back-in. After par's on the 37th hole, Irvin was bunkered on the 38th and could only manage a bogey as Shields two-putted from 10 feet to capture the title.

Local players such as Jo D Blosch lost their bid for the championship, but continued to compete in the lower flights, which amounted to consolation events. Blosch finally lost the first flight to Mizzou sophomore Letitia Moses 4 and 2.

The Western, which began holding tournaments for Women in 1901 at the Onwentsia Club in Chicago, was also held in St. Louis in 1908 at St. Louis CC and in 1922 at Glen Echo CC. Ms. Audrey Faust and Ms. Virginia Pepp, two of the areas outstanding players and both District Champions, contended for the title against the likes of Mrs. Melvin Jones of Chicago, the defending champion in the 1922 event. But neither would advance far.

The only St. Louisan who has made the finals of the Western was Grace Semple in 1908. The tournament is not without it's great champions, as the list of member clubs crosses the country. Former champions include Patty Berg, Nancy Lopez, JoAnne Gunderson Carner, Anne Quast Sander, Catherine Lacoste, Beth Daniel, Kathy Baker and Amy Benz. Kansas Citian Opal Hill is the only winner from the state as she captured the title three times in the 30's.

Ellen Port is a playing Director of the Western, and has competed for several years, reaching the quarterfinals on one occasion.

Women's Western Open

The *Women's Western Open* was inaugurated by Mrs. Paul Walker in 1930 and continued until 1967. Originally to give professional women golfers and amateurs an opportunity to compete in a Western Championship it was considered a major championship in women's professional golf until it was discontinued in 1967. As a result, the very best women players in the country competed and won this honor. A pin was awarded to the champion for one year and they received a silver cup for their year of reign. The winners include; Babe Zaharias, Mickey Wright, Patty Berg, Betsy Rawls, Kathy Whitworth, Louise Suggs, Opal Hill and Betty Jamison.

Tommy Armour Tour / Lou Fusz St. Louis Open

Held just a single year at Fox Run in 1994, the

Tommy Armour Tour has seen some winners that, at the time, seemed like no-names, but shortly proved themselves very capable.

One of these was Michael Campbell, the native New Zealander, who finished third in the 1995 British Open, after leading for two days. Few could forget his remarkable shot from the Road Hole bunker, at a seemingly impossible angle, and somehow leaving it only three feet away for his easy par. Campbell would win this event, the only time it was held in the area, and use it as a springboard for greater achievements.

Trans-Miss Championship

From the early 1900's till the present, the **Trans-Miss** championship for men and women was one of the "Major" amateur events of the season. Traditionally intended to counter the many "eastern" and "southern" events, only states between the eastern bank of the Mississippi and the Rockies were eligible, including states on the eastern bank. So how did Ohioan Jack Nicklaus win the event twice? Some rules change as time goes by, and this one did as well.

While many St. Louisans have ventured to play at sites throughout the country, it has been held in St. Louis only a few times. The first match here was

held at Glen Echo in 1905 where *Warren Dickinson* grabbed the crown. *Stuart Stickney* won the title in 1913, again at Glen Echo, defeating Ralph Rider. In 1919 at St. Louis CC, *Nelson Whitney* of New Orleans defeated *Richard Bockenkamp* of Sunset in a 40-hole match. Algonquin hosted the 1926 event where *Eddie Held* took top honors. Fifteen years later, in 1941, at Sunset CC, *Frank Stranahan* finished on top as he defeated John Barnum 6 & 5 in the finals. Sranahan was one of the top amateurs of his day. He finished as the low amateur in the Masters and US Open several times and 2nd in the US Amateur in 1950. He did win the 1948 and 1950 British Amateur and won the Tom O'Shanter 6 times. He was on the Walker Cup in 1947, 1949 and 1951. He turned pro in 1954 and won a few events.

The last event here was in 1962 at Old Warson when *Bob Ryan* defeated Harry Toscano. *Jimmy Jackson* was the first back-to-back winner of the Trans-Miss, having accomplished this in 1954-55. In the early 20's *Eddie Held*, *Jimmy Manion* and *Clarence Wolff* won the title for St. Louis in four consecutive years from 1923-26. Manion also finished 2nd in 1930. *Dick Bockenkamp* had the unfortunate luck of losing twice in the finals, first in 1919 in 40 holes, and lastly to Eddie Held in

Trans-Miss Championships involving St. Louis Players in the finals or played at St. Louis Clubs

	Winner	*Runner-Up*
1905	Warren Dickinson *Glen Echo*	Walter Fairbanks
1913	*Stuart Stickney* *Glen Echo*	Ralph Rider
1919	Nelson Whitney *St. Louis CC*	*Richard Bockenkamp*
1920	Robert McKee	*Clarence L. Wolff*
1923	*Eddie Held*	*Richard Bockenkamp*
1924	*Jimmy Manion*	Lawson Watts
1925	*Clarence Wolff*	Arthur M. Bartlett
1926	*Eddie Held* *Algonquin*	John Dawson
1928	Arthur M. Bartlett	*Bryan O. Winter*
1930	Robert MCCrary	*Jimmy Manion*
1931	Opal Hill *St. Louis CC*	Mrs. I.S. Hynes
1940	Betty Jameson *Glen Echo CC*	
1941	Frank Stranahan *Sunset CC*	John Barnum
1954	*Jimmy Jackson*	
1955	*Jimmy Jackson*	
1962	Bob Ryan *Old Warson CC*	Harry Toscano
1990	*Bobby Godwin*	
1994	*Ellen Port*	Shannon Hare

Note: St. Louis Players & Clubs are in italics.

The Championships

1923, 5 and 3. Clarence Wolff of Sunset also finished 2nd once in 1920, losing 3 and 2.

The Trans-Miss dates back to St. Joseph CC where, on August 11, 1900, they hosted the Omaha CC in a friendly challenge match. The event went over so well that soon fifteen clubs formed the Trans-Miss competition. Throughout the long history there have been many distinguished champions; Jack Nicklaus in 1958 and 1959, Deane Beman, Ben Crenshaw, Mark Brooks and Bob Tway have all worn the crown.

The Ladies portion grew out of the old Tri-State Golf Association which in 1924 became the Missouri Valley Golf Association. Then in 1926, as they were preparing for their championship in Omaha, a proposal was made to change the name to the Women's Trans Mississippi Golf Association. When the men's group agreed enthusiastically, the new group became a reality. The Trans has grown from the original Missouri-Kansas-Oklahoma area to 22 states as part of the organization.

Today the event is often referred to as the Trans-National, more in keeping with its national and international flavor than the Trans-Miss name, but the event is the same.

Ellen Port is the only lady to have won the title, claiming hers at the 1994 Trans-Miss over the Del Rio (Modesto, CA) CC course as she defeated Shannon Hare.

This was her first National title and marked the first time she had advanced beyond the quarterfinals in a major tournament. Winning it gave her the momentum to advance to the next level in her play and the results have been borne out during the last two years!

With the best amateur players throughout the country entered, the competition was very strong. Glenna Collett, Helen Hicks and Alexa Stirling, along with Barbara McIntire and Judy Bell are just a few of the ladies who thwarted the St. Louisians who entered. The Tans-Miss, along with the Western, offered some of the strongest fields of the day.

Virginia Pepp, *Audrey Faust Wallace*, *Marcella Rose*, *Betty Jane Haermerle*, *Marilyn Herpel*, *Doris Phillips*, *Jeannine Lewis* and of course, *Ellen Port* are just some of the ladies who have competed in the Trans.

Miscellaneous Titles

St. Louis has hosted other national events - those either not generally open to all players, or belonging to a fairly select group. One such title, held in 1940, was the **National Left-Handed Championship** at Norwood Hills.

Benny Richter had won this event the first two years it was held (1934 & 1935), but in 1940 Alvin Everett would win the title, as he would do two other times.

Future Events

While the following events are scheduled to be held there may be any number of factors which will preclude them from occurring as planned. The contracts for the US Mid-Amateur at Old Warson have been signed and it should be an exciting event. The US Publinks at Spencer T. is awaiting final signatures at press time, and an announcement should be forthcoming (if not already made prior to publication).

| 1999 | Old Warson | US Mid-Amateur |
| 1999 | Spencer T. Olin | US Men's Publinks |

It has been suggested that Bellerive will continue to pursue another Major event and that a PGA Tour event is also being pursued. With the LPGA having agreed to a three-year agreement with Michelob to keep their Classic at Forest Hills, the Senior Tour returning to Boone Valley (with a new TV contract and purse as well) and the Missouri Bluffs transplanting the Nike Tour event from Lake Forest, it would appear that major professional golf will be in the St. Louis area for several years to come.

"I saw a course you'd love Trent, you tee your ball on the first tee and declare it an unplayable lie."

...**Jimmy Demaret speaking to Robert Trent Jones**

St. Louis District Golf Association Championship

The SLDGA championship has had some of the areas premier players hold this title. For years this was the areas main amateur event. Other amateur events were held occasionally, but they never withstood the test of time.

Since 1916, the District, as it is usually called, has crowned some of the areas best players as its champion. Winning this is akin to the State Amateur, and some of the best players have not been able to capture the District as the stiff competition along with the heat and humidity wear-down only the most talented and well-conditioned. The fact that only Bob Cochran, Jim Holtgrieve and Jerry Haas have been able to win the event three consecutive years is testament to this. There have been eight back-to-back champions (Cochran did this in addition to his three-in-a-row) and another three players who have won the medal two or more times.

Bob Beckmann

From 1919 to 1929 Clarence Wolff, Jimmy Manion and Dick Bockenkamp won the title a total of ten times in this eleven year span. The triumvirate of Cochran, Jackson and Blair dominated the event during the late 50's to early 70's with one of them claiming the crown eight times in the 14 year span. During 1972 to 1989 Jim Holtgrieve, the Haas brothers, Jay and Jerry, along with fellow St. Clair CC member Mark Boyajian won the crown thirteen out of eighteen years. Today the competition gets tougher each year with only one repeat winner since 1988.

The 1996 matches were indicative of the new blood entering the competition. Two first-timers met in the finals, a day late because of heavy rain on Sunday, with University of Missouri player Dustin Ashby taking the championship. This is also unique since Dustin is not a member of a District Club and competed under new participation rules. An unusual event occurred during one of Bob Cochran's wins in the 30's. Father Eddie Donahoo, a very good player who qualified for three US Publinks, met Bob in the finals of the District. The Finals were scheduled for Sunday morning. Legend has it (at least I've been told this by another priest) that Cardinal Glennon got word to Father Eddie that he should be in church on Sunday and not on the golf course! Whether this affected his play or not is not known as Bob trounced him 8&7.

The winners with their club affiliation are;

1916	Roger Lord	Algonquin
1917	Christian Kenney	Glen Echo
1918	Stuart Stickney	St. Louis
1919	Clarence L. Wolff	Sunset
1920	Dick Bockenkamp	Midland Valley
1921	Dick Bockenkamp	Midland Valley
1922	Clarence L. Wolff	Sunset
1923	Jimmy Manion	Midland Valley
1924	Eddie Held	Algonquin
1925	Jimmy Manion	Riverview
1926	Clarence L. Wolff	Sunset

St. Louis Championships

1927	Jimmy Manion	Riverview
1928	Jimmy Manion	Riverview
1929	Clarence L. Wolff	Sunset
1930	Elliott Whitbread	Osage
1931	Bryan Winter	North Hills
1932	Bryan Winter	North Hills

Ken Highlander

1933	Bob Cochran	North Hills
1934	Bob Cochran	North Hills
1935	Tom Draper, Jr.	Sunset
1936	Elliott Whitbread	Sunset
1937	Eddie Held	Algonquin
1938	Chester O'Brien	Westborough
1939	Jonas Weiss	Meadow Brook
1940	Mark Schlude	Crystal Lake
1941	Bob Cochran	Norwood Hills
1942-45	No Tournament	
1946	Bob Cochran	Norwood Hills
1947	Bob Cochran	Norwood Hills
1948	Bob Cochran	Norwood Hills
1949	Ken Heilman	Greenbriar
1950	Jack Geiss	Norwood Hills
1951	Jonas Weiss	Meadow Brook
1952	Vince D'Antoni	Greenbriar
1953	Don Guariglia	Normandie
1954	Les Slattery, Jr.	Sunset
1955	Bob Goalby	St. Clair
1956	Jack Geiss	Norwood Hills
1957	Mel Wilke	Greenbriar

1958	Jim Tom Blair	Old Warson
1959	Rich Kohlman	Normandie
1960	Gene Fehlig	Westborough
1961	Bob Cochran	Norwood Hills
1962	Ken Lanning	Normandie
1963	Jim Jackson	Greenbriar
1964	Gene Fehlig	Westborough
1965*	Bob Cochran	Meadowbrook
1966*	Jim Jackson	Greenbriar
1967*	Newell Baker	Algonquin
1968*	Virgil Bernsen	Greenbriar
1969	Jim Tom Blair	Old Warson
1970	Jim Tom Blair	Old Warson
1971	Jim Jackson	Greenbriar
1972	Jay Haas	St. Clair
1973	Jay Haas	St. Clair
1974	John Johnson	Norwood Hills CC
1975	Jay Haas	St. Clair
1976	Jim Mason	Greenbriar
1977	Jim Holtgrieve	Westborough
1978	Jim Holtgrieve	Westborough
1979	Jim Holtgrieve	Westborough
1980	Jay Delsing	Norwood Hills
1981	Mark Boyajian	St. Clair
1982	Jeff Johnson	Norwood Hills
1983	Jerry Haas	St. Clair
1984	Jerry Haas	St. Clair
1985	Jerry Haas	St. Clair
1986	Mark Boyajian	St. Clair
1987	Mark Boyajian	St. Clair
1988	Ken Highlander	Sunset Hills
1989	Jim Holtgrieve	Westborough
1990	Sam Scheibal	Sunset Hills
1991	Richard Jarrett	Lockhaven
1992	Ed Schwent	Bogey Hills
1993	Scott Thomas	Norwood Hills
1994	Bob Beckmann	Norwood Hills
1995	Bob Beckmann	Norwood Hills
1996	Dustin Ashby	

- Denotes years competed at Medal play

St. Louis Women's District Golf Association

Founded in 1915, the Women have operated a separate championship from the Men since 1920. Many outstanding champions have worn the District crown, in particular Marilyn Herpel Conroy, Betty Jane Haemerle Broz, Peggy Hartenbach, Helen Dettweiler, Jeannine Dobbin Lewis, Dorothy Campbell and Judy Torluemke Rankin. More recently the champions have been Barbara Berkmeyer, Marcella Rose, Lynette Chrenka, Doris Phillips, Mary Gail Dalton, Jill Bertram and Barbara Beuckman.

In the early days Betty Jean Haemerle was the dominant player among district Women. Though oft challenged she bested most comers and was the premier player for years. Marilyn Herpel was one such foe, and she was quite a competitor. She began competing against the ladies in 1938, at age 8, and carrying only 4 clubs! The daughter of area pro Homer Herpel, Marilyn was Junior Champion and quickly rose to District Champion by 1945 at the ripe old age of 15. She set the Women's course record at Westwood in 1955 by firing a 73.

Another young player in the 50's was another 8 year old, Judy Torluemke. Judy won the District Junior in 1958 and 1959 but never the District Ladies crown, though she would claim two state crowns (1959 and 1961) before turning pro in 1962.

From the mid-60's through the present, there have been many multiple winners, but the ladies from Norwood have dominated. Barbara Berkmeyer, with 7 championships, and Barbara Beuckman with 5, Doris Phillips with three and Jill Bertram with two clearly show why the north-side layout is the club of champions. Add to the list Mary Gail Dalton from Westwood and Ellen Conant from St. Louis each with three, Lynette Chrenka with two representing Greenbriar, Jeannine Dobbin Lewis with four out of Normandie and Lockhaven, and Kathy Severson, Audrey Kopolow Hitch, Maria Palozola with two each and you have the core of the top ladies over the

Sara Louise Guth
Three time District Champion
(1934, 1935, 1936) and
1938 State Amateur Winner

past 35 years.

Barbara Berkmeyer, with those seven wins, is still the player to beat. While a shoulder injury kept her out of competition for awhile, it appears the problem has gone as 1996 saw her win the Metro and District titles within a two week. *"When Barb is on her game, she is awfully hard to beat"* was the phrase most spoken as she accepted the winners cup at Algonquin for the '96 title.

Conspicuous by her absence among District Winners is Ellen Port. During the 90's no area lady linkster has had a more brilliant career. But to accomplish this she has had to make choices about which tournaments in which to compete. To accomplish her goals to date meant concentrating more on

St. Louis Championships

national events than local competitions. Beginning with the 1997 campaigns, Ellen may begin to reduce her travel schedule, so her presence at local events should change, much to the dismay of local players as their chances of winning just dropped a bit.

1920	Mrs. E. Lansing Ray	St. Louis
1921	Mrs. Lynn Wasson	Glen Echo
1922	Virginia Pepp	Triple A
1923	Virginia Pepp	Triple A
1924	Audrey Faust	St. Louis
1925	Virginia Pepp	Triple A
1926	Virginia Pepp	Triple A
1927	Audrey Faust Wallace	St. Louis
1928	Mrs. Mahlon Wallace	St. Louis
1929	Mrs. I.S. Hynes	Normandie
1930	Virginia Pepp	Midland Valley
1931	Mrs. Mahlon Wallace	St. Louis
1932	Mrs. Mahlon Wallace	St. Louis
1933	Mrs. R.J. Kohn	Norwood Hills
1934	Sara Louise Guth	Algonquin
1935	Sara Louise Guth	Algonquin
1936	Sara Louise Guth	Algonquin
1937	Mrs. R.I. Caughey	Triple A
1938	Mrs. R.I. Caughey	Triple A
1939	Georgia Dexheimer	Normandie
1940	Mrs. R.I. Caughey	Greenbriar
1941	Mrs. Thomas Findley	
1942	Betty Jane Haemerle	Norwood Hills
1943-45	No Tournament	
1946	Betty Jane Haemerle	Glen Echo
1947	Betty Jane Haemerle	Glen Echo
1948	Betty Jane Haemerle	Glen Echo
1949	Betty Jane Broz	Glen Echo
1950	Jeanne Dobbin	Normandie
1951	Jeanne Dobbin	Normandie
1952	Susie Driscoll	Glen Echo
1953	Jeanne Dobbin	Norwood Hills
1954	Marilyn Herpel	Algonquin
1955	Marilyn Herpel Conroy	Algonquin
1956	Susie Driscoll	Glen Echo
1957	Ellen Conant	St. Louis
1958	Ellen Conant	St. Louis
1959	Ellen Conant	St. Louis
1960	Marcella Rose	Crystal Lake
1961	Barbara Beuckman	St. Clair
1962	Marcella Rose	Crystal Lake
1963	Doris Phillips	Norwood Hills
1964	Doris Phillips	Norwood Hills
1965	Doris Phillips	Norwood Hills
1966	Mary Gail Dalton	Westwood
1967	Barbara Berkmeyer	Norwood Hills
1968	Barbara Berkmeyer	Norwood Hills
1969	Mary Gail Dalton	Westwood
1970	Doris Phillips	Norwood Hills
1971	Barbara Berkmeyer	Norwood Hills
1972	Kathy Severson	Cherry Hills
1973	Audrey Kopolow	Meadowbrook
1974	Kathy Severson	Cherry Hills
1975	Mary Gail Dalton	Westwood
1976	Barbara Berkmeyer	Norwood Hills
1977	Lynette Chrenka	Glen Echo
1978	Barbara Berkmeyer	Norwood Hills
1979	Barbara Beuckman	Norwood Hills
1980	Audrey Kopolow Hitch	Meadowbrook
1981	Barbara Beuckman	Norwood Hills
1982	Barbara Beuckman	Norwood Hills
1983	Lynette Chrenka	Greenbriar
1984	Barbara Beuckman	Norwood Hills
1985	Jeannine Dobbin Lewis	Lockhaven
1986	Jill Bertram	Norwood Hills
1987	Jill Bertram	Norwood Hills
1988	Lindsey Murfin	Bogey Hills
1989	Marci Butler	Cherry Hills
1990	Lisa Minnihan	Bogey Hills
1991	Lee Vandiver	Sunset Hills
1992	Maria Palozola	Forest Hills
1993	Maria Palozola	Forest Hills
1994	Barbara Berkmeyer	Norwood Hills
1995	Barbara Anderson	Sunset Hills
1996	Barbara Berkmeyer	Norwood Hills

St. Louis Ladies City Golf Championship

Records on this event are sketchy. The ladies below won the event in the years listed, but other records cannot be found. With the rise in the importance of the District, perhaps this tournament was abandoned in favor of that event.

1902	Queen Rumsey
1903	Grace Semple
1920	Virginia Pepp
1921	Mrs. R.J. Kohn
1922	Virginia Pepp
1923	Virginia Pepp

St. Louis District Golf Association Senior's Championship

This initial seniors event began in 1929. It was sponsored by the District Golf Association and had, as its chairman, Bonner Miller, who was also secretary of the Missouri state golf association.

	Winner	Club
1929	E.H. Hatfield	
1930	C.E. Hope	
1931	Dr. C.W. Burrows	
1932	Al Stracke	Triple A
1933	Al Stracke	Triple A
1934	Thomas Clabaugh	
1935	Edward Grubb	Norwood
1936	Edward Grubb	Norwood
1937	Christian Kenney	Normandie
1938	Christian Kenney	Normandie
1939	Dr. I.R. Davis	Forest Park
1940	Christian Kenney	Normandie
1941	Dr. J.S. Homan	Triple A

St. Louis District Golf Association Senior Men's Championship

This recent event was formed by the District in 1991. The St. Louis Seniors' Golf Association, an organization separate from the District, has done such a terrific job of organization that seniors are clamoring to get in, but there is almost a five year wait. As a result, the District is offering this as an option to those over 55 to compete, while they wait to join the St. Louis Seniors' Group! Not strictly an "Open" event, the District polls member clubs for their top 6-10 Senior Players. From that list the invitations are sent and the field is formed. The event is held late in the season, in early October, and has been competed for over some terrific courses.

	Site	Winner
1991	Westwood	Dave Grossman
1992	Meadowbrook	Alex Nowicki
1993	Westborough	Jack Powers
1994	Sunset	Jack Powers
1995	Bellerive	Don Dupske
1996	Glen Echo	Jack Powers

St. Louis Senior Men's Championship

The St. Louis Seniors' Golf Association was formed in December 1954 for the purpose of "encouraging Fellowship and friendly competition in golf among senior players and to hold golf tournaments in which the members with a current established handicap may participate." Today the group awards trophies for the low Gross (noted below), the Low Net, the Buddy Warren team trophy, and the Sol Geller, L.I. Baker Memorial, Mervin Clark, George R. Krieger and Monte Lopata Trophies for various accomplishments. Comprised of members of the "core" fifteen private clubs (Algonquin, Bellerive, Forest Hills, Glen Echo, Greenbriar, Lockhaven,

St. Louis Championships

Meadowbrook, Norwood, St. Albans, St. Clair, St. Louis, Sunset, Sunset Hills, Westborough, Westwood) the organization's ranks are filled and membership is open only following a lengthy wait. Often confused with the District Seniors, the two groups are separate, although many are members of both groups.

Everett Hullverson Trophy - Low Gross -

1954	Les Slattery	Normandie
1955	Elliott Whitbread	Sunset
1956	Frank English	Algonquin
1957	Dave Mitchell	Norwood
1958	Hugh Hauck	Greenbriar
1959	John Dulaney	Norwood
1960	Bob Richardson	Normandie
1961	Joe Switzer	Old Warson
1962	Sly Schmidt	Sunset
1963	Bob Cochran	Meadowbrook
1964	E.D. Imboden	Normandie
1965	Bob Cochran	Meadowbrook
1966	E.D. Imboden	Normandie
1967	Bob Cochran	Norwood Hills
1968	Theodore Weiskotten	Normandie
1969	E.D. Imboden	Normandie
1970	E.D. Imboden	Normandie
1971	E.D. Imboden	Normandie
1972	Bob Cochran	Norwood Hills
	Charles Fawcett	Forest Hills
	Joe Switzer	Old Warson
1973	F. A. Pilliod	Westborough
1974	Bob Cochran	Norwood Hills
1974	Rev. Clarence White	Norwood Hills
1976	Jim Benson	Normandie
1977	Monte Lopata	Westwood
1978	Bob Cochran	Norwood Hills
1979	Wes Clark	Algonquin
1980	Bob Cochran	Norwood Hills
1981	Gene Fehlig	Westborough
1982	Bob Cochran	Norwood Hills
1983	George Frank	Norwood Hills
1984	Bob Nieberding	Glen Echo
1985	Bob Nieberding	Glen Echo

1986	Bob Croak	Algonquin
1987	Bob Wolak	Forest Hills
1988	Monte Lopata	Westwood
1989	Roy Daegele	Cherry Hills
1990	Herman Schwartz	Norwood Hills
1991	Russ Smith	Norwood Hills
1992	Russ Smith	Norwood Hills
1993	Rain Out	
1994	Jack Powers	Glen Echo
1995	Herman Schwartz	Norwood Hills
1996	Ray McCraine	Forest Hills

St. Louis Women's District Senior Championship

1985	Betty Von Rump	Westborough
1986	Audrey Hatlan	Cherry Hills
1987	Betty Von Rump	Westborough
1988	Alice Sampson	Greenbriar
1989	Mary Gail Dalton	Westwood
1990	Mary Gail Dalton	Westwood
1991	Mary Gail Dalton	Westwood
1992	Mary Gail Dalton	Westwood
1993	Mary Gail Dalton	Westwood
1994	Alice Sampson	Greenbriar
1995	Julie Holthaus	Bellerive
1996	Barbara Beuckman	Norwood Hills

St. Louis Women's District Junior Girls Championship

1936	Adele Baur	Glen Echo
1937	Mary Rosalie Sheridan	Forest Park
1938	Dorothy Jane Campbell	Norwood Hills
1939	Dorothy Jane Campbell	Norwood Hills
1940	Betty Jane Haemerle	Norwood Hills
1941	Dorothy Jane Campbell	Norwood Hills
1942-45	No Tournaments	
1946	Marilyn Herpel	Indian Meadows
1947	Marilyn Herpel	Indian Meadows
1948	Marilyn Herpel	Indian Meadows
1949	Susie Driscoll	Glen Echo

1950	Susie Driscoll	Glen Echo
1951	Susie Driscoll	Glen Echo
1952	Jacqueline Herpel	Indian Meadows
1953	Jacqueline Herpel	Algonquin
1954	Joan Greenberg	Meadowbrook
1955	Barbara Beuckman	St. Clair
1956	Kathleen Fawcett	Norwood Hills
1957	Barbara Beuckman	St. Clair
1958	Judy Torluemke	Triple A
1959	Judy Torluemke	Triple A
1960	Nancy Fawcett	Norwood Hills
1961	Nancy Fawcett	Norwood Hills
1962	Barbara Bubany	Algonquin
1963	Paula Smith	
1964	Paula Smith	
1965	Susie Sertl	Sunset
1966	Paula Eger	Greenbriar
1967	Paula Eger	Greenbriar
1968	Paula Eger	Greenbriar
1969	Paula Eger	Greenbriar
1970	Paula Eger	Greenbriar
1971	Cindy Barnard	Greenbriar
1972	Cindy Barnard	Greenbriar
1973	Allyn Frank	Greenbriar
1974	Linda McCabe	Norwood Hills
1975	Gail Kiplinger	Algonquin
1976	Susan Fromuth	Forest Hills
1977	Barbara Anderson	Sunset Hills
1978	Marcia McKinley	St. Clair
1979	Barbara Anderson	Sunset Hills
1980	Susan Fromuth	Forest Hills
1981	Jill Bertram	Normandie
1982	Jill Bertram	Normandie
1983	Cece Voigt	St. Clair
1984	Cece Voigt	St. Clair
1985	Cece Voigt	St. Clair
1986	Sara Hepler	Sunset Hills
1987	Lee Vandiver	Sunset Hills
1988	Robin Buck	Sunset Hills
1989	Robin Buck	Sunset Hills
1990	Lisa Wening	Norwood Hills
1991	Libby Mooney	Algonquin
1992	Libby Mooney	Algonquin
1993	Stacia Miles	Forest Hills
1995	Lizzie Uthoff	Norwood Hills
1996	Lizzie Uthoff	Norwood Hills

St. Louis District Junior Golf Championship

Begun in 1922 this honor went to the outstanding Junior Boys in the District competition. The event did include players from the public courses, at least through the 1930's, though their number was predetermined, usually at 10. The Champions include the following;

1922	William Medart
1923	E.K. Ludington
1924	Ben Goodwin
1930	E.J. (Mike) Roach
1931	Bob Cochran
1932	Joseph Switzer
1933	Frank Bredall
1934	Tom Draper
1935	Louis Fehlig
1936	Jonas Weiss
1937	Jonas Weiss
1938	Louis Wasson
1939	Gene Fehlig
1940	Jim Jackson
1941	Dan Biederman
1942	Jack Penberthy
1946	Clarence Norsworthy, Jr.
1951	Don Dupske
1954	Don Dupske
1966	Don Bliss
1983	Pol Montano
1985	Tom Wright

St. Louis Championships

St. Louis Publinx

The history of the Publinx goes back to 1959. The USGA had accepted an invitation to play the Public Links Amateur in Hawaii in July 1960. Mr. Milton Frank, who was the USGA Committeeman for the Public Links in this area, got together with Art Jennemann and several other public players to form the St. Louis Public Links Golf Association. The object was to develop a tournament to raise funds to help defray the expenses for players who qualified to represent St. Louis in Hawaii. Milton Frank continued to be the director until 1970 when it was turned over to Bart Collida, the new area committeeman.

The first Publinks Open was played on the first Sunday in May, 1960, and has continued to be played on that date since (except for the occasional rain-delay). The date usually marks the kickoff the season in the area, so golfers are primed and the turnout is high. The late Jimmy Jackson was the first back-to-back amateur champion, winning in 1962 & 63. In 1967, Jackson and Shaiper were tied with 70's. Jackson won the playoff after having been saved from the water on #1 & #2 by trees, before making birdie-two on the par 3 third. Beginning in 1974 ties were accepted and the playoffs ceased.

In the 1962 matches, Jackson was playing with Milon Marusic, Joe Switzer and Spinny Gould. As they were playing #15, at that time it was a straight-away par 4 about 255 yards downhill. The green sat about where the firs have been planted today at the end of the fairway. A good drive could put you on the

Bart Collida, "Mr. Publinx" for over 25 years (right) with St. Louis District Golf Association Secretary Larry Etzkorn. They devote hundreds of hours each year to promote amateur golf throughout the area.

green putting for an eagle! Jim hit a 4 wood and the ball flew straight and true toward the green; but he immediately noticed something else—his clubhead had shattered and was never found. He had an eagle putt (which he missed) but made an easy birdie 3. He went on to finish 3 under and win the medal.

Spinny Gould, an early financial supporter of the Publinx, was president of the Reliable Life Insurance Company. In those the early days entries were hard to come by, so Spinny had all of his employees come and play. The scores of some of the participants in the 1960 opening event reflected their good work-ethic; a 109 and a 117 were turned in that day along with 12 scores in the 90's! But that first event had it all. Johnny Manion was one of the starters, a Yale graduate came away as winner for the amateurs, a club-pro from Edwardsville claimed the pro title and 160 golfers all *"beat it 'round the park"*.

Some of the players who have played in this event are; Rich Poe, Phil Hewitt, Jim Bensen, Bob Nieberding, Joe Switzer, Dick Craden, Bob Riley, Tony Henschel, Paul McGuire, Frank Furlong, Curly Fryman, Walter Ambo, Vince Greene, Dave Douglas, Jim Barton, Milt Frank, Jim Jackson, Alan Schmidt, Dick Shaiper, Fred Wampler, Earl Parham, Pepper Moore, Booker Ford, Fleming Cody, Jim Tom Blair, Don Clarkson, Dutch Harrison, Milon Marusic and Frank Keller.

The early sixties were a great time at the Publinx. Not only were the best amateurs in the field, but the best area pro's competed for the top spot. Marusic, Shaiper, Jim Cochran, Terry Houser, Gene Webb, Dave Douglas, Eddie Johnson, Rich Craden and Cal Tanner were among the pro's who regularly participated. But the key word in the title is Publinx, and the top public players, with a sprinkling of club players, sought to put their names in the record book. Jim Jackson, the legendary Greenbriar tactician, won the event five times from the 60's to the early-80's, while Don Dupske won three times over a twenty year span, and Bill Moretti did the three-peat over seven years while Frank Furlong, long-time amateur and father of Dave Furlong, Pro at Ballwin was also a winner.

Dick Shaiper, Milon Marusic and Fred Wampler were perhaps the best of the early Pro's during the 60's as they each won twice. They were followed by Terry Houser who won twice in the 70's with five more times in the 80's. Cal Tanner and Wayne Morris also had their due, as did the steady Marusic who came back and won in 1978. During the 90's, Bob Gaus would have to be the pro to beat as he has won or shared the title four times. He won the title in 1983 as an amateur, making him the only player to accomplish that feat. Two amateur medals have been won by industry-reps, Dennis Osborne (Hogan) and Jerry Waitulavich (Ping). The first woman to compete was Ellen Port and in 1994 Jo D Blosch competed. We even have a former Billiken basketball player, Glen Mankowski, who won the 1964 event.

Today Bart Collida has little trouble filling the field, in fact he has had to turn many away, such is the demand from area golfers to play and support the Publinx effort. Results from 1960-1996 are;

Year	Amateur	Professional
1960	Roger Hemker	Howard Popham
1961	Ken Kreikemeier	Milon Marusic
1962	Jim Jackson	Fred Wampler
1963	Jim Jackson	Fred Wampler
1964	Glen Mankowski	Dave Douglas
1965	Pete Jones	Curly Fryman
1966	Jim Johnson	Jim Cochran
		Cal Tanner
1967	Jim Jackson	Dick Shaiper
1968	Don Dupske	Dick Shaiper
1969	Buddy Godwin	Bill Jones
		Milon Marusic
1970	Frank Furlong	Eddie Johnson
1971	Don Dupske	Rich Craden
1972	Bob Reynolds	Mike Delhougne
1973	Bill Matthews	Wayne Morris
1974	Gary Strickfaden	Rich Craden,
		Cal Tanner
		Bob Jones
1975	Jim Holtgrieve	Terry Houser
	Spencer Sappington	Cal Tanner
	Bill Moretti	Ed Griffith
1976	Jim Jackson	Wayne Morris
1977	Gary Strickfaden	Charles Dale
1978	Earl Burns	Milon Marusic
1979	Terry Tessary	Carey Austin
	Spencer Sappington	
1980	Dennis Osborne	Wayne Morris
1981	Bill Moretti	Terry Houser
1982	Mike Smith	Terry Houser
	Jim Jackson	
1983	Bob Gaus	None
1984	Mike Smith	Terry Houser
1985	Bill Bair	Earl Parham
	Richard Pruett	
1986	Barry Brown	Terry Houser
1987	Rain Out	
1988	Don Dupske	Terry Houser
	John Michaelis	
1989	Craig Hardcastle	Bret Burroughs
1990	Mike Fromuth	Bob Gaus
1991	Jerry Waitulavich	Tom Barry
		Dan Grenier
1992	Terry Tessary	Rich Fisher
	David Lucks	John Hayes
	Bo Smith	
	Bob Meeh	
1993	David Lucks	Bob Gaus
	Don Bliss	John Hayes
1994	Bill Bahn	Bob Gaus
		Bret Burroughs
1995	Mike Hartman	Bob Gaus
	Jim Dunn	
1996	Dan Donohoo	Earl Parham

Brian Fogt
1986 Bogey Hills Inv. Winner

Bogey Hills Invitational

In the early 80's golfers from all over the country descended on St. Charles to compete for the *"Mini-Masters"* held at *Bogey Hills CC*. In its time, this was the richest purse offered on a non-tour event; $40,000 to the winner out of a $300,000 purse. Held in late June, players who would later become household names would compete over the tough layout with demanding greens. The likes of Lee Janzen, Jay Delsing, Marco Dawson, Trevor Dodds, Jerry Heard, Greg Kraft and John Daly among others.

Beginning in 1972, the BHI was the closest thing St. Louis had to a legitimate pro tournament. It had high-quality golf with names that were becoming familiar as they used the BHI as a comeback vehicle. The 1978 event featured a 40-year old veteran Mike Hill shooting a 205 and downing Jay Haas by a stroke, despite Jay's brilliant 66 in the 2nd round.

The tournament ceased in 1993 following the cancellation of a round due to rain. When players voiced their very vocal displeasure at this situation, the tournament hosts decided enough was enough, and the tournament forever ceased. The winners have been the following;

	Professional	**Amateur**
1972	Cal Tanner	Bob Cochran
1973	Gene Gilliatte	Jim Jackson
1974	Vince Bizik	Jim Jackson
1975	Al Chandler	Bruce Hollowell
1976	Jay Haas	Terry Martin
1977	Al Chandler	Jim Holtgrieve
1978	Mike Hill	Buddy Godwin
1979	Jack Ferenz	Jim Jackson
1980	Tom Popa	Jim Holtgrieve
1981	William Lewis	Spencer Sappington
1982	Steve Spray	Craig Schnurbusch
1983	No Tournament	
1984	Tom Wargo	Spencer Sappington
1985	Richard Clark	
1986	Brian Fogt	
1987	Tray Tyner	
1988	Bob Estes	
1989	Steve Haskins	
1990	Marco Dawson	
1991	Tray Tyner	
1992	Clark Dennis	
1993	John Stacy	

Area players who have competed, and made the cut at Bogey include Jerry Tucker, Larry Emery, Tom Barry, Dale Boggs, Terry Houser, John Hayes, Jay Delsing and Jay Williamson.

Other competitors who have won Major events on the PGA or Senior PGA Tour include Lee Janzen (US Open), Hal Sutton, Payne Stewart, John Daly and Bob Tway (PGA Championships), and of course Tom Wargo (PGA Seniors)

The Course record for Bogey Hills was set during one of the events as Steve Lowry posted a record 61!

Mary Gail Dalton
1990 Ladies Winner of the
Tournament of Champions

Gateway Masters

Begun in 1994 as a "scaled-down" version of the Bogey Hills Invitational, this event is more local in scope than its predecessor. The Gateway Masters features more local pro's as well as amateurs, as they compete over the demanding Bogey Hills layout. The following are the winners in the Open, the Senior division and among the amateurs.

1994	Brian Fogt	Al Chandler (Sr)
		Don Bliss (A)
1995	Bob Gaus	Al Chandler (Sr)
		Scott Thomas (A)
1996	Bret Burroughs	Bob Jones (Sr.)
		Craig Schnurbusch (A)

Champion of Champions

This event, sponsored by the Triple A course, has been held in Forest Park or a few other area courses on occasion since 1941. Herbert B. Simon endowed the event and a perpetual trophy to this event, held in the early fall, is in his honor. Won many times by the likes of Jim Jackson and Bob Cochran (with Jim winning the event 12 times to Bob's 10), the event brings together club champions

from all area courses for a "champions tournament".

Since 1989, thanks to the efforts of Jim Offer, head pro at Triple A, both male and female golfers vie for the trophy. Other winners have included Howard Zacharitz, Jim Black, Jim Benson, Clarence Norsworthy Jr., Newell Baker, Dr. C.P. Leydecker and Ed "Brick" Imboden. Always one of the premier season-ending events, the winner here takes home one of the most treasured prizes.

Men

1941	Jim Black
1942	Bob Cochran
1943	Bob Cochran
1944	Jim Bensen
1945	Dr. C.P. Leydecker
1946	Howard Zacharitz
1947	Jim Jackson
1948	Jim Benson
1949	Bob Cochran
1950	Bob Cochran
1951	Bob Cochran
1952	Jim Jackson
1953	Bob Cochran
1954	Jim Jackson

Mark Naes - 1990 Winner
Tournament of Champions

St. Louis Championships

1955	Jim Jackson	
1956	E.D. Imboden	
1957	Clarence Norsworthy Jr.	
1958	Bob Cochran	
1959	Jim Jackson	
1960	E.D. Imboden	
1961	Bob Cochran	
1962	E.D. Imboden	
1963	Jack Berkley	
1964	Bob Cochran	
1965	Newell Baker	
1966	Jim Jackson	
1967	Bob Cochran	
1968	Earl Stamer	
1969	Clarence Norsworthy Jr.	
1970	Clarence Norsworthy Jr.	
1971	Jim Jackson	
1972	Jim Jackson	
1973	Jim Jackson	
1974	Mike Pendergast	
1975	Jim Jackson	
1976	Spencer Sappington	
1977	Jim Jackson	
1978	Chuck Bailey	
1979	Spencer Sappington	
1980	Spencer Sappington	
1981	Jim Jackson	
1982	Mike Smith	
1983	Karl Elbrecht	
1984	Craig Hardcastle	
1985	Don Bliss	
1986	Mike Smith	
1987-88	No Tournament	

	Men	_Ladies_
1989	Jim Jason	Di Di Derrick
1990	Mark Naes	Mary Gail Dalton
1991	Tom Moore	Alice Sampson
1992	Don Dupske	Mary Ann Beattie
1993	No Tournament	
1994	No record	
1995	Craig Hardcastle	Marcella Rose
1996	Tim Begley	Marcella Rose

The St. Louis Championships

There have been many Championships with this title, both men's and women's, though none have sustained through the years. At times different organizations sponsored an event, so determining continuity is almost impossible. They were called the City title, the Muny title or the St. Louis Open. Sometimes they were different events, but not always. While the District crown was open only to select public players [Jimmy Manion being one of these before he joined a club], the various City titles were competed-for by all.

One series was held in the pre and post-World War I days, while another was held at Algonquin from 1942 to 1951. In the early Championships Jimmy Manion was one of the winners in the 1929 event.

During the tenure at Algonquin, only 5 champions were crowned as Bob Cochran, Jim Jackson and Cary Middlecoff captured 8 of the 10 titles. The event was sponsored by the St. Louis District Golf Association, and the trophy was named in honor of Clarence M. Wolff, former secretary of the District. The Championship Trophy from the Algonquin years is on display at Algonquin CC. The 1951 championship marked the end of the tournament in St. Louis.

The LPGA events held in the 60's and 70's would also use this identification, and in some years add the title sponsor to it as well. (See the section on St. Louis Championships for this information) Auto-magnate Lou Fusz would sponsor a tournament which would carry the name and tradition on for several more years. Unfortunately the Fusz would die as it was closely tied to the Bogey Hills Invitational --the main draw that brought the pro's to St. Louis -- held a week before the Fusz event.

St. Louis Titles 1898-1980

The 1930 St. Louis Open edition offered some of the best golf in the country not played by Bobby Jones that year. Competed for over 72 holes at Sunset CC were the likes of Tommy Armour, the eventual winner, Walter Hagen, Horton Smith, Harry Cooper, Al Espinosa, Gene Sarazen, Ralph Guldahl, Paul Runyan, Joe Turnesa, Johnny Farrell, Jug McSpadden, Jim Foulis, Ky Laffoon, Denny Shute, Frank and Jim Fogertey and a young pro from Arkansas, Ernie (Dutch) Harrison. The area's top amateurs also played with Jimmy Manion shooting a 287 (-1) to claim low amateur honors, but still far back from Armour's (-12) 276 total. But it was not for want of trying. Jimmy played in the threesome with Gene Sarazen and Walter Hagen (who would finish second), and Jimmy would shoot a 66 to Hagen's 71 and Sarazen's 70 that day. Only an opening 78 prevented him from being in contention for the title.

In these days the event it was often referred to as the *City Championship.* Beginning in 1913 a *Municipal Championship* was competed for over the Forest Park Municipal links. This event was open to all comers. The *Muny Championship* is where Jimmy Manion, Eddie Held and others began their careers, as they did not belong to clubs.

The Republic Cup, first competed for in 1899 and won by Charles Scudder, was the early prize and this was the only area-wide event prior to 1912 when the first public courses came on the scene. The *City Championship* prior to 1916 was technically the beginnings of the District Tournament held today as it was mostly club players. Beginning in 1916, when the St. Louis District Golf Association was formed, three different events, were held for a few years. Eventually the *Municipal Championship* faded away, as would the *City Championship*, though this type of event would be revived under different names several times, thus the various St. Louis Open events.

Crowd watching the final putts at Sunset in the 1930 St. Louis Open

St. Louis Championships

As more players from around the country began to compete, it became more of an Open. During 1930-33 it was the first stop on the Pro Tour for the Fall/Winter season. From St. Louis they would head south and into Florida. (The Tour was not known as the PGA Tour at the time. It was just called the Pro Tour. In a given week there would be one, two and sometimes three Pro events held throughout the country. Pro's went where they could win or pick up a guarantee) The 1932 purse offered $65,000 to the players. In 1934, a small article in the paper announced that the event was indefinitely postponed and would not be rescheduled. In 1935 the St. Louis District Golf Association stepped up and sponsored an Open event with a Match Play format. This initial tournament was won by Norwood Pro Bill Schwartz as he defeated amateur Elliott Whitbread in the finals. This was held for a few more years, but it too ceased, and another event was reborn in 1942. Finally in 1950 and 1951 the event was once again a stop on the Pro Tour at Algonquin, but it too ceased after the 2nd year.

Listed below are individuals who won the City or Municipal titles, and later the Open crown.

Year	Winner	Site
1897	E.E. Steedman	St. Louis
1898	J.H. Brookmire	St. Louis
1899*	Charles Scudder	Field Club
1900	Bart Adams	Field Club
1901	Burt McKinnie	St. Louis
1902	Stuart Stickney	Field Club
1903	Stuart Stickney	Field Club
1904	Bert McKinnie	Glen Echo
1905	Ralph McKittrick	St. Louis
1906	Ralph McKittrick	St. Louis
1907	Arthur Stickney	Normandie
1908	Stuart Stickney	Glen Echo
1909	Arthur Stickney	St. Louis
1910	Christian Kenney	Normandie
1911	Arthur Stickney	Bellerive
1912	Arthur Stickney	Bellerive
1913	Harry Potter	Bellerive
1914	Eddie Limberg	
1915	Jimmy Manion	Forest Park

Year	Winner	Site
1916	No Record	
1917	Jimmy Manion	Forest Park
1918	Clarence Wolff	Forest Park
1919	Jimmy Manion	Forest Park
1920	George Koob	Forest Park
1921	Frank Pepp	Forest Park
1922	Eddie Held	Forest Park
1923	J.E. Mullin	Forest Park
1924	Reginald Belleville	Forest Park
1925	Michael Friedlein	Forest Park
1926	Jim Spencer	Forest Park
1927	Johnny Manion	Sunset CC
1928	Jimmy Manion	St. Louis CC
1929	Jimmy Manion	Bellerive CC
1930	Tommy Armour	Sunset CC
1931	Jimmy Manion	Midland Valley
1932	Walter Hagen	Meadow Brook
1933	Ralph Guldahl	St. Louis CC
1934	Postponed	
1935	Bill Schwartz (M)	St. Louis CC
1936	Bob Cochran (M)	Forest Park
1937	No Record	
1938-41	No Record	
1942	Bob Cochran	Algonquin CC
1943	Bob Cochran	Algonquin CC
1944	Ben Richter	Algonquin CC
1945	Bob Cochran	Algonquin CC
1946	Bob Cochran	Algonquin CC
1947	Frank Moore	Algonquin CC
1948	Jim Jackson	Algonquin CC
1949	Jim Jackson	Algonquin CC
1950	Cary Middlecoff	Algonquin CC
1951	Cary Middlecoff	Algonquin CC

Lou Fusz St. Louis Open 1980-1993

This event was held for 14 years, from 1980-1993, and was a favorite of players on the mini-tour. Some of the players who competed here are today some of the stalwarts on the Regular and Senior Tour as they played the Bogey Hills and then the Fusz in consecutive weeks.. These include; John Daly, Jeff Maggert, Jay Delsing, Jim Furyk, Brian

Claar, Tom Byrum, Tommy Armour III, Ted Schulz, Mike Hulbert and of course, Tom Wargo.

Current senior Bobby Stroble won the event twice and helped launch his career toward the elder statesmen. Next to the Bogey Hills Invitational, the Lou Fusz St. Louis Open was the next best thing for quality golf. The 1980 and 1981 events were held at Crescent CC (Players Club). From 1982 through 1993 it was held at Normandie GC. Bret Burroughs posted the record score in 1989 with a 198 for 54 holes. Amateur and Senior winners were awarded in various years, with Bob Mason capturing the initial amateur medal in 1980.

1980	Bobby Stroble	Bob Mason (A)
1981	Al Chandler	Jim Holtgrieve (A)
1982	Chuck Thorpe	Buddy Godwin (A)
1983	David Sann	Stan Utley (A)
1984	Chuck Thorpe	
1985	Bobby Stroble	
1986	Jeff Cooke	
1987	Dicky Thompson	
1988	Jeff Maggert (P)	Craig Hardcastle (A)
1989	Bret Burroughs (P)	Bob Welden (A)
1990	Greg Towne (P)	Bobby Cochran (A)
1991	Steve Ford	Terry Houser (Sr)
1992	Kevin Wentworth	Terry Houser (Sr)
1993	Dennis Postlewait	

1988 Lou Fusz-St. Louis Open Winner Jeff Maggert (second from right) with low amateur Craig Hardcastle.

Metropolitan Golf Association of St. Louis Championship; 1941-1949

The *Metropolitan Golf Association of St. Louis* was formed on July 23, 1941. The purpose was to bring together events for those *"...who cannot compete in midweek events and for those who are not members of private clubs..."*. Initially it began with an Amateur event in October, 1941, and later with an Open tournament a week later, though the amateur event would halt during the war.

Bill Edgar was the first secretary of the group with Riverview pro Joe Murray as chairman. Among the prominent individuals and professionals were behind the effort was Frank Moore, at the time serving in the military, but recognized as one of the top area professionals, Jim Black, Joe Dolan, Herbert Lorenz, Jerry Stanford, Charles Temple, Tom Draper, Arnold Hartenbach, Bud Bernhardt and Ted Bopp.

A total of 325 players entered the initial competition in 1941 played over the Forest Park links. With no entry fees, you only paid the regular greens fee. While intended to provide a competition for public-fee players, all players were welcomed to compete and the initial champion, Tom Draper playing out of Crystal Lake Club, was a former District champ. The event ceased at the end of the 40's, due in large part to their lack of getting access to the best courses and the lack of funds to continue the effort.

St. Louis Metro Amateur

This event was contested at match play, similar to the district and state matches today, with qualifying rounds narrowing the field. There were 5 classes in the "Met" with those listed below the winners of the championship flight. The finals of the inaugural event were held on October 12, 1941 at Forest Park. Tom

Draper defeated fellow Crystal Lake player Jack Purdum 2 and 1 in the finals.

1941	Tom Draper
1942-44	No tournaments
1945	Harry Pailer
1946	No record
1947	Bob Cochran
1948	Bob Cochran
1949	No record

St. Louis Metro Open

The initial Open was held in October 25-26, 1941 and was a two-day 36 hole medal event. Jim Fogertey came through on the 2nd day to capture the win. The second year was significant in that a relatively unknown 19-year old tied professional Frank Moore for the title a end of 36 holes. At the Monday playoff, they once more ended tied. Finally on Tuesday, Moore passed young Jimmy Jackson and claimed the victory.

1941	Jim Fogertey
1942	Frank Moore
1943	Bud Williamson
1944	Bob Cochran
1945	No record
1946	No record
1947	No record
1948	Bob Cochran
1949	Bob Cochran

St. Louis Women's Golf Association Metro Tournament

Begun in 1981, this ladies-only event was begun to determine the area-wide ladies champion. The SLWGA joined forces with the St. Louis District Ladies (SLWDGA) to sponsor an event to determine an area-wide champion. Kathie DeGrand was a major force behind this effort and was tournament director for the first few years when she passed the

torch to Pat Will. As was the case with many events, a lack of support caused it to cease after the 6th year.

Nancy Scranton, as a 19-year old at Florida State, won the first two events and showed area competitors a new level of golf as she thoroughly dominated the field. But Nancy will be remembered for two reasons; first is the quality of her play, and the second is perhaps more important; her character as a champion. The manner in which she won and her demeanor as champion will be long remembered by those who witnessed the tournament. Little wonder why Nancy continues to have success as a professional.

1981	Nancy Scranton
1982	Nancy Scranton
1983	Diane Daugherty
1984	Kathy Schaeffer
1985	Barbara Lehr
1986	Barbara Lehr

St. Louis Women's Golf Association Match/Stroke Play

Begun in 1976, this event was initially a 5-day match play tournament to determine the top public-player in the area. It soon went to a 3-day tournament as finding courses for 5 days, as well as the sheer time it took for the event, dictated the change. An early sponsor was Coors, so they held the tournament headline for several seasons.

Today this event rotates between stroke and match play as the group continues to determine the top public player in the area. Prior to 1990, all the events were at Match Play. Medal Play began in 1992 as part of this title. Of note would be the 1987 winner, Ellen Port. In one of her first wins at Bahnfyre, Ellen showed the talent that would carry her forward.

| 1976 | Cindy Kowert | Paradise Valley |
| 1977 | Francis Phipps | Bogey |

1978	Nancy Mitchell	St. Charles
1979	Barbara Lehr	Bahnfyre
1980	Barbara Lehr	Bahnfyre
1981	Pam Rothfuss	Paddock
1982	Barbara Lehr	Bahnfyre
1983	Barbara Lehr	Bahnfyre
1984	Micki Oulds	Creve Coeur
1985	Susan Jedlovec	Bahnfyre
1986	Marcella Rose	Normandie
1987	Ellen Port	Bahnfyre
1988	Pat Will	Normandie
1989	Joyce Queen	Raintree
1990	Pat Will	Normandie
1992	Dot Kurtzeborn (S)	St. Andrews
1993	Chris Clark (M)	Paddock
1994	Enid Harris (S)	Quail Creek
1995	Pat Will (M)	St. Andrews
1996	Jane Townsend (S)	Pomme Creek

Jimmy Jackson Memorial Tournament

Held in early September, this is named in honor of one of the best amateurs to play in the area. His death in 1983 saddened all who knew Jim, and this event keeps alive his memory for golfers throughout the Bi-state. Sponsored by the District Golf Association, with tremendous cooperation from Algonquin, it is an invitational event as club champions from District courses as well as winners of the Metro, District and Junior District along with Qualifiers for the Amateur, Mid-Am, St. Louis Publinks, US Publinks and Senior Amateur join past winners for the competition. The list of winners of his event would make Jim proud.

1985	Jim Mason
1986	Dennis Osborne
1987	Jeff Johnson
1988	Dennis Osborne
1989	David Lucks
1990	Jim Holtgrieve
1991	Ed Schwent
1992	Jim Holtgrieve

1993	Dennis Moore
1994	Jim Holtgrieve
1995	Scott Thomas
1996	David Estes

Michelob Open

Begun in the mid-70's this tournament was the brainchild of Bart Collida. With the help of Michelob and the writings of Bill Beck, from the Post Dispatch, Bart hoped to turn this into a true Open Amateur Championship.

Despite the lack of quality courses, he negotiated with the then-private Normandie CC for the host privileges, something that did not sit well at the time with many. Despite this, the event lasted from 1978 to 1986, though the last to years were played at Crescent CC. In the end, it was a familiar tune, lack of support that caused this event to fold. But for those eight years, some of the best area amateurs strutted like peacocks over Normandie and Crescent as they brought golf to a level not seen since

David Estes
1996 Jackson Champion

St. Louis Championships

the early 50's.

The event was played at Match Play, with a two-round qualifying preceding the serious play. Played during the week, players from all over entered, many using assumed names — not to cheat on their handicaps —but to avoid their bosses finding out. Still it did not stop one spiteful overseer, who found that one of his employees was playing and waited for him at the 18th green — where he asked him for the keys to the company car, and promptly fired him on the spot! Who said playing golf isn't dangerous!!

The 1982 Michelob Match Play Championship (l-r) Bill Joyce, Bart Collida (Tournament Director), Jeff Johnson (Winner), Peter Scott (representing Michelob) Bob Gaus (Runner-up), Tom Kammann (Head pro Normandie).

Some of the then-amateurs who competed in the event were; Russ Luedloff, John Hayes, Bob Gaus, Bret Burroughs, Paul Trittler, Pol Montano Tom LaBarbera, and other well-known amateurs Dennis Moore, Bob Beckmann, Jeff Johnson, Andy Frost, John Moore, Clay Smith, Gary Slay, Bill Matthews, Sam Loethen, Tom Barry, David Rhoads, Jim Holtgrieve, Clay Coates, Craig Hardcastle, Terry Martin, Dave Kaercher, Scott Edwards,

	Winner	**Runner-Up**
1978	Paul Trittler	John Hayes
1979	Bruce Thomas	Paul Trittler
1980	Russ Oldham	Earl Stamer
1981	Dave Kaercher	Jeff Johnson
1982	Jeff Johnson	Bob Gaus
1983	Dave Kaercher	Chuck Hull
1984	Tim Gehrig	Denny Alberts
1985	Scott Edwards	Chuck Hull
1986	Tim Gehrig	Bob Trittler

St. Clair Invitational

This tournament was held at St. Clair CC from the late 1950's until 1969 and then for a final time in 1977 & 1978. Pro's and amateurs from all over the area came to compete in what was the premier event of the era. Dutch Harrison, Bob Rosburg, Bob Goalby, Bob Cochran, Larry Ziegler, Jim Cochran, Joe Jimenez, Dick Shaiper, Milon Marusic, Phil Hewitt in addition to players like Sam Snead who ventured to Belleville for a shot at the top prize. Jay Haas got his a taste of a professional victory winning the last two events. Though the checks were small, averaging between $700 and $900 for the top spot, it was the winning that kept them coming back.

In 1966 Dick Shaiper set a course record in winning. Don Dupske and Bob Cochran were multiple winners on the Amateur side, while for a time it seemed as though Bob Goalby, playing out of his home course, would not relinquish the title, as he captured the 1960 & '61 crowns. The ever present Jim Jackson was also victorious here in 1959 setting the amateur record at that time of 139.

The tournament had ceased for 8 years then was given a temporary life for 1977 and 1978. Bob Goalby got his good friend, Sam Snead, to come to Belleville. Sam, still a spry 65 (67-70), tangled with Bob's nephew, Jay Haas before Jay eventually won the title by 3 strokes, but he had to shoot 65-69 to do so as Sam and Scott Bess tied with 137.

There was a forerunner to this; the St. Clair Open which began in June, 1939 and was won by Eddie Held with St. Clair Pro, Howard Popham, finishing 2nd a stroke back.

	Pro	*Amateur*
1958	Eddie Johnson	Dick Kohlman
1959	Dutch Harrison	Jim Jackson
1960	Bob Goalby	Onarion Gherardini
1961	Bob Goalby	Ken Lanning
1962	Frank Keller	Bob Cochran
1963	Fred Wampler	Dutch Miller
1964	Bill Emmons	P.J. Keeley
1965	Al Chandler	Don Dupske
1966	Dick Shaiper	Don Dupske
1967	Dutch Harrison	Bob Cochran
1968	Larry Suhre	Don Dupske
1977	Jay Haas	Jim Holtgrieve
1978	Jay Haas	Jim Holtgrieve

Normandie Amateur

Held at Normandie Park first in September, then from 1989 on in mid-May, the tournament is one of the non-organization sponsored events in the area. Initially the brainchild of John Hayes, today it is run

Don Dupske

Steve Irwin
1993 Normandie Champ

by Dave Smith, who also participates as a competitor. Sponsored recently by Firethorn, the tournament has also had Rainworld in a lead role as well as Ping.

1986	Tom Barry
1987	Tom Barry
1988	Scott Thomas
1989	Don Bliss
1990	David Estes
1991	Jeff Johnson
1992	John Kueper
1993	Steve Irwin
1994	Bill Bahn
1995	Scott Thomas
1996	Don Bliss

Ping Amateur

Ping initiated this event in 1995 after dropping it's former affiliation with the Normandy Amateur. This event is now held at the Eagle Lake GC in Farmington, MO.

1995	Scott Thomas
1996	Colby Robertson

St. Louis Championships

Championship

While only 6 years old, the Metro is already one of the most coveted titles in the area. The current Men's tournament is held mid-August with the ladies teeing off late in July.

The 1996 matches were held at Bellerive CC and marked a new chapter in amateur golf. When Tom Barry rolled in his final putt to claim the title, there was no doubt that the tournament had been a success, and the Metro, it appears, is here to stay. If it proves successful over the long run, it will accomplish what has eluded the area since the first putts were holed, an area championship for all amateur golfers. There have been several attempts at this, the *Michelob Open*, the *St. Louis Muny*, the *Metro* in the 1940's, and others. The current Metro appears to be on-track to putting the merry-go-round of *"area-championship pretenders"* to an end once and for all.

The Ladies event are held a bit earlier in the season, just a few weeks before their District Championship, and with Barb Berkmeyer capturing both the Metro and District in 1996, she clearly established herself as the player of the year.

The senior event was held in October and perennial contender Don Dupske once again showed his skill as he conquered the field at the Legends.

The MAGA held a banquet and honored the following as their golfers of the Year for 1996; Don Bliss and Ellen Port, along with Senior division winners Barb Berkmeyer and Don Dupske.

If there has been a common theme that has plagued all similar attempts, it has been lack of funding and support. Clearly Tom O'Toole and the Metro Board are on the right track. Access to courses, getting the top players to participate along with sponsorship is vital for long-term success. As new players approach the tees they must be welcomed with open arms. A parochial attitude or "too much owner-ship" could prove disastrous.

Men's Metro Tournament

**Tom "Toz" Barry
1996 Metro Champ**

1991	Don Bliss
1992	Derre Owsley
1993	Don Bliss
1994	Jim Holtgrieve
1995	Craig Schnurbush
1996	Tom Barry

Ladies Metro Tournament

1993	Ellen Port
1994	Ellen Port
1995	Jo D Blosch
1996	Barbara Berkmeyer

Senior Men Metro Championship

1995	Jack Powers
1996	Don Dupske

"Watson scares me. If he's lying six in the middle of the fairway, there's some kind of way he might make five."

...Lee Trevino on Tom Watson (1981)

The Missouri Amateur Championship

A very fine History of the Missouri Amateur was published in 1988 by Jack Garvin, a current member of the Missouri Golf Association Board. I will not attempt to duplicate his efforts for it was very thorough.

The information contained in that publication documented not only the winners and competition courses, but gave a complete listing of all the participants and the outcome, at least what could be reconstructed from existing records. This publication is being updated and should be available in the coming months.

The Missouri Amateur for men is the 10th oldest State Amateur in the country, having begun in 1905. Oddly, the state that has been holding their Amateur the longest is not located on the east coast, nor the west coast but in Utah where it began in 1899. Neighboring states to Missouri also have the distinction of some of the oldest; Iowa and Indiana in 1900, Colorado, Wisconsin and Minnesota in 1901, and Ohio in 1904. Only Rhode Island (1902) and Massachusetts (1903) reflect the early Amateur golf on the east coast. New York, site of the first club at St. Andrews-on-the-Hudson, and the second Amateur in 1896, did not play a state amateur until 1923.

The first US Amateur was played at Newport GC in Rhode Island in 1895. As most golf history buffs are aware, the Amateur was the first event played under the auspices of the USGA. The Amateur was considered the more elegant of the events, with the first Open played the day following the completion of the Amateur. The Open was primarily for professionals, considered the better players, but generally thought of as being of a "lower class" than the gentlemen who competed in the Amateur. Both were played over Newport GC, which at the time, was only a 9-hole layout.

Several area courses have played host to the Missouri Amateur, and many St. Louisans have held the title. The courses and number of times they have hosted are; Norwood Hills (3) 1931, 1938, 1981; Normandie (3) 1905, 1908, 1962; Sunset CC, (4) 1920, 1942, 1954, 1978; Glen Echo CC (4) 1906, 1910, 1915, 1949; Meadowbrook CC (Old) (3) 1924, 1940, 1956; St. Louis CC (2) 1907, 1946; Riverview CC (1) 1928; Westborough CC (1) 1933; Algonquin CC (2) 1917, 1951; Bellerive (1) 1984; Bellerive (Old) (1) 1935; Westwood (2) 1972, 1987; Old Warson CC (1) 1969; Meadowbrook (1) 1965; Greenbriar (1) 1959; CC at the Legends (1) 1991.

Jim Manion from Midland Valley CC (Meadowbrook) was the first to win 4 times ('1917, '21, '23, '26). But hot on his heels was Norwood Hills Bob Cochran who won in '40, '59, '62 and '65. Not to be outdone Jim Jackson from Greenbriar completed his quartet in 1976 to go along with his wins in '51, '54 and '59, a feat Don Bliss duplicated by winning in '72, '83, '86 and '88. In 1996 Don Bliss threatened to become the only five-time winner, but Wayne Fredrick took the better of Bliss in the finals 4&3. The only other four time winner was a relative unknown from Kansas City named Tom Watson. He first won in 1967 at age 17, and then won again in 1968, 1970 and 1971. Only Columbia CC's Scott Bess interrupted Watson march through the championship in 1969. Christian Kenney from Algonquin was the first three time winner, winning in 1908, 1909 and 1920, but could come no closer again.

Of the courses with the most winners, the nod goes to Norwood Hills, also known as North Hills prior to 1933, with 10 winners. Midland Valley, forerunner to Meadowbrook is next with 7, while Algonquin and Greenbriar follow with 5 each.

In the first champion was Harry Allen, a visiting lawyer from Massachusetts, he entered the tournament and promptly won. With such an introduction to St. Louis hospitality, he stayed in St. Louis and became one of the founders of Bellerive in 1910.

Perhaps the first of the early champions who earned a national reputations was Jimmy Manion. In 1921 Grantland Rice, the legendary sportswriter, named Manion as one of the top four amateurs in the country! He crossed clubs many times in the early 1920's with the likes of Bobby Jones, Jess Sweetser, Francis Ouimet, Robert Gardner Chick Evans and Jesse Guilford, all champions and Walker Cup members, as well as professionals like Tommy Armour, Walter Hagen and Horton Smith.

If you draw your attention to the list of winners you will see several eras where St. Louisans dominated. A small group of very talented golfers in each period ran roughshod over all comers. The first would be the 18 tournaments from 1917 to 1934. During this period 14 titles were won by only 8 St. Louis golfers with Jimmy Manion, Elliott Whitbread Chester O'Brien, Eddie Held and Richard Bockenkamp accounting for 11 of these. The next period was from 1951 to 1965 and during this 15 year period St. Louis golfers won 9 times with Jim Jackson and Bob Cochran winning six titles between them and St. Louisan-to-be Jim Tom Blair (at the time he was playing out of Jeff City CC) claiming another two. Only Springfield legend Bill Stewart was able to win more than once in this period. In the past 25 years the balance has been so even that St. Louis area golfers have won only 12 of these, with only Don Bliss and Jim Holtgrieve being able to repeat, winning 6 titles between them.

Year	Champion	Club
1905	Harry Allen	Field Club
1906	Bart Adams	Algonquin
1907	Albert Lambert	St. Louis
1908	Christian Kenney	Algonquin
1909	Christian Kenney	Algonquin
1910	Ralph McKittrick	St. Louis
1911	Robert Hodge	Evanston
1912	Stuart Stickney	St. Louis
1913	Raymond Thorne	Evanston
1914	Alden B. Swift	St. Joseph
1915	Cyrus More	Normandie
1916	Robert Hodge	Evanston
1917	James Manion	Midland Valley
1918	James C. Ward	Kansas City
1919	James C. Ward	Mission Hills
1920	Christian Kenney	Sunset
1921	James Manion	Midland Valley
1922	Richard Bockenkamp	Midland Valley
1923	James Manion	Midland Valley
1924	Donald Anderson	Normandie
1925	Eddie Held	Algonquin
1926	James Manion	Midland Valley
1927	Harold R. Wilson	Swope Park
1928	Elliott Whitbread	Osage
1929	Elliott Whitbread	North Hills
1930	Richard Bockenkamp	Midland Valley
1931	Bryan Winter	North Hills
1932	Frank Staller	Wood Hill
1933	Chester O'Brien	Westborough
1934	Chester O'Brien	Westborough
1935	Grable Duvall	Hillcrest
1936	Walter Blevins	Old Mission
1937	Glenn Oatman	Swope Park
1938	Walter Blevins	Swope Park
1939	Ted Adams	Chillicothe
1940	Bob Cochran	Norwood Hills
1941	James Black	Crystal Lake
1942	Don Smith	Fairview
1943-45	No Tournament	
1946	Jonas Weiss	Westwood
1947	Bob Willits	Kansas City
1948	Warren Riepen	Fairview
1949	Jack Geiss	Norwood Hills
1950	Warren Riepen	Fairview
1951	Jim Jackson	Greenbriar Hills
1952	Jim Tom Blair	Jefferson City
1953	Bill Stewart	Hickory Hills
1954	Jim Jackson	Greenbriar Hills

1955	Jim Tom Blair	Jefferson City
1956	Bob Barton	Normandie
1957	Bill Stewart	Hickory Hills
1958	Bob Cochran	Norwood Hills
1959	Jim Jackson	Greenbriar Hills
1960	Jack House	Milburn
1961	John Inman	Joplin
1962	Bob Cochran	Norwood Hills
1963	Jim Colbert	Santa Fe Hills
1964	Tom Garrity	Hillcrest
1965	Bob Cochran	Meadowbrook
1966	Jim Patton	Twin Oaks
1967	Tom Watson	Kansas City
1968	Tom Watson	Kansas City
1969	Scott Bess	Columbia
1970	Tom Watson	Kansas City
1971	Tom Watson	Kansas City
1972	Don Bliss	Norwood Hills
1973	Buddy Godwin	Westwood Hills
1974	Dale Kuntz	Mirror Lake
1975	Bruce Hollowell	Hickory Hills
1976	Jim Jackson	Greenbriar Hills
1977	Dennis Goettel	Carthage
1978	Jim Holtgrieve	Westborough
1979	Payne Stewart	Hickory Hills
1980	Buddy Ludwig	Blue Springs
1981	Jim Holtgrieve	Westborough
1982	John Hayes	Normandie
1983	Don Bliss	Norwood Hills
1984	John Sherman	Kansas City
1985	Don Walsworth	Marceline
1986	Don Bliss	Norwood Hills
1987	David Lucks	Algonquin
1988	Don Bliss	Norwood Hills
1989	Greg Gill	St. Louis
1990	Marty Sallaz	Kansas City
1991	Allen Rosen	Springfield
1992	Scott Thomas	Norwood Hills
1993	Bob Beckmann	St. Louis
1994	Tyler Shelton	Kansas City
1995	Jason Schultz	Columbia
1996	Wayne Fredrick	Hickory Hills

The Missouri Women's Amateur Championship

Golf for women has not always offered the opportunities it does today. Some of the early women champions had to sneak their way onto the course just to practice. Today women comprise a greater percentage of new players to golf than men, though the number of women players remains rather consistent.

We have had many wonderful champions through the years, from Grace Semple, who captured the first Amateur to Barb Berkmeyer with her five titles over twenty-five years. Betty Jane Haemerle-Broz, like her play in the District, dominated the late

***Betty Jane Haemerle-Broz
Won 5 District and 3 state titles from
1942-1949***

Missouri Championships

Mrs. E. Lansing Ray

40's, winning three titles after the War. Marilyn Herpel matched her with 3 titles after Betty Jane stopped competing. In their head-to-head matches, Betty Jane was virtually unbeatable for almost 10 years. Mary Gail Dalton has had a stellar career, though winning only once in the State, as have Kathy Severson, Paula Eger and Maria Palozola. Marcella Rose captured two titles, as did Judy Torluemke Rankin and Lindsey Murfin. Cathy Nelson and Ellen Port are two of the more recent champions whose names grace the trophy, with Ellen claiming two titles. The only out-state player to continually edge our best is Kansas City's Karen Schull MacGee who captured seven titles from 1960-1979.

Many of the ladies began very successful careers while in their teens, and younger. Marilyn Herpel and Judy Torluemke were two such players.

Marilyn, as noted earlier in the section on St. Louis Championships, began competing at age 4. Judy was slightly older, as she began play at age 6. A rather adept player by age 8, Judy had a rather unpleasant incident occur while she was playing in the 1953 Missouri Women's Amateur at St. Joseph CC. Members of her foursome made a mild protest at her presence and play was held up for a time as an official was consulted. It seems they believed that she was too young to compete in the Women's Amateur, but should have to compete as a Junior. She continued to compete and, as she has done most of her career, bested many of her competitors.

The following are the players who have captured the Women's State Amateur title.

1915	Grace Semple
1916	Laurie Kaiser
1917	Mrs. E. Lansing Ray
1918	Carolyn Lee
1919	Carolyn Lee
1920	Carolyn Lee
1921	Miriam Burns
1922-34	No Tournament
1935	Mrs. Opal S. Hill
1936	Mrs. Opal S. Hill
1937	Mrs. Opal S. Hill
1938	Sara Louise Guth
1939	Mrs. P.L. Pepper
1940	Mrs. P.L. Pepper
1941	Mrs. P.L. Pepper
1942-45	No Tournament
1946	Betty Jane Haemerle
1947	Jean Hutto
1948	Betty Jane Haemerle
1949	Mrs. Allen D. Broz
1950	Marilyn Herpel
1951	Maxine Johnson
1952	Marilyn Gault
1953	Marilyn Herpel
1954	Marilyn Herpel
1955	Kate Richards
1956	Patricia Rubelee
1957	Mrs. Robert S. Johnson

1958	Kaya Caldwell
1959	Judy Torluemke
1960	Karen Schull
1961	Judy Torluemke
1962	Karen Schull
1963	Marcella Rose
1964	Karen Schull MacGee
1965	Barbara Bubany
1966	Mary Gail Dalton
1967	Peggy Ludlow
1968	Karen Schull MacGee
1969	Marcella Rose

Jane Watson
The first lady of Missouri
Women's Golf

1970	Barbara Berkmeyer
1971	Paula Eger
1972	Karen MacGee
1973	Karen MacGee
1974	Barbara Berkmeyer
1975	Barbara Berkmeyer
1976	Cathy Reynolds
1977	Kathy Severson
1978	Lynn Ralston
1979	Karen MacGee
1980	Monica O'Hare
1981	Diane Daugherty
1982	Gayle Perryman
1983	Ann Marie Cain
1984	Barbara Berkmeyer
1985	Kelly Loy
1986	Elizabeth Smart
1987	Lindsey Murfin
1988	Lindsey Murfin
1989	Mary Ortelee
1990	Barbara Blanchar
1991	Cathy Nelson
1992	Ellen Port
1993	Maria Palozola
1994	Amy Smethers
1995	Ellen Port

On the 38th hole of the match, runner-up Lynette Chrenka (l) congratulates fellow Greenbriar member Paula Eger, new state champ, following their 1971 title match.

1996   Gina Spalitto

Missouri Men's Mid-Amateur Championship

Begun in 1995, the Missouri Golf Association falls in step with most national organizations in recognizing the needs of the "business-amateur" in establishing the Missouri Mid-Amateur. The inaugural winner, Scott Thomas, could not be a better representative, as he has established himself as one of the premier players throughout the state since the mid-80's. With Don Bliss capturing the 1996 trophy, St. Louis golfers once more, established their dominance in state wide events.

Year	Winner	Home Course
1995	Scott Thomas	Norwood Hills
1996	Don Bliss	St. Albans

Missouri Senior Amateur Championship

Ageless Bob Cochran went from winning the Amateur in 1965 to the Senior Amateur in 1969 (a good young player from Kansas City won the Amateur in 1967,'68, '70 & '71, Tom Watson), so in 1969 at age 57, Bob moved up, though he did compete in the 1971 & 73 championship, making it to match play both years.

Jim Jackson won back-to-back titles in 1980 & '81 shortly before his death in 1983. Other notable winners are Jim Manion, Joe Switzer, Bill Stewart (Payne's Father), and Bill Ludwig.

Through the years a variety of groups sponsored a Senior Championship. One prominent group was led by Don Faurot, the legendary Mizzou football coach who passed away during the summer of 1996. Without diminishing the significance of any of their tournaments, identifying which group was the sponsor of a particular event (and correspondingly, who was the winner) would be a monumental task. The champions listed below won "A Senior Event" in the year listed against good competition and were recognized as winning a Senior Missouri title.

Year	Winner	Course
1938	J.A. Shontz	
1959	Jimmy Manion	Normandie
1966	Syl Schmidt	Sunset
1967	Clarence McGuire	
1968	Joe Switzer	Old Warson
1969	Bob Cochran	Meadowbrook
1970	Tom Lawrence	
1971	Bob Cochran	Meadowbrook
1972	Bob Cochran	Meadowbrook
1973	Wilbur Bartles	
1974	Jack House	
1975	Jack House	
1976	Bob Willits	
1977	Bob Cochran	Meadowbrook
1978	Bob Cochran	Meadowbrook
1979	Bill Stewart	Hickory Hills
1980	Jim Jackson	Greenbriar
1981	Jim Jackson	Greenbriar
1982	No record	
1983	Charles Morgan	
1984	No record	
1985	No record	
1986	Jim McKinney	CC of Missouri
1987	Charles Talley	
1988	Jim Morris	
1989	Jim McKinney	CC of Missouri

Missouri Golf Association Senior Amateur

Beginning in 1990, the Missouri Golf Association began to formerly crown a Senior Amateur Champion. Among the winners have been the late Jim Plummer and the ever-present Roger Null. Sam Loethen, a transplanted St. Louisan, won the 1995 Senior shortly after qualifying for the US Senior Amateur.

Year	Winner	Course
1990	Ron Boyce	
1991	Bill Ludwig	Lees Summit

1992	Jim Plummer	Lake St. Louis
1993	Bob McBride	Cape Girardeau
1994	Bob McBride	Cape Girardeau
1995	Sam Loethen	Jefferson City
1996	Roger Null	Boone Valley

Missouri Senior Women

The following sections note the various championships that the Senior Women throughout Missouri compete for titles. None of these can be called the official championship, but in most cases, their champion has beaten some of the best around.

Senior Women's Missouri Golf Association

1975	Dottie Linsin
1976	Jane Hyde
1977	Dottie Linsin
1978	Dottie Linsin
1979	Peggy Ludlow
1980	Joyce Mahoney
1981	Joyce Mahoney
1982	Jeannie Lewis
1983	Joyce Mahoney
1984	Joan Thomas
1985	Joyce Mahoney
1986	RAIN
1987	Joyce Mahoney
1988	Joan Thomas
1989	Connie Morris
1990	Connie Morris
1991	Kay Chase
1992	Janet Gardner
1993	Pet Scherer
1994	Fern Carter
1995	Kathy Welsch
1996	Sally Wagner

Missouri Senior Women's Golf Championship

This Championship goes back to 1969 and held annual competitions for Senior Women. Unfortunately the number of players and their affiliations was limited to a fairly select group. While the winners below are, in most cases, outstanding in any competition, the event was not open to golfers outside of this group, and as a result, did not represent a true championship for Missouri Senior Women.

1969	Sue Faurot
1970	Florence Bush
1971	Mary Hoffman
1972	Mary Hoffman
1973	Florence Bush
1974	Ruth Foresman
1975	Mary Hoffman
1976	Betty McCarty
1977	Mrs. William Rush
1978	Mrs. William Rush
1979	Mrs. Lloyd Parker
1980	Peg Morgan
1981	Dottie Linsin
1982	Dottie Linsin
1983	Dottie Linsin
1984	Audrey Hatlan
1985	Mrs. William Parshall
1986	Betty Von Rump
1987	Mary Gail Dalton
1988	Mary Gail Dalton
1989	Mary Gail Dalton
1990	Alma Matthes
1991	Mary Gail Dalton
1992	Alma Matthes
1993	Mary Gail Dalton
1994	Alma Mattes
1995	Mary Gail Dalton
1996	

Missouri Women's Golf Association Senior Championship

This group was formed in an attempt to consolidate the Senior Women's Championship and make it available to all entrants. Though only a few years old, this group offers the best opportunity for a true Open championship for Missouri Senior Women. This annual event marks the initial tournament of the season for the MWGA. All members in good standing who have reached 50 years of age, and reside in Missouri or in Johnson County Kansas are eligible.

1993	Barb Beuckman
1994	Mary Gail Dalton
1995	Pat Scherer
1996	Betty Von Rump

Missouri Open Championship

Sponsored by a variety of groups at times, the Open may have met its maker. With no title-sponsor to be found the event is on hiatus and may stay there permanently if no one steps up to take charge. One significant event occurred in 1977 when the ever-present Jimmy Jackson became the only amateur to win the title.

1924	Al Espinosa
1975	Bob Stone
1976	Jay Haas
1977	* Jim Jackson
1978	Joe Jimenez
1979	Don Lee
1980	Robert Stroble
1981	Ray Goodman
1982	Robert Walker
1983	Phil Blackmar
1984	Bob Wolcott
1985	Steve Thomas

1986	Eugene Elliott	
1987	John Daly	
1988	Stan Utley	
1989	Stan Utley	
1990-94	No Tournament	
1995	Bob Gaus (P)	Jason Schultz (A)
1996	No Tournament	

* Amateur Winner

Missouri Junior Boys Championship

1951	Bob Reynolds
1965	Rich Carney
1966	No record
1967	Mike Farmer
1968	Jim Ruck
1969	Jim Ruck
1970	Jim Ruck
1971	Kenny Nicklaus
1972	No record
1973	Billy Helmbacher
1974	Lin Lentz
1975	Bill Landis
1976	Scott Gunther
1977	Bill Ludwig, Jr.
1978	Jeff Johnson
1979	Tom LaBarbera
1980	Stan Utley
1981	Tom Barry
1982	Tim Marlo
1983	Keith Gocal
1984	John Utley
1985	Brad Benbrook
1986	Brent Pennington
1987	Rollie Hurst
1988	Jason Johnson
1989	Joey Parr
1990	Jamie Schmitt
1991	John Stahlschmidt
1992	John McClellan
1993-95	No record
1996	Brian Sullivan

Missouri Junior Girls Championship

1961	V. Ann Beadle
1962	V. Ann Beadle
1963	Marsha Ann Feig
1964	Sue Ann Asher
1965	Pam Loyd
1966	Patty Duggins
1967	Paula Eger
1968	Paula Eger
1969	Paula Eger
1970	Paula Eger
1971	Leslie Peck
1972	Cathy Reynolds
1973	Judy Grayson
1974	Cathy Reynolds
1975	Cathy Reynolds
1976	Janie Robinson
1977	Kerry Speaker
1978	Linda Finders
1979	Susan Fromuth
1980	Diane Giolia
1981	Diane Giolia
1982	Kim Erickson
1983	Barbara Blanchar
1984	Ann Cain
1985	Barbara Blanchar
1986	Chris Morris
1987	Sandy Schwartz
1988	Amy Smithers
1989	Tami Fisher
1990	Tami Fisher
1991	Lisa Wening
1992	Sara Williams
1993	Brooke Hawkins
1994	Libby Howard
1995	Missy Robertson
1996	Missy Robertson

Missouri Cup Matches

Begun in 1994, the Cup matches have attempted to update a 25 year old series of competitions. The initial efforts had competitive matches in the early 70's, as Pro's went up against Amateurs. This was a combined match, featuring amateurs from around the state, usually selected by Ken Lanning, and Pro's from the two PGA's regions represented in the state, the Eastern Missouri PGA, today the Gateway Region, headquartered in St. Louis and the Midwest Region, based in Kansas City.

Later matches in the late 80's featured two competitions; one against the Gateway Pro's and a second against the Midwest PGA. But for a variety of reasons, none of which are quite clear, there was never a consistent amateur event throughout the state, pitting the top golfers in a season ending match.

The Missouri Golf Association-sponsored Cup Matches pit the teams in a Ryder Cup format in a two day event. Foursomes (best ball), alternate shot and finally singles matches are contested. In 1994 and 1995 the West squad reigned victorious as they proved they had the depth of talent to overcome some outstanding individual play on the East squad.

The inaugural Cup Matches were played over the Loch Lloyd CC in suburban Kansas City. The site of a Senior PGA Tour event, proved most demanding as the West played their home course advantage to the fullest as they pounced on the East 15 1/2 to 8 1/2 for a very lop-sided win.

The 1995 matches were held over the Oaks Course at Marriott's Tan-Tar-A, as challenging a layout as will be found as it meanders through narrow paths sliced in the mid-Missouri Ozark woods surrounding the Lake. Finding the fairways here is a must as there is little hope for recovery. Coming to the final hole of the final match, it was all square, and the winner of this match would decide the outcome. Unfortunately for the East, an errant tee shot found the woods, and the West had their second consecutive Championship.

In 1996 at St. Albans CC, the East put together

a team that was solid. Don Bliss was the player-captain for the East while Jack Garvin handled the duties for the West. Leading 9-3 going into the final day, the West would have to win 9 or more of the 12 points to keep the Cup. It was not to be. With Roger Null and Phil Keim, both playing in the Senior division, going out in the first group, Roger played magnificently, birdieing the par 5 11th and the par 3 12th to go 5-up over John Simmons, and the first points of the match were decided with a handshake on the par 5 14th with a 5&4 win. When Phil Keim closed out Grant Renne moments later, it appeared that victory was near. As Craig Schnurbusch took the better of Steve Bush moments later, the East had three points and only needed a halve in the final nine matches to win their first Cup. Subsequent wins by Barry, Estes and Thomas, plus a halve by Frost proved more than enough.

The matches offer some of the best match play to be found throughout the state. In 1996 there were six former State Amateur Champions in the field (Bliss, Holtgrieve, Thomas, Sallaz, Curry, Fredrick) and recent State Senior Champion Roger Null. Each year the play has offered some outstanding shotmaking under very competitive conditions. While the crowd consists mainly of friends and family, hopefully future matches will find more public attention. The 1997 matches will be held at Jefferson City CC, in early October.

1996 Results - St. Albans CC (East won 15 1/2 to 8 1/2)

Alternate Shot- Foursomes (East 4-2)
Groom & Moore (W) d. Frost & Kennedy; 3 and 1
Null & Holtgrieve (E) d. Fredrick & Greene; 1-up
Estes & Thomas (E) d. Renne & Simmons; 1-up
Bliss & Keim (E) d. Roberts & Cribbs; 1-up
Schnurbusch & Godwin (E) d. Bush and Curry; 3 &1
Sallaz & Schneider d. Barry & Rhoads; 7 and 6

Four-Ball (East 5-1)
Holtgrieve & Rhoads (E) d. Sallaz &Schneider; 2 &1
Kennedy & Keim (E) d. Roberts & Cribbs; 2 and 1
Godwin & Thomas (E) d. Fredrick & Greene; 1-up
Frost & Barry (E) d. Groom & Moore; 3 and 2
Estes & Bliss (E) d. Curry & Bush; 1-up

Renne & Simmons (W) d. Null & Schnurbusch; 1-up

Singles (East 6 1/2 to 5 1/2)
Roger Null (E) d. John Simmons; 5 and 4
Phil Keim (E) d. Grant Renne; 2 and 1
Monte Schneider (W) d. David Rhoads; 3 and 1
Steve Groom (W) d. Brian Kennedy; 3 and 2
Tom Barry (E) d. Chuck Greene; 5 and 4
Andy Frost and Bill Roberts; halved
Craig Schnurbusch (E) d. Steve Bush; 7 and 5
Marty Sallaz (W) d. Jim Holtgrieve; 2 and 1
David Estes (E) d. Kevin Cribbs; 2 and 1
Mike Moore (W) d. Bobby Godwin; 1-up
Scott Thomas (E) d. B.J. Curry; 1-up
Wayne Fredrick (W) d. Don Bliss; 2 and 1

1995 Results - Marriott's Tan-Tar-A (West won 12 1/2 to 11 1/2)

Foursomes (West leads 3 1/2 to 2 1/2)
Groom & Schorgl (W) d. Estes & Null; 1-up
Johnsen & Curry (W) / Godwin & Owsley; halved
Ludwig & Woodbury (W) / Frost & Fogarty; halved
Hollowell & Wilson (W) d. Mason & Keim; 6 and 5
Bliss & Lucks (E) d. Brewer & Rowland; 1-up
Sallaz & Sanders (W) /Thomas & Schnurbusch;halve

Four-ball (West 3 1/2 to 2 1/2)
Owsley & Null (E) d. Woodbury & Schorgl; 1-up
Johnsen & Sanders (W) d. Godwin & Keim; 5 and 4
Groom & Ludwig (W) d. Mason & Estes; 4 and 3
Lucks & Fogarty (E) d. Hollowell & Wilson; 2 and 1
Brewer & Rowland (W) d. Bliss & Thomas 1-up

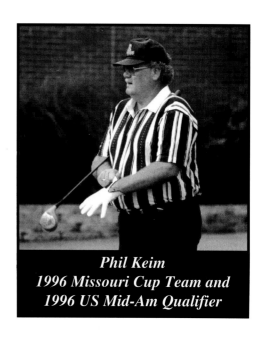

**Phil Keim
1996 Missouri Cup Team and
1996 US Mid-Am Qualifier**

Sallaz & Curry (W) / Frost & Schnurbusch; halved

Singles (East 6 1/2 to 5 1/2)
Phil Keim (E) d. Bruce Hollowell; 2 and 1
Bill Ludwig (W) d. Roger Null; 1-up
Craig Schnurbusch (E) d. Steve Groom; 4 and 3
David Estes (E) d. Fred Rowland; 1-up
Jim Mason (E) d. Ron Brewer; 6 and 5
Charlie Schorgl (W) d. Andy Frost; 3 and 2
David Lucks / Ryan Wilson; halved
Len Johnsen (W) d. Derre Owsley; 1-up
Andy Fogarty (E) d.Russ Woodbury; 7 and 5
Dee Sanders (W) d. Bobby Godwin; 2 and 1
B.J. Curry (W) d. Don Bliss; 1-up
Scott Thomas (E) d. Marty Sallaz; 2 and 1

1994 Results - Loch Lloyd CC
(West won 15 1/2 to 8 1/2)

Best Ball (East 3 - West 3)
Sallaz & Bush (W) d. Null & Meeh
Schnurbusch & McBride (E) d.Serrano & Fredenburg
Sinovic & Curry (W) d. Mason & Lucks
Groom & Sanders (W) d. Kootman and & Keim
Bliss & Frost (E) d. Rowland & Archer

Owsley & Bahn (E) d. Kirksey & Franks

Foursomes (West 4-2)
Rowland & Sallaz (W) d. Null & Schnurbusch
Sinovic & Curry (W) d. Mason & Kootman
Bliss & McBride (E) d. Groom & Sanders
Serano & Fredenberg (W) d. Meeh and Keim
Archer & Bucks (W) d. Owsley & Frost
Lucks & Bahn (E) d. Kirksey & Franks

Singles (West 8 1/2 - 3 1/2)
B.J. Curry (W) d. Bob Meeh
Antonio Serrano (W) d. Roger Null
Marty Sallaz (W) d. Mike Kootman
Chris Fredenburg (W) d. Jim Mason
David Lucks & David Kirksey; halved
Dee Sanders (W) d. Andy Frost
Archer (W) d. Bill Bahn
Steve Groom (W) d. Derre Owsley
Steve Bush (W) d. Craig Schnurbusch
Don Bliss (E) d. John Sinovic
Bob McBride (E) d. Rowland
Phil Keim (E) d. Franks

Paula Eger with her PeeWee National Championship Trophy in 1965. She would win 4 Missouri Junior titles, 5 District Juniors and the 1971 Women's State Amateur.

Miscellaneous State Championships

While the majority of area players have competed primarily in Missouri, with the Illinois State Amateur being the next most popular, there have been other State Championships that have been captured by area players. The list below includes Amateur and Open events. Unless indicated with an (O), the event is an Amateur only tournament. Some states have separate titles for Match and Medal play and are so indicated.

Arizona

1973 (O)	Steve Spray

Arkansas

1937 (O)	Dutch Harrison

California

1912	Jack Neville
1913	Jack Neville
1919	Jack Neville
1922	Jack Neville
1929	Jack Neville
1948 (O)	Smiley Quick
1949 (O)	Smiley Quick

Colorado

1939	Eddie Held (Match)
1963	Hale Irwin (Medal)
1964	Hale Irwin (Medal)
1965	Hale Irwin (Medal)
1966	Hale Irwin (Match)
1973	Jackie Herpel Heistand (Match)

Illinois

1963	Doris Phillips
1965	Doris Phillips
1967	Doris Phillips
1982	Jerry Haas (Medal)
1983	Nancy Scranton
1984	Jerry Haas (Medal)
1985	Cindy Mueller
1987	Cindy Mueller

Iowa

1963	Steve Spray
1964 (O)	Steve Spray

Maine

1928	Eddie Held

Michigan

1949	Tom Draper
1972	Tom Draper (Seniors)
1973	Tom Draper (Seniors)
1974	Tom Draper (Seniors)

Mississippi

1940 (O)	Dutch Harrison

Montana

1958 (O)	Smiley Quick
1961 (O)	Dutch Harrison
1963 (O)	Dutch Harrison

New Mexico

1973 (O)	Steve Spray

Ohio

1982	Brian Fogt

Texas

1939 (O)	Dutch Harrison
1949 (O)	Dave Douglas
1951 (O)	Dutch Harrison
1983 (O)	Frank Conner

Utah

1951 (O)	Smiley Quick

"No matter how hard I try,
I just can't seem to break sixty-four."
...Jack Nicklaus (1959)

Club Professionals

While each Professional affects the lives of the members and players they come in contact with there are a few who deserve special mention. The achievement of the Master Professional recognition is one such level that separates one PGA Professional from their peers. Induction into state or national shrines also indicates a high level of achievement in their field. On a more sentimental basis, length of service at a particular club or area, and level of teaching and competitiveness are also factors.

Each area professional is worthy of our recognition for the service they bring to the game. On the following pages are several who represent some of the best in PGA Professionals over the past 80 years.

Jerry Tucker

The pro at Bellerive since 1986, Jerry has developed quite a reputation in the area, both for his playing skills and his business acumen. The 1994 PGA Gateway Professional of the Year winner, Jerry has seen many of his assistants move on to head their own operations. As a player Jerry has played in four major championships and 11 national club professional championships and has been one of the top six players in the Gateway section for the last 12 years. He has qualified for two US Opens, 1981 at Merion and 1984 at Winged Foot. He has played in two PGA's, in 1989 at Kemper Lakes and 1992 at Bellerive. He was the Player of the Year in the Gateway section in 1993 and was Assistant of the year in 1981 and Assistant Player of the Year in 1988. In 1991 Jerry won the Gateway Shoot-Out against area Pro's and a guest touring Pro, PGA champion John Daly. Jerry's most recent achievement was earning the Master Professional designation in 1989, at the time only the 61st nationally. He has also served on the Board of Directors of the Gateway Section.

Jerry Tucker

A statistics buff, Jerry spends long hours developing and tracking his own performance, even collaborating to have a software package written specifically for that purpose. He established the Gateway and National Club Professional ranking system as well.

Some of his assistants who have moved on to head professional positions include; John Hayes (Forest Hills), Larry Emery (Norwood Hills), Steve Harris (CC at the Legends), Joe Schwent (Lake Forest), Mike Tucker, Alan

Clark (Fox Run), Jodi Weber (Players Club) and Brad Keating.

At age 47 he has aspirations of making a run at the Senior Tour, and has been honing his game in preparation for that challenge. Jerry has been grooming several of his assistants to make the transition to the duties of a head professional at Bellerive and the club recently announced that his brother, Mike Tucker along with Joe Schwent will be co-head professionals at the club.

Steve Spray

Steve has been head professional at St. Louis CC since 1979. In one of the most high-profile positions in the area, Steve has been one of the best professionals around. Like many who have the respect of their peers, Steve has been a past president of the Gateway Chapter and has served on the Board of Directors for years.

Dividing his time today between the Country Club and the Senior Tour, Steve has been able to not only play in many Senior Events, but do so not by exemptions, but via the qualifying route, a much tougher task. His playing credentials are excellent and are outlined in the next sections on the *Touring Pro's,* as Steve was on the PGA Tour for 10 years.

Steve Spray

Like any good administrator and teacher, he has worked to develop his assistants over the years. But the position is such that many do not choose to leave, or they do and come back later. Among those who have left for a head pro position is Ramona Twellmen who set up shop at Kokopelli CC in Marion, IL.

Steve and his wife Deanna formed a course management business in the early 80's. While this no longer occupies their time, Steve now hopes to have enough time to prepare for more play on the Senior Tour. Steve has been head pro at the Country Club longer than any other professional, and his tenure of over 22 years ranks among the longest of any current pro [Fred Clarkson was at Glen Echo for over 42 years, the longest of any area pro].

He played in the PGA Senior Championship in 1996 where he made the cut, and played in the 1996 Boone Valley Classic where he finished in the middle of the pack. He has played in three of the Majors in his career, (two while on tour) and is one of only four area players to have won a collegiate individual title. Not bad for a Club Pro from St. Louis!

Jerry Ray

Another Master PGA Professional in the area, Jerry has held down the duties at Paradise Valley for many years. While the landscape of courses has changed dramatically over the past several years, Paradise Valley has continued to remain among the top of the "old guard" of area courses, with a loyal and avid following. Jerry remains one of the main reasons for this. During the 1970's and early 80's, Paradise Valley was considered among the best courses in the area. However, as the "upscale" courses began to come to the area, golfers left many traditional layouts for different challenges. Jerry, like many professionals at the more-established courses, faced the

Jerry Ray

challenges of "giving the lady a facelift", or suffering the consequences.

Paradise Valley has undergone such a change. While the layout is essentially the same, many improvements have taken place that make it more challenging, yet allowing the regulars to still enjoy their game.

Jerry is also a past president of the Gateway PGA and has served in a variety of duties to support the organization. He serves as Director of Golf at Paradise.

Terry Grosch

Long considered one of the top teaching pro's in the area, Terry moved to St. Albans when Cherry Hills voted to make the transition in 1992. Born and raised in St. Louis, Terry spent his youth in Overland, doing what most kids do; playing a variety of sports...but golf was not one of them. He first ventured to Lakeside GC on Page Ave. to caddy, though by then it had been reduced to 9 holes. After attending UMSL in the late 60's, Terry spent a few years in the military and upon his return, he decided to give golf a try. After announcing his professionalism he applied for an assistants position at Cherry Hills in 1973 and to his amazement, he got the job! Terry has been associated with that organization ever since. Once he had the position he became determined to learn as much as he could about the game. He travels to Florida each winter, first to take a few lessons, then to watch and learn. And learn he did, from some of the best around; Peter Kostis, Hank Haney, Davis Love, Jack Grout, Bob Cooke, Gary Wiren, Tony Penna and Gardner Dickinson. He attended numerous clinics and sat in on many Golf Digest schools. What developed was a professional instructor who never stopped learning, hungry for new information, anything that would help him assist his students to improve their game.

Terry Grosch

Terry believes, with a passion, that each of us has a swing that is "right" for us. It is within each of us. But too often, we neglect to take into account our size, body type and athleticism as we attempt a swing that is counterproductive to our physique. In more detail, an individual with a long flowing swing will be better at hitting a draw, whereas a short, stocky individual would do better with a fade. It is the "resistance" factor of the lower and upper portions of our body that drives this concept. It is something we are born with and, rather than fight it, we should work with it as best we can.

Many of his present students are among the best players, amateur and pro alike. They include Trevor Dodds,

The Professionals

Jay Delsing, Scott Thomas, Scott Edwards, Jim Mason, Don Bliss, Jim Holtgrieve, Derre Owsley, Phil Keim and David Lucks. Why do they gravitate towards Terry? Probably because of his style and manner. The physical act of striking a golf ball is usually not their problem, it is wrapped inside the mental aspect of the game. Helping them focus, keep their concentration and learn to "trust their swing" is what makes them champions.

With small children at home, and a nagging hip injury, Terry doesn't play as much as he would like. Plus there is more of the "business" side of the game to manage. So he spends his time reviewing golf tapes and reading the latest on the swing; and of course, teaching.

He completed his work for the Master Professional title, except for his thesis, in 1988, but was awarded that recognition only two years ago, making him the areas fifth with this honor. As he approaches the half century mark, he reflects on what a wonderful career he has had and the many friends he has made. He can't think of anything else he would rather do!

Walter Siemsglusz

The Head Professional at Berry Hill Golf Course in Bridgeton since 1988, Walter is among the few area Pro's who have achieved the Master Professional designation, having received this honor in May, 1996. Prior to Berry Hill, Walter was at Shawnee Hills CC in Harrisburg, IL for several years. In 1995 and 1996 he was honored by his Gateway PGA peers with the Horton Smith Award for promoting educational programs throughout section.

Dick Shaiper

The dean of area professionals, Dick has held several positions at some of the top clubs around. Today he makes his home at Whitmoor and the Missouri Bluffs, but only after spending 15 years at Norwood Hills as Head Professional and prior to that as Head Professional at Glen Echo for 16 years. Always the consummate player, he has many championships to his credit.

Dick Shaiper

In 1951 Dick was the Junior District Medalist. Then in 1952 as a member of the Webster Groves HS golf team, Dick and his fellow golfers won the state title as Dick took individual honors. Another local Pro was on the St. Louis U. High team at the same time, Jim Cochran, though Jim matured into a much better player than some of the tournament results of the day show.

Dick moved into the professional ranks and captured the 1961 St. Clair Open and then again in 1964. He continued to be one of the better players in the area until the 1980's when he concentrated more on the business side of the game and left the playing to his assistants.

Dick and Peter Scott (now at Mexico CC) were the founders of the Gateway Junior Program. Using funds from the Gateway Golfing Society, they funded the birth and then growth of Junior Golf for many years with the help of many generous individuals, in particular Hal Richardson of Pepsi-Cola.

Benny Richter

Benny Richter

Benny served as Head Professional for 15 years at Triple A GC from 1928-42, and for another 16 (1942-1958) at Bellerive CC. Swinging from "the other side" Benny won the national southpaw championship several times in the 30's and worked with Wilson to develop a line of lefty clubs that bore his name. As a player he was outstanding. Finishing 2nd in the PGA Seniors' Championship twice, in 1947 to Jock Hutchison and in 1948 to Charlie McKenna. He continued to play competitively and finished in the top 10 at the Seniors' Championship into the early 50's. Benny was one of the stalwarts of the Eastern Missouri PGA Pro's for years and teamed with many of them during the years. During the 50's he partnered with Homer Herpel for an instructional program for players featuring a convex mirror to view your swing.

Gateway Missouri PGA Hall of Fame

Milon Marusic was the head Professional for 25 years at Algonquin CC. During his tenure he was one of the best playing professionals, competing and winning the St. Louis Publinx, The PGA Quarter Century Championships, and competing in the PGA, PGA Club Professional Championships, and many regional and local tournaments. Milon competed with the very best and was competitive through the 1960's, and continued playing in the St. Louis Publinx into the 70's, always posting competitive scores. He played in 14 PGA Seniors' Championships, 7 PGA Match Play Championships and 4 PGA's at Stroke Play. He also played in 7 PGA Club Professional Championships and was the PGA Quarter-Century Champion in 1982 and the Senior Match Play Champion in 1987. He was the first Pro inducted into the Missouri PGA Hall of Fame in 1992.

Jim Fogertey was the first PGA professional in the country to acquire the title "Master Professional" in 1972. He began his career as a caddie at St. Louis CC and was the head professional at Sunset CC for 37 years, from 1947 to 1974. During his caddie days he looped for Tommy Armour, fresh from Scotland as an amateur, in the 1921 US Amateur at St. Louis CC. During this time, many local players came under his direction and learned the game from him. He served for several years as the professional at the Myopia Hunt Club in the Boston area, one of its most exclusive clubs. Renown as an expert club-maker, particularly of hickory shafts, he always believed that the feel with the wood shafts was unsurpassed. Jim passed away on July 29, 1991 at his home in Kirkwood. He was inducted into the Hall of Fame in 1995.

Joe Dodich

of Fame in 1995. One special moment came at Sunset in the early 60's when Jim was out playing one Monday. He shot the front side in 27!! Nine straight 3's, including an eagle! A record that stood for many years as a recognized low 9 holes.

Dick Shaiper was inducted into the Hall of Fame in 1995. During his 35 year PGA membership, Dick has been head professional at Glen Echo, Norwood Hills and today at Whitmoor and The Missouri Bluffs as Director of Golf. He spent several years as an assistant to another great area professional, Milon Marusic at Algonquin. Dick was one of the area's premier players in the 1960's and 70's and won the St. Louis Publinx Professional division several times, as well as the St. Clair Open. Dick was Section President twice and was Golf Professional of the Year in 1968 and 1975.

Joe Dodich was head professional at Westwood for 22 of his 43 years as a PGA Pro. Joe was the oldest player to capture a Section event when he won at Normandie in 1979, shooting a 66 at age 48. He was a past president of the Section in 1976, 1977 and 1978 and was named Professional of the Year in 1978. Joe co-founded Crystal Highlands GC in Festus in 1988. He was inducted into the Hall of Fame in 1995.

Jim Fogertey

Gateway PGA Presidents	
1976-78	Joe Dodich
1978-81	Bob Kelsey
1981-83	Denny Walters
1983-84	Steve Sebastian
1984-85	Terry Grosch
1986-88	Jerry Ray
1988-90	Bob Jones
1990-91	Bill Hall
1991-92	Jon Johnson
1993-94	Steve Spray
1994-96	Russ Luedloff

The Range Pro's

There are another group of Professionals in the area. They do not serve members, but customers. They do not look over neatly manicured fairways, but a measured range. They see more Jim Furyk-like swings than they care to remember, and they attempt to help by offering a tip or two; [usually free and always accurate] to the masses who, by the bucket or basket, attempt to find the swing! These are the pro's who toil at the area driving ranges, those spots we drift-to when we just missed 18 consecutive fairways and greens and we try to figure-out how we can still do this and shoot in the 80's!

Perhaps the dean of the area is *Dick Lotz*. Dick has been riding herd over at Tower Tee for over 32 years. Assisted by Nike player Bob Gaus, Steve Lotz, and his wife Barbara, Dick still works the register as he greets his "members". With Tower Tee West open for a few years, Dick has now moved westward.

Dick Lotz

He also owns Crystal Tee in Festus and Yorktown Range in Belleville with Bob Goalby. At Tower Tee, they will see about 40,000 rounds per year, a very healthy number for the 18 hole par 3 layout.

Another veteran is **Dale Boggs** at Creve Coeur Recreation Complex. Dale has been plagued for years by the ever-changing fates of the Missouri River. His 18 hole putting course, built several years ago, show his ingenuity at attracting new players. Still others are **Tom DeGrand** at Pro-Am Golf Center on Union at I-55, and **Zeke Seeger** at Little Lakes. Others include **Dan Buffington** at The Falls Recreation Complex, **Dan Polites** at DP Golf Center in Belleville, **John Kokoruda** at Tee-Up in Collinsville, **Steve Lestmann** at Tree Court, **Dean Frankiewicz** at Chesterfield Valley, **Mike Brengard** at Pro Tee Golf Center in Wood River, **Tom Heyer** and **Lee VanDover** at The Golf Center in Valley Park and **Steve Williams** at Archwood Tee in St. Peters.

Dale Boggs

Through the years, many others have manned ranges. One of the most significant names was **Eddie Held** who had Held's range on Manchester for years. Ranges have come and gone. There were two where the dove at West County Shopping Center now flies, and the corner that now houses the Galleria in Brentwood saw two ranges (one by Walter Ambo) nearby as did the Page-Price location that now holds an empty Central Hardware. Another site was at the intersection of Lindbergh and Watson in South County. Another pro who operated a range was **Don Clarkson**, who had his indoors at Westport Plaza. Despite the loss of these, others have come forward, in many cases much better. The days of the "Tin Cup" type range is virtually gone. Today they offer not just golf but batting cages, miniature golf, restaurants, putting greens and basketball nets.

The Professionals

Ron Akin

Garth Bayer

Alex Bopp

Clarence Norsworthy

Tony Henschel

Stewart Maiden

Gene Webb and Dick Lotz (r)

Orville White

Steve Sebastian

PGA Professionals at Area Clubs

Algonquin (1899)[3]
D.K. White (1905-08)
David Patrick (1909-13)
William Kidd (1914-19)
Elmer Harrison (1929-53)
Don Harrison (1929-53)
Walter Harrison (1929-53)
Homer Herpel (1954-56)
Milon Marusic (1956-80)
Steve Sebastian (1981-Present)

St. Louis Field Club (1898-1910)
Ed McNamara (1997-98)
Robert Simpson (1899-1900)
George Norman (1899-04)[1]
David Ogilvie (1901-02)
Willie Duffy (1904)
Nick Kessler (1903-05)

Bellerive (Old-1910-1960)
Jack Gatherum (1911-1913)
Robert Foulis (1910-1942)[1]
Bob Jessiman (1931-42)
Ben Richter (1942-59)
Paul Maguire (1959-64)

Bellerive (New-1960)
Paul Maguire (1959-64)
Bob Ross (1965-70)
Nick Gustin (1971-76)
Gary Fee (1977-1986)
Jerry Tucker (1987-1996)
Mike Tucker (1996- Present)*
Joe Schwent (1996-Present)*
*Co-Head Pro's

Berry Hill (1967)
Ken Davis (1976-1988)
Walter Siemsglusz (1988-Present)

Bogey Hills (1961)
Russ Boudrais (1961-65)
Hershel Ross (1966-80)
Dennis Walters (1981-84)
Bob Jones (1985-Present)

CC at the Legends (1989)
Larry Emery (1989-1993)
Steve Harris (1994-1996)
Greg Mullican (1996-Present)

Cherry Hills (1964)
Jim Spencer (1964)
Phil Hewitt (1965-76)
Terry Grosch (1977-92)
Tim Krebs (1995-Present)

Clinton Hill (1971)
Clete Idoux (1971-74)
Brian Maine (1989-92)
Jim Knott (1993-1994)
Dan Polites (1995-Present)

Crescent CC (1979)
The Players Club (1988)
Don Clarkson (1979-82)
Terry Houser (1983-85)
Don Clarkson (1986-87)
Jodi Weber (1988-91)
Charlie Stock (1992-Present)

Creve Coeur (1924)
Wyndham Monroe (1928-29)
Jack Beirne (1929-38)
Arnold Hartenbach
Bob Jones (1968-71)
Al Oulds (1972-86)
Tom Heyer (1987-91)
Mark Lewis (1991-Present)

Crystal Lake (1929-1979)
Wyndham Monroe (1929-36)
Homer Herpel (1937-42)
Dave Sutherland (1947-49)
Alex Bopp (1950-79)

Duwe / Lakewood (1961)
Bill Duwe (1961-71)
Mike Halcomb (1972-73)

Eagle Springs (1989)
Tim Davenport (1989-91)
Barry Storie (1992-Present)

Forest Hills (1965)
Dutch Harrison (1965-74)
Roger Williams (1975-1986)
Jon Johnson (1987-92)
John Hayes (1993-Present)

Forest Park (1913)
Clarke Morse (1928-29)
Coleman Morse (1928-29)
Ed Duwe (1929-46)
Bob Riley (1947-1966)
Ken Sample (1969-1973)
Steve Sebastian (1974-76)
Kevin Schwartz (1986-88)
Roger Williams (1988-90)
Chris Blevins (1990-92)
Leonard Martin (1992-Present)

Four Seasons CC (1962)
Bill Whitfield (1962-77)
Gordon Ziegler (1983-87)
Russ Luedloff (1988-1996)

Fox Creek/Ballwin (1962)
Bob Green (1962-68)
Dave Furlong (1990-96)

Glen Echo (1901)
Robert Foulis (1901-07)[1]
Willie Duffy (1908-10)
Fred Clarkson (1911-53)
Don Clarkson (1954-62)
Dick Shaiper (1963-78)
Bill Hall (1979-93)
Larry Emery (1994-95)
Nash Haxel (1995-Present)

Glenwood (1970-79)
Clarence O'Hara (1970-73)
Bob Jones (1974-79)

Grand Marias (1935)
Clarence O'Hara (1974-79)
Mike Murphy (1993-96)

Osage (1926-1936)
Homer Herpel (1926-28)
Jim Fogertey (1929-35)

Greenbriar Hills CC (1937)
Frank Fogertey (1936-73)
Bob Kelsey (1974-81)
Scott Oulds (1982-Present)

Green Trails (1965-1985)
Monte Bradley (1965-68)
Allan Lucht (1969-72)
Ken Sample (1973-85)

Hillcrest/Sherwood (1928)
Homer Herpel (1929-32)
Ken Blume (1983-87)
Frank Hartzel (1988-89)
Stephen Kleiss (1990-Present)

Lake Forest CC (1978)
Joe Gradl (1979-82)
Jeff Hogge (1983-87)
Joe Schwent (1988-89)
Fred Friedman (1990-Present)

Lakeside GC (1950-1956)
Gene Webb (1950-56)

Lockhaven CC (1955)
Lou Miller (1955-62)
Ken Pruitt (1963-64)
Jim Barton (1965-69)
Jim Rohan (1970-75)
Tom Tatnal (1976-78)
Mike Halcomb (1979-92)
Bill Moser (1993-Present)

Midland Valley (1911-1932)
Charles Clarkson (1917-24)
Francis Schwartz (1925-33)
Ray Schwartz (1925-33)
Bill Schwartz (1925-1933)

Meadow Brook (1932-1961)
Orville White (1934-43)
Dale Morey (1944-45)
Frank Moore (1946-51)
Walter Ambo (1951-55)
Ky Laffoon (1956-57)
Ed Johnston (1958-60)

Meadowbrook (1961)
Ed Johnson (1961)
Monte Bradley (1962-65)
Tom Fonseca (1966-70)
Lee Van Dover (1971-85)
Mark Morgan (1986-93)
Bill Lansdowne (1994-Present)

Normandie (1901)
Willie Duffy (1902-04)
Willie Dow (1905-07)
Robert Foulis (1908-12)[1]
Sandy Auctherlonie (1927-30)
Coleman Morse (1931-44)
Clarke Morse (1931-1944)
Johnny Manion (1945-58)
Frank Keller (1959-65)
Walter Eiserman (1966-67)
Frank Keller (1968-75)
Tom Kammann (1976-84)
Steve Heath (1985-88)

North Hills (1922)
Norwood Hills (1933)
Louis J. Hamel (1922-26)
Bill Mehlhorn (1922-23)
Joe Henry (1927-50)
Ray Schwartz (1951-54
Dick Chassee (1955-56
Gene Webb (1957-69)
John Gerring (1970-71)
Ed Griffiths (1972-78)
Dick Shaiper (1979-94)
Larry Emery (1995-Present)

Old Warson (1954)
Dutch Harrison (1954-60)
Al Mengert (1961-62)
Don Clarkson (1963-78)
T.D. Morris (1979-86)
Bob Dickman (1987-88)
Garth Bayer (1989-Present)

Paddock GC (1960)
Ken Sample (1960-69)
Jim Barton (1970-72)
Terry Clark (1973-82
Mike Kirkpatrick (1990-91 &
95-Present)

Quail Creek GC (1988)
Mike Murphy (1988-91)
Doug Brown (1991-92)
David Bird (1992-93)
T.D. Morris (1994-Present)

Riverview GC (1914)
North Shore (1926-1994)
James Pairman (1929-31)
Joe Murray (1937-42)
Ken Capps (1963-74)
Dale Boggs (1975-77)
Bob Aldridge (1978-?)

Rock Springs GC (1912)
C.C. Graves (1926-32)
Homer Herpel (1933-35)
Lou Miller (1951-55)

Ruth Park (1931)
Les Switzer (1931-34)
Francis Schwartz (1935-36)
Les Scanlon (1937-38)
Clarence Norsworthy (1939-41)
Homer Herpel (1942-46)
Henry Christman (1947-78)
Paul Miller (1979-81)
Eric Engle (1984-90)
Ron Akin (1991-Present)

St. Albans (1993)
Terry Grosch (1993-Present)

St. Andrews (1967)
Frank Keller (1967)
Tim Davenport (1974-88)
Kirk Porter (1989-Present)

St. Ann (1950)
Tim O'Connell (1950-86)
Mark Ryan (1987-Present)

St. Charles GC (1956)
Clarence O'Hara (1956)

St. Clair (1911)
Walter Kossman (1922-31)
Harvey/Bill Merch (1932-40)
Frank Moore (1941-46)
Johnny St. Clair (1947-50)
Clarke Morse (1951-75)
Clarence Voigt (1976-86)
Paul Hooser (1987-91)
Jeff Hunter (1992-Present)

The Professionals

St. Louis CC (1896-1913)
Ned Mack (1897-98)
George Norman (1898-99)[2]
James Mackrell (1898-1900)
Robert Simpson (1901-02)
Gilbert Nichols (1902-04)
Will Leslie (1902-03)
Willie Duffy (1905-08)
Willie Anderson (1909)
Fred McLeod (1910-12)

St. Louis CC (1913) Ladue
Jim Foulis (1912-1915)
Stuart Maiden (1919-20)
Jim Barnes (1921-22)
R. A. Longworth (1923-31)
Ralph Guldahl (1932-33)
Alex Ayton (1934-48)
Fred Bolton (1949-51)
Ted Neist (1952-57)
Dave Douglas (1957-73)
Brian Boggess (1974-75)
Steve Spray (1976-Present)

Sunset Hill CC (1917) Sunset CC
Dave Robertson (1916-20)
Jim Barnes (1917-20)
John Manion (1927-44)
Dave Sutherland (1945-47)
Jim Fogertey (1948-73)
Mike Halcomb (1974)
Ben Johnson (1974-76)
Mike Murphy (1977-86)
Gary Fee (1987-Present)

Madison County CC (1922)
Sunset Hills [Edwardsville]
Howard Popham (1940-62)
Winton Dryden (1963-69)
Ross Horst (1970-78)
Bill Sowerwine (1979-88)
Victor Whipp (1989-93)
Brad Peck (1993-Present)

Tower Grove (1898-1903)
George Norman (1898-03)

Triple A GC (1897-1902) Original
Triple A GC (1902) Present site
Ed McNamara (1899-1900)
Mr. Sherwood (1900-02)
Harrison Brothers (1923-27)
Ben Richter (1928-32)
Clarence Norsworthy (1933-46)
Bob Green (1947-63)
Fred Kolb (1964-65)
Bob Riley (1966-67)
Ann Gavin (1968)
Frank Keller (1969-85)
Jim Offer (1986-Present)

Westwood Club (1908) [Glendale]
Westborough (1928)
Otto Hackbarth (1908-1911)
J.M. Watson (1911-14)
Arthur Smith (1928-29)
Clarence J. Coff (1929-31)
Orville White (1932-34)
Walter Ambo (1935-50)
Leroy Trotter (1951-53)
Tony Henschel (1954 -82)
Bob Nieberding (1983-84)
Phil Hewitt (1985-Present)

Westwood (1928)
Dave Sutherland (1928-31)
Jim Cockburn (1932-50)
Ed Furgol (1951-56)
Roger Pedigo (1957-59)
Fred Wampler (1960-65)
Robert Frainey (1966-67)
Bob Rosburg (1968-69)
Joe Dodich (1970-91)
Daryl Hartig (1992-Present)

Kirkwood CC (1912)
Woodlawn CC (1926-1936)
Earl Lancaster (1912-37)

[1] - Foulis was greenkeeper at several clubs at the same time. The term greenkeeper/professional was used extensively during the early 1900's.

[2] - Norman was the teaching pro and clubmaker, but not head pro at these courses.

[3] - Date next to club notes the date the Club/Course was founded. In some cases the original course may no longer exist, but the club can be traced to the date shown. Where two names are shown, the club changed names or reorganized. See section "COURSES" for more information on the club or course.

Clarke Morse

Frank Pepp

Touring Pro's

"I would rather win one tournament in my life than make the cut each week."

...Arnold Palmer

Among the many Touring Professionals who have called St. Louis home, there are only a few "native" Bi-Staters! A few lived here for a time in their youth, then moved on. Some married St. Louis spouses and settled here. Still others found head professional positions at area clubs and their stay ranged from a year to a lifetime! Those listed in the following section played the PGA Tour (and other Tours) while living in the area.

If this work were to categorize them by group then Bob Goalby and Judy Rankin would be among the top's for St. Louis area natives. Hale Irwin would rank a close second, having lived here for almost 30 years, as would have the late Dutch Harrison having settled here late in his career.

Jay Haas, Bob Tway, Steve Spray, Larry Ziegler, Frank Conner, Tom Wargo, Nancy Scranton, Trevor Dodds, Jay Delsing, Jerry Haas, Jay Williamson, Bill Hall, Jim Cochran, Jim Offer, Brian Fogt, Jim Mason, Doug Brown, Brian Fogt, Bob Gaus, Dick Hendrickson, Steve Reid and others that have been inadvertently overlooked have all played the Tour, and have enjoyed varying degrees of success in their chosen profession.

The Professionals

Jim Barnes

Jim Barnes was a tall (6'3"), lanky Englishman who migrated to St. Louis during WW1 and claims a place in history as the first winner of the PGA Championship in 1916. Jim worked as the club pro at several clubs, including Sunset Hill while competing on the early tour. Facing Jock Hutchison in the finals of the 1916 PGA (Hutchison would go on to win the 1920 PGA and 1921 British Open) Barnes would face an early 3 down situation, but would rally to trail by one at the end of 18 holes. In the days of the 36-hole finals in a single day, staying close in the opening round was critical. The final 18 would find Barnes winning 1-up as Hutchison missed his 5 footer on the final hole and Barnes rolled his in. Barnes would also win in 1919 in a match that was billed as a "David vs. Goliath" match as Barnes faced 5'3" Fred McLeod for the title. Once again Barnes proved unbeatable as he holed a 40 foot birdie putt on the 31st hole to claim a 6&5 win. He was perhaps the dominant player in the country in the year immediately preceding and the few years following the first World War. In addition to the PGA and the US Open, he would win the Western Open in 1914, 1917 and 1919 often with rounds in the 60's.

He would play in a total of 9 PGA's, reaching the Finals again in 1920 where he would lose to Walter Hagen in his first PGA victory 3&2. He would reach the Semifinals in 1921 and the Quarterfinals in 1923 and again in 1924, but would never again claim the title.

His record in the PGA of 24 wins and only 7 losses for a .777 winning percentage ranks him 7th all time in wins behind the likes of Snead, Hogan, Sarazen and Nelson. Snead with 50 wins ranks first in that category, and with players with over 20 wins, only Byron Nelson (37-8), Ben Hogan (22-5), Snead (50-14) and Walter Burkemo (27-6) have better winning percentages. As a champion of his day, he had few contenders. At match play, only Snead (3), Hagen (5) and Sarazen (3) have more titles to their credit and, of course, Jack Nicklaus (4) at stroke play.

Barnes was at Sunset Hill in 1919 and 1920. While there he won the 1919 PGA, so the layout must have agreed with his game. He left Sunset Hill and spent a year at St. Louis CC in 1921, winning the US Open that year. It is characteristic of the time that although he was the head pro at St. Louis in '21, he represented Pelham CC on the tour! He stayed at St. Louis until January, 1923 when he moved on. He would not win another championship after leaving St. Louis.

Frank Conner

Born in Vienna Austria, Frank made his home in Belleville for several years, and is an honorary member of St. Clair CC. While not a household name, Frank joined the PGA Tour in 1975 and was a regular on the Tour in the 80's, where one of his highlights was his win at the Deposit Guaranty Classic in Hattisburg, Mississippi as he shot a 13 under 267 to walk away with the first prize. Frank was involved in one of the largest playoffs in PGA history when 5 players tied for first at the 1981 Quad Cities. Dave Barr would wind-up being the eventual champion.

Frank is unique in that he has played both pro tennis and golf, and is one of only two players to compete in the US Open in both sports. After banging around the Nike tour from 1990-1995 Frank was eligible for the Senior Tour in 1996 and he took full advantage of the opportunity, competing in his first 13 events he cashed-in for over $150,000. He finished the season in great form with over $500,000 in winnings and number 20th on the list, guaranteeing him a spot on the '97 Tour. Frank now resides in Texas with his wife and two daughters.

Jay Delsing

The St. Louis U. High and UCLA grad grew up on the grounds of Norwood Hills, where he learned how to play the game to a greater and more refined skill. The 6'5" Delsing stands out among the tour players. Jay was the St. Louis District Champion in 1980 and joined the Tour in 1985. Jay is a very affable man and takes the trials of Tour life in stride.

A two-time All American as a Bruin, his teammates were Corey Pavin, Steve Pate and Duffy Waldorf. His play on the Tour could best be described as "streaky". In 1994 he made 10 of his first 11 cuts and finished in the top 10 in two events. While only making 16 cuts in 27

Jay Delsing and Dutch Harrison

events he was able to finish 124 on the List to keep his card. During 1993 he set a course record at the TPC at Southwind (61) and during 1992 Jay posted 4 top 10 finishes and finished 52nd on the money list.

His best finish was a 2nd at the 1995 St. Jude Classic. Competing in 28 events in 1995, he was able to make the cut in only 11, yet took home over $230,000. An interesting note; his scoring average of 71.7 (ranked 136) is only 2.3 strokes off Nick Faldo's leading 69.47, illustrating the fine line between leading the pack and trying to keep up. Jay returned to Q-school in 1996 and kept his card by shooting good rounds the last two days to make the cut.

Trevor Dodds

Born in Windhoek, Namibia (Southwest Africa) in 1959, Trevor played may different sports during his school years, including field hockey, cricket, soccer and swimming. His first introduction to golf came at age 12. His father was a tremendous influence on his development as he taught Trevor to enjoy the game above all else. Acquiring his first set of clubs at age 15, he began on sand greens and airways, but it didn't stop him as he became a 3-handicap quickly. He didn't play on grass until some time later.

At 17 he represented the Western Province Juniors in South African Junior golf on a team which travelled to the US. The team included fellow countryman David Frost and one of the opponents on a US Junior team was Mark Calcavecchia, who Trevor defeated in their match. Receiving a scholarship to Lamar College he "walked-on" the golf team and in his senior year he won two events and had 9 top 5 finishes and was a first team All-

Trevor Dodds

The Professionals

American selection along with Steve Elkington, Davis Love III, Duffy Waldorf, Scott Verplank and Sam Randolph.

He turned pro, made it through Q-School and in 1985 was on the PGA Tour. But it was short-lived. *"...my game wasn't developed to the level it needed to be to stay on Tour"*, and by 1995 he had left the Tour...but not left golf. Trevor's best finish was a 3rd in the 1993 AT&T Pebble Beach event, but after seven years he was not content with just also-ran finishes.

On the Sunshine (South African) tour in 1988 he finished first in scoring with a 69.0 average. He also finished 4th on the Order of Merit for 1988-89 after ending 1987-88 in the 14th spot. His best finishes that year were a 3rd place at the Lexington PGA, a 5th place tie at the AECI Classic, two 6th place finishes in the Helix Sun Classic and the Bloemfontein Classic. His biggest thrill came in 1990 when he won the South African Open, the National Title of the country. He competed in the World Series of Golf as a result and several other honors. In 1990 he finished 3rd on the Order of Merit and in 1995 11th with a 6th place finish in 1996.

His play in Canada during the past two seasons was extraordinary. He won two events in 1995 and finished 1st on the Order of Merit. During 1996 on the Canadian Tour, Trevor set all time records for wins, money and scoring average. With only 12 events on the tour during their season, Trevor won 4, the Henry Singer Alberta Open, ED TEL PLAnet Open, Infiniti Open and the Canadian Masters. In doing so he eclipsed Dave Barr's mark for money in one season and his four wins was another record on the Canadian Tour. Capturing the top prize in bunches, his wins came in two back-to-back weeks . So fickle is the game, as we all know, that in a five week stretch he finished first four times but amazingly finished tied for 42nd in the other tournament! His scoring average of 69.22 was also tops on the tour, though it had been as low as 68.7 during one stretch.

During his run in 1996 Trevor acknowledged that this was *"...the best five golfing weeks of my life."* Following his win at the Canadian Masters, Trevor became very emotional as he thanked the large gallery for supporting him. But his success was not all that easy. Beginning the final round up by three, he was caught and dropped into second as he bogeyed twice. But he regained his composure at the 15th with a birdie to regain a two shot lead and held on for the win.

Trevor believes that St. Louis is one of the best kept secrets in golf. With St. Louis CC, Bellerive, Old Warson we have three of the best in the country. Newer courses such as St. Albans, Boone Valley and Fox Run are exciting. But the traditional layouts draw his praise as well; Algonquin, Westborough and Westwood.

He feels fortunate to have met Terry Grosch early in his stay here. *"...he has become a great friend and a very good coach. He has helped me develop some of my strengths and has shown me drills to overcome some of my weaker tendencies."* Trevor also gets occasional help from David Leadbetter, Bob Rotella and of course his father.

The birth of his daughter, Audrey, has been a great blessing to he and Kristen. With his playing schedule, she will log over 40,000 miles before she turns one!

As far as playing the PGA Tour again, he knows that he has to first get through Q-school, not an easy prediction. *"I am much better prepared and am better equipped to succeed."* As fellow pro Ian Leggatt stated, *"He can most definitely make it again on the PGA Tour...he doesn't do anything great - he just does everything well."*

Heather Drew

Heather began playing at Old Warson when she was just 7 years old. Her father was the General Manager of KMOX in those days and Heather picked the game up as a junior. Unfortunately, her father was again transferred, first to Chicago and then to California, where they now live.

Heather Drew

It was when in the San Diego area that she became hooked on the sport. She attended the University of Arizona, and after a successful freshman season, she received a scholarship for her remaining years. Following graduation in 1981 she attempted to join the tour and finally did for the 1983 season.

At 5'4" Heather would not intimidate anyone physically, so she lets her game do the talking for her In her 14 seasons on tour, Heather has had several very successful tournaments. In 1990 in the Jamie Farr Toledo Classic she had a putt to tie Patty Sheehan and force a playoff. Unfortunately it didn't fall and she had to settle for second. Two years later she again was the runner-up in Toledo; the course suits her game very well!

From 1989 through 1992 Heather was the model of consistency; her stroke average was coming down and she was finishing high most weeks. The checks she was cashing each week were quite nice. Then in 1994 her mother passed away and her mental game went into the rough. During 1994 and 1995 she had to go back to Q-School but couldn't find the magic those weeks. Then in the 1996 Q-School, she had some physical problems that kept her from performing. You might think this would get her down, but you would be way off base. Heather's attitude is great! She knows what she has to do to regain her old form. Her short game has never left her and this is the key to playing well on the LPGA. Today she plays out of Lomas Santa Fe CC, about an hour north of San Diego. She has lined up several exemptions and will show up on Monday to qualify for others. She needs to get back to doing those things that allowed her to be successful, keep the ball in play and let your short game pick up birdies.

She has seen the influx of the foreign players, though most of them have played college golf in the states. They bring a unique attitude with them. They are not content to just compete; they are intent on winning. This is the new driving force on the Tour today and the level of competitiveness has risen to new high because of it. She knows that to remain out there, she too must develop a new attitude, with the game to match.

Bob Goalby

Known best for his victory in the *1968 Masters*, Bob was one of the most consistent golfers of his day. He went into the winners circle early as an amateur when at age 26 he was the 1955 St. Louis District Champion. Bob turned Pro the following year and joined the Tour in 1957.

In 1958, his first year on tour, he won the Greater Greensboro Open at Starmount Forest CC, shooting a 275. He was rewarded for a successful season by being named the PGA Rookie of the Year. In 1960 he won at Coral Gables and then in 1961 he won the LA Open at Rancho Municipal GC, shooting a 275 to claim the $7,500 top prize. He also won the St. Petersburg Open that year. The 1962 Hartford Classic, then known as the Insurance City Open, was won by Bob when he shot a 271 at Wethersfield CC. In 1967 he won the then San Diego Open at the

The Professionals

Bob Goalby in 1962

Two photos of Bob taken over 30 years apart (left) while on the PGA Tour the year after setting the mark of 8 consecutive birdies in the St. Petersburg Open and below, in a more recent picture from the Senior PGA Tour.

The idea for the Senior Tour was Bob's and when he brought it to Deane Beman he paid litle attention to it...at least not until it began to take off! Then guess who's idea it suddenly became!!

Bob Goalby in 1994

Bob Goalby and Jay Haas on the range

Stardust CC in San Diego shooting a 269. Other Tour victories were the 1969 Robinson Classic, the 1970 Heritage and the 1971 Bahamas Classic. He was also a member of the *1963 Ryder Cup Squad* and was second at both the *1961 US Open* to Gene Littler and the *1962 PGA Championship* to Gary Player.

One of the records Bob set on the PGA tour, back in 1961, has never been broken, though it has been tied twice. That is his record of 8 consecutive birdies in the St. Petersburg Open at the Pasadena Golf Club. Fuzzy Zoeller tied this in 1976 and Dewey Arnette did the same in 1987. Bob also had streaks of 7 and 6 consecutive birdies at other times in tour events. In 1995 Jay Delsing almost tied the mark as he recorded 7 consecutive birdies on his way to victory in the St. Jude Classic in Memphis.

One of the initial participants in the *"Legends of Golf"* series played in the late 70's --the forerunner to the Senior PGA Tour-- Bob was one of the founders of the Senior Tour and has participated every season since 1980. So successful was Bob in his early days on the Senior circuit that during 1982 he did not finish out of the top-10 in any event! Bob won his initial Senior title at the 1981 Digital Seniors Classic at Marlboro CC in Massachusetts over Art Wall by two shots. This tournament has turned into the Bank of Boston Senior Classic. He next teamed with Mike Reid as they claimed the 1983 Showdown Classic at Jeremy Ranch GC in Utah. He also won the *Peter Jackson Champions* event in Winnipeg over Gene Littler in 1982, shooting 15 under for the three rounds. However in 1986 Littler gained some revenge, downing Bob in the *Bank One Classic* in a playoff. He suffered another second in 1981 when Don January edged him by a stroke in San Francisco at the *Eureka Classic*. In 1992 Bob took the Super Senior title at the *Franklin Quest Championship*.

The former SIU Saluki continues to enjoy the competition and in 1995 entered 12 events, though he cut back on the 1996 events as the travel and business pressures persuaded him to stay closer to home. A nagging shoulder injury has added further discomfort and for the time being, Bob will be content to enjoy the time off.

NBC saw the value in having someone with Bob's experience on their team and he spent 13 years as an analyst for the network. He was also prominent in his color commentary at the 1987 Skins game at LaQuinta. This particular one was highlighted by Trevino's ace on the par-3 17th hole.

Locally Bob captured the St. Clair Invitational twice, in 1960 and again in 1964. He won the St. Louis Open twice and was the force behind the St. Clair Invitational becoming the premier Pro event during the late 50's and through the 60's. It was revived in 1977 and 1978 as Bob got the gang back together again. His nephew, Jay Haas defeated legendary Sam Snead for the title in 1978.

The Professionals

As one of the founders of the Senior Tour, he has served as a Player Director on the Board for 15 of the past 18 years. Bob continues to live in Belleville, and now spends part of his time as a course designer, having done *The Orchards* and recently has *Champions Trail GC* under construction. Besides golf, one of Bob's passions is Quail hunting. Bob was inducted into the Illinois Sports Hall of Fame in 1991.

Jay Haas

Jay Haas

Jay Haas, along with his uncle, Bob Goalby and his brother Jerry Haas, are, along with Jimmy Connors, the best known athletes from Belleville, and perhaps in all of Southern Illinois.

Winning District Titles in 1972, 1973 & 1975, Jay attended Wake Forest where he was a two time All-American. In 1975 he won the individual medal at the NCAA championships on the Scarlet Course at Ohio State, the excellent Alister Mackenzie design. Playing on the same team with Curtis Strange, they presented a formidable presence as Wake also won the team championship for the second consecutive year. Jay was honored with the Fred Haskins Award in 1975 as the outstanding College Golfer of the year . Other winners of this award have been Ben Crenshaw, Curtis Strange, Scott Simpson, Scott Verplank, Bobby Clampett, Bob Tway and Billy Mayfair. 1975 was capped-off by his selection to the Walker Cup squad. At the matches, played over the Old Course at St. Andrews, he teamed with Curtis Strange for two wins and won his singles match 2 and 1 over

Richard Eyles. In 1976 Jay continued his brilliant career, winning the Southwestern Amateur and then the Missouri Open as his initial professional event. He completed Q School in 1976 and joined the PGA Tour.

After turning pro, Jay began slowly, always doing well, but never quite getting to the top echelon. Then as he began to mature, so did his game and to date he has 9 career wins.

His first win came in 1978 at the San Diego Open. From there it was 1981 in Milwaukee when he won the Greater Milwaukee Open and later the same year, the B.C. Open at En-Joie GC in Endicott, NY. At the 1982 Texas Open Jay again tasted victory when he shot a 262 over the Oak Hills course in San Antonio, and once again had a two victory season, winning the Hall of Fame Classic. Jay's other wins include the Big "I" Houston Open in 1987, the Bob Hope Chrysler Classic in 1988, the St. Jude Classic in 1992 and the H-E-B Texas Open again in 1993. Jay finished 3rd at the 1995 Masters and for the 4th time, made a year ending appearance in the lucrative Tour Championship. Jay

Jay Haas - 1975

also competed for the US in the 1995 Ryder Cup at Oak Hill and the 1983 matches at PGA National. He was also a member of the inaugural Presidents Cup team in 1994.

Jay returned to St. Clair CC in 1977 & 1978 to compete in the revived St. Clair Invitational. Uncle Bob Goalby put on the classic one more time, much to Jay's enjoyment. He battled with Sam Snead for the title before besting the aging-legend for the title.

Surprisingly Jay never competed for the Missouri or Illinois State titles, St. Clair CC not belonging to the MGA and the Illinois Amateur conflicted with other events..

One of the true gentlemen in the game, Jay is always a favorite with the other players and the crowds. His mild manner and businesslike game are the trademarks of his success. At the recent Greg Norman Shark Shoot-out at Sherwood CC in California, Jay teamed with Tom Kite as they recorded a three shot win over a very competitive field, which included Hale Irwin, Lanny Wadkins, Tom Watson, Raymond Floyd, Brad Fabel, and of course the Shark himself.

Jay resides in Greenville, S.C. with his wife Janice, the sister of fellow pro Dillard Pruitt, and their five children.

Jerry Haas

Jerry & Lizzy Haas

Jerry Haas

Jerry continues to play on the Nike tour and part time on the PGA tour as he hones his game in an attempt to join his brother on the Tour permanently. Jerry was a District Champion in 1983, 1984 and 1985. He also won the Illinois Amateur three consecutive years in 1982, 1983 & 1984, and was a member of the 1985 Walker Cup. He also tied for 31st in the 1985 Masters, missing the top 24 (and an automatic invite) when he doubled the par 3 16th. He attended Wake Forest, like his older brother Jay, and was also an All-American. As a Junior, Jerry won the Pepsi Little Peoples Championship in 1978.

Jerry's game was in quite a slump during most of 1994. He had missed 11 consecutive cuts and his chances of moving up seemed even more in doubt. But at Highland Springs CC, Springfield's wonderful Robert Trent Jones layout, Haas revealed that not only did he have a new putting stroke, but his game was back in form. He won twice more (Tri-Cities Open and Sonoma County Open), and as result finished 9th on the money list and earned

The Professionals

Bob Goalby with nephews Jay Haas (center) and Jerry Haas. In 1985 they became the only family, since the first Masters in 1934, with three members to play in the Masters in the same year.

his PGA card for 1995. Such is the life of the struggling PGA tour player. Having played on the Tour in 1990 & 1991, Jerry knew the pressures that would be present. Attempting to remain in the top 125 to keep his card was his top priority, though he knew how difficult that would be. His best finishes in 1995 were at the Buick Classic and the Canon Greater Hartford Open where he tied for 18th at both. 1996 saw Jerry back on the Nike Tour, once again hoping to find the touch that will allow him to move a step closer to the Tour on a permanent basis

Though he missed qualifying for the Tour at the Q-School in December, Jerry is far from thinking about losing his desire. His crossroads now revolve around his wife and 16-month old daughter.

Jerry is among the group of professionals who have won pro events and know what it takes. He knows he has the game to compete, he just has to do it better. *"When I have played poorly it is usually because I took a chance on hitting that perfect shot, when one for the center of the green would have been good enough."* The strength of his game lies in his short game. Not a long driver, he went to the cavity-backed irons to help him with control and getting the ball up quicker with the long irons.

Bill Hall

Bill Hall

The former Head professional at Glen Echo, Bill went to the 1993 Senior Qualifying School hoping to make the cut for the Senior Tour and grab one of the eight spots. He did even better than that. He played so well that he finished as Medalist in the qualifying on the tough West Course at Grenelefe Resort.

During 1993 Bill honed his game by being part of the "rabbits" on the Senior Tour; taking the Monday Qualifying route each week. He performed well enough to play in two tournaments. He also entered several mini-tour events and capped the year by finishing second in the local qualifying for the Club Professional Championship at Palm Beach Gardens where he finished 41st He then grabbed the last spot for the 1994 Senior PGA Championship in 1994.

Early on, while at the University of Arkansas, Bill thought about the tour. He played in the 1965 US Amateur at Southern Hills and after a stint in the military in Vietnam, he returned to Arkansas to complete his degree. In 1971, while an assistant at Old Warson, Bill helped prepare for the Ryder Cup. By 1977 he finished high enough at the PGA Club Pro Championships to earn a spot as a "rabbit" on the Tour, so he became a nomad for eight months, travelling from stop-to-stop trying to qualify, which he did in six of the twenty events he attempted. But it was finally enough, so from 1979 till 1993, Bill settled in at Glen Echo and was one of the areas top club pro's.

Dutch Harrison

Dutch Harrison was one of those early champions whose colorful personality and brilliant game thrust him into the national limelight. Like most Pro's of the day, Dutch made a living on and off the Tour, as Club Pro at many area clubs including Old Warson and Forest Hills in the 1950's and 60's. But it was his play during the 40's and 50's that showed his greatness. In a book published in the late 80's *"Mr. Dutch - The Arkansas Traveler"* the story of the colorful Pro was told for all to marvel.

Dutch competed in the early days of the PGA Tour, and his first Pro win was in 1939 (though he did win the Arkansas Amateur in 1929 and the Arkansas Open in 1937) at the Texas Open held at the Brackenridge Park GC in San Antonio. (Brackenridge would become famous a few years later when Mike Souchak would shoot a 27 for 9 holes in 1955 and go on to shoot a record 257 over 72 holes for a 27 under par total). Winning the 1949 Canadian Open at St. Georges G&CC in Toronto and the Western Open at the Original Bellerive CC in 1953 Dutch would also finish 2nd in the 1962 PGA Seniors Championship behind Paul Runyan,. Four years later in 1966 he would again be a bridesmaid, this time to Fred Haas Jr.

Like most pro's of the 30's and 40's Dutch traveled with other pro's as they moved from site to site searching for wins, and more money to continue their adventure. Dutch and his wife traveled with Sam Snead, Bob Hamilton and Herman Keiser, sharing their expenses.

The Professionals

In 1937 Horton Smith, Springfield, MO native and two-time Masters champ, took Dutch under his wing and got him a job as an assistant in Chicago. This provided him some on-going income and allowed him to carry-on. During this period he won the Bing Crosby and placed 4th at the LA Open.

"The Arkansas Traveller"
E.J. 'Dutch' Harrison

Dutch played in three Ryder Cups, 1947, 1949 and 1951 and would go undefeated in singles, winning both his matches (8&7 and 5&4), and falling only in the foursomes match in 1949 with Johnny Palmer. Dutch would compete in 11 PGA Championships at Match Play, reaching the Semifinals in 1939 where he lost to Horton Smith. His 18 all-time Tour victories placed him in a tie for the 37th spot all-time. This during the time when the tour was dominated by the likes of Nelson, Snead, Hogan and Middlecoff. In fact from 1940 to 1953 one of the above four did not lay claim to the most wins in a season only twice, once in 1943, when the tour was for the most part halted during the war and in 1940 when Jimmy Demaret had 6 wins. During this period Hogan won 40 events, Snead 43, Middlecoff 13 and Nelson 26.

Dutch has a great ability to get to the finals, but winning was another matter. In playoffs he was 1 for 9, winning only the 1952 Texas Open over Doug Ford. This does not diminish his star. In fact he is in good company, Ben Crenshaw is 0-8 in playoffs, Raymond Floyd 4-11, Ben Hogan 8-12; on the other side Nicklaus is 13-10 and Palmer is 14-10 while Snead was 10-8 and Tom Watson 8-4. In 1954 Dutch won the Vardon Trophy for the best stroke average on tour, 70.41.

Finally, in 1952 Dutch took a head Pro job at Dornich Hills in Oklahoma where he met a young caddie named T.D. Morris. In 1955 when Old Warson was searching for a pro to open the new Robert Trent Jones layout, Dutch was lured back to St. Louis. He hired a young protege to work with, Doug Sanders. Dutch moved to Olympic Club in San Francisco in 1960, and the same year finished 2nd to Arnold Palmer at Cherry Hills in the US Open. He returned to St. Louis in 1965 to open Forest Hills CC, where he remained until his health faltered in 1974. He remained Pro-Emeritus until his death in 1982.

Countless stories abound about Dutch. One of the favorites occurred at Old Warson. Al Hayes, President and a founder of Old Warson, played with Dutch frequently, usually losing enough to pay Dutch's caddy with a little left over for the ponies! One day Hayes is on the very back of the 18th green with the pin at the front. Remarkably he rolls in the birdie putt to win the match. As they meet in the grill, Hayes is

Dutch and Bob Hope were such friends that when Dutch passed away Hope cancelled his engagements to attend his funeral.

giddy with excitement and tells anyone who will listen about his victory. Dutch, growing a little impatient, walks over to settle-up (it was all of $20). As he pulled the $20 from his wallet, he asked Al what he was going to do with it. To which Hayes stated, *"I'm going to frame this $20 and hang it over my mantle for everyone to see!"*, to which Dutch replied, *"Can I give you a check?!"*

Perhaps Ben Hogan summed up Dutch's' career best, *"He was a good friend who knew everybody. He was a very pleasant person. He was a heckuva good golfer, and I might say he didn't win as much as he should have. I thought he was a lot better player than his record showed. He should have won more of the major tournaments."*

Hale Irwin

Perhaps the best known of the area's Touring Pro's, Hale's illustrious career is just beginning on the Senior Tour, and beginning with a bang. Born in Joplin, Hale has lived in the area for over twenty years. He began winning while living in Colorado as he won four consecutive Colorado Amateur crowns, the first in 1963 just after his high school graduation. The first three, 1963, 1964 and 1965 were all won at stroke play, while the last, in 1966 was won at match play. The following year, while at the University of Colorado, he won the 1967 NCAA individual championship at Shawnee CC in Delaware, Pennsylvania, one of only four area residents to have ever accomplished this feat.. Hale has always been unique... you don't find many football players (especially one who was also a two-time all Big Eight defensive back selection) who have won three US Opens!

After joining the Tour in 1968 he was consistent, being one of the best drivers on tour. Being his best in the US Open, Hale is one of only 5 players who have won at least 3 Opens, with Willie Anderson, Bobby Jones, Jack Nicklaus and Ben Hogan being the others.

His first win in 1974 and the second in 1979, pointed to a strong, accurate game. But 11 years would pass until his comeback-sudden death win over Mike Donald in the 1990 Open at Medinah, making him the oldest player to win an Open. It would be the final tribute to a very successful Regular Tour career; but not his last Major. His 20 career Tour victories puts him in the top 25 all time while his career earnings place him in the top 15.

Since joining the Senior Tour in late 1995, Hale has earned almost $86,000 per start, and recently won the PGA Seniors Championship in addition to the Vantage Championship and has been near the top in nearly every tournament. He won the American Express Invitational and

An attentive Hale Irwin watches Sam Snead as Bob Goalby kneels in foreground.

finished second at the Tradition (won by Nicklaus) and the Royal Caribbean (won by Bob Murphy).

While most tend to focus on his US Open victories, and rightly so, Hale has been in contention for other Major championships. He finished second at the 1983 British Open, won by Tom Watson at Royal Birkdale.

Regular wins on the PGA tour include the Glen Campbell LA Open in 1976 where he shot a 272 at the tough Riviera CC. The Honda Classic fell victim to his game in 1982 at Inverrary G&CC, shooting a 269 to win $72,000. He also captured the 1976 Florida Citrus Open (today the Bay Hill Classic) at Rio Pinar CC in Orlando by shooting a 270. Hale obviously likes Hilton Head for it is one of three tournaments he has won more than once. The Sea Pines Heritage Classic title was his in 1971 and again in 1973 as he conquered the Harbour Town Links. His latest victory at Hilton Head was in 1994 when he once again solved the links at Sea Pines. Up until last years Classic, Hale held the record for the fewest putts in a round, one that was tied by Loren Roberts in 1996. Besides his Open titles, perhaps some of his most memorable wins were at Muirfield Village, with his first there at the 1983 Memorial. Shooting a 281 on the difficult layout, Hale used his accurate driving and iron play to remain in control. He returned 2 years later in 1985 to claim the $100,000 top prize, again shooting a 281. Another of Hale's multiple-win titles was claimed at the Atlanta CC in the Atlanta Classic (today the Bell South). Shooting 271 and 273, Hale won the 1975 and 1977 titles. 1975 was a very good year for Hale; at the Western Open, played at Butler National GC, Hale shot a 283 to add another title to his list of wins. In 1977 at the Texas Open Hale shot a 266 at Oak Hills CC in San Antonio to claim the top prize. At the 1981 Buick Open played over Warwick Hills CC, Hale shot a 277 to win in a playoff. Hale also won the 1984 Bing Crosby National Pro-Am at Pebble Beach. At the World Cup in 1979 Hale defeated Bernhard Langer and Sandy Lyle to capture the individual crown.

Hale was also the benefactor of the rise in the popularity of the Ryder Cup. A Member of 4 Ryder Cup teams, perhaps his most vivid memory would be his match with Bernhard Langer at Kiawah in 1991. Hale happened to be in the final match in the final day and his match with Langer would be the deciding factor in who won the Cup. When Langer missed the 8 footer on the 18th, the entire team (and America) let go with a collective "Ooooh", as the US won the Cup 141/2 to 131/2.

Among his lesser known achievements was his streak of 86 consecutive events without missing a 36 hole cut. Inducted into the PGA World Hall of Fame in 1992, this marked a fitting tribute to an outstanding Tour career. No doubt that they may have to put an asterisk by his name as he continues his play on the Senior Tour.

No biography would be complete without coverage of Hale's work for St. Louis Children's Hospital. Since 1976 Hale has brought players from the PGA tour, LPGA tour and Senior Tour, with a sprinkling of local Pro's as well, to Old Warson in May for his annual tournament. Area golfers ante up "big bucks" to play with the Pro's and donate to a most deserving cause. Over the years over 4 million dollars have been raised that allow Children's Hospital to continue to provide the best care to children throughout the Metropolitan Area. The Hale Irwin Pediatric Cancer Center was their way of honoring this great gentleman.

Jim Offer

The current head professional at Triple A, Jim has been at several clubs throughout the area in his career. But perhaps the highlight was the years Jim spent with Dutch Harrison, Ben Hogan, Byron Nelson, Jimmy Demaret and others as a player on the PGA Tour. Only an injury prevented him from competing longer.

Judy Rankin

Today Judy is most visible walking the fairways for ABC sports as she reports on the Tour. But in her playing days she was not only a formidable presence, but one of the best. In 1976 Judy Rankin became the first woman player to earn over $100,000 in a single season. She posted 26 career Tour wins including 11 over a two year period in 1976 & 1977. When she retired she was in the top 20 all-time leading money winners. Her wins in 1977 include the Sarasota Classic, the USX Golf Classic, the Mayflower Classic and the Cellular Ping-One Championship (with JoAnne Garner in a team event).

Judy won the 1976 and 1977 Rolex Player of the Year awards and the Vare trophy for scoring average in 1973, 1976 and 1977; and in '77 she finished among the top-10 in 25 events, a record on the tour that still stands. She had at least one win in each year from 1970-79 and unlike many it was not her game which forced her off the tour in 1983, but a chronic back problem. She had surgery in 1985 to correct this, but she forgo a comeback and instead uses her knowledge to make the game more interesting for us as she reports on play as a commentator.

Judy Rankin

Growing up in south St. Louis, living on Jamieson Avenue before moving to Ellisville when in high school, Judy began playing at Triple A at age 6, where she came under the tutelage of her father Paul, as well as Bob Green, Eddie Held and later Bob Toski. Receiving an "honorary" membership to Triple A, she had free run of the course. Unlike others who "played" to hone their skills, Judy practiced and practiced in preparation to compete in area tournaments. *"I remember one nine hole tournament, I was playing a girl named Jackie who was about 15. A very pretty girl, and like a lot of young girls - I was only nine at the time - I looked up to her. I wanted to be like her when I grew up. But I knew she couldn't compete with me. I felt horrible. I wanted her to like me, but at the same time we were competitors. I beat her 5 and 4. I don't think I slept that night I was so upset."*

Judy and her father watched as her mother became quite sick for several years. When she died Judy was only eleven. The toll her death took on Paul Torluemke

The Professionals

was tremendous. *"After she died I don't think my father picked up his clubs again, except on very few occasions. He basically just worked with me. We became much closer."* Financially, it also was a tremendous burden. But somehow her father kept things going. She attended the original Eureka High, a much smaller building than the sprawling complex on Hwy. 109 today. She was bussed to school from Ellisville, then after school she would meet with Eddie Held at his range on Manchester for lessons, usually on chipping and her short game.

In 1956, she captured the National Pee Wee Championship, the first among her many amateur wins. Remarkable as it sounds, she won the St. Louis Junior Girls Championship AND the State Amateur in the same year, 1959! In the '59 finals she faced Karen Schull, the Kansas Citian who would go on to win seven state titles. But this year she was no match for Judy. *"That was the first tournament I went to by myself. My dad and Bob Green really didn't expect me to do that well. They drove down for the finals. Dad tried he best to stay away, so I wouldn't get nervous."* Her victory in the 1959 Missouri Women's Amateur is of special note, as it was at age 14, which still ranks as a record as the youngest champion. The next year, 1960, she finished 24th in the US Women's Open, and was low amateur, another record for her age.

The 1958 District Junior Girls' Championship and the 1961 Missouri Amateur Championship also became hers over the next few years. Her two wins in the State Amateur were the culmination of her amateur days before she turned professional, at the ripe old age of 17. She played in three US Opens and two US Amateurs before joining the tour, and in most US Opens from 1962 until 1981.

One experience almost forced her to quit golf early on. *"It was 1953, I was about 8, and my dad and I were looking at pictures of the coronation of Queen Elizabeth. He told me that Ben Hogan, who had just won the British Open, might get to meet the Queen. He told me that if I ever won the British Amateur, I might get to meet the Queen as well. It became a goal of ours to try to play in the British Amateur."* When she finally got her chance, it turned out to be a disaster. At the Amateur in 1960, played at Carnoustie, things did not go well. She lost in the second round and seemed unprepared for the competition. When she came home, her dad asked her if she wanted to quit playing, and she said that she did. Several months went by and one day they got a call from Sports Illustrated. They were wondering if Judy was going to compete in the US Women's Open at Baltusrol. Paul told them he wasn't sure and asked why? SI told him that they wanted to do a story on Judy and put her picture on the cover! She did play and, as they say, the rest is history!

In 1974, Judy ventured to Europe to compete in the Colgate European Open. Not exactly widely known in Europe, several "sponsors" placed considerable sums on her play - legal in England - and when she won they benefited nicely. When she returned for a repeat performance a year later, the bookies were a bit wiser and stayed away from "unhealthy" wagers.

After a fall at the end of the 1977 season, her back had already been hurting, she played in pain for the next few years, but could never regain the same level. She would win once in 1978 and 1979 before she finally realized that it was time to put the sticks away and do something to relieve the constant pain.

Despite the successful 1985 surgery, Judy decided that she should stay retired, lest she should risk another injury. A side benefit to this was that she and her husband Walter were able to enjoy their son's high school years. But when the ABC job came along, it was the right situation at the right time. She has enjoyed it ever since.

Judy recently captained the victorious Solheim Cup squad as they defeated the combined European squad 17-11, despite being down 9-7 going into the final day's singles matches. This was the first victory by a visiting team on foreign soil, and the US now leads the series 3-1. Played over the St. Pierre Hotel and Country Club in Chepstow, Wales, only Annika Sorenstam could taste victory the final day as the US team won 10 of the matches, and halved the other. With the pressure off, Judy could finally begin to enjoy the victory.

Judy at age 9 with her trophies

Judy does have a bit of sadness at the experience. She knows that when a team must be selected, some feelings will be hurt when certain individuals are not included. She has seen it at the Ryder Cup and knows it will happen again. But she wouldn't have given up the opportunity for the world. She believes she made the right choice for this years' team and the result has borne her out.

As an on-course reporter, Judy has gotten to know many current St. Louisans, particularly on the senior tour. Hale Irwin, who she has known for years, Tom Wargo, Frank Conner and Larry Ziegler and of course Bob Goalby.

If one gains anything from Judy it is her sincerity and humility; rare traits in someone who has achieved so much, and who continues to be in the public limelight. *"I never felt totally confident. I always believed that if I didn't do my best I could be beaten. Maybe that's why I worked so hard."* Judy is well aware that like many others, she has been very fortunate. She knows that she has a god-given talent and she tried to do the best she could with it. There were many paths that could have been taken. Many times she could have lost a match or shot a poorer score. But somehow there was a plan to it all that allowed her to succeed.

Judy has been gone from St. Louis for many years. Her career, both as a player and reporter, keep her on the road. But there were two ladies she singled-out who treated that little 14 year old with great kindness and generosity, Ellen Conant and Mary Gail Dalton, for which she will always be grateful. These two ladies, as most of us know, are champions in their own right, and evidently in more areas than just golf!

Honors continue to follow Judy. She was inducted into the Texas Hall of Fame in 1987 and the All-American Collegiate Hall of Fame in 1993. In January 1997, Judy was inducted into the Missouri Sports Hall of Fame in Springfield.

Today Judy resides in Texas with her husband and son.

The Professionals

Nancy Scranton

There must be something in the water in Centralia! Growing up just an hour from the arch, Nancy was always a good athlete, regardless of the sport. She played on the golf team in high school and competed against area teams, but never really thought much about the game beyond just that. She took lessons from Gene Carello, the West Frankfort pro for several years, but it was her father and sister, who is a 4 handicap, who really excelled at that time.

Nancy attended the university of Florida for two years, then sat out a year before transferring to Kentucky. During this time she met Tom Wargo, who had moved into the area and purchased Greenview. The two have been inseparable since. Never really a mechanical player, he was the perfect instructor for her. While no one would ever accuse Tom of having the perfect swing, he taught her how to play.

In 1979 she won the Southern Illinois Amateur. Then she won it again in 1982 and 1983. She won the 1981 and 1982 St. Louis Metro Championship. Then in 1983 she won the Illinois Amateur. Her final year at Kentucky she won a few tournaments and was named All-Southeastern Conference and an All-American. When she made her first attempt at the Qualifying school she made it easily. She was 24 and a professional golfer! Life was good!!

Like most rookies, her first season was one of adjustment and she played in 27 events but won little as the travel and competition were challenging. After two more so-so seasons, she broke through in 1988 and was in the top 30. She would remain there for the next four years.

Nancy Scranton

 1991 was a break through season, not just winning for the first time, but winning her first "Major" at the du Maurier Ltd. Classic. It was the type of win you like, barely make the cut, shoot two great rounds (64 and 68) and win by three. Then in 1992 she would capture the Los Coyotes LPGA Classic which was a come-from-behind classic; down by seven shots beginning the Sunday round, she fired a 65 to ease by Meg Mallon for the win. 1993 was a let-down season, but 1994 and 1995 would be real problems. It seemed that her game had gone south. She was not only missing fairways consistently, normally one of her strengths, but she began to lose confidence in her swing. She began to experiment, and things got only worse. Fortunately they discovered the problem. It was physical; she had an injured shoulder that would require surgery to fix. She decided to have the surgery and took off 1996 to let it heal. (She went to the same doctor who did the surgery on Brian Jordan and Ozzie Smith. It was the same type of injury).

It was very tough taking a year off. All those things you take for granted now seem so far out of your reach. But the shoulder is doing great. She and Tom Wargo recently played in a mixed foursome and it felt fine, until she tried to keep up with Tom! Nancy has always been a hard worker. She loves to practice. She knows that she can't practice as much and still play now. She has to pace herself more.

Physically Nancy is in great shape. At 5'9" she hits the ball a long way (she averaged 240 with her drives) and was straight as an arrow. She is going to a biomechanics specialist to make certain she isn't doing anything that will put stress on her shoulder. Once she gets through that, she can put her mind at ease and concentrate on getting her old reliable swing back.

The nice thing about winning is that you know what it feels like. Nancy likes that feeling! During 1997 look for Nancy to return to championship form by mid-season.

Steve Spray

The head Professional at St. Louis CC, the former Eastern New Mexico All-American has had a long and successful career as a professional. At the NAIA school, Steve won the 1962 & 1963 Individual medal at the Championships, while he helped his team win the team championship in 1963. As a Junior, Steve won the 1959 Western Junior Championship.

Steve competed on the PGA Tour from 1965 to 1975 where he won the 1969 San Francisco Open and finished 5th in the 1968 US Open, before becoming a Club Professional. Steve can point to a back-nine at the 1968 US Open at Oak Hill when he shot a 30 in the 4th round, which at the time was a US Open record. In fact his 65 set four records at that time; the 30 on the back was a USGA record for the low 9 holes, the 65 he shot broke Ben Hogan's 67 mark, he had a record 8 birdies during the round and it was a record low score for the 4th round of a US Open. [Most of these have since

Centralia natives Nancy Scranton from the LPGA tour and Tom Wargo

been eclipsed, but at the time they were significant achievements]

When Steve turned fifty he quickly qualified for the senior tour and despite a shoulder injury, has competed successfully. But like any Club Pro, this is the area that draws his attention. Attending to the normal routine of carts, tee times, lessons, shop management and apprentice training is a full time job. A good group of assistants is important for the smooth operation of the shop, and keeping the members happy, perhaps the pro's most important "second job".

For the coming 1997 season Steve is still attempting to decide his best course of action. He will compete in a few events, and attempt to qualify for others, but he is not intent, for the moment, on making it a more permanent situation.

Steve Spray

The Professionals

Tom Wargo

PGA Club Professional Player of the Year for 1992. This accomplishment, to be honored as the top Playing Club Professional in the country among the 23,000+ professionals, especially at age 49, is the honor Tom is most proud of in his career. Certainly winning the 1993 PGA Seniors title was a tremendous thrill, but deep down, Tom has been and always will be a Club Pro!

Greenview CC in Centralia, Illinois sits alongside Highway 51, just a few miles north of I-64, about an hours drive from the arch. When Tom is in town, you can count on his buddies enjoying a cup of coffee in the clubhouse, waiting for him. *"I'll take 15 today Tom"*, shouts one prospective opponent, while Tom exhales a puff from the ever-present cigar. *"Whose playing with who today?"*, asks another. *"What's the bet?"* asks Tom. *"Two a side"* comes the response. *"I'll give you 14 today"* states Tom firmly. It's not the money...it's the winning that gets Tom excited!

"We went to Qualifying school in '93 and we led after the first two rounds. Then we shot a 76 the final round and finished in a playoff for the 10th spot. We won the playoff, but 10th place is going to get you only a few exemptions for the year (only the top 9 were exempt). *We had a lot of success early, and we played in about three events and won about $36,000 coming out of Florida so we felt if we could average about $14,000 over the next 20 events we could finish in the top-31 and get our card."* When Tom talks about his accomplishments, he frequently uses the "we" statement...for to him it hasn't been a journey alone, his wife Irene is a big part of that success.

"Winning the PGA Seniors at PGA National wasn't scary at all. The one thing no one ever asked me about, not the media or anyone, was the fact that I had played PGA National many times and had won over it before. I knew what club to hit, I knew the wind, I knew the greens. All I had to do was execute the shots."

Long considered one of the best playing professionals in the area, Tom was a favorite at local ProAms and charity events for years. Having competed in many Club Professional events and in the 1992 PGA at Bellerive, Tom was convinced that he could compete with the top Pro's on the Senior Tour. In late 1993, Tom was competing in the PGA Seniors' Championship at PGA National. His main competitor in the final round was long time PGA tour player, Bruce Crampton. Few in the media gave Tom any chance of keeping Crampton out of the winners circle. During the final round, as he played the "Bear Trap", the last 3 holes of the Nicklaus-designed course, Tom had a three stroke lead. Crampton made up ground with birdies and they were tied at the end of

Tom Wargo

regulation. The first playoff hole was halved with pars, and as they played the 2nd, the par-3 156 yard 17th, Crampton blinked first as his errant tee shot went right, and wet! Tom knew a 6 iron would put him in the trap and a 7 would put him on the green...but a mis-hit 7 would end up in the water! Tom pulled the 7 iron from his bag and calmly executed the shot. The ball ended up in the middle of the green and the victory was his. His score of 275 was so good that since 1980 only one man has posted a lower score in this Championship; Jack Nicklaus with a 271 in 1991.

Tom came to the area in 1972 with plans to run an eighteen hole course in Sandoval, Illinois. He was not a professional at the time and was looking to making a living. Running a course seemed like a good idea. The plan fell through, so he attempted to qualify for a few events, thinking that could lead to a few years on the PGA Tour with an eye on the Senior Tour. Tom went to the PGA Qualifying school *"...somewhere around '76 or '78 in Orlando at Disney World. I didn't play all that well and shot a couple 76's. I left town not real happy but I picked up a paper for the final results. Some of the guys who were there were Seve Ballesteros, Jerry Pate, Andy Bean. These guys were right out of college and here I was 33 at the time. I realized I had to work on my game a lot to compete at that level."*

Tom was the Gateway Section of the PGA Champion in 1988, and he also competed in the PGA Cup Matches against Great Britain & Ireland at the Belfry the same year. During that event he won his single match, and went 2-2 in the team matches. Tom also won the 1990 Club Professional Stroke Play Championship.

Tom has enjoyed considerable success on the Senior circuit compiling a total of three wins. In addition to the PGA Seniors, he won the Doug Sanders Celebrity Classic in Houston in 1994 with a one shot victory over Bob Murphy and during 1995 he had 14 top-10 finishes (including two 2nd place and two 3rd place finishes) and won the Reunion Pro-Am in Dallas by 7 shots. Tom also won the 1994 British Senior Open and in 1996 he had the thrill of competing in the British Open at St. Andrews. He played with Arnie in a practice round and during the competition, Tom was nearby as Arnie stood on the Swilcan Bridge and waved good-bye to his fans for the final time.

Tom loved competing over the courses in Great Britain, especially at St. Andrews. The style of play is so different that over there, one that he enjoyed tremendously. *"There is more respect for the game in Scotland than over here. They don't kick the ball from behind trees, they just go out and play the game. The game over here is too soft, the way the courses are set-up. In Scotland the courses are hard. You have to hit a different types of shots"*

Tom Wargo

A match with Tom could turn into a marathon event because he won't quit! He'll keep playing till he wears you out. If he loses, he just ran out of holes. As you might imagine, he also loves to practice. *"I get a bigger kick out of practicing than playing...I've been known to hit balls 8-10 hours a day at times."*

He struck up a friendship with Arnie and had the courage to ask him to play together in the Legends tournament. *"He's a hella'va fella. I asked him first because I know Arnold...and he can still make birdies. We have similar personalities and thought we could have some fun out there! He's one of the all time great personalities in the world."*

Tom would love to compete in the US Open and the Masters, but he recognizes the difficulty of getting spots in either. He would probably have to win the US Senior Open for both to occur. Aware of how fortunate he has been, he looks to have 3-5 more good years on tour before he cuts-back on his schedule to about 25 events. A true iron-man, Tom played in 33 events in 1995, leading the Senior Tour with 24 top 10 finishes. During 1996 he again played in over 30 events, finishing 15th on the list and expecting even better things in 1997. *"We're setting a lot of goals for ourselves now that we think are reachable, reaching the top 5 or 10 are some of them."* Suddenly, life in the Wargo household will never be the same!

Larry Ziegler

Larry Ziegler

Born in St. Louis, Larry joined the Tour in 1966 and continued through the 1970's and 80's, where he played consistently, but found the winners circle on rare occasions. He won the 1969 Michigan Classic in a playoff over Homero Blancas, the 1975 Greater Jacksonville Open and in 1976 he claimed the USF&G Classic at Lakewood CC in New Orleans, shooting a 274. This was also the year he tied for third at the Masters. Joining the Senior Tour in 1989, Larry was victorious at the 1991 Newport Cup and has had 3 other top 3 finishes.

On the regular Tour, Larry was long considered one of the longest hitters of his day. Compared to the likes of John Daly he would be considered an also-ran today. He has always been known as a hard worker, and while never achieving star status, his 22 year Tour career was rewarding, earning 1 Million dollars over his career. During 1995 Larry finished in the top 25 in 9 events and in the top 10 in 3 of those. Overall Larry competed in 31 events during 1995 and earned enough money to finish 45th on the money list.

Larry holds one record of note; in 1993 he recorded aces at two events, the Las Vegas Senior Classic and the Bruno's Memorial Classic, being the last time a player had multiple aces in a season. Legend has it (and Larry confirmed it) that on the par 5, 593 yard ninth hole at Forest Park (along Skinker Blvd.) that Larry reached the green in two! Those who have played this demon know what a feat that was.

Area Senior Pro's gather for a day on the links
Front (l-r) Jim Barton, Bill Whitfield, Joe Dodich, Phil Hewitt, Dick Lotz
Back; Jack Corbett, Lynn Rosely, Bill Moser, Lee McClain, Jim Cochran

PGA, Senior, Nike, Hogan, Armour and mini-tours

At any given time, there will be a few to a dozen or more St. Louisans competing on the various tours. In 1996 The Nike tour had Bret Burroughs, Bob Gaus and Jay Williamson competing while the Tommy Armour Tour had Dan Barry, Burroughs, Gaus and Todd Meyer on their circuit. Others such as the South Florida mini-tour include E.J. Brumm while Trevor Dodds still competes on the South African Tour, Asian Tour and Canadian Tour, where he was the leading money winner. The Ben Hogan Tour, which preceded the Nike Tour, was begun in 1990 as a way of preparing players for the grind of the regular Tour. Its affiliation ended in 1994, and then Nike took over sponsorship.

Of note in 1996 at the Kemper Open was where Bellerive's Jay Williamson gained a spot and was in contention from the first round and held the lead briefly in the third round. But the inexperience of not having played in the last group before, and playing with the eventual winner, Steve Stricker, took its toll and Jay shot a 78 in the closing round. It is this kind of experience that could prove invaluable, should he find himself in that situation again. Jay qualified for the Tour at the 1994 Q-School at Grenelefe on the tough Robert Trent Jones West course, over 7,000 yards of tough Bermuda and the 6,869 yard Ron Garl designed East course. Jay lost his card for the 1997 season and appears headed to the Far East to hone his game.

Other St. Louisans, not included elsewhere, who have competed on the PGA, LPGA, Senior PGA or Nike Tours at one time or another include; Wayne Morris, Al Chandler, Doug Brown, Brian Fogt , Tom Barry, Dan Barry, Steve Reid, Dick Hendrickson and Bob Gaus. Our apologies to anyone omitted from this list.

Professionals Championships

Championship Competitions by Area Professionals

While the Championships listed previously cover most local or regional events, and we have covered the major National events elsewhere, there are still events won by St. Louisans and St. Louis Professionals that deserve recognition. Some of these tournaments are no longer held, while others have been renamed or incorporated into others. Nevertheless, the following St. Louisans Professionals won titles, or qualified for our National Championships over the years.

Player & Club	Event
Anderson, Willie St. Louis CC	• US Open (1901, 1903, 1904, 1905) 1st • Western Open (1908) 1st
Ayton, Alex St. Louis CC	• PGA Seniors' Championship (1949) 17th • PGA Seniors' Championship (1947) 13th • PGA Seniors' Championship (1946) 6th • US Open (1920) • Western Open (1938)
Ambo, Walter Westborough CC Ambo River Valley GC	• PGA Senior Stroke Play (1986) 1st • PGA Championship (1947,1948) • Western Open (1938) • US Publinks Championship (1935)
Austin, Carey	• St. Louis Publinx (1979) 1st
Barnes, Jim Sunset Hill CC (Sunset)	• US Open (1913, '14, '15, '16, '19, '20, '22, '23, '25, '26, '27, '28, '29, '30, '32) • US Open (1921) 1st • PGA Championship (1916 & 1919) 1st • PGA Championship (1921) 2nd • PGA Championship (1924) 2nd • British Open (1920, '21, 22)
Barry, Tom Armour/Nike Tour	• St. Louis Publinx (1991) 1st
Benbrook, Brad	• Pepsi Little Peoples Championship (1983) 1st
Boggess, Brian St. Louis CC	• PGA Championship (1974) • PGA Club Professional Championship (2 years)
Boggs, Dale Creve Coeur Rec. Complex	• PGA Club Professional Championship (4 years)
Bradley, Monte Meadowbrook Norwood Green Trails	• US Open (1964, 1965) • PGA Championship (1967)
Braid, William	• US Open (1903)
Burroughs, Bret	• St. Louis Publinx (1994) 1st • St. Louis Publinx (1989) 1st • US Amateur (1985) • US Publinks (1985) • US Junior Boys (1980) • US Open (1991) • Lou Fusz St. Louis Open (1989) 1st • Gateway Masters (1996) 1st

Clarkson, Don
  Glen Echo CC
  Old Warson CC
	• PGA Championship (1963)
	• PGA Club Professional Championship (2 years)

Clarkson, Fred Glen Echo CC	• PGA Seniors' Championship (1947) 23rd

Cochran, Jim
  Twin Lakes GC
  Paradise Valley GC
  Crescent CC / Players Club
  Emerald Green
  Senior PGA Tour
	• PGA Seniors' Championship (1984) 28th
	• PGA Seniors' Championship (1987) 39th
	• PGA Seniors' Championship (1988) 54th
	• US Open (3 times)
	• US Senior Open (1989)
	• PGA Club Professional Championship (5 years)
	• St. Louis Publinx (1966) 1st

Cockburn, James Westwood CC	• PGA Seniors' Championship (1945) 6th • PGA Seniors' Championship (1946) 21st
Conner, Frank Senior PGA Tour	• PGA Championship (1985) 40th • PGA Championship (1980, 1982) • PGA Championship (1979) 23rd • US Open (1975, 1979) • PGA Deposit Guaranty Golf Classic (1988) 1st • Hogan Tour Knoxville Open (1991) 1st • Hogan Tour Tulsa Open (1991) 1st • King Hassan Morocco Open (1982) 1st
Craden, Rich St. Louis CC	• St. Louis Publinx (1974) 1st • St. Louis Publinx (1971) 1st
Dale, Charles Paddock CC	• St. Louis Publinx (1977) 1st
Delhougne, Mike Forest Park	• St. Louis Publinx (1972) 1st

Delsing, Jay
  PGA Tour
  Norwood Hills
	• PGA Championship (1991,1993)
	• PGA Championship (1990) 63rd
	• US Open (1991, 1992)
	• US Amateur (1981, 1982)
	• US Junior Boys (1978)
	• Missouri State Amateur (1981) Medalist
	• St. Louis District Golf Association (1980) 1st

Dodds, Trevor
  PGA Tour (1985-92)
  Nike Tour (1990)
  Canadian Tour
  FNB Tour
  Sunshine Tour
  South American Tour
	• US Open (1990, 1994)
	• Bogey Hills Invitational (1991) 2nd
	• South African Open (1990) 1st
	• Alberta Open (1996) 1st
	• Ed Tel Planet Open (1996) 1st
	• Infiniti Championships (1996) 1st
	• Canadian Masters (1996) 1st
	• Manitoba Open (1995) 1st
	• Canadian PGA (1995) 1st
	• Trustback Tournament of Champions (1990) 1st
	• Deer Creeek Hogan Tour (1990) 1st
	• Canadian Order of Merit winner (1995 & 1996)
	• World Cup (1996) 13th individual
	• NCAA 1st Team All-American (1985)

Dodich, Joe Westwood CC	• PGA Championship (1958) • PGA Seniors' Championship (1987) • Gateway Senior Championship (1981) 1st

Professionals Championships

Douglas, Dave St. Louis CC	• PGA Championship (1950) (QF) • PGA Championship (1949, 1958, 1962) • US Open (1947, '48, '49, '50, '51, '55, '56, '60, '61, '62) • St. Louis Publinx (1964) 1st • Ryder Cup Team (1953) • Western Open (1953, 1954, 1955) • Houston Open (1954) 1st • Canadian Open (1953) 1st • Texas Open (1949) 1st • Orlando Open (1951) 1st

Emery, Larry
  The Legends
  Glen Echo CC
  Norwood Hills CC
	• Gateway Section Championship (1980) 1st
	• Gateway Section Championship (1987) 1st
	• Gateway Section Championship (1990) 1st
	• PGA Championship (1990,1995)
	• PGA Club Professional Championship (1985) 84th
	• PGA Club Professional Championship (1989) 22nd
	• PGA Club Professional Championship (1990) 95th
	• PGA Club Professional Championship (1992) 91st
	• PGA Club Professional Championship (1993) 100th
	• PGA Club Professional Championship (1994) 5th
	• PGA Club Professional Championship (1995)
	• US Open (1987)

Fisher, Rich	• St. Louis Publinx (1992) 1st
Fischer, Mrs. David Meadowbrook	• US Women's Open (1966)

Fogertey, Jim
  Osage CC
  Sunset CC
  Myopia Club
	• PGA Championship (1941)
	• PGA Championships (3 years)
	• US Open (1932, '35, '36)
	• Western Open (1933)
	• St. Louis Metro Open (1941) 1st

Fogt, Brian
  Bellerive CC
  Nike Tour
  PGA Tour
	• Bogey Hills Invitational (1986) 1st
	• Kansas Open (1993) 1st
	• Ohio Amateur (1982) 1st
	• PGA Tournament Series (1 win 1977-95)
	• US Open (1991)
	• Porter Cup (1982) 2nd
	• Southern Illinois Open Assistants Championship (1991) 1st

Fonseca, Tom Meadowbrook CC	• PGA Championship (1964)
Fryman, Cecil "Curly" Forest Park	• St. Louis Publinx (1995) 1st
Furgol, Ed Westwood CC	• US Open (1954) 1st • US Open (1948, '55, '56)
Gaitherum, Jack Bellerive	• US Open (1911) • Western Open (1909, 1912)

Gaus, Bob Tower Tee Nike Tour	• US Amateur (1980) • US Publinks Championship (1981, 1983) 1st • US Open Championship (1990) • Southern Illinois Open (1985) 1st • Southern Illinois Open (1986) 1st • Gateway Assistants Championship (1987) 1st • Gateway Assistants Championship (1988) 1st • Gateway Assistants Championship (1990) 1st • PGA Club Professional Championship (1995) • St. Louis Publinx (1995) 1st • St. Louis Publinx (1994) 1st • St. Louis Publinx (1993) 1st • St. Louis Publinx (1990) 1st • St. Louis Publinx (1983) 1st Amateur
Goalby, Bob PGA Tour (1957-1979) Senior PGA Tour (1980-) St. Clair Events prior to 1957 were as an Amateur.	• The Masters (1968) 1st • US Open (1959, '61, '62, '66, '67, 68 '70, '71, '73) • St. Louis District Golf Association (1955) 1st • US Amateur (1956) • PGA Championship (1960) 32nd • PGA Championship (1961) 15th • PGA Championship (1962) 2nd • PGA Championship (1963) 17th • PGA Championship (1964, 1969, 1970) • PGA Championship (1965) 68th • PGA Championship (1966) 49th • PGA Championship (1967) 7th • PGA Championship (1968) 8th • PGA Championship (1971) 46th • PGA Championship (1972) 62nd • PGA Seniors' Championship (1979) 26th • PGA Seniors' Championship (1980) 4th • PGA Seniors' Championship (1981) 13th • PGA Seniors' Championship (1982) 3rd • PGA Seniors' Championship (1984) 13th • PGA Seniors' Championship (1984) 4th • PGA Seniors' Championship (1989) 58th • PGA Seniors' Championship (1990, 1994) • Greater Greensboro Open (1958) 1st • Coral Gables Open (1960) 1st • Los Angeles Open (1961) 1st • St. Petersburg Open (1961) 1st • Insurance City Open (1962) 1st • Denver Open (1962) 1st • San Diego Open (1963) 1st • Robinson (Ill) Open (1969) 1st • Heritage Classic (1970) 1st • Bahamas Classic (1971) 1st • Marlboro Senior Classic (1981) 1st • Peter Jackson Senior Champions (1982) 1st • Jeremy Ranch Shootout (1983) 1st with Mike Reid
Grenier, Dan Cloverleaf GC	• St. Louis Publinx (1991) 1st

Professionals Championships

Griffiths, Ed Norwood Hills CC	• St. Louis Publinx (1975) 1st
Grosch, Terry Cherry Hills / St. Albans CC	• US Open (2 times) • PGA Club Professional Championship (1983, 1984, 1985)
Guldahl, Ralph St. Louis CC	• US Open (1937 & 1938) 1st • Ryder Cup (1937) • St. Louis Open (1933) 1st • PGA Championship (1937, '38, '39, '40 '41) • Western Open (1936, 1937, 1938) 1st

Haas, Jay
  PGA Tour
  St. Clair CC
  Wake Forest University
	• PGA Championship (1978) 58th
	• PGA Championship (1979) 7th
	• PGA Championship (1980) 50th
	• PGA Championship (1981) 19th
	• PGA Championship (1982) 5th
	• PGA Championship (1983) 9th
	• PGA Championship (1984) 39th
	• PGA Championship (1985) 38th
	• PGA Championship (1986) 53rd
	• PGA Championship (1987) 28th
	• PGA Championship (1988) 38th
	• PGA Championship (1992) 62nd
	• PGA Championship (1993) 20th
	• PGA Championship (1994) 14th
	• PGA Championship (1995) 8th
	• PGA Championship (1989, 1990, 1996)
	• Presidents Cup (1994)
	• Ryder Cup (1983, 1995)
	• Andy Williams-San Diego Open (1978) 1st
	• Greater Milwaukee Open (1981) 1st
	• BC Open (1981) 1st
	• Hall of Fame Classic (1982) 1st
	• Texas Open (1982) 1st
	• Big "T" Houston Open (1987) 1st
	• Bob Hope Chrysler Open (1988) 1st
	• Federal Express St. Jude Classic (1992) 1st
	• H-E-B Texas Open (1993) 1st
	• Walker Cup Team (1975)
	• US Open (1996, '95, '94, '93,'92, '91,'90, '88, '85, '83, '82, '80, '77, '75(Amateur), '74 (Amateur))
	• US Amateur (1971, '72, '73, '74, '75)
	• US Junior Boys (1967, 1968, 1969)
	• St. Clair Open Pro event (1977, 1978) 1st
	• St. Louis District Golf Association (1975) 1st
	• St. Louis District Golf Association (1973) 1st
	• St. Louis District Golf Association (1972) 1st
	• NCAA Individual Championship (1975) 1st
	• Fred Haskins Winner (1975)
	• Missouri Open (1976) 1st
	• Southwestern Open (1976) 1st
	• Mexican Open (1991) 1st
	• National Pee Wee Championships (1960) 1st

Haas, Jerry
  PGA Tour
  Nike Tour
  St. Clair
(Events prior to 1986
  were as an amateur)
	• Illinois State Amateur Championship (1982) 1st
	• Illinois State Amateur Championship (1984) 1st
	• The Masters (1985) 31st
	• Walker CupTeam (1985)
	• US Open (1986, 1987, 1988)
	• US Amateur (1983, 1984, 1985)
	• Nike Tour Ozarks Open (1994) 1st
	• Nike Tri-Cities Open (1994) 1st
	• Nike Sonoma County Open (1994) 1st
	• US Junior Boys (1979)
	• St. Louis District Golf Association (1985) 1st
	• St. Louis District Golf Association (1984) 1st
	• St. Louis District Golf Association (1983) 1st

Hackbarth, Otto Westwood CC (Westborough)	• US Open (1908)
Halcomb, Mike Lockhaven CC	• Pepsi Invitational Championship (1983) 1st • Pepsi Invitational Championship (1984) 1st

Hall, Bill
  Glen Echo CC
  Senior PGA Tour
	• PGA Club Professional Championship (1974) 66th
	• PGA Club Professional Championship (1975)
	• PGA Club Professional Championship (1976) 61st
	• PGA Club Professional Championship (1977) 13th
	• PGA Club Professional Championship (1978)
	• PGA Championship (1978) 70th
	• PGA Club Professional Championship (1993) 41st
	• PGA Senior Club Professional Championship (1993) 16th
	• PGA Senior Club Professional Championship (1994) 24th
	• PGA Senior Club Professional Championship (1996)
	• PGA Seniors' Championship (1995)
	• PGA Tournament Series - Senior Div. (1 win 1977-95)
	• US Open (1972, 1977)
	• US Senior Open (1994) 32nd
	• US Amateur (1965, 1968)
	• Medalist Senior Tour Qualifying (1993)

Professionals Championships

Harrison, E.J. "Dutch" Old Warson CC Forest Hills CC	• Arkansas State Open (1937) 1st • Arkansas Amateur (1929) 1st • Ryder CupTeam (1947, 1949, 1951) • US Open (1936, '37, '39, '41, '46, '47, '48, '50, '51, '52, '53, '56, '58, '60, '65 '67) • PGA Championship (11 years-Match Play; 1 year Stroke Play) • PGA Championship (1939) Low Qualifier (T138); Semi-Finals • PGA Championship (1940, '41, '42, '45, '46, '49, '53, '54, '55) • PGA Championship (1952) Low Qualifier (136) • PGA Championship (1963) 49th • PGA Club Professional Championship (1968) 32nd • PGA Club Professional Championship (1969) 29th • PGA Seniors' Championship (1962) 2nd • PGA Seniors' Championship (1964) 3rd • PGA Seniors' Championship (1965) 7th • PGA Seniors' Championship (1966) 2nd • PGA Seniors' Championship (1968) 10th • PGA Seniors' Championship (1969) 5th • PGA Seniors' Championship (1970) 28th • PGA Seniors' Championship (1972) 25th • Canadian Open (1949) 1st • Texas Open (1939) 1st • Texas Open (1951) 1st • Bing Crosby Pro-Am (1939) 1st • Bing Crosby Pro-Am Invitational (1954) 1st • Western Open (1953) 1st • Western Open (1939, '40, '46, '47, '48, '49, '50(2nd), '51, 52, '53, '56, '59, '63, '65, '66, '67)
Hartig, Daryl Westwood CC	• PGA Club Professional Championship (1987, ;89, '92, '94) • Nike Gateway Classic (1995, 1996) • PGA Section Champion (Kentucky) 1981
Haxel, Nash Bent Creek GC Glen Echo CC	• PGA Club Professional Championship (2 years) • US Amateur (1983)
Hayes, John Normandie GC Bellerive CC Forest Hills CC	• PGA Club Professional Championship (1994) 88th • PGA Club Professional Championship (1989, '90, '91, '92, '93, '94, '95, 96) • PGA Club Professional Championship (1990) 43rd • Missouri Amateur Championship (1982) 1st • Gateway Assistants Championship (1985) 1st • St. Louis Publinx (1993) 1st • St. Louis Publinx (1992) 1st • Gateway PGA Player of the Year (1990)
Heckel, Steve Crab Orchard GC	• PGA Club Professional Championship (1986) 36th • PGA Club Professional Championship (11 years) • PGA Championship (1987) • US Senior Open (1996)
Hewitt, Phil Westborough CC	• PGA Senior Club Professional Championship (1989) 29th • PGA Seniors' Championship (1988, 1989,1990)
Hooser, Paul St. Clair CC	• PGA Club Professional Championship (2 years)

Houser, Terry The Falls Sunset Range Arlington GC	• Gateway Section Championships (1985) 1st • PGA Club Professional Championship (1984) 90th • PGA Club Professional Championship (1991) 71st • PGA Club Professional Championship (4 years) • PGA Senior Club Professional Championship (1991) 25th • PGA Senior Club Professional Championship (1992) 15th • PGA Senior Club Professional Championship (1996) • US Senior Open (1992) • PGA Seniors' Championship (1992) 68th • PGA Seniors' Championship (1993) • St. Louis Publinx (1988) 1st • St. Louis Publinx (1986) 1st • St. Louis Publinx (1984) 1st • St. Louis Publinx (1982) 1st • St. Louis Publinx (1981) 1st • St. Louis Publinx (1975) 1st • St. Louis Publinx (1974) 1st
Hunter, Jeff RaintreeCC St. Clair CC	• US Open (1983,1985, 1991) • PGA Club Professional Championship (4 years) • PGA Club Professional Championship (1992) 91st • Spalding Series Championship (1991) 1st • Gateway Section Championship (1991) 1st • Gateway Section Championship (1993) 1st • Gateway Assistants Championship (1989) 1st

Professionals Championships

| Irwin, Hale
　　PGA Tour (1968-1995)
　　Senior PGA Tour (1995-)

Events Prior to 1968
　　were as an Amateur. | • US Open (1974) 1st
• US Open (1979) 1st
• US Open (1990) 1st
• US Open (1966 (Amateur), '71, '72, '73, '75, '76, '77, '78, '81, '82, '83, '84, '85, '88, '89, '91, '92, '93, '94, '95, '96)
• Atlanta Classic (1975) 1st
• Atlanta Classic (1979) 1st
• Australian PGA (1978) 1st
• The Memorial (1983) 1st
• The Memorial (1985) 1st
• San Antonio Texas Open (1977) 1st
• Western Open (1975) 1st
• Buick Open (1981) 1st
• Buick Classic (1990) 1st
• Bing Crosby Pro-Am (1984) 1st
• Glen Campbell LA Open (1976) 1st
• Honda Classic (1982) 1st
• Florida Citrus Open (1976) 1st
• Sea Pines Heritage Classic (1971) 1st
• Sea Pines Heritage Classic (1973) 1st
• Sea Pines Heritage Classic (1994) 1st
• Colgate Hall of Fame Classic (1977) 1st
• Hawaiian Open (1981) 1st
• Broadmoor Invitational (1967) 1st
• Colorado Amateur (1963) 1st
• Colorado Amateur (1964) 1st
• Colorado Amateur (1965) 1st
• Colorado Amateur (1966) 1st
• Ryder Cup Teams (1975, 1977, 1979, 1981, 1991)
• South African PGA Championship (1979) 1st
• Won World Cup Individual title (1979) 1st
• PGA Championship (1970) 30th
• PGA Championship (1971) 22nd
• PGA Championship (1972) 11th
• PGA Championship (1973) 9th
• PGA Championship (1975) 5th
• PGA Championship (1976) 34th
• PGA Championship (1977) 44th
• PGA Championship (1978) 12th
• PGA Championship (1980) 30th
• PGA Championship (1981) 16th
• PGA Championship (1982) 42nd
• PGA Championship (1983) 14th
• PGA Championship (1984) 25th
• PGA Championship (1985) 32nd
• PGA Championship (1986) 26th
• PGA Championship (1990) 12th
• PGA Championship (1991) 73rd
• PGA Championship (1992) 66th
• PGA Championship (1993) 6th
• PGA Championship (1994) 39th
• PGA Championship (1995) 54th
• PGA Championship (23 years) |

	• Japanese Bridgestone Classic (1981) 1st • World Cup Team (1974, 1979) • World Match Play Championship (1974) 1st • World Match Play Championship (1975) 1st • Bahamas Classic (1986) 1st • Brazilian Open (1982) 1st • US Senior Open (1995) 5th • Ameritech Senior Classic (1995) 1st • Vantage Championship (1995) 1st • Ameritech Senior Open (1996) 1st • The Tradition (1996) 2nd • PGA Seniors'Championship (1996) 1st • Senior Players Championship (1996) 2nd • US Senior Open (1996) 2nd
Jessiman, Robert Bellerive	• Western Open (1938)
Johnson, Eddie Cherry Hills	• St. Louis Publinx (1970) 1st
Jones, Bill Forest Park	• St. Louis Publinx (1969) 1st
Jones, Bob Bogey HillsCC	• St. Louis Publinx (1974) 1st
Kelleher, Tom Normandie	• US Open (1927, 1928)

Keller, Frank
   Normandie CC
   St. Andrews GC
	• PGA Championship (1959, 1963, 1965, 1967)
	• US Open (1965)

Kokoruda, John
   TapawingoGC
   Tee-Up Golf
	• Newport News Amateur Championship (1979) 1st
	• Hampton Open Championship (1980) 1st

Kossman, Walter St. Clair CC	• US Open (1927, 1928, 1930)

Laffoon, Ky
   PGA Tour
   Meadow BrookCC
	• PGA Championship (11 years)
	• PGA Championship (1937) Semi-Finals
	• US Open (1933, '34, '35, '36, '37, '39, '42)

Lansdowne, Bill Meadowbrook CC	• PGA Club Professional Championship (1995)
Lotz, Dick Tower Tee	• US Senior Open (1981, 1985)

Manion, John
   Normandie CC
   Sunset CC
	• PGA Seniors' Championship (1946) 18th
	• PGA Seniors' Championship (1947) 19th
	• PGA Seniors' Championship (1948) 15th
	• PGA Seniors' Championship (1949) 17th
	• US Open (1927, 1928, 1930)
	• Western Open (1938)

Marcuzzo, Mark
   Belk Park
   Spencer T. Olin
	• US Open (1993)

Professionals Championships

MarusicMilon Algonquin CC	• PGA Championship (1949,'52,'53,'54,'56,'57, '58,'62) • PGA Championship (1960) 46th • PGA Championship (1961) 45th • PGA Club Professional Championship (1975) 48th • PGA Club Professional Championship (1980) 43rd • PGA Club Professional Championship (1980) 43rd • PGA Quarter Century Club Championship (1982) 1st • PGA Senior Stroke Play Championship (1987) 1st • PGA Seniors' Championship (1967) 27th • PGA Seniors' Championship (1968) 19th • PGA Seniors' Championship (1969) 10th • PGA Seniors' Championship (1970) 39th • PGA Seniors' Championship (1971) 33rd • PGA Seniors' Championship (1972) 25th • PGA Seniors' Championship (1973) 4th • PGA Seniors' Championship (1974) 24th • PGA Seniors' Championship (1975) 14th • PGA Seniors' Championship (1976) 4th • PGA Seniors' Championship (1978) 18th • PGA Seniors' Championship (1979) 45th • PGA Seniors' Championship (1980) 43rd • St. Louis Publinx (1961) 1st • St. Louis Publinx (1969) 1st • US Open (1952, 1961) • US Senior Open (1980) • Western Open (1952, 1953, 1954)
Maguire, Paul Bellerive	• US Open (1954)
McLeod, Fred Sunset Hill CC	• US Open (1910, '11, '12, '13, '14, 15, '16, '19, '20, '21, '24, '28, '29) • US Open (1908) 1st • PGA Championship (1919) 2nd • PGA Championship (1921, '23, '24, '26)
Melhorn, William E. North Hills CC/ Norwood	• US Open (1923,'24,'25,'26,'27,'28,'29,'30,'31,'32,'34,'37) • PGA Championship (1925) 2nd • PGA Championship (1919, '20, '24, '27, '28, '29, '30, '31, '34, '36, '37) • Western Open (1924) 1st

Moore, Frank
   Meadow BrookCC
   St. Clair CC
	• PGA Championship (1942) QF
	• PGA Championship (1934, 1938)
	• US Open (1932, '33, '36, '37, '39, '47, '48)
	• Hale America Open (1942)
	• Western Open (1936, 1938)

Dale Morey Meadow Brook	• US Amateur (1953)

Morris, Wayne Algonquin CC	• Irvin Cobb Invitational (1975) 1st • Irvin Cobb Invitational (1976) 1st • Irvin Cobb Invitational (1977) 1st • PGA Championship (1973) • PGA Club Professional Championship (1972) 11th • PGA Club Professional Championship (1974) 74th • PGA Club Professional Championship (1975) 48th • PGA Club Professional Championship (1976) 27th • PGA Club Professional Championship (8 years) • PGA Senior Club Professional Championship (1990) 69th • PGA Senior Club Professional Championship (1993) 68th • PGA Seniors' Championship (1988, 1989) • US Open (1974) • US Senior Open (1989, 1993) • St. Louis Publinx (1976) 1st • St. Louis Publinx (1973) 1st • St. Louis Publinx (1980) 1st
Morse, Clarke Normandie	• US Publinks (1926, 1927 Medalist) • US Open (1931, 1932) • Western Open (1938)
Morse, Coleman Normandie	• Western Open (1928, 1938)
Moser, Bill Lockhaven CC	• PGA Senior Club Professional Championship (1989) 76th
Nicholls, Gilbert St. Louis FC	• US Open (1900, 1902, 1903, 1904 (2nd), 1905, 1909) • PGA Championship (1922)
Nieberding, Jr. Bob Westborough CC	• PGA Championship (1981) • PGA Club Professional Championship (1978) 57th • PGA Club Professional Championship (1980) 35th • PGA Club Professional Championship (1981) 76th • PGA Club Professional Championship (1990) • Gateway Section Champion (1994) 1st
Niest, Ted St. Louis CC	• US Open (1955)
Norsworthy, Clarence Sr. Ruth Park Triple A	• PGA Championship (1941) • Western Open (1936, 1938)
Offer, Jim PGA Tour Triple A	• US Junior Boys (1960)
Oulds, Scott Greenbriar Hills CC	• Gateway Section Championships (1986) 1st • PGA Championship (1987) • PGA Club ProfessionalChampionship (7 years) • PGA Club ProfessionalChampionship (1986) 20th
Parham, Earl Forest Park	• US Senior Open (1991, 1992) • St. Louis Publinx (1996) 1st • St. Louis Publinx (1985) 1st
Patrick, David Algonquin	• US Open (1911)

Professionals Championships

Peck, Brad Sunset HillsCC	• PGA Club Professional Championship (1994) • PGA Club Professional Championship (1993) 106th
Popham, Howard Sunset HillsCC	• St. Louis Publinx (1960) 1st

Rankin, Judy Torluemke
   LPGA Tour
   Triple A
   (Events prior to 1962 were as
   an Amateur)
	• Missouri Women's Amateur (1959) 1st
	• Missouri Women's Amateur (1961) 1st
	• St. Louis District Junior Girls' (1958) 1st
	• St. Louis District Junior Girls' (1959) 1st
	• US Junior Girls (1957, '58, '59, '60, '61)
	• US Junior Girls (1961) semi-finalist
	• US Women's Amateur (1960, 1961)
	• US Women's Open (1959, '60, '61, '62, '63, '65(10th), '66(7th), '67, '68(9th),'72(2nd), '73(6th), '75(9th), '76, '77(10th), '78, '79, '81,)
	• US Women's Open (1960) Low Amateur
	• US Junior Girls (1960) semi-finalist
	• Ladies British Amateur (1960)
	• LPGA Tour Wins (26)
	• Corpus Christi Open (1968) 1st
	• George Washington Classic (1970) 1st
	• Springfield Jaycee Open (1970) 1st
	• Lincoln-Mercury Open (1970) 1st
	• Quality-First Classic (1971) 1st
	• Lady Eve Open (1972) 1st
	• Heritage Village Open (1972) 1st
	• American Defender (1973) 1st
	• Lady Carling Open (1973) 1st
	• Pabst Classic (1973) 1st
	• GAC Classic (1973) 1st
	• Baltimore Classic (1974) 1st
	• Colgate European Open (1974) 1st*
	• National Jewish Hospital Open (1975) 1st
	• Burdine's Invitational (1976) 1st
	• Colgate Dinah Shore Winner's Circle (1976) 1st
	• Karsten PING Open (1976) 1st
	• Babe Zaharias Invitational (1976) 1st
	• Borden Classic (1976) 1st
	• Colgate Hong Kong Open (1976) 1st
	• Orange Blossom Classic (1977) 1st
	• Bent Tree Classic (1977) 1st
	• Mayflower Classic (1977) 1st
	• Peter Jackson Classic (1977) 1st
	• Colgate European Open (1977) 1st
	• LPGA National Team Championship (1977) 1st*
	• WUI Classic (1978) 1st
	• WUI Classic (1979) 1st

Richter, Ben Triple A Club Bellerive CC	• PGA Championship (1936, 1937) • PGA Seniors' Championship (1946) 4th • PGA Seniors' Championship (1947) 2nd • PGA Seniors' Championship (1948) 2nd • PGA Seniors' Championship (1949) 10th • PGA Seniors' Championship (1951) 9th • PGA Seniors' Championship (1952) 23rd • PGA Seniors' Championship (1953) 31st • National Left-handers Amateur (1934 & 1935) 1st • Western Open (1938)
Robertson, Dave Sunset Hill (Sunset)	• US Open (1912)
Rosburg, Bob WestwoodCC	• US Open (1953, '55, '56, '58, '59, '69) • PGA Championship (1959) 1st
Sanches, Mrs. Wanda Sunset CC	• US Women's Open (1964)
Schirmer, Ray	• US Open (1936)
Schwartz, Francis Midland Valley	• US Open (1928, 1930)
Schwartz, Ray Midland Valley Norwood Hills	• US Open (1933) • Western Open (1938)
Schwartz, Bill	• St. Louis Open (1935) 1st
Schwent, Joe Bellerive	• PGA Club Professional Championships (1993) • PGA Club Professional Championships (1994)
Scranton, Nancy LPGA Tour	• Illinois Women's Amateur Championship (1983) 1st • du Maurier Ltd. Classic (1991) 1st • St. Louis Metro Women's Championship (1981,1982) 1st • Illinois Amateur (1983) 1st • US Women's Open (1986) • Los Coyotes LPGA Classic (1991) 1st • Southern Illinois Amateur (1979, 1982, 1983)
Shaiper, Dick Glen EchoCC NorwoodHills CC Missouri Bluffs GC	• PGA Club Professional Championship (5 years) • PGA Club Professional Championship (1969) 54th • PGA Club Professional Championship (1970) 69th • PGA Club Professional Championship (1974) 45th • Missouri State High School Championship (1952) 1st • Senior Club Championships • Senior Open Championship • St. Louis Open (1968) 1st • US Open (1962, 1966) • St. Clair Invitational (1961, 1964) 1st • St. Louis Publinx (1967) 1st • St. Louis Publinx (1968) 1st
Siemsglusz, Walt Berry Hill GC	• PGA Club Professional Championship (1995)
Simpson, Robert Field Club Country Club	• US Open (1900, 1901) • Western Open (1907, 1911) 1st

Professionals Championships

Spray, J. Steve
(also as John Spray as Amateur)
  PGA Tour
  Senior PGA Tour
  St. Louis CC
	• Iowa Amateur Championship (1963) 1st
	• Iowa Open Championship (1964) 1st
	• New Mexico Open Championship (1973) 1st
	• PGA Championship (1970, 1978,1979,1980,1989)
	• PGA Championship (1971) 78th
	• PGA Club Professional Championship (1977) 19th
	• PGA Club Professional Championship (1978) 17th
	• PGA Club Professional Championship (1979) 23rd
	• PGA Club Professional Championship (1988) 34th
	• PGA Senior ClubProfessional Qualifying (1995) Medalist
	• PGA Club ProfessionalChampionship (9 years)
	• PGA Senior Club Professional Championship (1991) 14th
	• PGA Senior Club Professional Championship (1995) 27th
	• PGA Seniors' Championship (1992) 68th
	• PGA Seniors' Championship (1996) 30th
	• San Francisco Open - PGA Tour (1969) 1st
	• The Masters (1968)
	• US Amateur (1963)
	• US Open (1968 (5th), 1970)
	• US Senior Open (1995) 57th
	• US Senior Open (1991 (40th), 1995 (57th), 1996)
	• Western Open (1965, 1966, 1967, 1968, 1969, 1971)
	• Gateway Section Championships (1977) 1st
	• Gateway Section Championships (1979) 1st
	• Gateway Senior Section Champion (1995)
	• Bogey Hills Invitational (1982) 1st
	• Western Junior Championship (1959) 1st

Stock, Charlie The Players Club	• PGA Senior Club Professional Championship (1994) 50th • PGA Senior Club Professional Championship (1995) • PGA Seniors' Championship (1991) 75th • PGA Seniors' Championship (1995)

SutherlandDave
  Crystal Lake
  Westwood
	• PGA Seniors' Championship (1949) 13th
	• PGA Seniors'Championship (1948) 7th
	• PGA Seniors'Championship (1947) 9th
	• PGA Seniors'Championship (1946) 3rd
	• US Open (1927, 1928, 1930)

Tanner, Cal Forest Park	• St. Louis Publinx (1966) 1st • St. Louis Publinx (1974) 1st • St. Louis Publinx (1975) 1st • Bogey Hills Invitational (1972) 1st

Professionals Championships

Trittler, Paul	• US Publinks (1978, 1979)
Tucker, Jerry Bellerive CC	• PGA Championship (1989,1992) • PGA Club Professional Championship (13 years) • PGA Club Professional Championship (1983) 78th • PGA Club Professional Championship (1984) 79th • PGA Club Professional Championship (1988) 34th • PGA Club Professional Championship (1990) 92nd • PGA Club Professional Championship (1994) 37th • PGA Club Professional Championship (1995) 60th • PGA UST Match Play Championship (1996) 2nd round • PGA Tournament Series (1 win 1977-95) • US Open (1981, 1984) • Gateway Shoot-Out Championship (1991) 1st • Gateway Match Play Championship (1993) 1st
Tucker, Mike Bellerive CC	• PGA Club Professional Championship (1995)
Wampler, Fred Westwood CC	• US Amateur (1948) • PGA Championship (1967) 38th • PGA Championship (1975) 54th • PGA Championship (1965) 54th • PGA Championship (1964) 44th • PGA Championship (1960) 49th • US Open (1953, 1959) • PGA Championship (1959, 1961, 1968, 1969, 1972, 1974) • PGA Seniors'Championship (1975) 2nd • PGA Seniors'Championship (1976) 2nd • PGA Seniors'Championship (1977) 8th • PGA Seniors'Championship (1978) 10th • PGA Seniors'Championship (1979) 29th • PGA Seniors'Championship (1980) 4th • St. Louis Publinx (1962) 1st • St. Louis Publinx (1963) 1st • St. Clair Invitational (1962) 1st

Professionals Championships

Wargo, Tom
  Greenview GC
  Senior PGA Tour
	• PGA Seniors' Championship (1993) 1st
	• British Senior Open (1994) 1st
	• Bogey Hills Invitational (1984) 1st
	• PGA Stroke Play Champion (1991) 1st
	• Gateway Section Championships (1988) 1st
	• Gateway Section Championships (1992) 1st
	• Gateway Player of the Year (1991)
	• PGA Championship (1987,1988,1991)
	• PGA Championship (1992) 28th (Low Club Professional)
	• PGA Championship (1993) 31st
	• PGA Club Professional Championship (1985) 49th
	• PGA Club Professional Championship (1986) 3rd
	• PGA Club Professional Championship (1987) 5th
	• PGA Club Professional Championship (1990) 15th
	• PGA Club Professional Championship (1991) 5th
	• PGA Club Professional Championship (1992) 23rd
	• PGA Cup Team (1988, 1989, 1990, 1991, 1992)
	• PGA Section Champion (Illinois) 1990 & 1991
	• PGA Senior Club Professional Championship (1992) 2nd
	• PGA Senior Stroke Play Championship (1993) 1st
	• PGA Seniors' Championship (1994) 10th
	• PGA Seniors' Championship (1995) 30th
	• PGA Tournament Series Senior Div. (2 wins 1977-95)
	• PGA Tournament Series (10 wins 1977-95)
	• Senior PGA Tour Doug Sanders Celebrity Classic (1994) 1st
	• Senior PGA Tour Reunion Pro-Am (1995) 1st
	• US Senior Open (1993) 17th
	• US Senior Open (1994) 4th
	• US Senior Open (1995) 27th
	• US Senior Open (1996)

Webb, Gene
  Norwood Hills CC
  Lakeside GC
	• PGA Club Professional Championship (2 years)
	• PGA Championship (1959)
	• PGA Championship (1968) 70th
	• US Open (1948, '49, '50, '51, '52, '56, '67)
	• The Masters (1950)

Whipp, Victor Sunset Hills CC	• PGA Club ProfessionalChampionship (1991) 75th • PGA Club ProfessionalChampionship (1995) 93rd • PGA Club ProfessionalChampionship (4 years)
White, D.K. Algonquin	• US Open (1906)
White, Orville Meadowbrook	• US Open (1934)

Williamson, Jay PGA Tour	• Kansas Open (1991) 1st
Williamson, Justin	• US Open (1991)
Ziegler, Larry PGA Tour Senior PGA Tour Terre Du Lac	• PGA Championship (1968) 73rd • PGA Championship (1969) 5th • PGA Championship (1970) 45th • PGA Championship (1971) 46th • PGA Championship (1973,1975,1976,1981) • US Open (1968, '70, '73, '74) • PGA Championship (1974) 32nd • PGA Seniors' Championship (1990) 9th • PGA Seniors' Championship (1992) 22nd • PGA Seniors' Championship (1993) 39th • PGA Seniors' Championship (1994) 24th • PGA Seniors' Championship (1995) 21st • PGA Seniors' Championship (1991,1996) • PGA Senior Club Professional Championship (1995) 21st • Michigan Classic (1969) 1st • Greater Jacksonville Open (1975) 1st • First NBC New Orleans Open (1976) 1st • Newport Cup (1991) 1st

Note: The PGA Championships prior to 1958 were Match Play Championships. Since 1958 they have been Stroke play. If no finishing position is noted behind year played in an event, player failed to make the cut at stroke play. In Match Play only players advancing to quarterfinals are noted. Clubs or other affiliations are noted below players name. Some players noted as Professionals are not affiliated with area clubs, but compete for prize money in area events.

The Architects

"Except where the course has been designed and the construction work supervised by the modern golf architect, there is hardly a golf club of any size which has not frittered away hunderds of dollars in doing bad work all for the want of the best advice in the first instance."
...Alister MacKenzie (1934)

Golf course architecture has long been the conversation on the course, any course. Few sports offer each participant the opportunity to determine their own line of play with few restrictions. Men who have spent their lives in the study of course construction have their work criticized by the newest of competitors. Almost everyone who has set foot on a course has something to say, good and bad, about the layout.

What then is a golf course architect? What do they offer that makes them valuable to the success of a project (besides their name). The professional architect brings together the principles of **Art** (harmony, proportion, balance, rhythm and emphasis), **Tradition** (classic holes and designs from other courses), **Play Design** (penal, strategic or heroic), **Functionality** (for a long approach, the larger the green; for the shorter approach the more contouring of the putting surface or placement of a bunker closer to the surface) and **Shot Values** (what is the relative reward or punishment for good and bad shots). Combine these with the three Basic Considerations of golf course design, namely the game itself, eye appeal and maintainability of the course.

Today there are also the environmental, zoning and commercial issues that the architect must deal with in their plan. Courses that are poorly maintained may be the fault of the architect (or lack of one) who failed to take into account turf conditions, rainfall, erosion, grasses, course maintenance budget

and number of rounds played. Mounding, bunkers, water, large greens all place strains on budgets that must be taken into consideration if the course is to be properly maintained over the years.

Below are architects from the area who practice much of their design work here. Unfortunately a few are nor longer alive to give us their accounts of their designs. Some are native St. Louisans like Homer Herpel who was not only a designer but also a PGA Professional at many area courses from the mid-20's to the 50's. Others such as Hale Irwin and Gary Kern, have made St. Louis their home for many years. These gentlemen have had tremendous influence on area golf and on other cities who have contracted for their considerable talents.

Gary Kern

Gary studied engineering at Texas A&M and Purdue, where he became a licensed surveyor in Indiana. In the course of his survey work he had the

opportunity to assist Bill Diddel as he was laying out a course in the area. During this time he found course architecture fascinating. He continued to work with Diddel during the actual construction, gaining knowledge and some practical insights.

Gary Kern (above) and with son Ron (below)

Shortly after this he decided to moonlight as a designer and in 1969 landed his first design job. By the mid-70's, Gary had enough work to practice full-time. In the 1980's he moved from Indianapolis to St. Louis where he teamed with Hale Irwin. In 1986 he was joined by his son Ron in the practice and the two of them have collaborated on many area projects.

Gary is credited with over 20 new constructions and over 30 where he has done remodeling projects. Some of his best designs are Quail Creek, Fox Run, Bent Creek, Fourche Valley, Sun Valley, Eagle Lake, Fox Creek and Rolling Hills. His remodeling efforts include Cape Girardeau, Norwood Hills (East), Lake Forest Lake Valley, Meadowbrook, Union Hills, Westborough, Cherry Hills, Sunset Hills and Cardinal Creek at Scott AFB.

The Architects

Hale Irwin

Hale joined other Tour pro's in forming his design company in 1986. Like his counterparts Nicklaus, Palmer, Player, Trevino, Weiskopf and a handful of others, Hale moved into the design business at a time when he may have believed his Tour career would begin to subside. Hale did not have the national reputation the others enjoyed and, despite his two US Open victories, could not command the "signature" prices the others did. So he continued on the tour and a magical thing happened, he won another US Open in 1990 at Medinah. Not only did he become the eldest winner, but he was the only winner in sudden death, having dueled with Mike Donald in regulation and tying him in the 18 hole playoff before claiming victory on the 19th hole of the day.

From his offices in Ladue, Hale has used his contacts to develop his design business on a world-wide basis. Area courses include Quail Creek (with Gary Kern) and the Legacy in Granite City. Hale may have little time for design work now that he is one of the leading money winners on the Senior Tour. But he has an excellent staff to support his up-front efforts and continue to provide the service and quality work for his customers.

Hale formed a partnership with Dick Phelps, a Colorado designer, and the two of them developed several courses through-out the nation in the early 90's. The relationship was such that Phelps' son worked for Hale in his office as

Hale Irwin

did other Phelps employees.. Some of the courses completed with Phelps include; Cordillera Resort and Lafay-ette GC in Colorado (1992), Panther Creek CC in Springfield, IL (1992) Blackrock CC in North Carolina (1992), The Lakes at Sycamore GC in Indiana (1992), Southern Woods CC in Florida (1992), Cerro Plata CC in California (1992).

His management company continues to manage several area facilities, most notably Quail Creek and Lakewood GC in Fenton.

Bob Goalby

Bob has built only a few courses, but they have enjoyed been very well received. One of his first efforts was in Palm Springs where he built the Springs, a retirement community facility that continues to enjoy huge success. Bob captured the hearts of area golfers when he put *The Orchards* on our list of "must plays" in 1991. With the completion of the new clubhouse, the Orchards has a tremendous following of golfers on both sides of the river. His latest venture, with his son Kye, is *Champions Trail* in Fairview Heights, just north of I-64 on Hwy 159. Situated on Old Collinsville Road, Champions Trail is a course that *"allows golfers, regardless of their ability, an opportunity to play, have fun and, if they take advantage of the terrain, enjoy a good round."*

Originally *Champions Trail* was the brainchild of Goalby, Jay Haas, Curtis Strange and Jimmy

Bob Goalby

Conners. But the need to have additional financing brought other investors into the picture and the four original "players" have now bowed out as owners.

Bob takes a basic premise about golf and applies it to his design; *"golfers don't need trouble, they'll find enough of it on their own!"* As a result, his courses are very playable. Mounds are positioned so that slightly errant shots may find their way back into the fairway. Bunkers are present, but usually you have alternate routes to avoid them. The greens are medium in size so three putts are not the norm if you put your approach where you're supposed to on them.

Keith Foster

To sit with Bob is like spending an afternoon with your uncle. He has been just about everywhere and seen just about everything! Bob has played the best courses in the world and shot some outstanding rounds. But he also knows that finding the fairway can be a problem from time-to-time -- for anyone, including him. He wants the game to be enjoyable. He wants you to come back again and again. When he speaks about *Champions Trail* it is with the confidence that you'll find it not only enjoyable, but will want to return very soon.

Al Linkogel

St. Louis-born Linkogel was responsible for the design of many courses in the 50's and 60's throughout the area. St. Ann GC Columbia (IL) GC, Cherry Hills CC, Bogey Hills CC and St. Charles GC were the area courses designed or remodeled by Mr. Linkogel. He served as superintendent at Westwood

Al Linkogel

CC for 27 years, before retiring in 1953. Following his retirement from Westwood he opened Links Nursery, a nursery and garden supply business. The nursery stood on Conway road, across from Westwood until 1984 when the family sold the land. Al began to work throughout Missouri and Illinois converting sand greens to grass, and performed this task for over 40 courses, among them Sparta CC and Elmwood GC in Belleville. His frequent partner on many of these projects was Ray Freeburg, an architect from Purdue University, who assisted on many designs.

For many Al was the grandfather of zoysia in the area. His work with this tough, wiry seed would impact almost every area course, and some not-so-ordinary facilities. When Busch Stadium decided it wanted to put grass in, who did they turn-to? Links Nursery and Al, who put together a zoysia and bluegrass mixture for them.

His work at Bellerive, Old Warson, Westwood and others can be seen in the excellent condition these courses have been in over the years. When superintendents at any club had a problem, Al was frequently the first person they called for help.

Al died in 1982 at age 74 in Marthasville, Missouri. Links Nursery continued for a few years but was finally sold in the mid-80's.

Keith Foster

The newest addition to area architects has been in town about a year, but he has already begun to make his mark. Keith grew up in southern Florida

The Architects

and was exposed to the Miami area courses; expansive, large greens, bermuda grasses, water and sand. He also saw the designs of Dick Wilson, Red Lawrence and Joe Lee. He began his career in course maintenance and took a position with the Nicklaus staff. After a short while, it was time for a decision; did he stay on the maintenance side of the business or move into the design. The Nicklaus folks wanted him to stay in the course maintenance area, but Keith had other ambitions. He left and landed a position with Arthur Hills where he became exposed to some outstanding facilities, and where he began to hone is talents. After leaving Hills he joined the Wadsworth group where he got his first exposure to the midwest. But he soon went on his own and opened an office in Arizona. At the urging of the Wadsworth people, Keith relocated to the Midwest, and St. Louis had another designer. At only 38 years of age, he has crammed a lot of experience into his resume!

Keith is from the younger group of architects that has come to value the great courses from the past. He gets excited when he speaks about St. Louis CC, Normandie or Glen Echo, the same way as when he talks about Oakmont. Some of the courses he has done have gotten national acclaim; Champions CC in Kentucky, the #1 rated club in the state, The Quarry in San Antonio,

Homer Herpel

Born just one years after the 1905 Worlds Fair, Homer worked as a cartoonist for local newspapers. He began caddying at the original St. Louis CC on Davis Place and when the course moved to the Ladue location he stayed for a few years before turning professional in 1925. He became a member of the PGA in 1937 and served as a club professional at

Homer Herpel

many area courses, including Algonquin CC Ruth Park, Osage (Greenbriar), Indian Meadows, Crystal Lake, Rock Springs, Poplar Bluff and Hillcrest GC (Sherwood). He was elected to many positions in the Eastern Missouri PGA and served as president in 1942. Like many professionals of the day, he did not spend his full year at the club, and for a time in the 50's he spend two years developing the Surf & Turf GC in Tarpon Springs, FL.

Long considered one of the best teaching professionals in the area, Homer taught such golfers as Mark Schlude, Gene Fehlig, Jonas Weiss, Jimmy Jackson, Lou Wasson, Jim Black and Jim Benson. In 1950 Homer developed one of the most unique teaching methods of the day, the "Tel-A-Form" which was a convex mirror which showed a players position during the swing. This was the forerunner of today's more advanced video teaching methods. He also teamed with Ben Richter of Triple A and they developed an Indoor Golf Center in downtown St. Louis and ran it for 4 years from 1938-42. This was one of the first such centers in the country.

After retiring in 1955 he began designing and supervising construction of area courses. He worked in conjunction with designer-architect Chic Adams and the two of them did several layouts. Among his best known area layouts are Ballwin GC, The Executive course at the Lodge of the Four Seasons, North Shore, Paddock CC and the first 9 at Union Hills CC. He also spent two years in Poplar Bluff developing the new course there. Homer died in 1977 at age 72 in University City.

His daughter Marilyn, a competitive golfer in her own right, attended Washington University and in the 1948 Association of Intercollegiate Athletics for Women, was runner-up for the individual championship. She was also a Missouri State Champion three times and a District Champion. She is highlighted in the Amateur section. Another daughter, Jackie Herpel Heistand, was a Colorado State Amateur champion in 1973 as well as a St. Louis Women's District Champion and a two time Girls Junior District titleholder

Jack Neville

Born in St. Louis in 1891, Jack moved to California as a young man an won the first California State Amateur in 1912 and then again in 1913, 1919, 1922 and 1929. He co-designed the Pebble Beach Links with Douglas Grant and the course opened in 1918 and won his last two amateur titles over the links. He also designed nine holes of the Pacific Grove municipal GC which opened in 1932,

He won the 1914 Pacific Northwest Amateur and was a member of the 1923 Walker Cup Team. He was employed by the Del Monte Properties Corporation until his retirement in 1971,

Jack Neville
Designer of Pebble
Beach Links

Lee Redman

Lee came to the St. Louis area over 28 years ago as he was seeking a position as a Course superintendent. The US Open had been at Bellerive and in 1969 they were in need of the talent to refresh the course. Lee was there ready for the challenge.

With agree from Purdue University, where he studied under the renowned Dr. William Daniel, Lee began to search for the right grasses to rebuild the RTJ beauty.

Over the years Lee has built or remodeled 8-10 courses, quite a lot considering the

Lee Redman

part-time nature of the activity. One of his first was Mehlbrook in south county. This was a fine 9 hole facility that was developed during the early 70's when a resurgence began. Unfortunately it fell prey to homes, and by 1980 it was gone. In 1974 when he did Parkwood Oaks at I-270 and McKelvey. Working amid huge Oak trees, Lee carved a wonderful 9-hole tract that survived almost 7 years before the zoysia was overtaken by condo's.

His next effort was at Montgomery County GC where he transformed their sand greens to the real thing. Then in 1992 he would secure a contract for Roseland in Alton. Working with a fairly flat piece of land, he used the wind and natural lake, with a little mounding for character, to create a sporty 9-hole layout. He also did work at Westwood Hills in Poplar Bluff, Memphis CC in northern Missouri and Doe Run in Van Buren.

But the course he is most enthused about would be Royal Oaks in Troy, Missouri. This 18 hole layout sits just north of the Troy exit and was completely laid-out and routed in 60 days. The natural contour of the land created some problems, but he was able to work around them to create a first class course for the area.

Lee approaches a design project with usually three things in mind; playability for the golfers, maintenance cost control and traditional course design. In short, the owner must be able to make money, golfers must like the course and it should not penalize them unduly. At Royal Oaks most knowledgeable golfers believe Lee has

The Architects

Wayne Stiles
Designer of the two courses at Norwood Hills, these were the only two Missouri designs for Stiles, who did most of his work in the northeast, particularly Massachusetts and New Hampshire.

Marvin Ferguson
Designed Bahnfyre CC in the mid-80's.

William Diddell
Crystal Lake CC (1929-1979) was his lone design in the area, but his influence on Gary Kern, like other mentors of the era, will be his legacy for the area.

Dr. Michael Hurdzan
This Ohio State graduate has given us Crystal Highlands (1988), Annbriar (1992) and more recently the new 18 at St. Albans. He also did remodeling at Sunset CC.

accomplished this.

"You're only as good as your last greens" is how Lee summed up his position at Sunset CC. Following 18 years at Bellerive, Lee has called Sunset home for the last 10. He is quick to credit much of his success to the work and research of the USGA green section as well as David Stone, superintendent of the Honors Course in Tennessee. Stone developed a method of selectively killing Bermuda when it is mixed-in with zoysia, something all too frequent in this area.

The winter kill that affected almost every area course last year was a nightmare to course superintendents. Members ran through the halls of many courses screaming for the supers head! But in reality there is little that could have been done to prevent the problem. Every 12-15 years Bermuda takes a hit and all Lee or any other super can do is overseed a little with rye to keep the course green and hope the damage will be minimal.

To help with the overall plan, Sunset has contracted with Dr. Michael Hurdzan to work with Lee to develop a 5 year master plan. From this the work will be staged so that minimal disruption occurs.

Another course that summoned Lee was Warrenton GC as he constructed the back nine and the greens for them in 1975.

Lee tries to take things in stride. Missouri is tough on superintendents and they must constantly be on the lookout for new grasses to keep their courses in top shape. "Quickstand" bermuda, developed by Dr. Pyle from the University of Kentucky looks very promising for the area, if the members don't cave in and just resod the whole course with zoysia!

Paula Eger

Paula grew up in Kirkwood, where she attended Nipher Junior High and then Kirkwood. As a Greenbriar junior, she played on many of the inter-club tournaments with the Mason and Marx brothers. During the 60's Paula would win 5 consecutive Junior

Paula Eger

District titles before attending the University of Arizona to play golf. Scholarships for women's golf were virtually non-existent at the time, so she played for the enjoyment of the game. It was during this time she decided that whatever she did, she wanted to be a part of golf as a career. So she rearranged her classes to take as much in agronomy and landscape as she could, and got her degree. The question was, what to do with it now?

Dozens of stamps were applied to the envelopes holding her resume as she mailed them to architects throughout the country. Joe Finger responded and he and Byron Nelson, who were partnering at the time, flew to Tucson, met with Paula, and she had her first job. She was hooked.

Beginning in the maintenance side of the business, her knowledge of grasses and turf were tops here, she began to get involved in the construction of several courses. But this would be short lived. Like the housing industry, the golf construction business is a business, and it goes through peaks and valleys. Paula would experience these throughout her twenty-plus year career. When she left Finger, she joined Jim Hardy, a part-time Senior tour player and partner of Peter Jacobsen in a design business. Together they have worked all over the globe from Australia to Panama to Scotland to Kansas City and Dallas. The

The Architects

Golf Services Group combines the best of Eger, Jacobsen and Hardy to give their clients a quality, playable and interesting course. Paula's talents in the technical and creative end of the business are superb.

A very detail driven person, Paula still likes to take pen to paper as she eschews the computer-driven process for more of the personal, hand-on view. The recently have contracted to work with Nicklaus on four projects in Tennessee to give them even added exposure.

Another unique aspect of her career is her partnership with Carol Mann, former LPGA star. She and Carol teamed up in 1994 to for perhaps the only all-women design and development organization. From the start their aim was to listen to women about how to design and

Jim Cochran

renovate courses to be "golfer friendly." Then the Woodlands CC came asking about renovating the Course. It seemed the members did not want to play the layout, thus taxing the other courses. After watching women play the courses several times, they established a formula for various skill levels. While increasing the number of tees from three to five they also helped the club enjoy a 12 percent increase in member play over the new tract.

The PeeWee, Junior and State Champ has done much more than make golf her career; she has given back to the game through her skills, so that others might enjoy it just as much!

Jim Cochran

Jim turned professional in 1962 and won his first tournament, the Tri-State, and has been compet-

ing ever since. Prior to 1980, Jim was a consistent choice for the Missouri Cup teams which pits Pro against Amateur. In 1980 Jim was chosen as Gateway Player of the year as he earned the most points in UP Open qualifying, the various pro opens, the Missouri Open and the Bogey Hills Invitational. It was during the Pro-Open at Cherry Hills when Jim first realized he had a chance to upset Al Chandler as the leader. At the Bogey Hills Invitational Jim was paired with Jim Mason, Richard Poe and Tom Wargo. He birdied the last two holes to finish with a 140 total and the Player of the Year title

As an architect, Jim built several area courses, beginning with Twin Lakes GC in 1960. This land was later needed for the construction of I-270 so Jim moved on and built Paradise Valley CC in 1965. During the late 60's and early 70's, Paradise Valley was one of the areas premier facilities. Tee times were as hard to get as finding a cool day in July. Though relatively short, it offered some exciting opportunities for the brave with risky carries, huge elevation drops and plenty of woods. The 12th hole has always been talked about; a tram takes golfers from just beyond the 11th green up a steep hill to the devilish par 3 12th. For the walkers, which dominated here for years, this was a godsend in the heat of our summers.

For you trivia buffs, the different 9's at Paradise Valley have interesting story. Originally the concept was for a 27-hole layout with the present front to be part of a short 9-holes and the back to be 9-holes of the longer 18 hole course. However, as is often the case, the plans changed so the course remained only 18, with the two very different nines.

In 1977 Jim sold Paradise Valley and had every

intention of getting out of the golf business. But when he heard about the site at the Players Club (then known as Crescent CC) Jim jumped at the opportunity. The championship layout was completed in 1979 with Lawrence Packard doing considerable work with Jim on the layout. Jim remained at The Players Club until 1988 when he sold the club to a member group.

Jim competed on the Senior Tour from 1988 through 1990. In 1988 he finished 48th on the Money list and 34th in scoring. But as the Senior Event's purses grew, so did the number of previous PGA Players who wanted to partake. The competition got much greater. Always a good player, Jim was able to be competitive, but the travel and lack of the big payday would eventually take its toll.

Never one to sit still, Jim began negotiations with the Pipefitters to construct a course on their property in North County. Emerald Greens GC became a reality in 1994 as Jim had completed his 4th area course.

While many don't remember Twin Lakes, the rest are stable members of the golfing community. His growth as a designer is apparent as you see the move from Paradise Valley to The Players Club to Emerald Greens. Emerald Greens has two personalities; the front with rolling hills while the back is more links-links, especially when the wind is howling. Jim took a piece of land and carved away those pieces that were not part of the course!

As an owner, Jim has been a tough taskmaster. Anyone who has played these courses and drove their cart off the path on "Paths Only days" were likely to suffer his wrath. He cared deeply about the courses and their upkeep, for it was his sweat that went into creating them.

Robert Foulis - 1927

Jim is also the nephew of Bob Cochran. Jim's father was also named Jim Cochran, and he was a St. Louis city policeman who at times could post some pretty good rounds. In one event he beat his brother Bob in competition, though this was an exception to the rule.

As Jim noted in an earlier article, *"Ninety-nine out of a hundred people don't like their jobs. I thoroughly enjoy what I do. I enjoy being outside and enjoy the people."*

Robert & James Foulis

No discussion of Golf Course architecture in the St. Louis Area would be complete without a lengthy tribute to Robert and Jim Foulis. These two, as noted in sections elsewhere in this book, were responsible for almost every early course construction and, in the case of Robert, their on-going maintenance through the 1920's.

Born in St. Andrews Scotland, Jim was the 2nd oldest son (behind Dave), with Bob being the 2nd youngest boy. They, along with their father James Sr. worked for Tom Morris in his shop, making clubs and balls for golfers. Bob first learned how to make "featheries" even sewing the leather and stuffing the feathers into the ball through small holes. He next

The Architects

C.D. Wagstaff Redesigned Greenbriar in 1937 following the change from Osage CC and later, when land for I-244 (now I-270) forced a routing change, he added 9 holes in 1958.

Robert Bruce Harris Designed Ruth Park in 1931 (with help from Robert Foulis) and Meadowbrook CC as they moved from Overland to the present site in 1961. Lockhaven (1955) in Alton is also one of his excellent designs.

made clubs and "gutties" for Old Tom. After mastering this art, Tom taught Bob about course design; first at St. Andrews and then on other courses throughout Scotland. Jim at this time was not as interested in architecture as making money, so he was traveling about the country selling products.

In 1894, as the Chicago Golf Club was nearing completion of its 18 holes in Wheaton, Illinois, Charles Macdonald sent for his friend, a real Scottish pro from St. Andrews to be its first professional. But Bob would decline this offer, so his brother Jim took the position. After arriving in Wheaton, he shortly sent for Bob and he arrived in 1895 and with Jim laid out the course at Lake Forest, today Onwentsia CC.

James designed the initial 9 holes for St. Louis CC in 1896 and consulted on the 2nd 9 in 1898. He also did the 9 holes for the Jockey Club in 1898.

Robert came to St. Louis and began work on Normandie in 1901 and when Jim joined him, they both completed Glen Echo in May 1901. Normandie was opened in October of the same year. Robert consulted on Algonquin, Forest Park, Triple A, Woodlawn CC, Midland Valley CC, The Bogey Club, Log Cabin Club, Riverview CC. Jim and Bob did the 18 holes at Sunset CC in 1917 and Jim, Dave and Bob did the 18 holes at Bellerive in 1910.

Walter Ambo

James returned to St. Louis in 1912 and served as head pro at St. Louis CC for 3 years before returning to Chicago. Robert remained in the area, primarily at Bellerive until 1942. There wasn't a club in the area that didn't seek his advice on their greens, grass mixtures and course conditioning.

The direct line of descent from St. Andrews to Glen Echo and Normandie is evident. While the courses are worlds apart, both in terrain as well as distance, the features which make them unique and the careful eye of the architect in positioning the tee, greens and routing makes our courses unique in the world.

Other Area Designers

Clete Idoux

Known better throughout Illinois than Missouri, Clete Idoux has designed many facilities in the near Illinois area. North County (Red Bud), Clinton Hill, Twin Oaks (Greenville) are among his layouts. Most of his courses are 9 holes - Clinton Hill being the exception - but they are very enjoyable to play.

Joe Idoux

Joe designed only one layout, Elmwood in Belleville in 1959. Very popular with the regulars,

Joe Idoux

Joe designed only one layout, Elmwood in Belleville in 1959. Very popular with the regulars, his family still runs the course.

Wilber & Larry Suhre

In 1972 this father-son duo opened Oakbrook in Edwardsville with 9 holes. The back 9 was added two years later. Larry continues as professional at the course.

Walter Ambo

Perhaps not as prolific as others, Walter was concerned primarily with only one layout, Ambo

Golf links which he tended with the care of the gardner he was. The course was known as River Valley before Walter took over in 1970 and named it Ambo River Valley. A nice 9 hole layout, Ambo was content to keep it that way for several years before deciding to add 9 holes in 1978. The course was renamed Ambo Chesterfield GC at that time and Walter groomed the course as best as could be for the locale and confines. Despite the apparent confines of the course and the course yardage, the greens offer some of the most difficult targets in the area. The former head professional at Westborough CC competed in several professional championships; most notably the 1948 PGA at Norwood Hills.

Walter was also pro at Greenbriar during the 50's and taught a young Paula Eger her game!

The 12th hole at Old Warson CC, the 1955 Robert Trent Jones gem.

The Signature hole at the Weiskopf-Morrish designed 18 holes at St. Albans - the par 3 12th.

The Architects

The first driving range built in the area (and perhaps in the country) was on Ladue Road at Forsyth, where the Brown Shoe Company now resides. The range moved to Clayton Road and Brentwood in 1927 and was called Swat Ho. Swat Ho was owned by future St. Louis Blues owner, Sid Salomon. In 1935 Ray and Francis Schwartz built a range adcross the street from Swat Ho. The Cross Roads Sandwich Shop is at #4. Visitors to the shop would get a hamburger and milk shake then come across to hit balls. Some of the visitors to the range include Bob Hope and his wife along with George and Babe Zaharias. The picture shows Clayton Road running from left to right and Brentwood running from top to bottom! The picture is taken looking to the north.

"We had some great head-to-head matches. Nine times out of ten she won."
...Kathy Whitworth speaking of Mickey Wright

The Writers

Over the years there have been many sports-writers who have covered golf for our local papers. A few of them have been outstanding. Others were the Brent Musberger of the day, try as they may, they just didn't get it!

Each group of players related to these men and women - and many had their favorites. Frequently the writers themselves were strong proponents of the game and fought to get space. At other times, they were at the mercy of their editors who relegated space to seemingly lesser events.

During the early days of the sport coverage was spotty; writers knew very little and articles were written often to explain what "goff" was to their readers. But as "personalities" came into vogue, articles about Jimmy Manion, Eddie Held, Virginia Pepp, Audrey Faust, Eddie Held and others were present. Readers would read about their exploits through the eyes of the author. Their descriptions of a particular shot or putt took on an air of excitement and anticipation. Their next match would be highlighted, as these athletes represented themselves and their city in the sport.

Gradually, golf began to have a regular column. Coverage came from the local writer, but frequently a former national winner, such as Snead or Hagen, would syndicate their writings throughout the country.

The *St. Louis Republic* was the first that took on the campaign to increase the number of public courses throughout the area. Their year-long series of articles finally got the mayor and city council to approve the use of city parks for golf. Unfortunately

Harold Tuthill

this came in 1917, with World War 1 on the horizon, and golf quickly got lost in the commotion.

There were four papers in town; the *Post Dispatch*, the *Globe-Democrat*, The *Republic* and the *Star Times*. Each covered the events in their own style and the space allocated varied. Some focused on instruction, while others concentrated more on national events. Still others had their individual "players"; those who got significant coverage of their play. Their coverage in competing papers would change accordingly as each looked for their own slant. The competition for readership began very early!

There have been eras where the coverage of a group of men or women was outstanding. In other years the focus was more on the events then the individuals. As we hit the 20's and 30's the writers became more knowledgable and their writings reflected this. Men such as O.B. Keeler, Grantland Rice and Bernard Darwin wrote so eloquently that they shamed many writers into becoming better -- or moving to other areas! Their coverage into the 40's and 50's was equally strong. First we needed diversions from the War and golf still had heroes. In the 50's it was just that we had more free time and we were looking for heroes. Nelson left in '46 but Snead and Hogan were still winning consistently. "Little" Ben Hogan, as he was called, was transformed into the "Hawk" as he went from runner-up to champion.

Special writers have made their impact on the area from time-to-time. Until the Globe-Democrat ceased Reno Hahn and Vern Tietjen were among those who carried the torch. To many golfers, these two were unsurpassed in their love and expression

The Bards

of golf. They too, had their favorites and articles about their exploits were numerous. Vern was a Triple A member who developed a championship game as well as a talent for describing the matches as though you were one of the participants! Reno Hahn is considered by many players as the best the area had as his words seemed to take you to the course.

Harold Tuthill was another such writer. To the players, his coverage was accurate, fair and extensive. He wrote not only in the papers but also for local magazines as he described life on the fairways.

More recently, Bill Beck was the crown prince. The former president of the Golf Writers Association of America was brought to St. Louis by the *Post* specifically to cover golf. His coverage was unique for the insight into the structure of the game as well as the players. He covered it for almost 15 years, perhaps as no one else had done before. He took up causes that would benefit the area, and was instrumental in helping the *Michelob Match Play* move forward in the late 70's and early 80's. Respected by most, he did have his detractors who said he took liberties with the facts from time-to-time. But his writing style and knowledge of the game were outstanding. Many current players attribute their media exposure to his writings during this time, as golf grew significantly throughout the area during his tenure.

When Dave Dorr picked up the beat he immediately sensed one of the areas major problems; the lack of an area-wide championship. He was focused on helping the area get such an event, one that would crown a single amateur champion. This became his crusade, one that would culminate with the present-day Metro Championships.

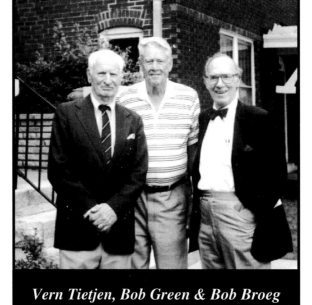

Vern Tietjen, Bob Green & Bob Broeg

If you speak with golfers today, there is a common belief that the *Post-Dispatch* is not focused on golf. We have turned into the Cardinals-Rams-Blues-Famous Barr paper! Focusing on professional sports makes icons of the soon-to-be free agent, while ignoring the exploits of the amateur athletes. Winning a national title (or two in a row) receives less coverage than our newest recently acquired .200 utility infielder or back-up outside linebacker!

The players, especially the top amateurs, are quick to point out that when they play out of town they frequently get better coverage there. And if you are a woman golfer, you might as well be playing bridge for the coverage their events receive.

This is not to state that individual writers do not try to improve the situation, but their hands are frequently tied by management with other agendas.

At times the writers became too close to the players, and their objectivity became skewed. Where groups waged mini-contests, they picked sides; where individuals were not cooperative, they were ostracized; and depending on who was connected to whom, the articles took on a selective slant. Objectivity seemed to vanish and subjectivity took over

Despite the sometimes difficult conditions, the following writers did their best to highlight the accomplishments of area linksters. Some of these writers and the eras they did their work are;

St. Louis Post Dispatch
Beatrice Wolf (early 20's)
Joseph F. Holland (early 20's)

Gerald Holland (early 20's)

J. Roy Stockton (early 20's)

W.J. (Bill) McGoogan (late 20's)

Dent McSkimming (mid 20's)

John H. (Jack) Alexander (mid 20's)

Alan W. Price (mid 20's)

Les Harrison (early 30's)

Clarissa Start (late 30's)

Harold Tuthill (1970's)

Bill Beck (late 1960's - 80's)

Jerry Marshall (70's)

Dave Dorr (1970's - early 90's)

Steve Kelley (1980's)

Bob Pastin (1980's-early 90's)

John Sonderegger (early 90's)

Dan O'Neill (mid-1990's)

St. Louis Globe Democrat

John J. Sheridan (mid 20's)

Marion F. Parker (mid 20's)

Alan W. Price (early 30's)

John G. Scott (mid 30's)

Maurice O. Shelvin (late 30's)

Justin L. Faherty (late 30's)

Patti Newbold (late 30's)

W. Vernon Tietjen (40's -50's)

Reno Hahn (70's)

Kathy Beebe Burns (1980's)

Julie Ward (1970-80's)

St. Louis Star

Ted Drewes (mid 20's)

James M. Gould (20's-30's)

L.K. Spear (early 30's)

Jim Toomey (early 40's)

W. Vernon Tietjen (late 30's)

Photojournalists

Bill Knight

Apart from the individuals on the preceding pages who put words to paper to document the events, perhaps men and women such as Bill Knight ["shooter" on AOL] are equal in their importance to the sport. They are the ones who document with pictures the players, clubs and events. Without them we would have to imagine what the Royal and Ancient clubhouse at St. Andrews looks like against the setting sun, or only imagine Hogan's swing as he made that majestic follow-thru at Merion, or the almost mystical manner in which Sam Snead coils before unleashing his power.

Since 1971 Bill has traversed the country trekking after the pro's with his assortment of camera bodies, lenses, filters, film and tripods as he searched for the "shot". When we see a photo in a magazine or paper, we seldom look at the credit. Often it is hidden in the back of the book where you must reference back to see whose "eye" caught the moment.

Bill became aligned with the Tour almost by accident. A friend knew of his interest in photography and suggested that he take some photos and see what he could

Bill Knight in front of his Wall of Fame

sell. To his amazement, almost $3,000 worth were purchased. He had the bug and know he knew what to do.

His collection is extensive as he criss-crosses the country documenting the Tours. From his shots of the 1971 Ryder Cup at Old Warson to the 1996 Boone Valley Classic, if it happened in golf, chances are Bill was present.

Dave Preston

Compared to Bill Knight, Dave is a relative newcomer to golf. But he will also be found at countless events going through roll after roll in search of the "shot". The Glendale native is quickly earning quite a reputation for his talent.

John and Brian Hayes

George Pietzker

In this area, he is the grand-daddy of photographers. His shots dating back to the 20's captured some of the most memorable moments in sport throughout the country. Sadly most of his film and negatives have been lost or mis-placed. But if you are lucky enough to have a shot with his moniker on the print, you have a shot from one of the best.

Publications

At times it must appear that golfers cannot get enough instruction or information. If one surveys the magazine racks at almost any store you will find not just the national publications; *Golf Digest, Golf Magazine, Golf for Women, Senior Golfer* etc., but a host of regional magazines. Many of these appeal to the golfers seemingly insatiable lust for par, and the "tricks" to achieve it. Everything from new clubs to glasses, hats, braces, nets, "jointed" clubs, "whippy" clubs, guides, and a host of products.

Local publications, directed exclusively at area players have appeared throughout the area since the early teen's. The first publication that can be found , was *The Nineteenth Hole,* published in the post-WW1 era. *The St. Louis Athlete* was another, published in the early to mid 20's. While not focused entirely on golf, it did have several memorable stories on local players and championships.

While locally produced magazines and newspapers did survive for a time, others that arrived in the area were more "cookie-cutter" in their design. They sell advertising nationally then sprinkle in a few local businesses and some local articles and pass them off as local or regional magazines. We must remember that most magazines are present to sell advertising, golf or whatever topic is portrayed is just the vehicle. And too often the content takes a back seat to the ad space.

Golf Scene Magazine (1988-1992) was an exception to the rule. Begun in 1988 by brothers John and Brian Hayes along with other family members, this was entirely a St. Louis regional publication. From the April 1988 premier issue to the final in November/December 1992, it provided outstanding coverage of events from the Ozarks through Southern Illinois. It attempted, as few others had, to provide *complete* coverage of professional, amateur, college, high school and tournament golf.

And it did it well. If anyone has attempted to publish anything they have a passion for, you know the problems. Finding the information, meeting deadlines, getting the photographs, proofreading, editing, printing and distributing. Perhaps the hardest part is the most important, finding the advertisers willing to ante up the money to keep it going. It is quite amazing, given the five years *Golf Scene* was present, that Brian and John still speak to each other, much less continue to work together at Forest Hills CC.

From their featured foursome, to the numerous instructional articles, to the course reviews, *Golf Scene* gave exceptional coverage to amateur as well as professional golf, from the high schools [despite the often lack of cooperation at getting the results] and colleges to the local and regional championships and to the area pro events. They honored pro and amateur alike with player of the year honors and ranked courses [always a dangerous task] and provided an annual listing of courses.

Some of the interviews they brought us were memorable; Jim Fogertey discussing his 50-plus years career in golf, Hale Irwin as an architect and player, Tom Wargo in his pre-Senior Tour days, Jerry Tucker, Larry Emery, Don Bliss, Scott Thomas, David Lucks, Jim Holtgrieve, Ellen Port and others It was a magazine golfers awaited the next publication with great anticipation.

Perhaps it was the change to take the publication to a publishing company that foresaw it's demise. Or maybe it was just the stress of doing this for four years, along with their 'real jobs'. Whatever caused the end of *Golf Scene*, it was a loss for the area. It will always be preserved in our minds as providing some of the best coverage seen in the area.

Another magazine was *"Where to Golf in St.*

Louis" that was published in 1983. Craig Lovasz was the publisher and like many others, it promised to be an annual publication, though the Editor's Note inside indicated that a favorable response was needed to see an '84 edition. Within the pages are several events worth noting; the 1982 Junior League Challenge Cup featuring Sam Snead, Judy Rankin, Pat Bradley and Tom Kite at Glen Echo CC and the upcoming 1983 event at Sunset featuring Rankin and Kite against Jan Stephenson and a to-be-named Top PGA Pro.

There was also a feature article on Hale Irwin which sounded more like a final tribute to the then-sixteen year career. The Senior Tour at this point, was not even a blip on his radar screen!

A color insert on the Lake of the Ozarks as a golfing destination was included as were complete listings of area public courses and a listing of private facilities. Interestingly, there were 40 public courses listed and 21 private. These were the days when Crescent and Lake Forest were public/semi-private and Normandie and Arlington were private. North Shore was listed as 18 holes, and Bahnfyre and Arrowhead still were part of south county golf. Of the public courses listed, 16 were in Illinois with 24 in Missouri; 18 were 9-holes including Lake Forest, Rolling Hills, Ambo Chesterfield and St. Peter's.

In 1992 **Missouri Fairways** made it's debut. Bryan Edwards, Publisher of the magazine, hoped to provide *"...an informative guide to a wide variety of public golf courses in the sate of Missouri, as well as offering the avid golfer tremendous savings on greens fees, pro shop merchandise..."!* The vehicle for this was an Annual Club Membership. For $24.95 you received discounts on golf, hotels, travel and rental cars. The magazine featured full-color shots of various courses (there were 25 in the initial edition) that were spread throughout the state.

Another publication that has come and gone [and come back again, at least in one form or another] is *Missouri Fairways & Greens.* The most recent birth took place under

the direction of William Mathis. The new Vol. 1 No. 1 was distributed at the Boone Valley Classic in hopes of drawing a large readership for future editions. Featured articles on Bob Goalby, Hale Irwin, Tom Wargo, Boone Valley, and a summary of Missouri Golf Association events were included.

Of note is the name of Warren Mayes, a contributor to *Missouri Fairways & Greens* and a former Editor of *Missouri Golf*, another statewide publication that was begun in cooperation with the Missouri Golf Association in 1991 and died after only a few editions. The original Missouri Golf was part of the aforementioned "cookie-cutter" approach; a multi-state publication that included Utah, Kansas, Texas, Florida, Sun Country and Missouri. However Warren Mayes is a first-rate writer with tremendous insight into the St. Louis golf community. So the articles and related material had more of a St. Louis "flavor" than other magazines.

Bill Mathis also has a good track record as a publisher so chances are better that *Missouri Fairways & Greens* will survive. But readership, advertisers and time will be the eventual standard.

Another magazine was **National Golfer** which boasts a 20,000 plus readership in over twenty states. While this publication focuses on the same geographic area as the Gateway PGA (Eastern Missouri and Southern Illinois) early editions included about 24 pages [out of 56] of local information with the remainder regional or local stories. Jay Randolph Jr. and Dennis Green were the primary local drivers behind this.

The Golf Directory was begun in 1989 by this author and Pete Gallagher as a way of providing a directory of all area courses. The initial edition included eastern Missouri and Southern Illinois courses, while the second, published in 1990 included all of Missouri as well as Southern Illinois.

Gradually the books settled into a St. Louis-only Directory as the 1993 and 1996 editions were distributed.

Unlike other publications, a single page is devoted to each course; thus the Directory is over 150 pages as it lists all courses within a two hour drive of the area. Today it lists 136 courses, public and

private, in the greater Bi-State area. There have been other directories published in the past few years, but, with a little self-promotion here, we believe it is the most complete course listing in the area! It continues to be updated annually as new courses are completed in the area and changes occur to the existing layouts.

Another annual publication is the *Gateway Golfer* a publication of the gateway PGA. While this focuses mainly on the Professional activities in the area, it also addresses many of the major amateur events and golfers. Published under the direction of Gateway PGA Executive Director, Jeff Smith, it highlights the top Professional honors for play, marketing and teaching. Recent PGA Pro's of the Year have included Russ Luedoff, Steve Spray, Garth Bayer, Terry Houser, Larry Emery and Jerry Tucker. This is entirely presented for the Gateway PGA

member clubs and the advertising and stories reflect the successes of the past season, and upcoming events. The earliest editions of the Gateway Golfer, dating from 1978, were published bi-monthly and later quarterly, as they had more of a "total golf" approach. It would be accurate to state that early on, it was more like *Golf Scene magazine*, than the current version of *Gateway Golfer*!

Golfing newspapers have also made frequent appearances in the area. One such paper was from the early 70's and was *Metro St. Louis Golfing News*, and was published by Dan Grothaus. Similar in nature to the Annual *Post-Dispatch Golf Guide*, another great area golfing resource, the Metro highlighted courses, players and events. Interviews included Jay Haas as a youthful amateur, Barb

The Bards

Berkmeyer as the recent 1975 Missouri State Champion, as well as articles by Jay Randolph and Harold Tuthill. A more recent paper is **Club Lynx** which is distributed free throughout the area. It too features articles, course listings and interviews with 12 issues to be published annually, according to President Dave Stevens.

Other magazines are **Golfers Dream** and The **Golfer's Pocket Guide of St. Louis Golf.** Both are smaller, pamphlet-size editions. The **Golfers Dream** is another "cookie-cutter" type with 16 pages of local information sandwiched around 48 pages of national golf stories and advertising. The premiere issue of this was in 1995. The **Pocket Guide** has been around since about 1993. It's format is all local, with basic course information and local advertising.

In 1979 St. Louis-based Creative Sales Corporation, a Color Art Division, combined with the PGA of America to produce **The Golfers Atlas.** While the purpose was to utilize the maps that the company produced, it documented golf courses throughout the country with locations, professional, holes, yardage and amenities. While only produced one time, it was a very useful tool for the early traveling golfer.

Perhaps one of the more interesting coverage of golf takes place each Thursday on KFNS-AM590 with the **Fairways & Greens** show, with hosts Jeff Smith and Jay Randolph Jr. The show offers interviews and insights into local and national golf coverage. Begun in 1992, the show has also had cable TV exposure. It grew from a 30 minutes radio broadcast to 3 hours, now competing with the mid-day talk shows from 11 am to 2 pm. Jay Randolph Jr. also has a Saturday morning solo stint **Tee One Up** that begins at 9 am, also on KFNS.

The Internet - World Wide Web

A more recent series of Golf related activities have sprung up — on the Internet — and St. Louis has several sites for golf and related activities.

GolfMasters, formed by St. Louisan Kevin Cantwell, is one such Web Site. *GolfMasters* attempts to consolidate all local events in a single, easy to use and find site. Featuring Pro tips, tournaments (amateur and professional) regional tournaments, charity events and a Pro Shop, where you can purchase goods, GolfMasters is an excellent reference site for area golf and offers many golf-related features and activities.

Another golf related site,

Mike Weinhaus

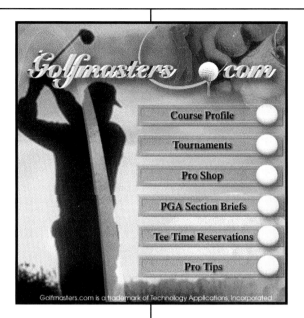

specializing in the rules of golf, is **at** *Golfcircuit* called *"Haus Rules"* by Mike Weinhaus. Mike, a Meadowbrook member, is a USGA certified rules specialist, whose site on the Web features local PGA Tour events, Rules Q&A, Golf News, a Pro Shop and Classified areas. Mike will respond to a golf rules question from all who send. He also offers a Rules Quiz to test your knowledge (with or without the Rules Book). Those of you who compete regularly in area events will know Mike and "surf-into" his site.

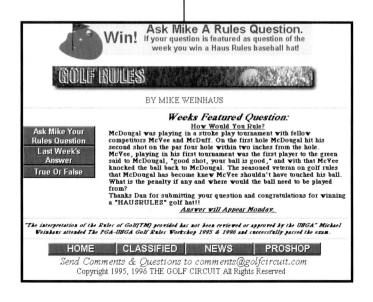

The Courses

St. Louis Area Golf Clubs - A Chronology

Course	Founded	Designer	Holes	Par	Yards
Algonquin CC Founded as a Golf Club in 1899. Original 9 holes in the Webster Groves Park in 1900 near Gore and the RR Tracks. Moved to present site in 1903 with 9 holes. Completed 18 holes in 1914 at present site. Remodeled by Marvin Ferguson (1980). Remodeled by Geoffrey S. Cornish and Brian Silva (1984) One of the original members of the St. Louis District Golf Association in 1916	1904	Robert Foulis George Andrews & Bart Adams 1931 Layout 1910 Layout (for 18 holes) 1903 Layout	18 18 18 9	71 71 74 37	6155 6203 6730 3016
Alton CC	1903		9		
Alton Municipal GC A 9 hole course	1934		9	35	3092
Ambo Chesterfield GC (See Chesterfield)					
American Legion GC (Edwardsville)	1968	Howard Popham	9	35	2652
Annbriar GC (Waterloo, IL)	1993	Dr. Michael Hurdzan	18	72	6841
Arlington CC (Granite City)	1964	Robert Bruce Harris	18	72	7104
Arrowhead GC Course was located on Telegraph at Arrowhead GC Drive. Originally a private course, it went public in 1969. Course closed in 1988.	1955		9	35	2522
Bahnfyre GC (see also Southmoor) Course was located on Tesson Ferry Rd. just west of Wells Rd. Originally named **Southmoor**, renamed when new 9 holes built in 1981. Closed in 1987.	1981	Marvin Ferguson	18	70	6014
Ballwin Municipal GC Formerly **Fox Creek CC**, renamed in 1974. Remodeled in 1987 by Bob Lohman.	1962	Homer Herpel	9	36	3382
Belk Park GC Back 9 holes added by Lawrence Packard (1970)	1957	Lawrence Packard & Brent Wadsworth	18	72	6812
Bellerive CC Remodeled by Ron Kirby, Denis Griffiths (1985); Remodeled by Robert Trent Jones (1990)	1960	Robert Trent Jones	18	72	7302
Bellerive CC (Original) Originally the **St. Louis Field Club** which was organized in 1897, the members moved to this site in 1910 and constructed an 18 hole course. Located at the present site of the University of Missouri-St. Louis the club moved in 1960 to the new Bellerive CC on Ladue Rd. One of the original members of the St. Louis District Golf Association in 1916	1910	James, David & Robert Foulis	18	71	6421
Belleville CC (See Westhaven GC)	1926		9		

Bent Oak GC (Jerseyville, IL)	1991		9	36	3290
Berry Hill GC Originally operated as a semi-private club, it was sold to the city of Bridgeton in 1979.	1967	Fisher & Fritchell	9	36	3117
Biltmore GC (Fenton) Course closed in early 1940's.	1930		9		
Bogey Club A 9 hole course, 18 when combined with the 9 holes at the Log Cabin Club. One of the original members of the St. Louis District Golf Association in 1916.	1910	Robert Foulis	9	36	2764
Bogey Hills CC Original site of the **St. Charles CC**. Initially had 9 holes. Additional land was acquired in 1971 and the back 9 was built.	1961	W. Clark & Dennis Walters	18	71	6556
Boone Valley CC (Augusta, MO)	1992	P.B. Dye	18	71	7056
Cajun GC (See also Desoto CC) Renamed in 1990 when new management took over. Also known previously as **Suburbia GC** in the '50's	1929		9	36	2911
Camelot GC (Collinsville, IL) A 9 hole course. Course closed in late 70's.	1969		9	35	2394
Cardinal Creek CC (Scott AFB) Remodeled by Gary Kern (1985)	1976		18	72	6484
Carondelet Park Links (Tower Grove Park) An all Ladies Club established in 1896. Initially 6 holes then 9 holes in 1898.			6 9	25	1100
Cedar Creek GC (See Wentzville GC)					
Centennial GC (Jerseyville)	1993	Pat Goetten	9	35	2835
Champion Trail GC (Fairview Heights, IL) Course set to open in 1997 with 27 holes.	1997	Bob & Kye Goalby	9 9 9	36 36 36	3563 3487 3395
Cherry Hills CC Remodeled by Gary Kern (1985) Went public in 1992. Majority of membership went to **St. Albans CC**.	1964	Al Linkogel and Ray Freeborg	18	71	6367
Chesterfield GC (see also River Valley) Back 9 added in 1978 by Walter Ambo	1963	Walter Ambo	18	68	5540
Clinton Hill GC (Fairview Heights)	1971	Clete Idoux	18	71	6601
Cloverleaf GC (Alton, IL)	1931	Paul Gabriel	18	70	5535
Columbia Bridges (Columbia, IL)	1996	Gary Kern	9	36	3123
Columbia GC (Columbia, IL)	1968	Al Linkogel	18	71	6280

The Courses

Cottonwood GC (Desoto, MO)	1981		9	36	3335
Country Fairways GC (N. Alton, IL) Closed c. 1980.	1968		9	35	2856
Country Lakes GC (Warrenton, MO)	1993	Bob Garrard	18	71	5708
Crescent CC (See The Players Club)					
Creve Coeur GC Originally an 18 hole course. The part of the course closest to Olive closed in 1969 to make way for Office Park. Course remodeled to existing 9 holes. Course owned by the City of Creve Coeur.	1924	Present 1929 Layout	9 18	35 70	3008 6371
Crystal Highlands (Festus/Crystal City)	1988	Dr. Michael Hurdzan	18	72	6542
Crystal Lake CC Course was located on Bopp Rd. between Manchester and Clayton Rds. Closed in 1979.	1929	William Diddel 1929 Layout	18 18	70 71	6019 6257
Dardenne Lake GC (see St. Peters)					
Deer Creek GC Course opened as a public facility, went private for two years and then went public again.	1989	Brooks McCarthy	18	72	7008
Desoto GC (See Cajun GC and also Suburbia GC)	1929		9		
Duwe GC (See Lakewood GC)					
Eagle Springs GC Facility has 27 holes, including a 9 hole par 3 course	1989	David Gill	18 9	72 27	6454 1309
Elmwood GC (Belleville, IL)	1959	Joe Idoux	9	36	3030
Elmwood GC (Washington, MO)	1968		9	36	3154
Emerald Greens GC	1994	Jim Cochran	18	70	6258
Fairmont GC (Fairmont City, IL)	1953		9	33	2248
Falls GC, The (O'Fallon, MO)	1995	Ed Schultz, Terry Allen and Mike Null	18	71	6394
Ferguson CC Course closed in early 1940's.	1930		9		
Florissant 600 GC Course closed in mid-70's	1968		9	27	1252
Florissant Valley CC Course plowed under by 1903 (see also **Normandy Heights Club**)	1899	Ned McNamara	9		
Forest Hills CC Remodeled by Dennis Griffiths (1987) and Dick Nugent (1990) Remodeled by Keith Foster (1996) [Valley Course]	1965	Chic Adams	18 9	72 30	6735 1931

Forest Park GC Originally opened with 9 holes. Added 9 holes in 1913 and 9 more in 1915. The "hill" 9 were the last added, those running by Art Hill.	1912	Robert Foulis	18 9	70 35	5865 2552
Four Seasons CC Semi-Private with limited outside memberships.	1962	Sid Kandel & Harland Bartholomew	9	35	2806
Fox Creek CC Renamed **Ballwin Municipal GC** in 1974.	1962	Homer Herpel	9	36	3382
Fox Creek GC (Edwardsville)	1993	Gary Kern	18	72	7025
Fox Run CC (Eureka)	1994	Gary & Ron Kern	18	72	7031
Gateway National Golf Links	1997	Keith Foster	18		
Glen Echo CC Remodeled by Robert Foulis (1904). One of the original members of the St. Louis District Golf Association in 1916. Course was named **Ridgedale CC** following the sale of the club for indebtedness in 1915. Name reverted back to **Glen Echo** in 1921. The club was originally to be the **Mound City Golf Club**, but this was changed prior to the construction of the course.	1901	Jim & Robert Foulis 1931 Layout 1910 Layout	18 18 18	71 71 74	6382 6182 6108
Glenwood GC (Maryland Heights) Course was located near McKelvey and Marine Roads. Closed in 1979.	1974		9	34	2900
GolfMohr GC (Collinsville, IL) Course closed in 60's	c.1950		9		
Governors Run GC (Carlyle, IL) Regulation course plus a 18 hole par 3.	1994	Donald Horrell	18 18	72 54	7013 1093
Grand Marias GC (East St. Louis) Originally known as **Lake Park GC**.	1935	Joseph Roseman	18	72	6706
Granite City GC (See Rivers Edge GC) Located in the Melvin Price Support Center.	1958	Lawrence Packard & Brent Wadsworth	9	36	3265
Green Trails CC Course was located on Ladue Rd. just west of Woods Mill (Hwy. 141). Course was only 9 holes by 1970. Course closed in 1982	1960	Original At closing 1982	18 9	 36	 3436
Greenbriar Hills CC (formerly Osage CC) Changed name to Greenbriar in 1937. 9 holes added by C.D. Wagstaff (1958) Remodeled by Ron Prichard (1988). Remodeled by Don Sechrest (1990).	1926	C.D. Wagstaff	18	71	6427
Greenview GC (Centralia, IL) Closed in the 1930's.	1922	Tom Bendelow	9		
Greenview GC (Centralia, IL) Course owned by Senior PGA star Tom Wargo	1966	Oral Telford	18	72	6441

The Courses

Course	Year	Designer	Holes	Par	Yards
Green Trees GC (Lake St. Louis, MO) A 9 hole course. Course closed in late 70's.	1973		9		
Hawk Ridge GC (Lake St. Louis, MO)	1995	Larry Flatt	18	72	6679
Hidden Valley CC Originally opened as a 9 hole club. Expanded to 18 holes in 1980.	1962	Tim Boyd	18	70	6189
High Point GC (See Northland)					
Hill Crest GC (See Kirkwood CC) Course was leased by Kirkwood CC in 1914.	1910		9		
Hillcrest GC Course renamed **Sherwood CC** in 1971.	1964	Homer Herpel	9	33	2637
House Springs GC	1978	Everett Tuggle	9	36	2995
Incline Village GC Originally named **Ponderosa GC**, renamed **Incline Village GC** in 1979. Course added a back 9 in 1994.	1960	Links Nursery (Al Linkogel)	18	71	5934
Indian Meadows GC (Olivette) Course was located off Olive St. Road between Price and Warson Rd. Course closed in 1956.	1946		18		
Indian Mounds GC (Fairmont City, IL)	1995	Dave Murray	9	29	1711
Innsbrook Estates GC (Wright City) Back 9 added in 1989.	1982	Mark Waltman & Jay Randolph	18	70	6465
Jefferson Barracks GC (Columbia, IL)	1991	Tony & Jim Watkins	9	36	3090
Jefferson Barracks Links Course closed by 1903.	1898		9		
Jefferson Barracks Officers Club GC Course was located in the Jefferson Barracks Military base. Closed in 1940's	1927		9		
Joachim GC (Herculaneum, MO) Originally opened with sand greens. In 1934 grass replaced the sand.	1929		9	36	3092
Kenrick Seminary GC Located on the grounds of Kenrick Seminary. Course had sand greens. Closed around 1978.	1928		9	34	2300
Kickapoo GC (Ellsberry, MO) Course located near Mississippi River. Closed c.1970 due to persistent flooding.	1960		9		
Kinloch Club Course was closed by 1902.	1898	Jim Foulis	9		

Course	Year	Designer/Remodeler	Holes	Par	Yards
Kirkwood CC (See also Hill Crest GC) Originally leased Hill Crest GC which had 9 holes. Additional 9 holes added in c.1919. Renamed **Woodlawn CC** in 1927. Closed in 1937. One of the original members of the St. Louis District Association in 1916.	1914	Remodeled by Robert Foulis 1919	18	72	6079
Lago Bello GC (See St. Peters)					
Lake Forest CC (Lake St. Louis. MO) Originally called **Lake St. Louis GC**, the name was changed when the Back 9 was added and course remodeled by Gary Kern in 1986.	1978	Neil Sellenriek	18	72	7141
Lake James GC	1991		18	72	5937
Lake Park GC (See Grand Marias)	1935	Joseph Roseman	18		
Lake St. Louis GC (See Lake Forest)					
Lakeside GC Course was on Page near Woodson Rd. Originally an 18 hole course, part of it was sold off and was a nine hole around 1960. Course closed in 1970	1950		18		
Lakewood GC Originally **Duwe GC**, renamed in 1972. Remodeled by Hale Irwin in 1991	1961		9	34	2555
Legacy GC (Granite City, IL)	1991	Hale Irwin	18	71	6327
Lockhaven CC (Alton, IL)	1955	Robert Bruce Harris	18	72	6701
Locust Hills GC (O'Fallon, IL) Originally a 9 hole course, it was completely rebuilt as 18 holes and re-opened in 1970.	1965		18	71	6005
Log Cabin Club Remodeled by Robert Foulis (1935). One of the original members of the St. Louis District Golf Association in 1916. A 9 hole course, 18 when combined with the 9 holes at the Bogey Club.	1909	Robert Foulis & Jim Mackrell 1929 Layout	9 9	36 34	2708 2463
Madison County CC (See Sunset Hills)	1922		9	36	3110
Meadow Brook CC (See Midland Valley) Original club (**Midland Valley CC**) and renamed when new owners took over in 1932.	1912	Robert Foulis			
Meadow Woods CC (Centralia, IL)	1927		9		
Meadowbrook CC (see Midland Valley) Remodeled by Gary Kern (1988) Seven holes remodeled by Brent Wadsworth (1996)	1961	Robert Bruce Harris	18	72	7081
Mehlbrook CC A 9 hole course located on Ringer Rd near Mehl Rd. Course closed in 1979	1973		9		
Meramec Shores GC (St. Clair, MO)	1994	Jerry Reible	18	72	5897

The Courses

Course	Year	Designer	Holes	Par	Yards
Mid-Rivers GC (St. Peters, MO)	1993	Ned Storey	18	72	6604
Midland Valley CC Remodeled by Donald Ross (1919) Remodeled by William Diddel (1928). Course was located on Ashby Rd. north of Page. It sold in 1932 and renamed **Meadow Brook CC** by new owners. Club moved to Clayton Rd. in 1960 and renamed **Meadowbrook CC**. One of the original members of the St. Louis District Association in 1916.	1913	James Foulis	18	72	6239
Mound City Golf Club (See Glen Echo)					
Missouri Bluffs GC	1994	Tom Fazio	18	72	7047
New Melle GC (New Melle, MO)	1991	Ted Christner	18	71	6348
Nor-Lakes (See Northland)					
Normandie GC Originally **Normandie CC**. Second oldest existing club in the area. A private Club from 1901-1985, it was renamed **Normandie Park** in 1985 when it went public. Reverted back to **Normandie GC** in 1995 under new management. One of the original members of the St. Louis District Golf Association in 1916.	1901	Walter Gilliam Robert Foulis 1931 Layout 1910 Layout	18 18 18	71 72 73	6534 6361 6133
Normandie Heights GC (See Florissant Valley Country Club)					
North County GC (Red Bud, IL) A 9 hole course	1969	Clete Idoux	9	35	2664
North Hills CC (See Norwood Hills) Renamed **Norwood Hills** in 1933. Originally had 45 holes (East, West and a 9 hole layout) Joined District in 1925.	1923	Wayne Stiles Layout in 1929	18 18 9	71 71 36	6543 6434 3120
North Shore CC (See Riverview)	1916	1931 Layout	18	72	6156
Northland GC Par 3 course located off West Florissant near Chambers. Course changed name to **Nor-Lakes GC** in 1964. Changed name to **Village GC** in 1970. Changed name to **High Point GC** in 1977. Course closed in 1980.	1961		9		
Norwood Hills (East) Formerly known as **North Hills** until 1933. Remodeled by Roger Null (1989) Remodeled by Gary Kern (1987)	1923	Wayne Stiles	18	70	5972
Norwood Hills (West) Formerly known as **North Hills** until 1933. Remodeled by Roger Null (1992)	1922	Wayne Stiles	18	72	6804

Oak Brook GC (Edwardsville) Second 9 was added in 1974.	1972	Larry & Wilbur Suhre	18	71	6151
Old Warson CC	1954	Robert Trent Jones	18	71	6926
Orchards, The (Belleville)	1991	Bob Goalby	18	71	6405
Osage CC (See also Greenbriar) Osage went bankrupt in 1935. 9 holes added in 1937 and reorganized as **Greenbriar Hills** a year later in 1938. Course lost 9 holes when Highway took the land in 1958 and C.D. Wagstaff added 9 holes then.	1926	1929 Layout	18 18	71 71	6275 6156
Pacific GC A 9 hole course. Course closed in 1972.	1967		9		
Paddock GC	1964	Homer Herpel	18	72	6493
Paradise Valley GC	1965	Jim Cochran	18	70	6186
Parkwood Oaks GC (Maryland Heights) A 9 hole course located at I-270 and McKelvey Rd. Course closed in 1981.	1975	Lee Redman	9		
Pebble Creek GC Course located at Clarkson and Kehrs Mill Rd. Closed in 1977	1972		9		
Persimmon Ridge GC	1998	Keith Foster	18	71	6850
Pevely Farms GC (Crescent, MO)	1997	Arthur Hills	18		
Players Club Formerly **Crescent CC** (Public) went private in 1988. Roger Packard added 9 holes in 1991.	1979	Larry Packard Roger Packard	18 9	72 30	7014 1722
Point Prairie GC (See Wentzville GC)					
Pomme Creek GC	1991	Gary Kern	18	66	5031
Ponderosa GC (See Incline Village GC)					
Prairies GC, The (Cahokia, IL)	1996		18	72	6670
Quail Creek GC	1986	Hale Irwin /Gary Kern	18	72	6805
Raintree GC (Hillsboro, MO)	1980	Butler & Associates	18	72	6122
Ridge GC (Waterloo, IL) Back 9 added in 1994.	1992	Donald Horrell	18	72	6522
Ridgedale CC (See Glen Echo) Glen Echo was renamed in 1916 following the sale of the club for indebtedness. Course resumed using the Glen Echo name in 1921.					

The Courses

			Holes	Par	Yards
Riverdale GC Course closed in 1941. Located near Telegraph and the Meramec River.			9		
River Lakes GC	1996	Tony & Jim Watkins	9	35	2705
River Valley GC Originally only 9 holes, course was renamed **Ambo River Valley GC** in 1970. Back 9 holes added in 1978. Renamed **Chesterfield GC** in 1985.	1963	Walter Ambo	18	68	5540
Rivers Edge GC A 9 hole course. Also known as N.I.S.A. in mid-70's. Located on the Melvin Price Military Base. Also known as **Granite City GC**	1954		9	36	3380
Riverside GC A 9 hole Par 3 course was built in 1991	1966	Jack Wolfner	18 9	69 27	5505 948
Riverview CC (See North Shore GC) Course was located on Riverview Drive just north of I-270. It opened with 9 holes as a private course. Completed 2nd 9 in 1923. Renamed **North Shore GC** in 1930. Course closed in late 30's. Reopened in 1959 when it added land to make 27 holes. Remodeled in 1959 by Homer Herpel and Chic Adams. Course closed in mid-1980's then reopened in 1989. Closed during floods of 1993. Reopened as a 9 hole public course in 1995. Closed end of 1995.	1916	Robert Foulis Layout in 1993 Layout in 1931 Layout in 1923	18 9 18 18	71 35 72 71	6460 3129 6456 6464
Rock Springs CC (Alton, IL) Course opened as a private club. In the early 60's course was donated to the city of Alton.	1913	Tom Bendelow	9	35	3053
Rolling Hills GC (Godfrey, IL) Originally opened as a 9 hole course. Gary Kern added the back 9 in 1992.	1965	Gary Kern	18	71	5718
Roseland GC (Alton, IL)	1992	Lee Redman	9	36	3378
Royal Oaks GC (Troy, MO)	1994	Lee Redman	18	72	6206
Ruth Park GC Originally known as **University City GC**. Assistance on original design from Robert Foulis.	1931	Robert Bruce Harris	9	35	3139
Sherwood CC (See Hillcrest)					
Southmoor GC Closed 9 holes in 1981. Opened new back 9 in 1981 and renamed **Bahnfyre GC**.	1952	Terry Moore	18	70	5800
Spencer T. Olin (Alton, IL)	1988	Arnold Palmer & Ed Seay	18	72	6941

Course	Year	Designer	Holes	Par	Yardage
St. Albans CC Originally opened with 18 holes. 3rd 9 completed in 1996. Final 9 under construction by Dr. Michael Hurdzan and will be complete in 1997.	1993 1996	Tom Weiskopf & Jay Moorish Dr. Michael Hurdzan	18 18	72	7180
St. Andrews GC	1967	Stewart Mertz	18	68	5866
St. Ann GC 9 hole course is owned and operated by the City of St. Ann.	1951	Al Linkogel	9	34	2615
St. Catherine-Villa 9 hole course	1974		9	35	2856
St. Charles CC Course opened with 9 holes. Closed in 1942. Land later became site of **Bogey Hills CC**, but only after having been a farm for almost 20 years.	1929		9		
St. Charles GC Opened with 18 holes. Added 9 holes in 1963.	1956	Al Linkogel	18 9	68 36	5317 3115
St. Clair Golf While not strickly the forerunner of St. Clair CC, members from this 1908 layout on the bluffs overlooking the Mississippi River, were some of the founders in 1911 of the present day St. Clair CC.	1908		9		
St. Clair CC (Belleville, IL) Originally opened with 9 holes. Added 9 holes by William Langford (1927)	1911		18	72	6536
St. Louis Athletic Club Course closed in early 1901 when space was needed for expansion of Forest Park to accommodate the 1904 Worlds Fair pavilion construction. Club opened with 9 holes then added 9 more in 1900 when it was located in the northwest corner of Forest Park. Forerunner to the **Triple A** club today.	1898		18		
St. Louis Country Club Original club founded in 1892 as St. Louis Polo Club in Bridgeton. When club burned, it moved and built initial 9 holes on what is now Polo Place in Clayton in 1896. In October, 1903 9 holes were added making 18 at the Hanley Road site. An additional short course was built for the ladies in the northwest portion of the club. Course moved to present location in 1913 and new course opened in 1914. Course remodeled by Robert Trent Jones (1952). First Golf Club & course in the Area. One of the original members of the St. Louis District Golf Association in 1916.	1896 1913	James Foulis (Clayton site) 1910 Layout Charles Blair Macdonald & Seth Raynor	9 18 18	36 73 71	2935 5760 6484

The Courses

St. Louis Field Club (see Bellerive) (Bissell, MO) Third course to open in the Area [May 1898]. Course closed in 1910 when membership moved to the newly established Bellerive CC in Normandy.	1898	D.O. Ives & A.L. Kenneth John McGee	9	39	2436
St. Louis Jockey Club (also called St. Louis Golf Club) Second course opened in the area [April, 1898]. Located on the infield of the Jockey Club racetrack. Course closed in 1905 following the abolition of para-mutual wagering by the Missouri Legislature.	1898	James & Dave Foulis	9	39	1916
St. Peters GC Originally opened as a private 9 hole course. Renamed **Dardenne Lake** and went Semi-Private in late 60's. Later renamed **Lago Bello CC** in 1975. City of St. Peters acquired the layout in 1977 and name reverted back to **St. Peters GC**. Course remodeled and second 9 added by Garrett Gill (1996).	1962	Original Present	9 18	37 71	3480 6016
St. Vincent Hospital GC Located on the grounds of St. Vincent Hospital on St. Charles Rock Road. Course closed in mid-60's. Owned by the Daughters of Charity Order.	1930		9		
Stonewolf G&CC (Fairview Heights, IL) Course opened in September, 1996.	1996	Jack Nicklaus	18	72	6891
Suburbia GC (see also Cajun & Desoto) Course renamed Cajun GC in 1990.	1929		9		
Sugar Creek CC Back 9 added in 1992	1990		18	71	6299
Sun Valley GC (Ellsberry, MO) Back 9 added in 1991.	1988	Gary Kern	18	70	6395
Sunset CC Originally named **Sunset Hill CC**, renamed Sunset CC in 1930's. Remodeled by Lawrence Packard (1962); Remodeled by Mike Hurdzan in 1988 and additional work in 1990 & 1991. One of the original members of the St. Louis District Golf Association in 1916	1917	James & Robert Foulis 1917 Layout 1929 layout	18 18 18	72 71 72	6323 6265 6250
Sunset Hills CC (Edwardsville, IL) Originally the **Madison County CC**, the name changed in the 50's. Back 9 added by Lawrence Packard, Brent Wadsworth (1955); Remodeled by Gary Kern (1987)	1922	Present layout 1922 layout	18 9	71 36	6743 3110
Sunset Lakes GC	1988	Bob Lohmann	18	72	6461
Tamarack GC (O'Fallon, IL)	1954	Pete Dye	18	71	6450
Tanglewood GC (Pacific, MO) Course closed around 1980.	1973		18	68	5600

Tapawingo GC	1994	Gary Player	18	72	7151
Teamsters GC (See Union Hills)					
Terre Du Lac CC (Bonne Terre, MO)	1967	R. Albert Anderson	18	72	6743
Tower Grove Park Club Originally a 6 hole course, expanded to 9 holes in 1898. A Ladies only club. Mistakenly referred to as the Carondelet Park Club in an 1899 Golf Guide. Course closed in 1903.	1897	George Norman	9		
Tower Tee GC Back 9 holes built in 1974 by Neil Sellenriek.	1969	R. Albert Anderson	18	54	2000
Tree Court GC Renamed Family Golf Centers in 1996.	1993	Dave Murray	9	27	777
Triple A GC Remodeled by Robert Foulis. Also referred to as St. Louis Sportsman's Club or the St. Louis Amateur Athletic Association. First course was 9 holes then 9 more were added in 1901. Club moved to present site in 1903 and built 9 hole course. One of the original members of the St. Louis District Golf Association in 1916	1898	Robert Foulis 1910 Layout	9 9	35 35	2799 2610
Triple Lakes GC (Milstadt, IL)	1961	Mert Richmond	18	72	6232
Twin Lakes GC (Sunset Hills) Course closed in 1967 to make way for I-44 / I-270.	1955	Jim Cochran	9	34	2556
Union Hills GC (Pevely, MO) Originally named the Teamsters GC changed names in 1988. Back 9 added by Gary Kern (1988)	1976	Homer Herpel	18	72	6502
University City GC (See Ruth Park)					
Village GC (See Northland)					
Warrenton GC	1969	Luecke Family	18	70	5557
Waterloo CC	1927		9	34	2780
Wentzville GC Formerly known as Point Prairie and Cedar Creek. Changed name to Westzville GC in 1994	1958		9	36	3157
West Par GC Located at Clarkson & Kehrs Mill Rd. Closed in 1983	1963		9	34	2900
Westborough CC Originally opened in 1908 as the Westwood CC. Renamed Westborough in 1928 when members moved to the present Westwood CC opened on Conway Rd. Remodeled by Gary Kern (1990) One of the original member courses of the St. Louis District Golf Association in 1916	1908	Tom Bendelow 1910 Layout	18 18	68 74	5814 6011

The Courses

Western Military Academy GL (Alton, IL) Course closed prior to 1910.	1899		9		
Westhaven GC (Belleville, IL) Originally named **Belleville CC**, was built with sand greens until mid-50's.	1926		9	35	3013
Westwood CC Originally 27 holes (Red, White & Blue) spread over 300 acres. Only 18 holes survived after WWII. Remodeled by William Diddel (1961); Remodeled by Marvin Ferguson (1969)	1928	Harold Paddock	18	72	6785
Whitmoor CC (East) Changed to North course in 1995.	1988	Karl Litton	18	71	6646
Whitmoor CC (West) Changed to South course in 1995.	1990	Karl Litton	18	72	7004
Woodlands GC	1994	Hansen Dev.	18	71	6401
Woodlawn CC (See Kirkwood)					
Woods Fort GC (Troy, MO)	1994	Picket Ray & Silver	18	72	6804
Yorktown GC (Belleville, IL)	1961	Pete Dye	18	54	2166

All courses 18 holes except where noted. Holes, Par and Yardage is given for either present conditions or at the time of the closing of the course.

The Author and friends at Grand National GC on the Robert Trent Jones Trail
Front (l-r): Bruce Daughtry, Larry Cardinale, Charlie Brown,
Ed Neusel, Mike Crider, Bob Barlow, Ted McBride.
Back (l-r) Jim Healey, Steve Neusel, Jeff Neusel, Pat Brady and Jim Brady.

The opening hole at Algonquin CC

Breakdown of Area Courses

138 Courses in covered area*

Area Wide Statistics		Missouri		Illinois	
		Total Courses	**87**	**Total Courses**	**51**
Public Courses	101	Public	56	Public	45
Private Courses	37	Private	31	Private	6
18 holes	93	18 holes	62	18 holes	31
9 holes	45	9 holes	25	9 holes	20
18 holes - Public	64	18 - Public	37	18 - Public	27
18 holes - Private	29	18 - Private	25	18 - Private	4
9 holes - Public	37	9 - Public	19	9 - Public	18
9 holes - Private	8	9 - Private	6	9 - Private	2

* Includes some courses under construction

Chronology of Golf Courses by Year Founded

St. Louis Country Club [Clayton]	1896	Lakeside GC	1953
St. Louis Field Club [Bellerive CC]	1897	Old Warson CC	1954
St. Louis Amateur Athletic Club [Triple A]	1898	Tamarack GC	1954
Tower Grove Park Links	1898	Arrowhead GC	1955
Jefferson Barracks Links	1898	Lockhaven CC	1955
Kinloch Club	1898	St. Charles GC	1956
St. Louis Jockey Club	1898	Belk Park GC	1957
Log Cabin Club	1899	Cedar Creek GC [Wentzville GC]	1958
Florissant Valley CC	1899	Granite City GC [Rivers Edge GC]	1958
Algonquin CC [Original]	1899	Elmwood GC [Belleville, IL]	1959
Western Military Academy GC	1899	Bellerive CC [Ladue]	1960
Glen Echo CC	1901	Green Trails CC	1960
Normandie CC	1901	Ponderosa GC [Incline Village]	1960
Algonquin CC [Present]	1903	Bogey Hills CC	1961
Alton CC	1903	Duwe GC [Lakewood GC]	1961
Triple A GC [Present]	1903	Meadowbrook CC	1961
Westwood CC [Westborough CC]	1908	Northland GC [Nor-Lakes/High Point]	1961
Bellerive CC [Normandy]	1910	Triple Lakes GC	1961
Bogey Club	1910	Yorktown GC	1961
Midland Valley CC [Meadow Brook]	1911	Four Seasons CC	1962
St. Clair CC	1911	Fox Creek CC [Ballwin GC]	1962
Hill Crest CC [Kirkwood CC / Woodlawn]	1911	Hidden Valley CC	1962
Forest Park GC	1912	St. Peters GC [Lago Bello/Dardenne]	1962
Rock Springs GC	1912	Carlyle Lake GC	1962
St. Louis Country Club [Ladue]	1913	River Valley GC [Chesterfield/Ambo]	1963
Riverview CC [North Shore GC]	1916	Rolling Hills GC	1963
Sunset Hill CC [Sunset CC]	1917	West Par GC	1963
Greenview GC [Original]	1922	Kickapoo GC	1963
North Hills CC [Norwood Hills] (West)	1922	Arlington CC	1964
Madison County CC [Sunset Hills CC]	1922	Cherry Hills CC	1964
North Hills CC [Norwood Hills] (East)	1923	Hillcrest GC [Sherwood CC]	1964
Creve Coeur GC	1924	Paddock CC	1964
St. Charles CC	1925	Forest Hills CC	1965
Osage CC [Greenbriar Hills]	1926	Locust Hills GC	1965
Belleville CC (Westhaven GC)	1926	Paradise Valley GC	1965
Jefferson Barracks Officers Club	1927	Greenview GC [Present]	1966
Waterloo CC	1927	Riverside GC	1966
Westwood CC [Conway Rd]	1928	Berry Hill GC	1967
Kenrick Seminary GC	1928	St. Andrews GC	1967
Crystal Lake CC	1929	Terre Du Lac CC	1967
Desoto GC [Cajun GC]	1929	Pacific GC	1967
Joachim GC	1929	American Legion GC	1968
Biltmore GC	1930	Columbia GC	1968
Ferguson CC	1930	Elmwood GC (Washington, MO)	1968
St. Vincent Hospital GC	1930	Country Fairways GC	1968
Cloverleaf GC	1931	Florissant 600	1968
Ruth Park GC [University City GC]	1931	North County GC	1969
Alton Municipal GC	1934	Tower Tee GC	1969
Lake Park GC / Grand Marias GC	1935	Warrenton GC	1969
Indian Meadows GC	1946	Camelot GC	1969
St. Ann GC	1951	Clinton Hill GC	1971
GolfMohr GC	1951	Oak Brook GC	1972
Southmoor GC [Bahnfyre GC]	1952	Pebble Creek GC	1972
Fairmont GC	1953	Mehlbrook CC	1973

Green Trees GC	1973	Ridge GC	1992
Tanglewood GC	1973	Roseland GC	1992
Glenwood GC	1974	Annbriar GC	1993
St. Catherine-Villa GC	1974	Centennial GC	1993
Parkwood Oaks GC	1975	Country Lakes GC	1993
Cardinal Creek CC	1976	Fox Creek GC	1993
Teamsters GC [Union Hills CC]	1976	Mid-Rivers GC	1993
Lake Forest CC	1978	St. Albans CC	1993
Crescent CC [Players Club]	1979	Tree Court GC	1993
Raintree GC	1980	Emerald Greens GC	1994
Bahnfyre GC [Southmoor]	1981	Woodlands GC	1994
Cottonwood GC	1981	Fox Run GC	1994
Innsbrook Estates GC	1982	Governors Run GC	1994
Quail Creek GC	1986	Meramec Shores GC	1994
Crystal Highlands CC	1988	Missouri Bluffs GC	1994
Spencer T. Olin CGC	1988	Royal Oaks GC	1994
Sun Valley CC	1988	Tapawingo GC	1994
Sunset Lakes GC	1988	Woods Fort GC	1994
Whitmoor CC (North)	1988	Hawk Ridge GC	1995
Deer Creek CC	1989	Indian Mounds GC	1995
Eagle Springs GC	1989	The Falls GC	1995
Sugar Creek CC	1990	Columbia Bridges GC	1996
Whitmoor CC (South)	1990	Sugarloaf GC	1996
Bent Oak GC	1991	Prairies GC, The	1996
Jefferson Barracks GC	1991	River Lakes GC	1996
Legacy GC	1991	Stonewolf G&CC	1996
New Melle GC	1991	Champions Trail GC	1997
Orchards, The	1991	Crystal Springs GC	1997
Pomme Creek GC	1991	Pevely Farms GC	1997
Lake James GC	1991	Gateway National Golf Links	1998
Boone Valley CC	1992	Persimmon Ridge GC	1998

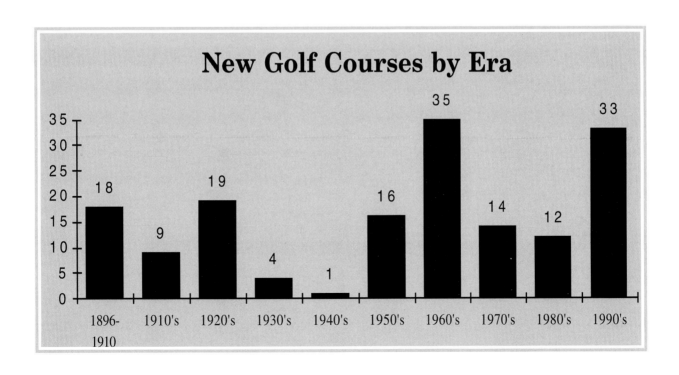

323

Directory of Current Clubs and Courses

Algonquin CC
340 North Berry Rd.
Glendale, MO 63122
(314) 962-2320
Pro: Steve Sebastian

Alton Municipal GC
Homer Adams & Golf Rd.
Alton, IL 62002
(618) 465-9861
Mgr. Don Gore

American Legion GC
St. Louis Rd.
Edwardsville, IL 62025
(618) 656-4653
Mgr. Helen Richert

Annbriar GC
1524 Birdie Lane
Waterloo, IL 62296
(618) 939-4653
Pro: Jon Lark

Arlington GC
Arlington Rd.
Granite City, IL 62040
(618) 344-5232
Mgr: Sue Fallert

Ballwin Municipal GC
333 Holloway Rd.
Ballwin, MO 63011
(314) 227-1750
Pro: Dave Furlong

Belk Park GC
111 North Wood River Rd.
Wood River, IL 62095
(618) 254-9065
Pro: Chris Nobbe

Bellerive CC
12925 Ladue Road
Creve Coeur, MO 63141
(314) 434-4405
Pro: Jerry Tucker

Bent Oak GC
1725 S. Broadway
Breese, IL 62230
(618) 526-8181
Pro: Butch Kellerman

Berry Hill GC
11919 Berry Hill Rd.
Bridgeton, MO 63044
(314) 731-7979
Pro: Walter Siemsglusz

Bogey Club
9266 Clayton Rd.
Ladue, MO 63124
(314) 993-0161
Mgr:

Bogey Hills CC
1120 Country Club Road
St. Charles, MO 63303
(314) 946-1511
Pro: Bob Jones

Boone Valley CC
1319 Schluersburg Rd.
Augusta, MO 63332
(314) 928-5200
Pro: Bob Ross

Cajun CC
Hwy. 21 & Old Boyd Rd.
Desoto, MO 63020
(314) 586-8999
Mgr. Don Reed

Cardinal Creek GC
Scott AFB
Belleville, IL 62225
(618) 744-1400
Pro: Brian Maine

Carlyle Lake GC
Rte. 127
Carlyle, IL 62231
(618) 594-2758
Pro: John Kueper

CC at the Legends
625 Legends Parkway
Eureka, MO 63025
(314) 938-5548
Pro: Greg Mullican

Cherry Hills GC
16700 Manchester Rd.
Grover, MO 63040
(314) 458-4113
Pro: Tom Krebs

Chesterfield GC
815 River Valley Rd.
Chesterfield, MO 63017
(314) 469-1432
Pro: Ken Sample

Clinton Hill GC
3700 Old Collinsville Rd.
Belleville, IL 62221
(618) 377-3700
Pro: Dan Polites

Cloverleaf GC
3555 Fosterburg Rd.
Alton, IL 62002
(618) 462-3022
Pro: Mike Graner

Columbia GC
Box 67A8
Columbia, IL 62236
(618) 286-4455
Pro: Bob Furkin

Columbia Bridges GC
1655 Columbia Bridges Rd.
Columbia, IL 62236
(618) 281-3900
Pro: Bob Furkin

Cottonwood GC
Hwy. Y
Desoto, MO 63030
(314) 586-8803
Mgr: Dick Portell

Country Lake GC
15 Country Lake Dr.
Warrenton, MO 63383
(314) 456-1165
Mgr: Wayne Knapheide

Creve Coeur GC
11400 Olde Cabin Rd.
Creve Coeur, MO 63141
(314) 432-1806
Pro: Mark Lewis

Crystal Highlands GC
3030 US Hwy. 61
Crystal City, MO 63028
(314) 931-3880
Pro: Don Brozio

Deer Creek GC
5300 Dulin Creek Rd.
House Springs, MO 63051
(314) 671-0447
Mgr: Brooks McCarthy

Eagle Springs GC
2577 Redman Rd.
St. Louis, MO 63136
(314) 355-7277
Pro: Barry Storie

Elmwood CC
1400 Eiler Rd.
Belleville, IL 62223
(618) 538-5826
Pro: Joe Idoux

Elmwood GC
#9 Elmwood Dr.
Washington, MO 63090
(314) 239-6841
Pro: Cary Ziegler

Emerald Greens GC
12385 Larimore RD.
St. Louis, MO 63138
(314) 355-2777
Pro: Jim Cochran

Fairmont GC
Collinsville Rd.
Fairmont City, IL 62201
(618) 874-9554
Mgr: Margaret Juenge

Family Golf Center
3717 Tree Court Indus. Dr.
Kirkwood, MO 63122
(314) 861-2500
Mgr:

Falls GC, The
1170 Turtle Creek Drive
O'Fallon, MO 63366
(314) 240-4653
Dir Golf: Terry Houser

Forest Hills CC
36 Forest Club Dr.
Chesterfield, MO 63017
(314) 227-1528
Pro: John Hayes

Forest Park GC
5612 Grand Dr.
St. Louis, MO 63112
(314) 367-1337
Mgr:

Four Seasons CC
615 Broadmoor
Chesterfield, MO 63141
(314) 469-5386
Pro:

Fox Creek GC
655 Fox Creek Dr.
Edwardsville, IL 62025
(618) 692-9400
Mgr:

Fox Run GC
1 Putt Lane
Eureka, MO 63025
(314) 938-4653
Pro: Alan Clark

Directory of Current Clubs and Courses

Glen Echo CC
3401 Lucas & Hunt Rd.
St. Louis, MO 63121
(314) 382-5780
Pro: Nash Haxel

Governors Run GC
3300 Governors Dr.
Carlyle, IL 62231
(618) 973-1290
Pro: Steve Hanks

Grand Marias GC
4600 Pocket Rd.
East St. Louis, IL 62205
(618) 398-9999
Pro: Mike Murphy

Greenbriar Hills CC
12665 Big Bend Blvd.
Kirkwood, MO 63122
(314) 821-7565
Pro: Scott Oulds

Greenview GC
2801 Putter Lane
Centralia, IL 62801
(618) 532-7395
Pro:

Hawk Ridge GC
18 Hawk Ridge Dr.
Lake St. Louis, MO 63667
(314) 561-2828
Pro: Tim Faulkner

Hidden Valley CC
17409 Hidden Valley Dr.
Eureka, MO 63025
(314) 938-5373
Pro: Tom Linard

House Springs GC
Dulin Creek Rd.
House Springs, MO 63051
(314) 671-0560
Mgr: Dan Tuggle

Incline Village GC
1240 Fairway Dr.
Foristel, MO 63348
(314) 463-7274
Pro: Todd Toma

Indian Mounds GC
Hwy. 111
Fairmont City, IL 62201
(618) 271-4000
Pro: John Kokoruda

Innsbrook Estates GC
#1 Innsbrook Dr.
Wright City, MO 63385
(314) 928-3366
Pro: Mark Waltma

Jefferson Barracks GC
2305 Ramsey Rd.
Columbia, IL 62236
(618) 281-5400
Mgr: Steve Willis

Joachim GC
Scenic Drive
Herculaneum, MO 63048
(314) 479-9737
Mgr:

Lake Forest CC
300 Yard Drive
Lake St. Louis, MO 63367
(314) 625-1946
Pro: Fred Friedman

Lake James GC
7555 St. James Dr.
Edwardsville, IL 62035
(618) 656-4653
Mgr:

Lakewood GC
1015 Bowles Ave.
Fenton, MO 63026
(314) 343-5567
Mgr: Dan Schweiser

Legacy GC
3500 Cargil Rd.
Granite City, IL 62040
(618) 931-4653
Mgr:

Lockhaven CC
PO Box 47
Alton, IL 62002
(618) 466-2441
Pro: Bill Moser

Locust Hills CC
1015 Belleville St.
Lebanon, IL 62254
(618) 537-4590
Pro: Fred Paskvan

Log Cabin Club
1140 Log Cabin Lane
Ladue, MO 63124
(314) 993-0154
Mgr:

Meadowbrook CC
Clayton & Kehrs Mill Rd.
Ballwin, MO 63011
(314) 227-5361
Pro: Bill Lansdowne

Meramec Shores GC
2164 Gravois
St. Clair, MO 63077
(573) 629-0900
Pro: Rick Marquart

Mid-Rivers GC
4100 Mid Rivers Mall Dr.
St. Peters, MO 63376
(314) 939-3663
Pro: Bev Miller

Missouri Bluffs GC
18 Research Park Circle
St. Charles, MO 63304
(314) 939-6494
Dir. Golf: Dick Shaiper

New Melle Lakes GC
404 Foristell Rd.
New Melle, MO 63365
(314) 398-4653
Mgr: Henry Barry

Normandie GC
7605 St. Charles Rock Rd.
Normandy, MO 63133
(314) 862-4884
Mgr: Greg Wolfner

North County GC
703 West Market
Red Bud, IL 62278
(618) 282-7963
Mgr:

Norwood Hills CC
#1 Norwood Drive
St. Louis, MO 63121
(314) 521-4802
Pro: Larry Emery

Oakbrook GC
RR3; Fruit Road
Edwardsville, IL 62025
(618) 656-5600
Pro: Larry Suhre

Old Warson CC
9841 Old Warson Rd.
Ladue, MO 63124
(314) 961-0005
Pro: Garth Bayer

Orchards GC, The
1499 Golf Course Dr.
Belleville, IL 62221
(618) 233-8921
Pro: Bill Bals

Paddock CC
50 Country Club Lane
Florissant, MO 63033
(314) 741-4334
Pro: Mike Kilpatrick

Paradise Valley GC
Old Hillsboro Road
Valley Park, MO 63088
(314) 225-5157
Pro: Jerry Ray/Jeff Hogge

Players Club, The
745 Lewis Road
Crescent, MO 63025
(314) 938-6200
Pro: Charlie Stock

Pomme Creek GC
#1 Golfview Drive
Arnold, MO 63010
(314) 296-4653
Pro: Stanley Abraham

Prairies, The
300 Tri-Centennial Dr.
Cahokia, IL 62206
(618) 332-6944
Pro: Mike Walsh

Quail Creek GC
6022 Wells Rd.
St. Louis, MO 63128
(314) 487-1988
Pro: T.D. Morris

Raintree GC
5925 Plantation Drive
Hillsboro, MO 63050
(314) 797-4020
Pro:

Ridge GC
600 Floraville Rd.
Waterloo, IL 62298
(618) 939-4646
Mgr: Ken Osterhage

River Lake GC
Ramsey Rd.
Columbia, IL 62236
(618) 281-6665
Mgr: Jim Watkins

Directory of Current Clubs and Courses

Rivers Edge GC
Melvin Price Center
Granite City, IL 62040
(618) 452-4444
Mgr:

Riverside GC
1210 Larkin Williams Rd.
Fenton, MO 63026
(314) 343-6333
Mgr:

Rock Springs GC
Rock Springs Park
Alton, IL 62202
(618) 465-9898
Mgr: Kim Wheeler

Rolling Hills GC
5801 Pierce Lane
Godfrey, IL 62035
(618) 466-8363
Mgr: Bob Van Hatten

Roseland GC
200 Wonderland Dr.
Alton, IL 62002
(618) 462-7673
Mgr:

Royal Oaks GC
533 North Lincoln Dr.
Troy, MO 63379
(314) 462-8633
Pro: Brent Branstetter

Ruth Park GC
8211 Groby Road
University, MO 63132
(314) 727-4800
Pro: Ron Akin

Sherwood CC
8100 Fine Road
St. Louis, MO 63129
(314) 846-8850
Mgr: Pat Hiller

Spencer T. Olin GC
4701 College Ave.
Alton, IL 62002
(618) 463-3111
Pro: Mark Marcuzzo

St. Albans CC
St. Albans Road
St. Albans MO 63038
(314) 458-3062
Pro: Terry Grosch

St. Andrews GC
2121 St. Andrews Lane
St. Charles, MO 63301
(314) 946-7777
Pro: Kirk Porter

St. Ann Municipal GC
4100 Ashby Road
St. Ann, MO 63074
(314) 423-6400
Pro: Tim Ryan

St. Catherines-Villa GC
Old Carpenter Road
Edwardsville, IL 62025
(618) 656-4224
Mgr: John Luketiott

St. Charles GC
500 Friedens Rd.
St. Charles, MO 63303
(314) 946-6190
Mgr: Frank Phillips

St. Clair CC
S. 78thth Street
Belleville, IL 62223
(618) 398-3402
Pro: Jeff Hunter

St. Louis CC
400 Barnes Rd.
Ladue, MO 63124
(314) 994-0017
Pro: Steve Spray

St. Peters GC
200A Salt Lick Rd.
St. Peters, MO 63376
(314) 397-2227
Pro:

Stonewolf G&CC
7125 N. Illinois
Fairview Heights, IL 62208
(618) 624-9653
Pro: Wayne Ockovic

Sugar Creek CC
5224 Country Club Dr.
House Springs, MO 63051
(314) 677-4070
Pro: Brad Hulett

Sun Valley GC
Rte 2; Box 52
Elsberry, MO 63343
(314) 898-2613
Mgr: Kerry Davis

Sunset CC
9555 Geyer Road
Sunset Hills, MO 63127
(314) 843-1100
Pro: Gary Fee

Sunset Hills CC
2525 Highway 157 South
Edwardsville, IL 62025
(618) 656-8088
Pro: Brad Heck

Sunset Lakes GC
113366 West Watson Rd.
Sunset Hills, , MO 63127
(314) 843-3000
Pro: Jeff Hansen

Tamarack GC
800 Tamarack Lane
O'Fallon, IL 62269
(618) 632-6666
Mgr: Marvin Vogt

Tapawingo GC
13001 Gary Player Dr.
Sunset HillsMO 63127
(314) 349-3100
Pro: Julie Brown

Terre Du Lac CC
Hwy. 47
Bonne Terre, MO 63628
(573) 562-7091
Pro: Rob Sedorcek

Tower Tee GC
6727 Heege Rd.
St. Louis, MO 63123
(314) 351-1353
Pro: Dick Lotz

Triple A GC
5163 Clayton Ave.
St. Louis, MO 63110
(314) 535-9140
Pro: Jim Offer

Triple Lakes GC
6942 Triple Lakes Lane
Millstadt, IL 62260
(618) 476-9985
Mgr:

Twin Oaks GC
21916 Route 127
Greenville, IL 62246
(618) 749-5611
Mgr: Kimberly Laws

Union Hills GC
1230 Abbey Lane
Pevely, MO 63070
(314) 296-0291
Mgr: Neal Spencer

Warrenton GC
South Hwy. 47
Warrenton, MO 63383
(314) 456-8726
Mgr: Larry Luecke

Wentzville GC
350 North Pointe Prairie Rd.
Wentzville, MO 63385
(314) 394-6686
Mgr:

Westborough CC
631 S. Berry Rd.
Oakland, MO 63122
(314) 968-4180
Pro: Phil Hewitt

Westhaven GC
8 Maple Dr.
Belleville, IL 62220
(618) 233-9536
Mgr: Art Buesch

Westwood CC
11801 Conway Rd.
Town & Country, MO 63131
(314) 432-2311
Pro: Daryl Hartig

Whitmoor CC
1100 Whitmoor Drive
St. Charles, MO 63303
(314) 926-2266
Pro: Russ Luedloff

Woodlands GC
2839 Harris Lane
Alton, IL 62002
(618) 462-1456
Pro: Todd Cress

Woods Fort GC
#1 Country Club Dr.
Troy, MO 63379
(314) 462-6600
Mgr: Dick Crosby

Yorktown GC
300 Goalby Drive
Belleville, IL 62221
(618) 233-2000
Pro: Dick Lotz

Index

Index

Index

Index

Index